CLASS STRUGGLE
IN HOLLYWOOD

GERALD HORNE

CLASS STRUGGLE IN HOLLYWOOD

1930–1950

*Moguls,
Mobsters,
Stars, Reds, &
Trade Unionists*

University of Texas Press, Austin

LIBRARY OF CONGRESS CATALOGING-IN-PUBLICATION DATA

Horne, Gerald.
  Class struggle in Hollywood, 1930–1950 : moguls, mobsters,
stars, Reds, and trade unionists / by Gerald Horne.— 1st. ed.
      p.   cm.
  Includes bibliographical references and index.
  ISBN 0-292-73137-X (cl. : alk. paper) —
  ISBN 0-292-73138-8 (pbk. : alk. paper)
  1. Motion picture industry—Employees—Labor unions—
California—Los Angeles. I. Title.
PN1993.5.U65 H67   2001
331.88'1179143'0979494—dc21   00-025950

CONTENTS

PREFACE

This is a book about labor-management conflict in Hollywood. It concerns the attempt of the Conference of Studio Unions (CSU), a federation of craft unions led by painters and carpenters, to confront not only the major studios but also a competing union, International Alliance of Theatrical Stage Employees (IATSE) and its allies in organized crime. CSU went on strike in 1945 and was locked out in 1946. However, it fought its antagonists to a standstill in 1945. They were routed in 1946. The vanquishing of CSU erased progressive trade unionism for generations to come in one of this nation's most significant industries.

CSU's enemies wielded one major charge—that the organization was led and dominated by members of the Communist Party. However, this allegation was wildly inaccurate. The CSU's leader—Herb Sorrell—was a painter and former boxer who appeared to have absorbed one too many punches to the skull. He was militant and fearless, but lacked tactical skills. He was publicly hostile to the Soviet Union and insensitively clumsy in addressing the needs and aspirations of Southern California's African American population. Despite the fact that these actions were clearly not the hallmarks of Communist leadership in the first half of the twentieth century, the explosive cry of "Communist" effectively disrupted CSU's effort to win victories for its membership.

The union's downfall amounts to a controlled experiment that demonstrates vividly that accusations of communism were not just designed to drive out practicing Reds with ties to Moscow. This it did, most definitely, but these bombardments were also intended to damage militant non-Communist labor, which suffered fatal collateral damage. With the latter ousted, the path was primed for management to seize greater control of the production process and garner more profits by reducing once powerful mastifflike unions to the status of tiny, toothless terriers. The experience of Hollywood labor demonstrates that the Red Scare was in many ways an attack on militant "unionism," conducted under the guise of an attack on communism.

The strife of the mid-1940s was also important for other reasons. At stake was nothing less than control over an industry that was essential in forging people's consciousness. The titans of Hollywood had invested mightily in creating a "star system" that had captivated the imagination of millions worldwide who followed the doings of actors—on and off the screen. Hollywood was surely a "dream factory," and these iconic actors lived lives that were the stuff of dreams as they instructed and mesmerized. But how would the multitudes respond to the sight of their favorite stars on picket lines, embroiled in a class struggle? How would the masses react when the Oz-like curtain of illusion was ripped away, revealing that the issues in Hollywood were not that different from those in Detroit, Pittsburgh, and other labor-management battlefronts? Yet there was at least one significant difference: class struggle in Hollywood could grab attention and provide lessons in ways unmatched by other labor-capital conflicts.

Other factors help explain the ferocity of the onslaught on Hollywood labor. The screenwriters, which did include a complement of Communists, were indispensable in the production process. Though the moguls sought to show otherwise, making a decent movie without a competent screenplay based on a sound idea was tough. Even in the digital era of the twenty-first century, dispensing with writers—unlike other guilds and unions—will be difficult. Moreover, screenwriters, who were genuinely interested in intellectual exchange and foreign film were countered by moguls who were desperately interested in constructing firm protectionist walls to keep international cinema out of the U.S. market. When the screenwriters—who actively fought against tariff walls that kept foreign films from U.S. audiences—were denuded of Communist influence, it became easier for the moguls to bar foreign films while conquering markets abroad. This protectionism provided a comfortable cushion of profitability that proved critical to the industry in the post–World War II era in the face of a stiff challenge from television, independent film producers, and a successful antitrust lawsuit that disrupted the vertical integration of Hollywood. In fact, labor unrest in Hollywood erupted at an unpropitious moment for the moguls, confronted as they were by all manner of challenges—not least of which was anti-Semitism. Bulldozing csu seemed all the more important in a context where nettlesome problems seemed to be proliferating and metastasizing.

As Communist and other leftist screenwriters like John Howard Lawson, Abraham Polonsky, Dalton Trumbo, Donald Ogden Stewart, Lester Cole, and Ring Lardner, Jr., were driven into purgatory, the ideological content of movies spiraled downward. Making films concerning racism, not to mention gender and class inequality, became more difficult and the road was paved for more "beach blanket" fluff. According to one analyst, weighty " 'social problem' films decreased from 20.9 percent of the studios' output in 1947 to 9 percent in 1950 and 1951."[1]

To be fair, csu and the left had reason to be taken by surprise, for the anticommunist upsurge swept through the industry like a fast-moving, Southern California late-summer blaze. As late as the fall of 1946 Hollywood's chief spokesman, Eric Johnston—and the likeminded actor Ronald Reagan—were dismissing bedrock anticommunist notions. A shrewd businessman, Johnston was proud of his association with Josef Stalin during the war. By 1947 Johnston and Reagan had emerged as avatars of anticommunism and the "blacklist." Apparently it was the intensity of the class struggle led by csu that forced many in Hollywood to reconsider the utility of anticommunist tactics and to proceed fatefully toward an industry-wide blacklist.

csu and the left had other problems. By the time the unions went on strike in 1945 the studios had squirreled away so many films that even if production were halted, fresh product would continue to reach the theaters. Moreover, the studios were the ones exhibiting "class consciousness," standing shoulder-to-shoulder to confront a common foe, while the unions were busily knifing one another. The conflict in Hollywood illustrated an age-old lesson: class consciousness does exist in abundance in the United States; it is just painfully deficient among the working class.

It seems clear that fear of a Communist-led union leadership was not the catalyst that inspired fear and loathing of csu. After all, leading Communists were contemptuous of Sorrell and initially opposed the group's 1945 strike, which was viewed widely as a blatant violation of the wartime "no-strike" pledge. Then again, Communists had their own problems in Hollywood. They purported to be the party of proletarians but, in fact, few painters, carpenters, and truck drivers joined their ranks in Hollywood.

Communist leaders in the industry—like the screenwriter John Howard Lawson—were, unlike Sorrell, eloquent in their denunciation of racial bias; they also penned some of the more effective antiracist screenplays. In creating films like *A Medal for Benny, Home of the Brave, Intruder in the Dust,* and *Broken Arrow,* progressive writers and directors were far in advance of their mainstream counterparts. The roles Communists provided for women like Katharine Hepburn were far more sophisticated than the fare Hollywood provided ordinarily. Hollywood leftists rose to the defense of Mexican Americans in the 1943 "Sleepy Lagoon" case, in which authorities falsely accused a dozen young Latinos of murder; and at that time, this group was invisible to most Americans. When an appeals court overturned the conviction and reprimanded the trial court judge for his prejudice and hostility toward the defendants, Communists could claim justifiably a share of the credit.

Firm challenges to racism and sexism were more than just benevolent "do-goodism." Overcoming bigotry was at the core of repulsing reactionary anticommunism—or anti-Semitism, for that matter.

Yet, Communists too could have done more in bringing talented black writers like Langston Hughes, Countee Cullen, and Shirley Graham to the gilded trough of screenwriting. A key reason that Hollywood unions weakened in the 1940s was their seeming hesitation to forge alliances with the rising number of African American workers.

Moreover, at touchy moments requiring tactical flexibility, some Communist leaders proceeded awkwardly and, in the process, alienated other potential allies. I speak of a fabled incident involving the writer Albert Maltz (to be addressed below) and the age-old question of whether a "good" writer can have "bad" politics—be it Balzac, a favorite of Marx and Engels, or James Farrell, the "Trotskyite" whose name so inflamed Communists.

Still, dwelling unduly on the real and imagined foibles of the Communists is deceptive ultimately. First of all—and this must be understood and repeated—CSU was *not* a Communist-dominated union, as was the National Maritime Union, for example. The leading Hollywood Reds were screenwriters and directors and—despite their admitted strength in Southern California—they were clearly not CSU's leaders nor at the heart of the dramatic events of 1945 and 1946.

Nonetheless, Hollywood was a pillar of the Communist Party in Los Angeles—a district probably second only to New York City in Red strength. Why? The reasons were many but chief among them was the fact that the labor policies of studios—like Disney—were so draconian and their profits were so significant that workers felt compelled to organize. Furthermore, the party and the unions received critical assistance—

material and otherwise—from moneyed screenwriters and leftist stars and directors. This advantage was shared by few workers outside of Hollywood.

Another organized force, however, played a pivotal role in the electric developments of 1945 and 1946. It too was highly centralized. It too was secretive and often circumspect—at best—about its membership, which stretched from coast to coast. It too often took cues from across the Atlantic. It too was led by cadre. It merits attention, not least because its actions in the political economy are too often veiled. I speak of organized crime.

The cronies of Al Capone himself helped to maintain the odious Willie Bioff and the detestable George Browne in the leadership of IATSE. The muscle of the mob crushed union dissidents. Johnny Roselli, the mob's main man in the West, was a pal of Harry Cohn, the boss at Columbia. Studio executives paid mobsters tens of thousands of dollars, claiming dastardly extortion: CSU labeled these payments bribes designed to buy "labor peace." Meanwhile, mobsters were on both sides of the class divide: investing in studios while controlling labor.

The moguls had other problems beyond their shady partners. These mostly Jewish men were running an often fabulously profitable industry in a nation tainted with anti-Semitism. Inevitably, bigoted circles muttered about the moguls' actual and imaginary affluence and influence. That the leader of the Hollywood Reds—John Howard Lawson—was also Jewish only confirmed in narrow minds that these co-religionists were involved in a conspiracy so immense that it implicated capital and labor alike: the infamous anti-Semitic concoction *The Protocols of the Elders of Zion*—positing a plot by Jewish Communists and capitalists to seize control of the planet—was confirmed in these fevered imaginations.

The strike and lockout provided the moguls with an opportunity to demonstrate that they would be true to their class interests by crushing CSU with an energetic relish. They could show that they were not "foreigners," but "Americans." A spasm of anti-Semitism erupted in Los Angeles as the postwar era began, reinforcing the conservative assault on labor. When "Bugsy" Siegel, the notorious Jewish mobster who controlled an important "movie extras" union, was murdered and his varied interests in Los Angeles and a soon to boom Las Vegas were gobbled up by his onetime Italian American comrades, a loud signal was transmitted to the moguls that if they did not shape up appropriately, they too could be expropriated—albeit in a more sophisticated manner than that used on the unfortunate Siegel. When the moguls "did the right thing" and smashed CSU, they showed that they could set aside presumed ethno-religious interests and that they were qualified to advance further within the ruling elite. This transition also presupposed—as the scholar Karen Brodkin has put it [2]—that Jewish Americans too could "become white."

Reactionary blitzes were as much a part of the Southern California landscape as palm trees and beaches. In contrast to its northern rival, San Francisco, where union labor had flexed its brawn during the tumultuous general strike of 1934, Los Angeles was a reliable redoubt of the right. Not coincidentally, two of the United States' more important postwar leaders emerged from this Communist-hating region: Richard Nixon and Ronald Reagan.

Reagan was a significant player in this drama. As a leader of the Screen Actors Guild and a certified liberal, he could have helped avert the crushing of CSU. However, he was beginning a short journey that would lead him to the right. Why? He believed that CSU was a perfidious "Communist front" bent on exerting the will of Moscow in Hollywood; this was—by his own admission—the major reason that he helped to engineer the crossing of CSU's picket lines.

The lockout of 1946 set the stage for the blacklist of 1947. This epochal development is—perhaps understandably—interpreted generally as a blanket penalty that applied exclusively to the "talent" guilds: actors, writers, directors. Yet, a prelude to this movement was the bludgeoning of CSU, whose members were likewise barred from the industry.

Not only did the vanquishing of CSU mold the trajectory of what was to become the nation's most populous state, it also squashed the possibility that reform-minded unions might have impact on an industry increasingly capable of adroitly kneading the popular consciousness. The elimination of CSU placed Hollywood labor in a disadvantageous position while global production and technological change loomed as the twin keynotes for a new century.

⭐ Part I of this book contains the Introduction, which expands on the broad outlines of the Preface and sketches a story that reaches a climax in later chapters, which focus on the strike of 1945 and the lockout of union labor in 1946. The Introduction provides a broad base of understanding for these events by examining their impact on the movies, anticommunism and the Communist Party, anti-Semitism and the movie moguls, and labor and the mob in Southern California.

Part II consists of Chapter 1, which outlines labor-management jousting in the film industry before the mid-1940s, and Chapter 2, which examines the Communist Party and its chief local antagonist, the "Red Squad" of the L.A. Police Department.

Part III—more specifically, Chapter 3—explores the role of the mobsters, who allied with the moguls to squash union activism, and the stars who were torn between supporting csu and standing aside, fearful that lending aid would lead to their own demise. Chapter 4 probes the moguls.

Part IV, Chapters 5 and 6, is the core of this book, giving a detailed examination of the tumultuous events of 1945 and afterward when militant labor confronted the moguls and wound up being driven from the industry.

The Epilogue updates the trends noted in the rest of the book—e.g., the film industry's place in the economy of Southern California; the changing nature of race and ethnicity in the region and the industry, particularly as it concerns organized crime; the continued value of export markets; and, most importantly for this study, the weakened state of labor in Hollywood—which is a direct outgrowth of the crushing of csu.

ACKNOWLEDGMENTS

In researching and writing this book, I incurred numerous debts, including officials, librarians, and archivists at the University of Southern California; University of California, Los Angeles; New York University; National Archives; Library of Congress; Boston University; University of California, Berkeley; Stanford; San Francisco State University; Eastern Washington Historical Society; Brigham Young University; Museum of Modern Art; California State University, Northridge; University of Texas at Austin; Academy of Motion Picture Arts and Sciences; American Film Institute; Screen Actors Guild; International Alliance of Theatrical Stage Employees; University of Wisconsin; Wayne State University; California State Library, Sacramento; New York Public Library; Southern Illinois University; Columbia University; Hoover Institute; Center for Jewish History; Southern California Library for Social Studies and Research; Reference Center for Marxist Studies; and the Niebyl-Procter Library.

The librarians at the University of California, Santa Barbara (my academic home when this study commenced) helpfully retrieved important books and documents. The same holds true for librarians at the place where I now teach, the University of North Carolina: As with all of my work since I arrived in Chapel Hill, Trevaughn Brown-Eubanks and work-study students too numerous to mention have been indispensable in performing the numerous chores necessary to produce this manuscript. Chris and Mary Young, Oliver Jones, and Annie Chamberlin have been likewise helpful.

PART

1

INTRODUCTION

In March 1945, as victory over fascism loomed, the Conference of Studio Unions (CSU)—a federation of craft unions in the film industry that was accused of being dominated by Communists—went on strike in Los Angeles.

By October the strikers' patience was dissipating, just as temperatures in Southern California were reaching record highs. The studio executives' discontent was also rising as the strike dragged on.

Then a dramatic moment occurred that was encapsulated neatly in a *Los Angeles Times* headline: "Film Strike Riot." Dozens were injured in a melee at the entrance to Warner Bros. studio in Burbank as strikers confronted scabs and police officers. Some among the hundreds of strikers and their supporters were "knifed, clubbed and gassed," while others were swept off their feet by spray from fire hoses. The glass of smashed windshields littered the pavement. There were "tear gas bomb blasts" and overturned cars. Periodic fistfights at times engaged a dozen men or more. The studio had built "barricades of long tables against the barrage. The pickets pulled the three overturned cars together to form a defense of their own. . . . Their ammunition was replenished by soaked and bedraggled women strikers."[1]

This event was not the last—just the most dramatic—episode of violence to punctuate that bitter struggle. A year later violence flared once more, this time as CSU charged the studios with a "lockout." Douglas Tatum, a set erector at Warner Bros., was driving to work in September 1946. Objecting to Tatum's crossing of the picket line, a striker "shoved his hand or some object into the right front window," which "immediately disintegrated into a thousand small particles," one of which "penetrated" Tatum's right eye. Earlier, Arthur Maurer, also a painter at Warner Bros., had been riding to work in a company bus. Security on the vehicle was insufficient, for a "large man . . . swung at the driver of the bus with his fist and began to beat the driver about the face, head and body." The assailant then shellacked Maurer, before being joined by a dozen other men who began to break the windows of the bus. Maurer was left with damaged teeth, a jaw that felt "paralyzed," and "pain in chewing or using his mouth."[2]

Ronald Reagan, a leader of the Screen Actors Guild, recalled later that during this time "homes and cars were bombed. . . . [W]orkers trying to drive into a studio would be surrounded by pickets who'd pull open their car door or roll down a window and yank the worker's arm until they broke it, then say, 'Go on to work, see how much you get done today.'" Reagan crossed the picket lines, albeit with some difficulty. The studio provided transportation, but one day when he approached the bus for the always adventurous ride to work, he found it "going up in flames, the target of a fire bombing." Reagan was outraged by this "Soviet effort to gain control over Hollywood and the content of its films." His shock and fury compelled him to collaborate with the FBI. It had "a profound effect on me. More than anything else, it was the Communists' attempted takeover of Hollywood and its worldwide weekly audience of more than five hundred million people that led me to accept a nomination to serve as president of the Screen Actors Guild, and indirectly at least, set me on the road that would lead me into politics." These harrowing days convinced Reagan that "America faced no more insidious or evil threat than Communism."[3]

Reagan was not alone in arriving at this apocalyptic conclusion. California State Senator Jack Tenney also captured the sentiments of many when he told Governor Earl Warren that this labor agitation was a "Communist" plot. How else to explain the "pickets armed with blackjacks, chains, broken bottles, etc.[?]" Tenney asked. This unrest, he argued, was the "spearhead of [the] long range Communist strategy to control [the] motion picture as [a] potent medium of propaganda."[4] Grace Dudley told Governor Warren that it might be "necessary for us to organize the vigilentes [sic] in true California tradition. . . . I have never seen anything like [this violence] in this state," she complained, "and I was born here."[5]

⭐ If Grace Dudley were paying attention to the troubled state of labor-management relations in the film industry, she would not have been overly surprised that such strife gripped the industry. For years, film labor had been controlled by the International Alliance of Theatrical Stage Employees (IATSE), which had historic ties to organized crime; the union originated in the 1890s, though its mob ties did not accelerate until the 1930s.[6] In the years leading up to the strike of 1945, CSU—which was led by painters and encompassed film workers ranging from carpenters to screen story analysts—had become embroiled in increasingly tense jurisdictional disputes with IATSE, which had a similar mix of members. For years the studios had buttressed their hegemony by playing one union faction against another; in the 1930s, for example, IATSE battled the International Brotherhood of Electrical Workers.[7]

When Johnny Roselli, the mob's main liaison with the industry and IATSE, was indicted, tried, and convicted of extortion in 1944, insiders thought that CSU's fortunes would expand, enabling this latecomer to oust the previously established IATSE from its preeminent position among film workers. However, this optimism proved premature. After the lockout of 1946, CSU was never again a meaningful force in the industry.

According to one study, CSU's demise likewise meant the end of "decentralization and democracy" within the film union movement; it "took away from the other progressive unions and guilds throughout the film industry a dependable source of labor solidarity."[8] Carey McWilliams agrees, arguing that the crushing of CSU set the stage for the purges and blacklists, a process that culminated in the case of the Hollywood Ten, a group of screenwriters and directors who resisted this trend.[9] More than this, says blacklisted screenwriter Abraham Polonsky, blacklisting was "mainly an attack on the major unions"; the "blacklist," he argues, "went on among them before it hit" the writers, directors, and actors.[10]

In the following pages, I will portray in detail the labor unrest that rocked the film industry in 1945 and 1946; but more than this, I will examine the major forces—moguls, mobsters, stars—and above all, trade unionists and Communists, that drove this crisis. During the few years between 1945 and 1950, as the Red Scare took hold, the influence of militant trade unionism in the film industry was drastically reduced. Of course, this drama took place in many venues nationally, but Hollywood—where illustrative drama has been a primary staple—presented this well-known story in a way that gripped the public's imagination; the dramatis personae, from Ronald Reagan to Gene Kelly to Katharine Hepburn, were familiar faces that audiences from coast to coast watched routinely with rapt attention. The creation of celebrity actors seemed to spawn a group of uncontrolled Frankenstein's monsters who might use their tremendous influence on behalf of labor, not management.[11] With the Cold War dawning and those on the left—particularly alleged Communists—being demonized, this struggle gained a resonance that was echoed by analogous trends in literature, drama, and painting.[12]

A contributing element to this explosive mix was the backdrop of California, the heart of the western United States: for "perhaps nowhere in the country was the effect of decades of Cold War felt more intensely than in the lands west of the Mississippi River." Not coincidentally, two of the leading Cold War politicians—Richard Nixon and Ronald Reagan—hailed from Southern California, where enormous defense spending helped to reinforce notably virulent anticommunist politics.[13]

Inevitably, the role of ideology—principally anticommunism and anti-Semitism—will be a primary concern in these pages. The strike and the lockout formed not only a momentous chapter in the history of the film industry and in the increasingly important region of Southern California; they were also critical in the evolution of the Red Scare and the concomitant undermining of unions—and Communists—that accompanied it.

★ As an industry that produced great wealth while massaging the public consciousness, film had long received the keen attention of labor and capital alike. In 1929 the movie moguls met in Manhattan at the Hotel Montclair to assess their handiwork. Film, those gathered were told, "represents an investment of two and a half billion dollars. . . . It costs between $70,000,000 and $100,000,000 a year to advertise the product in our newspapers. 235,000 people are employed. . . . 100,000,000 people go to the moving theatres weekly. . . . More silver is used [in film developing and related processes] than in the minting of coin." Cotton was used by "the hundreds of bales" for the "basis of celluloid film is cotton."

Colonel F. L. Herron, treasurer and manager of the Foreign Department of the Motion Picture Producers and Distributors, was almost giddy in noting the ideological content of this product; Hollywood showed "people having fun. They depict freedom; prosperity; happiness; a higher standard of living in clothing, houses . . . motor cars—in fact, all the components of good living. And the world, seeing these things, quickly responds and demand the same thing. . . . American pictures do more to sell our products than 100,000 salesmen."[14]

A few years before these gleeful words were uttered, the Senate Finance Committee estimated that in the United States between $750 million and $1 billion were spent on movies. The industry—taken broadly—employed 250,000 in 1921, and investments that year totaled a hefty $250 million. Before the rise of the aerospace industry in Southern California during World War II, the film industry was the prime engine for growth in this region whose population increases were establishing records.[15]

By 1950 the film industry's economic importance had not diminished dramatically despite being challenged by television. One analyst concluded that the "building industry, electricity supply trade, transportation, printing, heating equipment, fuel, installation, and servicing of sound among others, are . . . dependent for a considerable portion of their prosperity upon the continued growth and stability of the [film] industry."[16]

Though often viewed as irrelevant fluff, the film industry actually rested close to the heart of the U.S. economy. As the lockout of 1946 got under way, Communist screenwriter John Howard Lawson filed away information that the Chase Bank was the largest shareholder in 20th-Century Fox. The Rockefeller interests had holdings in Metro-Goldwyn-Mayer (MGM). Radio-Keith-Orpheum (RKO) was owned by Irving Bank and Atlas Corporation at various periods. The other studios, including Columbia and Warner Bros., all had strong ties with major banks. The iconoclastic pundit George Seldes concluded that "all movie companies are dependent upon the House of Morgan."[17]

The industry was dominated by eight companies: the aforementioned plus Paramount, Universal, and United Artists. The industry was integrated vertically with the studios also controlling theaters that garnered 75 percent of box office revenues.[18]

Because of Hollywood's involvement with major financial interests, the strike and lockout assumed dramatic importance. Filmmaking was notoriously labor intensive, but it also involved substantial financial outlays; the studios spent $50 million to build sound stages in 1929, while production cost per film averaged about $300,000 at Warner Bros. and $500,000 at MGM during the Depression. Banks particularly had been active investors; though much has been made—understandably—about directors as "auteurs" of films and the different film styles of various studios, banks with their ability to "review . . . scripts and production projects" had an "awesome potential for control" of the industry. Their "lending policies" could "validate or disapprove a company's plan for future operation." The California-based Bank of America was known as the "movie bank": its board membership over the years even included, e.g., Will Rogers, Wallace Beery, Harry Cohn of Columbia, Jack Warner, Daryl Zanuck, et al.

The banks, which were apprehensive about the impact that alleged Red domination of unions might have on their sizable investment, reportedly initiated the blacklist—formalized in November 1947—against alleged Communists and their sympathizers in the industry. Of course, the bankers were also displeased by the spectacle of supposedly Red film strikers marauding in the streets of Los Angeles.[19]

Capitalists and Communists alike took the movies seriously. IATSE frequently cited the portentous words of the Bank of America's A. P. Gianinni: "They who control the cinema can control the thought of the world."[20] From Moscow, V. I. Lenin concurred, arguing that "of all the arts the cinema is the most important."[21] Left and right alike agreed that investment in—and attention to—the cinema industry was of paramount importance.

Diana Altman has written that "New York was the financial center of the industry. . . . If Hollywood had collapsed, the film industry in America could have continued pretty much as it was . . . but when New York collapsed, the whole industry changed completely."[22] This slight exaggeration does downplay the crucial role of the San Francisco–based Bank of America, but insofar as it points to the critical role of the banks in Hollywood, her point is valid.

By the late 1940s, bankers became intensely concerned with "audience decline" and a related "unexpected phenomenon, the failure of a number of films produced with bank loans to return sufficient funds sufficient to repay those debts." The "eight studios released 388 films in 1939, but only 252 in 1946." This fall in production inevitably stalled hiring, further undermining CSU; employment in craft unions fell from 22,100 in 1946 to 13,500 in 1949. This drop influenced the kinds of films that could be made; "for a while certain kinds of film were eschewed—such as epics requiring large crowds, massive and costly sets, and intricate costumes. Films which emphasized contemporary realism were favored, and many of them were shot on location."[23] The ubiquitous market forces proved to be a potent auteur. More than this, the fall in craft union employment made CSU even more nervous about what was taking place in the industry and helped to spawn the feeling that this radical decline in numbers had to be met with a radical response.

Bankers' and financiers' investment worries represented an abrupt turnabout from the situation during the war. The quality of movies may have been hurt by wartime conditions—allocation of film stock to studios was reduced and "no reprints of scenes were permitted, and only one take was ever printed"—still, "everyone went to the movies," which "produced stratospheric attendance figures." In 1946 "theaters had their best year ever," and "every company made huge profits."[24] Earlier figures were equally rosy: "net profits in the fiscal year" ending in November 1945 for Universal Pictures alone were a hefty $3.9 million, the "largest in the history of the company."[25] It was at this time that the Legislative Research Service of the Library of Congress reported that daily attendance at public schools was 19 million and weekly attendance at church services was 18 million, while weekly attendance at the new cathedral and school—the movie house—was 95 million.[26]

The end of the war may have brought ecstasy to some, but it seemed to bring only gloom to the movie moguls. After the war, the studios faced several challenges: foreign quotas limiting markets for U.S. exports; competition from the nascent television industry; the unfavorable conclusion of an antitrust lawsuit seeking to disrupt the vertical integration of the industry; and a proliferation of independent producers as a partial result of new capital gains tax advantages for individuals forming their own companies. In fact, the antitrust litigation that had forced studios to divest themselves of theaters reduced their need to supply "product" for themselves, which in turn opened the door for more nonstudio film productions. Janet Wasko reports that "between 1939 and 1947," there was intense "competition among banks to provide funds for film production," but this ended abruptly by 1948. Allegations about Red labor leaders in the industry repelled capital, for there were many other less "tainted" areas in which to invest.[27] Moreover, this decline was detectable by 1946, helping to feed the months'-long lockout.

In sum, there was a "post-war decline in cinema going."[28] This sharp shift captured the attention of the Screen Writers Guild. In September 1948 an editorial in their organ lamented the "drop in box office through July 1948 as compared with July 1947." This was not all that concerned them: "[T]here has been a noticeable increase in the number of writers going to work for independents in the last few weeks. In fact, the pattern of independent companies operating on major lots and releasing through major distribution channels has become more definite." This trend had major implications for studio labor. Employing legions of workers in "dream factories," as Karl Marx might have predicted, inevitably sparked unions with demands that management deemed encroachment on their unique responsibilities, e.g., working conditions, setting of wages, even creative control. The spawning of "independents," which was not driven exclusively by the decline in studio productions, blunted this trend while still leaving the powerful weapon of distribution in the studios' arsenal. Simultaneously this development eroded the leverage of labor.

The Guild was not unaware of these epochal changes. Their organ noted that "the balance of power in the labor situation has changed greatly since the CSU has been decidedly defeated. . . . With at least 25% of 'back-lot' labor unemployed, concern for security is paramount—hourly wages aren't so important."[29]

"The Big Eight," note historians Clayton Koppes and Gregory Black, "reaped 95 percent of all motion picture rentals in the United States in the late 1930s" and controlled "80 percent of the metropolitan first-run houses, and all exhibitions in cities of more than 1,000,000 population." However, as time passed, the independents began to nip at the heels of Paramount, Fox, MGM, RKO, Warner Bros., Columbia, Universal, and United Artists.[30] The latter three, which were less integrated vertically than the "Big Five," faced even greater jeopardy.

In 1945 there "were about 40 independent producers, 70 the following year, 90 in 1947 and about 165 a decade later." Hollywood had, in effect, anticipated a widespread business trend of the 1990s: the sacking of needed employees and the rehiring of them as independent contractors, but sans benefits. This massive shift in Hollywood employment patterns had the side effect of eroding the distinctive signature and "look" that had helped to distinguish the work of one studio from another.[31]

To be sure, industry changes were not solely driven by the desire to disperse a concentrated force of wage laborers. At the time the guild's editorial lament was published, efforts increased to produce films abroad. This move helped avoid "high labor costs" and helped "circumvent the foreign restrictions [on imports of U.S. films] which came with the world dollar shortage," thus enabling producers to make "films in those countries which had blocked their funds."[32] The immobility of labor and the mobility of capital effectively undercut CSU as well as Hollywood labor generally.

But labor did not face crisis alone; 1947 marked the beginning of a real dilemma for the Hal Roach Studios, for example, which was considerably smaller than the "Big Five." Population had begun shifting to the suburbs, away from downtown theaters, while the aforementioned challenge of television grew. The diminishing fortunes of the industry as a whole simultaneously boosted smaller independents and forced the larger studios to compete much more intensely with midrange entities like Roach.[33]

Movie executives were not the only business leaders feeling increasingly anxious. After interviewing sixty major executives during the winter of 1945–1946, Professor E.W. Bakke of Yale reported that collective bargaining so far had inspired "anxiety . . . about the future; uncertainty as to where the process will end; a fear that it will eventually culminate in such stringent impairment of management's freedom that it will not be able to do its job satisfactorily." Management perceived that the antifascism of the war years—which had encompassed proleft, prolabor sentiments—undermined the "foreman's authority. Rank-and-file militancy commonly elevated the shop steward to co-equal status." Though the Communist Party had been supposedly undermined by the Hitler-Stalin nonaggression pact of 1939, by 1945, Reds led "14 of 31 CIO international unions . . . and shared or contested for power in half the others. At the 1946 convention the left wing commanded nearly a third of the delegate strength."[34]

Executives thought the Reds' rise to be inevitably linked to the erosion of management rights on the shop floor. One auto executive bluntly stated that "if any manager in this industry tells you he has control of his plant he is a damn liar."[35] One scholar in 1947 wrote of a "revolutionary shift in power from business to labor in the United States. . . . A laboristic society is succeeding a capitalistic one."[36]

These perceptions were no minor matter. Union strength could force drastically higher wages, thus inflating the costs of producing a film. In the industry, union strength could allow labor to influence the content of movies, even if only by objecting to negative portrayals of unions. Given Hollywood's vast influence on popular thought, strong unions there could potentially have affected the trajectory of the Cold War.

In the year following Japan's surrender in August 1945, unionists launched 4,630 strikes involving 5 million workers and costing more than 120 million workdays. These strikes encompassed more than just mass-production industries; citywide general strikes paralyzed such medium-sized industrial cities as Rochester, New York; Stamford, Connecticut; and Lancaster, Pennsylvania.[37] Like latter-day Lenins, executives faced the inexorable question: What is to be done? As management moved to reassert its authority in the workplace, it quickly discovered that anticommunism was one of the most potent weapons in its arsenal; anticommunism was the cover, antiliberalism the essence of the "Great Free Enterprise Campaign."[38] Executives orchestrated a multi-million-dollar public relations campaign that relied on newspapers, magazines, radio, and, later, television to reeducate the public in the principles and benefits of "free enterprise." People began viewing the postwar strike wave, symbolized by the CSU strike, as "nothing less than catastrophic civil war." Studio executives, whose very product was viewed by some as propaganda, were uniquely poised to influence this campaign. By 1951, business-sponsored movies reached a weekly audience of 20 million, more than one third of the nation's commercial movie attendance. That figure represented a 30 percent larger audience than in 1950 and a 500 percent larger one than in 1946.[39]

Simultaneously, business launched an all-out assault on the Communist Party and, as demonstrated by the CSU job action, sought to link all labor unrest with this increasingly unpopular organization—even when doing so was palpably misleading.

★ Those familiar with Los Angeles' well-deserved reputation as an antiunion bastion may have been surprised that the CSU strike and subsequent lockout turned out to be one of the pivotal worker struggles of the postwar era. The era of conservatism in L.A. labor-management relations is usually marked from 1910 and the bombing of the *Los Angeles Times* building—allegedly by labor activists—as the result of sharp political conflict. However, as early as the "printers' strike of 1890 the open shop" was the "dominant 'system' of labor relations in the city" and remained so "until World War II."[40]

Admittedly, "we know far less about the history of the labor movement in Los Angeles" than about its counterpart in San Francisco. However, despite Los Angeles' status as a beacon of conservatism, "in most respects" the local American Federation of Labor (AFL)—to which CSU and IATSE were affiliated—was "more progressive" than the national AFL. David Montgomery has argued that "the AFL unions have attracted far too little attention from historians of the war and postwar years, even though four of the five citywide general strikes of 1946 were initiated by AFL affiliates."[41] Likewise, the AFL in Los Angeles has not received the kind of attention that it so richly merits.

California's relative isolation from the national labor market enhanced workers' bargaining power; in addition, the state's early dependence on San Francisco as a port gave stevedores—who were influenced deeply by the left—enormous power.[42] This union proved influential in the early organizing of CSU.

Labor in Hollywood faced unique issues. There was a mix of proletarians (carpenters, painters, electricians) and entrepreneurs (such as
screenwriters). There was casual labor and craft unionism. There was the
highly speculative nature of profits in the industry, often with little connection between costs and result.[43] This was a truly labor-intensive industry. For a single scene of one mid-1930s movie, *Cleopatra,* "four hundred
miscellaneous devices were used on the stage and two hundred electricians were not underused to survey, adjust, operate light boxes, arc lamps,
sunlights, stage lights, spotlights, incandescents, floods, follow spots,
babies, light guns, torches. A chief electrical engineer must know how
to light an ensemble shot like an impressionist painter or as Rembrandt
knew how to distribute light in his eaux-fortes."[44]

Rembrandt aside, making movies was a unique combination of art
and mass production. Besides screenwriters, there were lawyers, who
negotiated employment contracts, monitored copyrights and insurance,
and handled lawsuits ranging from simple torts to complicated plagia-
rism and defamation actions. A budgeting office often studied the scripts
and divided them into numerous slices for other units to handle, with de-
cisions on sets delegated to set decorators and carpenters, for example.
There were researchers to find out what kinds of dresses women wore
in the United States in the 1890s, and what current structure does the
Place de l'Alma in Paris resemble. There were makeup artists. There were
plumbers and blacksmiths. There were wardrobe workers (from tailors to
florists to jewelers to cobblers), special effects workers (who could part
the Red Sea and stage earthquakes), and camera operators, projectionists,
photographers, sound engineers, editors, and laboratory workers who
developed the sixty prints typically processed for each finished film. There
were analysts who read novels and magazine articles for script ideas and
scores of secretaries busily typing away. There were editors and truck
drivers and food service workers. There were hundreds of jobs in Hollywood and scores of crafts. Perhaps the best way to envision a film studio
is as a virtual factory cum small town, with the concomitant difficulties in
getting all the workers to cooperate. With almost as many unions as job
categories, numerous debilitating jurisdictional battles took place among
various unions searching for new members and the resultant dues payments.

Yet unlike in any other "factory," the entrepreneurs—the writers—
"have always composed the most militant labor organization in Hollywood." Influenced by the Communist Party since its inception, the Screen
Writers Guild became associated with Red militance and thus lost some

negotiating power. The proliferation of craft unions, as opposed to the mass production unions preferred by the Congress of Industrial Organizations (CIO), contributed to mind-numbing jurisdictional conflicts.

The "normal" job insecurity of U.S. workers was exacerbated in this industry; it produced the arts, and the arts have a unique brand of insecurity. For example, unemployed autoworkers in Michigan may relocate to Texas; however, filmmaking's concentration in Southern California gives industry workers few other places to go, and since film is a "glamour" industry, its workers are typically less willing to accept alternative types of employment.[45]

Of course, more than glamour was keeping workers in Hollywood. Days before the lockout of 1946, *Variety* reported that the "average weekly pay of workers in [the] film industry was $87.27, a jump of $7.48 over the corresponding month in 1945"; the "hourly wage rate for the month was $1.86, the highest in any California industry. With the postwar decline of airplane and shipbuilding, film workers are tops in this state."[46]

Variety was worried, however, about an "impending unionization of everyone in the picture industry except the top executives. . . . [A]ll signs point in that direction in the not too distant future."[47] With alleged Communists leading the CSU, what would unionization mean for this hugely profitable industry?

Despite film's lucrativeness, however, the situation for Hollywood workers worsened with the war's end. A labor surplus developed as the defense industry began laying off workers and as veterans returned from the war in search of jobs. Management thus had created a ready-made pool of scabs eager to violate CSU picket lines in order to gain a foothold in this glamorous industry.[48] By the time of the 1946 lockout wily studio executives had stashed away 130 unreleased films and "with a minimum number of pictures in production, the studios apparently were not caught napping" by CSU's decision to reject management's final, draconian offer.[49]

★ The strike of 1945 was a direct result of a jurisdictional dispute between CSU and IATSE. The conflict originally concerned seventy-seven set decorators who had formed their own organization, the Society of Motion Picture Interior Decorators (SMPID), which had negotiated a contract in 1937 and renewed it in 1942, though this renewal was not certified by the National Labor Relations Board (NLRB). In 1943 SMPID affiliated with CSU, which tried to negotiate for the group in 1944.

IATSE intervened, arguing that 10 percent of the decorators were members of its Local 44. This battle dragged on until October 1944, when CSU leader, Herb Sorrell, demanded immediate recognition for his group of set decorators. The War Labor Board appointed an arbitrator who ruled that the producers should deal with CSU until the set directors held an election. In February the producers requested an election and a hearing was held on 7 March 1945 to follow up on this and other issues. Dissatisfied, CSU launched a strike five days later.

After the Warner Bros. film-strike riot in October 1945 the NLRB ruled in favor of CSU. As part of the settlement, CSU incorporated SMPID into its ranks but CSU's key affiliate—the Carpenters—lost jurisdiction over hundreds of set erectors to IATSE, thus forming the basis for the next major conflict: the lockout of 1946.[50]

Other jurisdictional quarrels also drove the unions' conflicts—e.g., disputes between IATSE and CSU over who would incorporate the Machinists. These problems—perhaps more so than the usual bread-and-butter issues of wages and working conditions—are what ultimately led to the triumph of IATSE and the demise of CSU.

This class struggle in Hollywood left a lasting legacy outside the film industry. The formulators of the Taft-Hartley legislation, which has been criticized as antiunion by some on the left, were influenced profoundly by the startling scenes of violence from Hollywood and the torturous elections and jurisdictional battles that characterized union struggles there. One congressman who was instrumental in shaping this bill called the Hollywood conflict "a very, very important consideration when we were drafting" this legislation.[51]

Film moguls and press barons alike charged repeatedly that CSU was led by the Communists and that the party cadre included CSU leader Herb Sorrell. Sorrell himself repeatedly denied these charges. Sorrell admitted to a congressional committee that he had met the Hollywood Communist leader John Howard Lawson "two or three times. All I know is that he has a great big nose," he said with his typical dismissive irreverence.[52] The screenwriter Philip Dunne also denies that Sorrell was a Red: "I knew Herb and he wasn't a Communist at all. He was a militant."[53] My own conclusion is that Sorrell was not a Communist: in fact, he squabbled with the Communists frequently. However, charging him with being a Red was useful in destabilizing CSU and bolstering IATSE. Repeatedly Sorrell was dragged before investigative bodies and pummeled with questions about his alleged party membership.[54]

Sorrell was born in Deepwater, Missouri, in 1897 but soon his family

moved to Alabama and then to California. Raised a Methodist and bap-
tized in the Baptist church, he showed few signs during his early life of
aspiring to be a Communist. He boxed under the name Jack Downey, and
during his career as a labor leader, he used his quick and sturdy fists more
than once. By the 1920s he had a job at Universal Studios, but was fired for
joining the union. By the time the 1937 strike erupted, he was back on the
job, serving as a picket captain. IATSE's friends in organized crime hired
goons to disrupt the strike, and during this time, Sorrell met the notorious mobster Frank Nitti. Sorrell later recalled the strike as the roughest
labor conflict of his life, and he concluded that his faction's ability to use
violence was the key to his members' not being wiped out.

The hypermasculine Sorrell boasted that despite his often violent
confrontations with these "thugs," he did not fear pain or death at their
hands. "I have had physical pain to the extent that I know that you only
have [to] endure so much and nature takes care of you—you pass out."[55]

Despite his denial of Communism, Sorrell did have progressive instincts. As he boldly told Congress, "I am a union man and my clothes
are union. Everything I buy is union." When in Washington, D.C., he
stayed at the Hamilton Hotel because it was the only "100 percent union
hotel."[56] He supported Upton Sinclair's campaign for governor in 1934
and worked closely with the Labor Non-Partisan League, which included
both CIO leaders and Communists. On the other hand, he attended Ku
Klux Klan meetings while living in Oakland in 1922, and he refused to
contribute to one of the left's most hallowed causes—the plight of J.J.
McNamara, who was convicted of blowing up the *L.A. Times* building in
1910. Sorrell was philo-Semitic, alleging that Jews made the best union
members and suggesting that if one hundred people were present at a
meeting, half would be Jewish. His opinion of African Americans, however, was not so elevated. He claimed that they just paid their dues and
"went along with whatever we said . . . I suppose that shows something
too." Apparently, concepts of racial privilege, penalty, and intimidation
lacked a place in his thinking.[57]

Earlier, before a congressional committee, Sorrell infelicitously described his earlier financial condition as "nigger rich."[58] Sorrell, who
spoke proudly of tracing his ancestors back to the *Mayflower*, recalled a
strike during his youth in which black strikebreakers were brought in.
Blandly and without critique, he added that the strikers "probably killed
some of them, drowned some of them. No Negroes came to that town
any more to stay overnight."[59] He also recalled meeting some Italian immigrant laborers as a young worker; "at that time a foreigner was—he

might as well have been an animal to me."[60] Sorrell often referred to himself in a self-deprecating manner. "I am not smart. . . . I am just a dumb painter," was his frequent comment.[61] Unfortunately, this comment was not altogether inaccurate.

Such weaknesses led him ineluctably into conflict with the Communist Party, which prided itself—inter alia—on its staunch defense of African Americans. Many Communists viewed Herb Sorrell with some contempt. The Los Angeles party's labor secretary, Ben Dobbs—whose father was a studio painter—felt that "it was a horror to listen to this man. . . . [H]e would scratch his head and look at me and say . . . 'I'm just a dumb painter.'" Like the party itself, Dobbs adamantly opposed the strike of 1945: "I could see no way in which the strike could possibly be won." He was appalled by Sorrell's casual endorsement of violence, particularly his statement, "I love to hear the cracking of bones on a scab's legs." After CSU had made itself vulnerable to the 1946 lockout, Dobbs recalled sadly that this defeat "just swept the progressive movement straight out of the AF of L here in [Los Angeles]. And the AF of L with all due respect, was at least ten times bigger than the CIO ever was in this area. This city was and is an AF of L town."[62]

Ben Margolis, the party's top lawyer in Los Angeles, also spoke sourly of Sorrell. Margolis recalls fondly the thousands of studio workers who were "arrested during this [lockout]. . . . It was a very bitter struggle in which the workers were very militant." But his recollections of Sorrell lack fondness; "he looked like a beer drinker . . . had kind of a florid face, heavy built, with a pot [belly]. A dynamic speaker, not a polished speaker" though he was "really a rough, tough guy." Although he was "a thousand percent honest" and "one of the most stubborn men I've ever met in my life," his "judgment left an awful lot to be desired." Margolis admitted that if "there was ever . . . a class conscious man, it was Herb Sorrell," but "he was not, in my opinion, a particularly good organizer." Margolis contrasted the less polished, less thoughtful Sorrell with the San Francisco longshore leader Harry Bridges, who "fought with judgment and understanding."[63] Sorrell, he maintained, "was totally apolitical and totally lacked leftist grounding. He was a terrible tactician." When Margolis' clients—the "cartoonists, the office workers and the screen story analysts"—wanted to return to work after the 1946 lockout was initiated, Sorrell stubbornly objected, noting ominously, "you'll have to go through my lines."[64]

Fundamentally, the Communists and their allies considered Sorrell to be headstrong, for he was unwilling to accept counsel about the direction of an immensely complicated industry. They appreciated his militance, yes, but even this strength could become a weakness if depended on alone, irrespective of the objective conditions that obtained.

These harpoons launched at Sorrell were not just ex post facto rationalizations. When the 1945 strike was called, the Communists objected strenuously, feeling that it disrupted antifascist unity and broke the unions' vow not to strike during the war. The West Coast party organ immediately issued a front-page editorial declaring, "End the Movie Strike at Once!" Though praising CSU and "its leader Herbert Sorrell" for its "record of progressive and patriotic unionism," the party unequivocally proclaimed that strikes "in this war period are impermissible under any circumstances."[65] Subsequently, the party stated that the strike was "playing into the hands of the worst enemies of the organized labor movement"; and that CSU had "fallen into a trap" set by the studios and William Hutcheson, the "reactionary . . . labor boss of the Carpenters Union and close ally of John L. Lewis." Sorrell's actions, said the party, were "highly individualistic and irresponsible." The Communists found themselves on the same side of the barricades as film technicians, who initially termed the events of March 1945 a "wildcat strike." Film technicians joined the actors, directors, writers, and camera operators in crossing the picket lines established by the "set crews . . . secretaries, stenographers, guides, cooks, waitresses, and dishwashers." This position was uncomfortable for the self-proclaimed party of the working class, helping explain why the party reversed field and endorsed the strike as the war was winding down.[66] Still, the Communists felt that the strike allowed the studios and IATSE to collaborate by locking out CSU workers,[67] enabling the crushing of progressive trade unionism in 1946.[68]

The Communists backed CSU in its 1946 conflict, but their enthusiasm for Sorrell remained wan. By early 1947 it was apparent that this would be a difficult struggle to win. John Stapp, chairman of the party's "Hollywood section" published an unvarnished critique of recent events. He criticized the "penetration of some 'top viewpoint' from the AFL upper crust. This causes some of the CSU members to look toward their internationals instead of their own efforts. . . . Rumors of 'something big happening next week between Hutcheson and the producers' are circulated constantly to stifle the independent action of the locals." He feared a "blight of syndicalism and Trotskyism" in CSU's "ranks. A few old-time craftsmen in the industry were members of the IWW (some still are!). They push a sectarian line of 'trusting no one but the militant workers.'"[69] From the Communists' point of view, syndicalists, with their single-minded devotion to militant labor action, and Trotskyites, with their hostility to Moscow, were beyond the pale; that CSU included many such forces deeply troubled the party.

Sorrell in turn was equally critical of the Reds and, particularly, their beloved Soviet Union. Before a congressional committee in 1948 he confessed, "I don't think I would live very long in Russia." Over there, if you "disagree with somebody . . . I'm sure they wouldn't do like they do in Hollywood, drag you out in the desert and leave you out there"—which is what happened to him after the lockout—no, "they'd actually shoot you."[70] Sorrell was a member of the Republican Party until the early 1930s: "I would have voted for Hoover when he ran in 1928, but I happened to be a little bit filthy rich and I had hit the stock market, and my wife and I were on tour." He then became a supporter of the New Deal, voting for Franklin D. Roosevelt "every time he ran." Unlike Communist labor leaders, Sorrell did not hesitate in signing the non-Communist affidavit required by Taft-Hartley. This fact did not prevent the L.A. Central Labor Council from hauling him into a hearing for supposedly supporting Communism. Despite these false accusations, Sorrell himself filed charges against Frank Spector, one of CSU's key operatives, for being a Red.[71] Sorrell treated Spector harshly, cracking that "if he is a scenic artist, I am a monkey. He could not draw nor anything else. He is not even a good painter."[72] "If I had my way," said Sorrell, "no Communist would be an officer or an organizer or a business agent of the union, because he would spend all his time organizing Communists instead of spending it organizing the workers." Before a congressional committee, Sorrell linked one of his closest aides, William Pomerance, to the Reds, charging that he "did everything in his power to destroy [CSU] and I understood that was the Communist line. I don't say he is a Communist but I feel that he is."[73]

Sorrell also accused Clarence Thompson, a painter who opposed his rule, of being a Communist. Exposing the seams of homophobia in Hollywood, he added that Thompson "has a squeaky voice. . . . [It] is very repulsive to a man, you know. He became repulsive to me in 1945[;] I would be ashamed to hit him so I slapped his face. . . . I slapped his face and told him if he was a man he wouldn't take an insult like that, but being a woman probably he deserved to be slapped."[74]

Many such statements indicate that Sorrell was no Communist: his public attacks on Communists, his disagreements with them on the timing of strikes, his racist statements regarding Jews and African Americans, and his critique of the Soviet Union. Even so, it was the spurious assertion that CSU was led by a Communist that led to the demise of the Conference of Studio Unions.

The same authorities who accused Sorrell of being a Communist maintained records showing otherwise.[75] The L.A. Police Department's "Red Squad"—along with several allied agencies—maintained incredibly tight surveillance of the Communist Party. They knew members' pen names, they knew internal gossip, they had membership lists, and they knew how much money the party had in the bank; beginning in 1941 they made reports almost weekly, providing an amazingly detailed account of what the organization was doing. Though the reports mention numerous Hollywood luminaries—some rightly, some wrongly—as Communists, Sorrell did not make the list.[76]

And so few Communists lived in Los Angeles that the authorities could not possibly lose track of the presumed Communist leader of one of the most powerful union federations in the nation. David Caute observes that between the 1930s and 1950s, about three hundred Communists worked in the film industry.[77] Max Silver—a party member from 1927 until 1945 and its organizational secretary in L.A. County—reported that the maximum number of comrades at any particular moment in all industries (film, auto, oil, etc.) and communities was four thousand.[78]

Communists were accused repeatedly of making Hollywood a membership priority, but strong evidence suggests otherwise. In 1945 *New Masses,* a journal in which the party wielded significant influence—printed articles on painting, novels, music, theater, and radio, but the "profit swollen film industry" was given short shrift.[79] The journal hardly covered the continual labor strife in this industry.

To be sure, "Marxism and socialist struggle are not newcomers, they are central to film history. . . . [F]ilm is unique, among all arts and mass media, in the defining role these traditions have played."[80] However, the Communists felt that industries like steel, auto, and rubber should occupy their primary attention.

Still, Communists in the film industry often were taken more seriously than their counterparts in other industries; not only did they directly influence public consciousness, but the highly paid screenwriters in particular donated large sums to the party. Public influence and money combined with star power to generate massive attention for the Hollywood labor conflict.

The columnist Eugene Lyons hinted at this concern with his flippant references to "$2000-a-week proletarians, the swimming pool peasantry, the caviar-and-champagne Communists." The party was stronger in Los Angeles, he felt, than anywhere else in the nation and these affluent members were one reason why.[81]

By the end of the 1930s California was second only to New York in its number of Communists, with a membership of almost 10,000. The California party was distinctive, with 46 percent of its members being women; indeed, there were "more women in party leadership in California than in any other state party."[82] The ability to tap into this traditionally peripheral group indicates the party's strong influence. A private intelligence agency that worked closely with military intelligence agreed. In 1943 an agency operative remarked with frustrated sarcasm, "well folks, some people declare the Communist movement is a lot of baloney. Recently, the party put on a membership drive, they picked up only 15,650 members in one period." California's catch was second only to that of New York.[83] The party's strength in the state guaranteed that the authorities would scrutinize labor federations, such as CSU, that had militant leadership.

Strikes, of course, were one of the Communists' most high-profile activities. To the Communists, strikes presented a special opportunity for working-class advance; "every strike is a dress rehearsal for revolution" was an oft-cited dictum. Party patriarch William Z. Foster, leader of several strikes, painstakingly analyzed the dynamics of strikes and made strong statements that unsettled employers. During strikes, he proclaimed, "we must attack always, or at the worst be preparing to attack. . . . The workers, like soldiers . . . fight best on the offensive. . . . When the employers take the initiative from us we must take it back with a counter-offensive. If they force a lockout upon us we must turn it into a strike, placing counter demands and involving more workers." He counseled against Sorrell's specialty, "secret negotiations," for such tactics often lost at the table what had been won on the battlefield. Also, unlike Sorrell, he specifically said, "[C]all off the strike officially when it is manifestly lost."[84] Though the 1946 lockout was truly lost as early as the spring of 1947, it actually dragged on until the 1950s. Contrary to the newspaper headlines and the moguls, however, the Communists did not lead CSU into this battlefield.

John Weber, a leading Red in the 1940s, has confirmed the absence of Communist leadership. The "Hollywood Section," he avers, not only did not lead this strike, it "was not actively involved" either. Because these Reds—who were disproportionately well-paid writers, directors and actors—were so concerned with "job security," they barely had a relationship with the county- and statewide party apparatus, let alone a bunch of defiant trade unionists.[85]

★ Though the press and studio executives focused incessantly on the presumed role of Communists within Hollywood labor, they had considerably less to say about gangsters—though their role was both open and notorious. Demonstrating mob influence is difficult, for gangsters require secrecy, and their later recollections are often unreliable. Yet available evidence does suggest that the mob held significant influence in Hollywood, and organized crime there was a classic example of a sizable entity being hidden in plain view.

CSU was founded in 1941 in the wake of the "successful conclusion of a nine-week strike of screen cartoonists" at Disney; however, a primary reason for the formation of the federation was to "fight against the gangster interests" in the industry.[86]

The gangster narrative has become a staple of Hollywood; it even supplanted westerns.[87] This trend is more than a case of art imitating life—and vice versa. Johnny Roselli, the mob's chief operative on the West Coast, held various posts in the film industry, including one in the office of Will Hays, who—inter alia—was the industry's chief censor. After leaving prison following his 1944 conviction for extortion, Roselli, formerly married to the actress June Lang, became a producer of some repute, working at Eagle-Lion studios "in an advisory capacity." According to the *Los Angeles Times*, "[H]e acquired a financial interest in at least one production on which he was technical adviser, 'Canon City' "—appropriately—"a story of a prison break."[88] Roselli was something of a "gangster auteur," lionized for his production credits on *T-Men* and *He Walked by Night*, which were "popular with critics and fans and became a major influence on early radio and television shows such as *Dragnet*." That Roselli's ties with powerful elites was no fluke became readily apparent when he did freelance work for the Central Intelligence Agency in Guatemala and Cuba.[89]

The role of organized crime in the nation's political economy has received significant attention of late. Stephen Norwood has written convincingly about Ford Motor's relationship to Harry Bennett—a mobster who was close to "Detroit's underworld"; he was instrumental in organizing goons to break up strikes and bash labor. According to Norwood, the United States is "the only advanced industrial country where business corporations wielded coercive military power"—power that often derived from mob ties.[90] Victor Riesel has substantiated this point in averring that "only America has a racketeering labor underworld."[91] John Gerassi and others have pointed to crime's centrality in directing the U.S. economy.[92]

Nevertheless, when it comes to the West Coast, "historians have been negligent" in sketching the role of mobsters. Los Angeles is a prime example. Guy McAfee, chief of the LAPD vice squad in the 1930s, built a career in bookmaking and casino operations beginning in the 1920s. Later he helped to build the Golden Nugget casino in Las Vegas—a city whose postwar boom was fueled by the likes of Roselli and his gangster comrades.[93]

But even the walking conflict of interest that was McAfee pales in significance compared with Johnny Roselli. He, after all, was the mob's chief representative in both Los Angeles and Las Vegas, and was "very much involved in [Howard] Hughes' entry" into Vegas "and his subsequent purchase of Strip gaming properties"; the billionaire Hughes also invested heavily in films and was a hysterical anticommunist.[94] In 1943 Roselli and some of his close mob confederates were indicted by the federal government, supposedly for extorting money from film producers. Just after the indictment was handed down, his comrade Frank Nitti (sometimes spelled Nitto) was found with a bullet in his skull, presumably a suicide.[95] The indictment charged that the mobsters were extorting a king's ransom from the studios in order to maintain labor peace; others, however, thought that the studios were bribing the mobsters to keep the mob-run IATSE in line. By providing the mob and their minions with hundreds of thousands of dollars, the moguls, it was said, avoided paying millions to CSU and its allies.[96]

Columbia pictures executive Harry Cohn confessed to a close—if not intimate—relationship with Roselli when he testified at the trial that the two of them had lived in the same apartment building in Los Angeles. Under oath he admitted having known Roselli "socially" and "well" since 1934. They played tennis and went swimming together. They traveled to Palm Springs and went to the horse races together. They exchanged expensive gifts. Cohn lent the thug tens of thousands of dollars. While on the stand, Cohn displayed proudly the ruby ring that Roselli had given him; in return he had given the gangster a cigarette case. Roselli tried to get the American Society of Cinematographers to accept two refugee cameramen recommended by Cohn. It was Roselli who encouraged Cohn to dump Eastman Kodak film stock in favor of DuPont's and offered him a partnership in the Agua Caliente race track in Mexico. It was Roselli who encouraged Cohn to release the film *The Hoosier Kid,* starring Mickey Rooney.[97] Cohn was not like the ingenues who littered his films, however; it was suspected that he "had been on the Capone payroll since the early 1930s."[98]

He was not alone in maintaining such ties. As the Las Vegas writer Hank Messick has argued, with the deepening of the Great Depression, "the only persons with liquid, unencumbered cash were the big bootleggers." After the mob entered the "boardrooms of motion picture companies as a silent partner," gangster movies proliferated with "Chicago gangsters" acting as "unofficial consultants" to ensure the proper authenticity. Roselli arranged for the East Coast gangster Longy Zwillman to provide the capital for Harry Cohn to take over Columbia; Zwillman in turn became the lover of the platinum blonde star Jean Harlow.[99] Arnold Rothstein, accused of fixing the 1919 World Series in baseball, was reputed to be an early investor in Loew's, the parent company of MGM. He often deployed his "gangster armies" on behalf of political machines and corporations alike.[100] The "closest friend" of MGM's Louis B. Mayer was Frank Orsatti, yet another hoodlum.[101]

Sidney Korshak was an attorney for the Chicago mob who later migrated to Los Angeles, where in the words of an FBI agent, he became by the time of his death in 1996 the "primary link between big business and organized crime." This son of a wealthy Chicago contractor graduated from law school at De Paul and became an attorney for Al Capone. His name came up repeatedly during Roselli's 1943 trial as a key operative who could be trusted. Lew Wasserman, a major donor to the Democratic Party and a high-level studio executive, considered him "a very good personal friend." Korshak's clients included "several Fortune 500 companies," along with stars like Frank Sinatra, Kirk Douglas, George Raft—and Ronald Reagan. He worked closely with Jimmy Hoffa as "overseer" of the Teamsters' investments in hotels. Former Teamster leader Jackie Presser was impressed with him: "There's nothing he can't fix. He don't even have an office. He don't even have a briefcase. He keeps everything in his head."[102]

Even before Roselli's trial, it was apparent that IATSE was riddled with gangster influence. In 1941 the mob puppets who led IATSE—Willie Bioff and George Browne—were convicted of extortion and sentenced, respectively, to eight- and ten-year prison terms. Joseph Schenck, head of 20th Century Fox and the producers' liaison with Bioff and Browne, was also sentenced to a year and a day in prison. Though the studios tried to downplay this scandal and their involvement, a federal judge denounced them for participating in these nefarious activities with full knowledge of the facts.[103]

While much was made of CSU's supposed Communist ties, less attention was paid to the moguls' actual mob ties. CSU vainly tried to highlight this irony, but was generally ignored—particularly after the dawning of the Red Scare. When labor strife was reaching its peak, CSU warned that the "gangsters are coming. . . . The pay-off boys, slot machine kings, brothel keepers and underworld characters kicked out of town when the people recalled Mayor Frank Shaw." "The movie magnates," the group warned fruitlessly, "have again allied themselves with the underworld."[104]

Though mob influence in IATSE supposedly fizzled with the conviction of Roselli and the ouster of his puppets Willie Bioff and George Browne, by 1946 the press was reporting that the latter two still maintained some influence.[105] In 1947 the powerful columnist Walter Winchell was blaring, "Don't look now but isn't that Willie Bioff back in Hollywood. Allegedly having secret meetings with movie producers in connection with the strike."[106] Later, the press reported that Bioff was in Los Angeles once more. "His host, who was the general manager of one of the great movie studios, called him Willie and took him around to meet the Beverly Hills elite and say hello to old friends, chiefly big wheels in the cultural art of making motion pictures."[107] The *Los Angeles Daily News* proclaimed that Bioff was "feted here," welcomed with open arms. The roly-poly Bioff "always seems to have a rising movie starlet on his arm," it was reported. Though Bioff and his gangster allies were responsible for "numerous beatings and at least half a dozen long, unhappy rides for hapless theater owners, small union officials and others who opposed him," he was being hailed like a glamorous movie star. Bioff was even in town during the lockout for a "conference with several big shots of the picture industry."[108]

Once Raymond Chandler saw a "band of studio executives trooping back from lunch one day and paused to marvel at the sight. 'They looked so exactly like a bunch of topflight Chicago gangsters moving in to read the death sentence on the beaten competitor' he wrote a friend. 'It brought home to me in a flash the strong psychological and spiritual kinship between the operations of big money business and the rackets. Same faces, same expressions, same manners. Same way of dressing and same exaggerated leisure of movement.'"[109]

As Chandler suggested, movie moguls and mobsters had more in common than most imagined. Corruption—the dark sides of both the

"California Dream" and the genre of film noir—is a reflection of their influence. Moguls' mob ties heightened when CSU went on strike in 1945 and escalated again with the lockout of 1946.

The Hollywood figure Faith Hubley has maintained that the mob, anticommunist unions, and right-wing Republicans were linked in a corrupt triangle: to continue working, the blacklisted artists could provide payoffs that ultimately made their way into the pockets of each side of this triangle.[110] She has a point. The central—though tacit—metaphor for the postwar United States was the simultaneous rise of organized crime and decline of the organized left, and the fulcrum of this seesaw was the film industry and the crushing of CSU.

The role of organized crime in the entertainment industry's political economy is a subject worthy of fuller exploration.[111] Suffice it to say at this point that the mob often allied itself with certain moguls, particularly when their mutual antagonist on the left appeared to be rising.

★ One major problem did pose challenges for both the studios and the unions: anti-Semitism.[112] From the industry's infancy, bigots had commented on what they perceived as the over-representation of Jewish men in the highest ranks of the studios. As early as 1922 a widely circulated pamphlet wondered, "who is to blame for the menace of the movies?" The answer was simple: "the producers are to blame for the indecent, rotten, putrid films which are defiling our land." And who were the producers? "Four or five Hebrews, such as Messrs. Lasky, Loew, Fox, Zukor and Laemmle."[113] Unfortunately, studio labor—particularly IATSE leader Richard Walsh—sometimes deployed anti-Semitism in its Hollywood struggles.[114]

When the strike erupted in 1945, bigots had another target. The most visible leader of the Hollywood Communists, John Howard Lawson, was Jewish, as were over half of those who would constitute the Hollywood Ten. Lawson's hate mail reflected anti-Semitism as often as it reflected anticommunism; in 1947 one correspondent told him, "Louzinski: You are a bright looking kike parading as an American. Your face, nose, ears, and eyes give you away as to what your race is." Another writer called him "the rat of Russia, a Jew louse."[115]

Anti-Semitism haunted the picket lines as well. On 26 October 1946 near the entrance to Columbia Studios on Gower Street, Henry Bernheim was "observing the picket line across the street when a plain clothes detective named Stevens said to me, 'You have a yellow streak down your spine like any Jew.'" At the same time, a hulking cop told Florence Cohen, "[B]eat it, hook nose."[116]

The perception reigned that Jews were hegemonic on both sides of the class barricades in Hollywood. Yet the film industry, which was initiated by Jewish men, was ultimately controlled by non-Jewish financial giants, "the Morgans and the Rockefellers." When the industry became successful, it was suggested, "Gentiles demanded that Jews relinquish their control."[117]

Despite the banks' pervasive power, the perception persisted of Jewish control—and this perception of control extended to the unions. "Jews were associated with labor agitation throughout the twentieth century, but the belief in a Jewish Communist conspiracy received a great deal of attention with regard to the Hollywood Question."[118] An official of the Anti-Defamation League of B'nai B'rith put it this way: "our evaluation of the general mood was that people felt if you scratch a Jew you can find a Communist."[119]

This simplistic analysis was not limited to the hoi polloi. Early in 1946 a "confidential" intelligence report detailed how "Hollywood and the immediate area now have become one of the main centers of CP [Communist Party] propaganda and activity in the United States." The writer of this report was mystified as to why studio executives had not cracked down harder on CSU.[120] A chief congressional investigator of Hollywood, John Rankin of Mississippi, well known for his hostility to Jewish Americans, was similarly baffled.[121]

CSU faced a perilous national shift. The country was moving rapidly away from the relative liberalism of the wartime era to an illiberal Red Scare. Besides, the moguls—who were mostly Jewish—faced pressure to show which side they were on by demonstrating they could crack down on a union that was allegedly dominated by Jewish radicals.

Nationally the ultraright had been placed on the defensive, given Washington's enmity toward fascism and its alliance with Moscow. But as the war began to wind down, this situation began to change. On cue in the fall of 1945 the Reverend Wesley Swift and his "Anglo-Saxon Christian Congregation" began radio broadcasts in Los Angeles. His focus included "Jewish Communism" and he was closely allied with the zealot Gerald L. K. Smith. Throughout the strike and lockout, Swift spewed forth hateful sermons, stating, "if I had my way I would take all Jew-Commies, line them up against the wall and shoot them." The "Detroit riots," he exclaimed, "were nothing compared to what is going to happen here in Los Angeles, the land of the Jews."[122]

Early in 1946 the L.A. Chapter of the American Jewish Committee was meeting in the Terrace Room of the Beverly Hills Hotel. Their executive director, John Slawson, was happy to report a "great decline" in anti-Jewish organizations during the war. "But since D-Day and following V-E Day and then V-J Day," he warned, "the curve began to go up until now we have approximately 125 organizations of a subversive nature which have in their platform anti-Semitism as a purpose."[123]

Anti-Jewish sentiment was another strike against CSU. Not only were CSU's bosses under pressure to show they could stand up to their supposed co-religionists, but anti-Semites were becoming more clamorous in Los Angeles and thus strengthening the overall atmosphere against unions and other forms of supposed radicalism. The strike wave of 1946 and the dislocation it helped to engender were being ascribed by some not just to radicals but to "Jewish radicals." Toxic radio broadcasts transmitting such perverse messages routinely poisoned the airwaves. With the end of World War II, however, the bigotry that Hitlerism represented was discredited, thus marking a turning point in the battle against anti-Semitism. Some Jewish Americans were able to climb the socioeconomic ladder, while anti-Semites suffered heightened anxiety. This smog of conflicting tendencies complicated life for CSU. And the international climate, which only recently had seemed so favorable to unions and even to the left, seemed to be changing dramatically as well.

★ Before World War II, foreign markets for years had supplied the U.S. film industry with "about a third of its revenue," but during the war the Axis powers were able to squeeze Hollywood out of a number of lucrative markets abroad. In turn Hollywood began paying more attention to the Latin American market, spurring the proliferation of Carmen Miranda movies and a decline of the "offensive, cardboard stereotype of the Latin American as a bloodthirsty villain."[124] This expansion south of the border led to the virtual dismantling of the Argentine industry, as U.S. authorities withheld film stock to punish this nation for its neutral stance. Meanwhile, Nelson Rockefeller's Office for Coordination of Inter-American Affairs pushed Washington to encourage U.S. companies to invest in Mexico.[125] This overseas expansion hurt CSU; opening production to low-wage shops abroad increased the number of "runaway shops."

The moguls themselves faced challenges abroad. European nations accused Hollywood of dumping films on them after the war, and they responded by adopting tariffs and quotas to halt the influx of U.S. movies.[126] But European nations, devastated by war, were hardly in a position to withstand Hollywood's blandishments, particularly when they were standing in line, tin cup in hand, awaiting aid from Washington to rebuild their economies. In addition, Communist nations provided a stiff challenge to Hollywood, putting the CSU leadership—which was being charged with being dupes of the Reds—in an uncomfortable position.

Early in 1946 when the wounds of the 1945 strike were still fresh, Eric Johnston—head of the industry's trade association—"disclosed that Soviet Russia is a potent contender for foreign market[s]." This page-one story in the *Los Angeles Times* quoted the "film czar" as stating that "the Czech government has recently concluded an agreement with Russia that 60 per cent of the motion pictures imported by Czechoslovakia must be Soviet films."[127] The Communist-influenced government in France was moving in a similar direction. Already Hollywood had refused to sell pictures to Prague "because . . . [it] 'has nationalized its film theaters and thereby established a state monopoly of film.'"[128] "Donald Duck is seeing red," cracked one writer. "Revenue from foreign distribution is the lifeblood" of Hollywood, Johnston explained in a more serious vein,[129] and growing Communist influence in Europe could restrict the flow of this lifeblood.

Moscow may have had difficulty in producing certain consumer goods to compete with the leading capitalist nations, but Sergei Eisenstein had shown that the Soviets could produce movies that the world hungered to watch.[130] CSU's problem was that many in the industry perceived the group's leadership as surrogates of this foreign competitor—a Trojan horse within the gates of Hollywood. As a result, some of the most fiendish opposition to the Reds emerged in the film industry, which unlike some other sectors faced significant competition from Moscow. Unsurprisingly, the U.S. president who emerged from Hollywood—Ronald Reagan—is the one who proved instrumental in bringing the Soviet Union to its knees.[131]

Hollywood worried that Communist officials in such countries as France and Italy would push for collaboration with Moscow's film industry, thus excluding U.S. movies. The neorealism trend in Italian cinema, which was hailed and propelled by Italian leftists, disturbed Hollywood. Before World War I France and Italy each exported more films than the United States did, but afterward they had difficulty reclaiming lost ground. By the 1920s about 95 percent of the films in Great Britain, 85 percent in Holland, 70 percent in France, 65 percent in Italy, and 60 percent in Germany were U.S. imports.[132]

This huge share of the global market provided a comfortable cushion of profits for Hollywood but Eric Johnston feared that the post–World War II dispensation could fracture this rosy picture. May Day in 1947 found Communists and unions on the march globally—including in the United States—but on this spring day Johnston was testifying before the House Ways and Means Committee in Washington, D.C. about the film industry. Hollywood, he told the attentive congressmen, "can't exist without a world market. . . . [O]ur remittances from foreign countries last year ran about $125,000,000, which is almost exactly the total profit of the motion picture producing companies the same year."[133]

Clouds were gathering on the horizon that could mar this pristine profit picture. Johnston was worried about a "sharp rise in the nationalistic trend in film production in other countries," including the barring of U.S. products. This situation was particularly troubling, he thought, because "the American motion picture is perhaps the [Unites States'] fastest growing export item. It is an important part of the American economy, and it has two great by-products: it helps to create a market for other American goods and it conveys American ideas and ideals."[134]

In the fall of 1947, weeks before the Waldorf meeting that led to the formalizing of the blacklist, Johnston took off for Europe to directly address his critics. Hollywood was issuing "loud yells of indignation" about a London proposal to slap a 75 percent tax on U.S. films, while industry "hotheads clamored" for "retaliation."[135] But as Johnston saw it, "his most difficult operation" was "to get our films past the Soviet iron curtain." Only ten U.S. films had been shown in the Soviet Union in the "past five years," and this was a nagging concern.

At this point, Johnston did not favor outlawing the Communist Party in the United States, but "he did advocate the barring of Reds from holding offices in unions, co-operatives and corporations"; some suspected that the ambitious Johnston had "an eye on the White House."[136] He could not help but notice the irony that two of his major concerns involved Communists—in Los Angeles and in Moscow. The moguls' battle with CSU involved not only domestic but global issues as well: anticommunism also drove the struggle to dominate foreign markets—a fact that helps explain why the strike and lockout were fought so tenaciously.

During his globe-trotting tour, Johnston met with many world leaders, including Yugoslavia's Tito.[137] Johnston was able to mend fences in many of Hollywood's prime markets in Western Europe but was largely unsuccessful in Eastern Europe, thus deepening the anticommunist mood among the moguls.

Yet with all of its advantages, globalization created problems for the moguls. Richard Walsh of IATSE recalled a deathly fear that workers in Mexico—and perhaps in other nations—would support CSU. He flew to Mexico City to try to halt pro-CSU actions by the unions: "they were trying to close all the theaters in Mexico for 1 day as a token strike to support their comrades in Hollywood."[138] Strong, ongoing solidarity by Mexican unions did not materialize, but this kind of transborder solidarity emphasized to the moguls that life would be simpler without CSU.

Ultimately this realization drove the desire for a blacklist. As one analyst put it, "[B]y entering into a Faustian bargain with the state, Hollywood moguls were hoping they would ensure the state's assistance in opening of foreign markets while, at the same time, limiting the power of the independent unions and guilds in Hollywood itself." The moguls' plan had some success.[139] The anticommunist upsurge generated opposition to Communists in Moscow and unions in Los Angeles alike.

★ Competition was not the moguls only reason for moving production offshore. The events of 1945 led to "millions in strike losses" that were "mounting hourly." The work stoppage affected quality, according to one producer: "[W]e used to put 20 painters on a set and finish it tonight for tomorrow's shooting, whereas now we get along with two painters [and] wait 10 days for them to get it ready." Another producer complained, "we've rewritten so many scenes, to take them outdoors and beat the set delays, that the damned thing's going to look like a horse opera without horses."[140]

The strike had other effects on production. The set decorators were the crux of this strike, and their role in movie making was crucial. As the attorney Burt Zorn put it, "[Y]ou cannot make a picture without having a set ready, because a set is just as important as a star, it is just as important as a camera. . . . If you do not have a set and have it completed, you cannot shoot a scene in the picture. . . ."[141] The director Robert Siodmak recalled that the strike erupted as he was cutting his film *The Spiral Staircase;* studio executives became so distracted with the unions that "they let me alone."[142] The strike seriously disrupted the filming of the David O. Selznick production *Duel in the Sun,* however, running up costs in some areas and causing cuts in others.[143]

Films involving Communists were particularly affected. Herbert Biberman had played a key role in helping to bring to the screen *New Orleans,* which featured Billie Holiday; as the film was winding down, he was called before a congressional committee and the film's message of tolerance was diluted.[144]

Biberman, the moving force behind the 1950s independent classic *Salt of the Earth,* had been targeted by the anticommunists for some time. Days after the 1945 strike began, the FBI had obtained a copy of his script for the film *The Master Race* and worriedly produced a lengthy analysis—worthy of a film graduate student—dissecting its possible political implications.[145] The FBI routinely obtained scripts from a "confidential source." In fact, the agency dreaded the day when in order to discredit a production, "it will not be sufficient to state that a certain known Communist wrote, directed, or produced a particular motion picture which follows the [CP] line."[146]

Other organizations also worried about the impact of the presence— or absence—of Communists on the content of films. By the fall of 1947 the NAACP leadership had grasped that a new day was arriving in Hollywood—and that this day did not bode well for people of color. Thurgood Marshall felt that "Negro and other minorities will now revert to the old line treatment by Hollywood producers" because the dominant definition of " 'communist propaganda' is anything in opposition to the status quo of the country." He recalled a recent unnamed script in which "there was a line providing for a white actress to call a Negro actress 'Mrs. Bigby.' This has been changed so that the Negro actress will be called by her first name. In another script, a white actress, in talking to a Negro actor at a race track, asked him to give her the name of a horse to bet on and he [replied] very politely, 'Madam, I do not know anything about horse racing or gambling.' This line has been struck out entirely." This situation further justified "abolition" of the "damn" House Un-American Activities Committee (HUAC), which was boosting racists while harassing those who were trying to improve African Americans' image in film.[147]

Commonality of interest failed to propel alliances for Hollywood progressives. The NAACP leadership—despite its unease about the blacklist's impact on film content—hesitated to rally to the banner of the Hollywood Ten or the CSU leadership. Both the FBI and Thurgood Marshall were concerned primarily with the handiwork of screenwriters and directors, but the studio executives well understood that the strike and lockout involved a critical issue of film content that implicated CSU and not just the so-called talent guilds: the look and direction of films. The unions shaped the look in part by their insistence on maintaining sharp jurisdictional lines among the different workers' groups.

The business journal *Fortune* sought to trivialize this question by recounting a conflict between Makeup Artists/Hair Stylists and the Costumers over who had the right to install false bosoms, based on whether they were made of cloth or rubber. "Movie labor is like nothing else in the world," the journal concluded with wonder.[148] The unions were also like "nothing else," because their expert labor was so crucial to the look and success of movies. Testifying before a congressional committee, Sorrell reminded the solons that shadows in films were "put in by paint" not light since the "intense lights of the set eliminate all shadows." Hence, he concluded, when the competent CSU painters were routed, the quality of movies deteriorated.[149]

For the 1946 film *Dead Reckoning,* the producers wanted to include a large bar in a nightclub scene. However, the construction could not take place without a jurisdictional argument between IATSE Local 44 and CSU's Carpenters Local 946 over who would be in charge. To avoid conflict, the producers changed the design of the bar, thus requiring the director to change the action—and the script—accordingly.[150] In numerous films from *Unfinished Dance* to *Till the Clouds Roll By* to *The Mighty McGurk* to *Speak to Me of Love,* the battles between CSU and IATSE forced directors and producers to make a multitude of changes: from lighting and shadow to the use of steel cots over bunks to the appearance of signs in fictional towns.[151] Diminishing such disputes provided another motivation for the moguls to seek the weakening of union strength.

Why were there so many jurisdictional problems in Hollywood? B. B. Kahane, a vice president at Columbia, said that in other factories, contentious issues are debated and settled. But at the studios, he maintained, "each set, each mechanical or other device designed to provide an illusion, presents a separate problem." The industry was highly unionized and split between two warring factions—CSU and IATSE—with the former being a federation of craft unions and the latter being an organization somewhat akin to an industrial union. Overlap and interdependence created many problems. Grips (IATSE) often used tools employed by carpenters (CSU); IATSE electricians did lighting work claimed by IBEW; prop men (IATSE) made metal parts—a job claimed by the machinists (CSU).[152] Students of theater know that "each aspect of the production—direction, acting, set design, lighting, costumes and so on—adds shades of meaning, intended and unintended, to the dramatization of the play's words."[153] In cinema, the importance of these "shades of meaning" heightened the shades of jurisdictional distinction that existed between and among unions.

Executives all over the nation were complaining about the perceived erosion of management's rights and responsibilities, but the jurisdictional spat between CSU and IATSE gave Hollywood's version of this story a special resonance. By ridding itself of CSU, the moguls were able to re-assert almost absolute control over the production process and thus to make the movies look like they wanted them to look, while avoiding the restraints imposed by "union auteurs."

The Communist film critic David Platt was among those who felt that directors were given far too much credit in movie-making; he felt it was "high time that the film critics paid more attention to the work of the screen-writer."[154] The L.A. branch of the FBI and Thurgood Marshall would have agreed with him, for they paid close attention not just to movies, but also to scripts. Interestingly, the director's authority increased as the screenwriters' guild seemingly became dominated by Reds.

Nevertheless, as Thomas Guback has reminded us, moviemaking is a collaborative, labor-intensive industry; film analysis often stresses only content—which it ascribes solely to members of the "talent guilds," notably directors and actors and screenwriters, ignoring production relations. However, factoring the latter into the equation "shifts the terms of analysis from what we see to the social relations that are implicit in the industry and that govern the terms on which the industry operates."[155]

An analysis of production relations inevitably prompts an analysis of labor, the too often forgotten "actor" in the production of films. Michael Nielsen has observed that "if one single quality distinguishes Holly-wood's product from the bulk of world cinema productions, it is the quality of unobtrusiveness—the refusal of the film to draw attention to the process of filmmaking itself by weaving a seamless whole that engages the viewers' attention completely. That quality is rooted in the craftsman-ship [sic] at every level of production."[156]

Agreeing with both Guback and Nielsen, Michael Chanan cautions that a trend has been developing towards cumbersome intellectual systems of analysis, purporting to reveal the ideological superstructure of the cinema, as if this were possible without first understanding the basic conditions of production. Perhaps this trend away from plain speaking, he suggests, is symptomatic of a general social and cultural condition in which the intellectual believes that he has it within his grasp to discover the real solution to our cultural ailments.[157]

Denise Hartsough has called for the inclusion of labor in film criticism. "If a union was on strike," she argues, "perhaps the absence of skilled workers limited the director's choices, affecting the look or sound of the film. If enmity existed at that time between a union [like] the Screen Actors Guild" and a craft union, perhaps the latter subtly "sabotaged the actors' performances." "The aesthetic approach to film history," she continues, "centers around film texts, but that is only one approach. The socioeconomic approach to film history focuses on cinema's political economy." [158]

Hartsough, Guback, Nielsen, and Chanan all make valid points. Actually a more complete understanding of movies may be within the "intellectual's grasp," but it cannot be reached, in my opinion, absent an understanding of the basic relations of production within the film industry. Such an analysis involves many elements but it should at least engage political economy (including the roles of labor, management, the state, and global markets), independent "actors" (e.g., organized crime, the organized left), ideology (particularly anti-Semitism, anticommunism, and the cult of free enterprise), and the motion of history (e.g., the coming of the Cold War and the Red Scare).

In the following pages, I will seek to incorporate these elements—and more—as I sketch what happened not only during the 1945 strike and the 1946 lockout but also what happened to class struggle in Hollywood generally.

PART

2

CLASS VERSUS CLASS

To understand the intensity of the labor unrest that pockmarked the film industry, it is necessary to understand the repressive atmosphere that characterized California in the years leading up to the strike of March 1945.

The writers, whose organizing efforts were sparked by Communists, were not the first to organize in Hollywood: they were preceded by the craftsmen—painters, carpenters, plumbers. In the summer of 1918 some five hundred of these workers went on strike and stayed on the picket lines until September, forcing several producers to close down in the process. This unrest continued in 1919 and 1920. By 1921 a number of the studios—thoroughly exasperated—locked out the unions; jurisdictional disputes hampered the unions' ability to forge unity, and by 1922 this era of labor militancy had come to an end.

Earlier, Theodore Roosevelt had told Congress that "every far-sighted patriot should protest, first of all against the growth in this country of that evil thing which is called 'class consciousness.' " By the end of World War I and the outbreak of unrest among studio labor, many in the United States had begun to agree with him; 1919 was a year "like none other in American history. Industrial conflict reached unprecedented levels as more than 300 strikes involved over 4 million workers. . . . The world had been turned upside down."[1]

The initiation of the Academy of Motion Picture Arts and Sciences in 1927 was a direct response to this earlier growth of union sentiment in Hollywood. A prime purpose of this new entity, which became fabled for its lavish and glittering "Oscar" ceremony, was a conscious attempt to "promote industrial harmony"; in effect, it "functioned as a company union."[2]

At the turn of the century, the Golden State contained one of the nation's largest socialist parties, which helped to spawn a fierce police-state apparatus designed to stamp out all traces of labor radicalism. The Socialist Party (SP) mirrored CSU in several ways. Both were influenced heavily by craft unions, both were deemed terribly radical, and both were weak on race matters. In retrospect, the SP's attraction to "oriental exclusion" laws weakened the party's attempt to broaden its base. Thus, with the Red Scare brought by World War I and its aftermath, the SP quickly found itself on the defensive as "vigilante methods . . . organized along military lines and with arms" were wielded against the quickly fading organization. Though the SP's Robert LaFollette, running on a third-party ticket, received more votes for president in 1924 in California than his Democratic counterpart, working-class radicalism was basically squashed in the state during this decade.[3]

Los Angeles pioneered the crushing of labor dissidence. The Los Angeles Police Department's (LAPD's) Red Squad was headed by a former "labor spy" for employers. The City of Angels was ruthless in its handling of strikes or any other form of dissidence; "picket lines were assaulted with nightsticks followed by tear-gas projectiles and guns. . . . [A]s official routine, the unit broke up every demonstration of organized communists and similar groups, raided communist halls every two weeks, confiscated literature, broke up Depression-related gatherings." There was "indiscriminate targeting of political figures, writers, ministers, journalists and prominent citizens." The Red Squad served as the "operational arm" of the powerful Merchants and Manufacturers Association, an influential group of businessmen. Carey McWilliams charged that in the 1930s "at least one member of the board of directors of every liberal-reformist organization in town turned out to be a police spy." In Los Angeles a "powerful alliance of businessmen, boosters, superpatriots and right wing evangelists" combined to make this rapidly growing city a hell on earth for those who went on strike.[4]

Hollywood did not escape the snare of repression. This fact immediately struck the British émigré Cedric Belfrage when he arrived there in the 1920s.[5] He noticed the pervasiveness of the "gangster element" who were integral to the industry's political architecture. Class stratification was a signal aspect of the film colony, and the ostentatious luxury in which so many lived helped to engender a rampant fear that the great unwashed might seize it all; this fear in turn sparked a desperate desire for an ever-growing apparatus of repression. Belfrage felt that "the contrast" between and among classes "was so much greater here than it was anywhere else"; there was a "great emphasis on how much people made" and a reluctance to "consort with people who were in a different [class]." Along with this wealth came an almost hysterical concern with the rudiments of class, said Belfrage, who noted a particular fascination with English butlers, titles, and the like.[6]

The authorities seemed to fear that Depression-influenced art was much too oriented toward working-class radicalism. John Howard Lawson, Clifford Odets, Bennett Cerf, Malcolm Cowley, and other luminaries published a pamphlet in 1935 providing gruesome detail about the arduous plight of progressive theater. They decried "police terrorism: nightsticks, tear-gas, riot calls and jails. Municipal persecution: violation of non-existent fire regulations, condemnation of theaters used for years, trumped-up charges of 'blasphemy' or 'obscenity,' the threat of losing your regular job if you appear in an amateur production of a play of social protest. And the kidnapping and beating and robbing of actors and directors—such are the dangers that confront the vital, sincere theaters in America today!"[7]

As so often happens, there were other "crimes"—large and small—undergirding a number of the great fortunes of Hollywood. There was the flood of capital from mobsters propping up the industry and there were the small indignities exacted on employees to garner profits. Studios routinely worked employees like latter-day slaves, "from sunup to sundown."[8] Dangerous stunts often led to broken bones—and worse. Agents routinely cheated their clients.[9]

Writers, the fulcrum upon which the industry rested, were subject to a special exploitation; their recognition of their plight and the presence within their ranks of more than one trade union militant ensured that writers would attract the angry attention of management.

When industry titans met in Manhattan in 1929, one concluded that "the dominant, I might say the menacing force in moving pictures [is] the scenario writer." Because good writers were few and far between, producers were "afraid to quarrel" with them and, thus, "let [them] do pretty much as [they] liked. The result was a type of picture which should never have reached the screen."[10] This situation must end, agreed management.

But it was not only the writers who were being targeted by the moguls. Edward M. Gilbert of the Screen Set Designers, Illustrators and Decorators recalled that in the early days of the industry "six designers were discharged by MGM studio for no other reason than attending a committee meeting in a private home where the possibility of organizing was discussed."[11] The studios maintained their own corps of spies to ferret out information about labor organizing. In 1933, for example, a top official of the Pinkerton's detective agency forwarded "a report" to Universal Pictures concerning the "IWW"—the anarcho-syndicalist "Wobblies"—and its alleged influence on unions.[12]

But it was the Red Squad that was the most pervasive organ of surveillance. The group's files included mailing lists of anarchists, "radicals" of various stripes, immigrant groups, and the like; it compiled "weekly intelligence reports" that scrutinized virtually every twitch made by every presumed agitator in Southern California.[13] In the fall of 1936 William Hynes of the Red Squad was hailed by an entrepreneur who told him, "I believe our boat builder's strike at San Pedro is practically over and, due to the wonderful protection that you gave us in maintaining law and order, I am happy to say that the shops are running non-Union. . . ."[14]

The Red Squad also kept in close touch with the right wing globally. In 1934, for example, Hermann Schwinn of the "Freunde des Neuen Deutschland" informed William Hynes about an upcoming mass meeting in Southern California protesting the anti-German boycott. He went on to "thank" Hynes "personally . . . for the splendid service your department has given during the visit of the officers and men of the German cruiser 'Karlsruhe.' "[15] The LAPD also shared information concerning various Italian radicals in the region with the consulate of Italy.[16]

However, being on the West Coast, the Red Squad maintained a keener interest in ties with Imperial Japan, which too had an interest in cracking down on Japanese and Japanese American radicals in the vicinity. In 1937 Kaoru Nakashima, secretary of Tokyo's consulate, sought information from the LAPD on the "organization and system of [the] Communist Party in California," including the "approximate number of Communists in California." Amazingly, this information was forwarded, and it might have proved helpful to Tokyo after Pearl Harbor if an invasion of California had come to fruition.[17] The consulate sought specific information about "Geo. Ishinge (his false name is Geo. Tauda) who is a member of the RED COMMUNIST PARTY [sic]."[18] Hynes contacted General Ralph Van Deman of military intelligence about information on Harry Steinmetz and "his possible association with prominent San Diego Japanese, who may or may not be members of the Communist Party."[19]

But Japanese and Japanese Americans with Hollywood connections interested the Red Squad as well. The group was seeking information on Charlie White, who was "supposed to be half Japanese and half Russian or English." He was "posing as a costume expert and character actor; he is understood to have mingled with John Reed Club members in Hollywood." Supposedly he was engaged in an unspecified espionage mission. He was "sort of slant-eyed (but not as much as an Oriental)," and "almost passing as a white man"; he was "said to be running around with a white girl from Seattle." He was born in Japan and spoke "English, Russian and Japanese fluently." Imperial Japan, which a few years later attacked the United States, was thankful to the LAPD for its aid, e.g., when it routed "Communists who were picketing in and about the entrance of the Yamato Hall, where a Japanese statesman was addressing . . . the members of the Japanese community."[20]

The Red Squad collaborated with domestic as well as foreign elites. LAPD provided pistol permits and gold badges to numerous directors and executives and some actors. According to *New Masses,* "[T]his award is bestowed with the understanding that the recipient will be ready when called upon to fight in . . . the 'War on Reds.'"[21] What seemed to rile these rightists particularly was the idea that radicals, driven by the exigencies of the Depression, were diverging sharply from the stereotyped image they had enjoyed previously. Hynes noted bitterly that "in past years the popular conception of a revolutionist was that of a vicious looking individual, broad shouldered, deep chested and wearing bushy whiskers, whose eyes blazed with the fiendish light of maniacal fury and hatred—clothed in uncouth garments—and carrying a bomb in his pocket and a sword in his hand." But now "the most dangerous apostles of Communism and revolution today are fresh-faced [and] fair-haired."[22] The provost at UCLA, Ernest Moore, agreed, calling his campus "one of the worst hotbeds of campus Communism in America."[23] Despite the ferocious repression visited upon Southern California, the 1930s witnessed an upsurge of radicalism that the Red Squad could not arrest totally.

The Red Squad saw its solemn duty as preventing the blooming of radicalism. It went to extraordinary lengths to accomplish this goal. Though it did not hesitate to collaborate with Nazi Germany, it also ceaselessly monitored anti-Nazi efforts. In 1937 its report on a gathering of the Hollywood Anti-Nazi League noted that the "Jewish nationality" was "in predominance." This assemblage included the actor Paul Muni, "who, by the way, was just voted recognition in the Jewish Hall of Famous Jews [*sic*]."[24]

As a result of such suffocating monitoring, the upsurge of labor proceeded fitfully in Hollywood. In 1933 production in Los Angeles was shut down for a while by striking electricians, but scabs were brought in.

James G. Stewart, who was involved in this fracas, recalled that these new-comers helped to produce some flawed movies. After the regular workers returned, he had to dub *Little Women,* which had been poorly recorded during the strike.[25] Even after the official settlement, there was "continued disruption and conflict between . . . International Sound Technicians" and the International Brotherhood of Electrical Workers, Local 40.[26] The transition from silent films to "talkies" predictably inspired further juris-dictional disputes between and among unions.

The 1933 strike provided bitter lessons for IATSE. IBEW was able to use its studio and political ties, along with its organized crime connec-tions, to subdue IATSE.[27] By the 1940s CSU was accusing IATSE of em-ploying similar tactics.

Little Women was not the only film reportedly affected by the un-steady state of labor-management relations. *New Masses* charged that MGM's *Riff Raff* and Warner's *The Frisco Kid* were designed to bolster the antiunion movement. Worse, Paramount was contemplating doing a fea-ture on the strikebreaker Allan Pinkerton, with the emphasis on him "not as an enemy of labor, but as a hero of capital."[28]

Yet at this juncture, despite the beginnings of a budding radicalism, studio labor remained relatively weak. In fact, studio labor had taken a voluntary 10 percent wage cut in 1932. Such outrages led to the 1933 strike but disaster struck as not only scabs but also fellow workers—e.g., Team-sters and Musicians—freely crossed the picket lines while the loyalties of others—e.g., Cameramen—were bought with handsome raises.

This was a difficult time for Hollywood. Small studios like Tif-fany, Sono Art-World Wide, Invincible, and Mayfair disappeared.[29] Para-mount, which was to control 1,200 theaters in the United States, some 230 in Canada, and more in other nations, owned more movie houses than any other entity in the world; however, by early 1933 the company was in receivership and voluntary bankruptcy, which lasted for almost two years.[30]

Studio labor too had reached its nadir. Though Jack Warner was brag-ging in the fall of 1933 that the studios had just enjoyed the "biggest month as far as motion picture extras are concerned since talkies began"—with a startling "'increase' in the number of people on the payroll," at al-most "100%"—the unions were on life support.[31] Warner had reason to celebrate; by the end of 1934 he and his studio comrades had played a pivotal role in repulsing the profound challenge provided by Upton Sin-clair's race for governor; this victory was viewed as a permanent bruise for labor and the left.

Edmond DePatie, a vice president at Warner Bros., recalled that workers were "exploited en masse." It was "almost sickening" and "not uncommon to work people as late as eleven and twelve o'clock at night" and "every Saturday night, fifty two weeks a year."[32] And if you objected to this regimen, unemployment was your alternative. An official of the Screen Publicists Guild noted that "insecurity played a big role in [the] growth of the union. It was not uncommon for a man employed several years to be told on Friday morning that he wasn't working after Friday afternoon. It's nice to be able to call the stars by their first names, but when the reward for 15 years' service is a salary of $40," the privilege was hardly worth it.[33] The idea of a "reserve army of labor" was not a theoretical figment in Hollywood. Pat Casey, a studio executive, observed that before the advent of the CSU "there were thousands of fellows hanging around those gates trying to get jobs in the studios."[34]

Joseph North lamented the plight of screenwriters, who "punched a clock, sat in cubbyholes, writing to order like tailors cutting a suit. Actors worked when they worked; up early in the morning, on location till all hours."[35] Like others, he too was struck by the pervasive insecurity of the industry; actors and other creative types who had to dig deep into their psyches to tap their muse, were driven further into psychological turmoil by the instability of the industry in which they toiled.

★ Willie Bioff was born in Russia in 1899; he once organized kosher butchers in Chicago and had served a stint as a pimp before taking over a weakened IATSE local in the early 1930s with his close colleague George Browne—who once operated a soup kitchen. Browne, born in about 1893, had been defeated by a 2–1 margin as early as 1932 in his effort to lead an IATSE local.[36] At that juncture, the projectionists—the heart of the local—were an essential part of the industry, for if a film could not be screened, no revenue could flow to the studios. Indeed, the critical role of the projectionists convinced studio labor generally that it should align with IATSE—which had this worker group within its ranks—rather than another labor organization, such as CSU. The projectionists were the weak link seized by Bioff and Browne.

This link was seized—and maintained—with violence. Bioff, it was charged, "beat" Herbert Green, an official of the projectionists local "mercilessly with a blackjack, as the result of which [he] died."[37] In 1935 Clyde Osterberg was "rubbed out" while trying to organize an independent union of projectionists.[38] Days later, "Two-Gun" Louis Altrie was murdered while trying to organize a union comprising janitors who worked in theaters.[39]

One night Bioff and Browne were celebrating their good fortune at a Chicago nightspot, Nick Dean's One Hundred Club, a known hangout of Al Capone and his cronies. The two were gambling and lost huge amounts, but their sizable bankrolls caught the eye of resident mobsters. Shortly thereafter they were called to a meeting on Michigan Avenue across from the Carleton Hotel, where they were asked to turn over half of the union's revenues, a figure which later rose to two thirds—or else. They complied. Later Frank Nitti—the "enforcer"—installed his man, Isidore Zevin, as IATSE's accountant to make sure that there was no funny business when the time came for the mob's cut. Browne, who later became a vice president of the American Federation of Labor, also testified under oath that the attorney Sidney Korshak sat in on the meetings between himself and Nitti, as the latter's representative.[40]

In 1934 Bioff and Browne were invited to a dinner at the Casino de Paris in Manhattan. Bioff later testified on pain of being charged with perjury—that "the dinner was on the balcony of the theater cafe"; they sat at a "long table on the balcony. It was to introduce George Browne and me to Charlie Lucky"—i.e., the infamous gangster "Lucky" Luciano. "I am sure that Frank Costello was there and Jack Dragno [sic]" a leader of the L.A. mob. Browne and Bioff were told "many times to be free to call on Charlie Lucky or on Frank Costello if we find any difficulties here in our work, and if we need anything to call on them and be free to call on them, because that is their people." Later they met with Capone himself at his estate in Miami. With the connivance of the mob, Bioff and Browne were installed as leaders of IATSE nationwide. In return, the two received mob muscle to help in persuading nonunion movies houses to sign up with IATSE.

Later, Bioff recalled, "the time came when we all sat together, [Nicholas] Schenck [of MGM], [Sidney] Kent [of Fox], myself and Browne and agreed to take $50,000 from each of the major producing companies and $25,000 from each of the independent companies." CSU later argued that these payments were bribes to ensure labor peace, while the studios argued that they were being extorted by the mob. Undeniably, the centralized structure of IATSE, which forbade local strikes without the president's authorization, made control of this office a valuable prize indeed.

For individuals claiming they were being extorted, the executives were quite friendly toward Bioff. Joseph Schenck, a top executive at Fox, arranged for Bioff and his wife to be transported to Brazil and Europe in

1938 when tax agents wanted to query the union leader about the sources of his wealth—some of which came from the Schencks. Bioff longingly recalled the "Normandie . . . the finest cruise afloat." Onboard was the wife of Louis B. Mayer, "a very sweet woman," he noted fondly. Harry Warner and his wife—acting strangely for victims of extortion—sent a bon voyage telegram and orchids to Bioff's wife. The Bioffs were feted by producers in London, where reservations had been made for them at the posh Dorchester.

Nor was this the extent of the gratuities and hospitality Hollywood extended to Bioff. Joseph Schenck sold him some shares of Fox "when it was selling for $25 or 21 1/2 or something like that. He let me make that profit." Bioff also went to religious services with Harry Warner and visited his sprawling ranch, though he denied meeting the glamorous actress Claudette Colbert there. Bioff admitted to being just as close with Spyros Skouras of Fox as he was with the Warners. He often met with Harry Cohn and Jack Dragna at Roselli's apartment. And yes, Johnny Roselli visited Bioff's L.A. office at least twice a month to pick up the money that was supposedly extorted from the studios.[41]

To be fair, executives claimed to fear that great harm would befall them if they were not nice to Bioff and Browne. Nicholas Schenck insisted that "in one of our theaters . . . we found a bomb under the roof of the theater, that holds between 3800 and 4000 seats. We have reported it to the prosecutor and we got no help and were never able to find out who put it there."[42] However, the executives could not bring themselves to admit that their close relationship with the mob's union puppets stemmed from the need for mobster capital during the Great Depression. Nor could they answer satisfactorily why they didn't broach these illegal dealings with their board or their counsel, not to mention the L.A. district attorney.

Why did Nicholas Schenck fear that the government would find out about payments to the IATSE leadership? Most people being extorted would not be so anxious about the foul deed being discovered. Why did Schenck invite Browne to visit his Long Island estate so frequently and to take yachting trips with him? Why did the two intimately address each other as "Nick" and "George"? Why was there "discussion about the painters" at their meetings? Why did the film executive Sidney Kent speak at IATSE conventions and praise Browne effusively?[43] Why did Bioff and Browne claim that the moguls gave them money as an insurance policy to guard against the rise of a more progressive, CIO-like union?[44] How could Bioff, when he went to the chief editor of *Variety* to demand the printing of "complimentary" articles about the IATSE leadership, promise that the producers would withdraw advertising from the trade paper unless this demand were heeded? Why, after the editor refused, did one official at a congressional hearing claim, "I have all the *Varietys* of this period and I can assure you that there is no advertising in them."[45]

The studios' largesse allowed Bioff and Browne to live like latter-day rajahs. The 5'6", 200-pound Bioff was an incredible sight; he appeared to be neckless, with a head that seemed to rise directly from his muscular torso and shoulders. His moon-shaped face supported multiple chins, and the ugly scar under his lip accentuated this unpleasant visage. His boast about drinking "100 bottles of a certain brand of beer a day" meant that he had a distinctive odor, slurred speech, and occasionally, a confused mind.[46]

Yet the decidedly nonglamorous Bioff owned eighty acres in the lush San Fernando Valley "hard by the estates of Tyrone Power and Annabella, Clark Gable and Carole Lombard" and other glamorous stars; his ranch included "$600 olive trees . . . 'the biggest and oldest in California.'"[47] Browne was no pauper either. When Roselli introduced him to the patrician Alfred Vanderbilt at a plush club in Hollywood, it was just part of another ordinary day consorting with the privileged few.[48] Both leaders lived extremely well thanks to the sweaty toil of thousands of studio workers.

In the fall of 1935 more workers joined IATSE, while the mobsters were investing in the industry; in other words the mob was supplying both labor and capital to Hollywood. Using the subsequent leverage, the mob enabled thousands of workers—including "soundmen, the property-men, the greensmen, the electricians and the laboratory workers"—to enter IATSE with the studios' acquiescence. Ironically, the mob-led IATSE was closer to the ideal of an industrial union—a harbinger of the CIO—than CSU, a federation of craft unions.[49] Thus, one IATSE local with only two hundred members in 1933 had five thousand by 1937.[50] Correspondingly, organized crime's influence over the film industry grew dramatically during the 1930s.

This reality was little known, for media figures such as the columnist Victor Riesel were busily perpetrating the myth that studio labor was dominated by Communists. "By 1935" the "Communists and their comrades," he thundered, "dominated or controlled the movie cameramen's union, the sound men's outfit, the laboratory technicians (which they seized by blackmailing its leaders into resigning), the costumers and the studio editors."[51] Roy Brewer, a leader of the anticommunist forces that routed CSU, agreed: "[Y]ou see," he recalled, "in 1934, the Soviet Union dispatched funds to certain American Communists in order to finance the takeover of the motion picture industry. The idea was to use motion pictures as propaganda to soften the peoples of the world toward communism."[52] The public had difficulty becoming outraged about the domination of organized crime while being fed a steady diet of propaganda about domination by the organized left.

Soon after the Red Squad and its minions had thoroughly blunted labor radicalism, studio labor began clamoring against the misrule of Bioff and Browne. With the advent of their leadership, already bad working conditions apparently became worse. Scenic artists, costumers, plumbers, et al. were "on tap twenty-fours a day . . . and you better hug the telephone or someone else will get the call. You can be snatched to work on location for a couple of hours, then not see a paycheck for weeks." Sexual harassment was as common as boring movies.[53] By 1937 there was already a "merciless . . . blacklist" in operation that kept many workers from protesting.[54] Even so, the Screen Writers Guild, with the Communist John Howard Lawson leading the way, had demonstrated what was possible when it organized in the face of stiff resistance from the studio and their creation the Screen Playwrights.[55]

Thus, when Hollywood labor struck in 1937, ostensibly over a special 2 percent levy that lined the pockets of Bioff and Browne, the workers had two formidable forces to contend with—the studios and IATSE. The reporter Florabel Muir recalled later that at the strike's "height" a "group of strange outlanders arrived in town. Some of these men told around that they came from Chicago. . . . I saw these fellows in action. They all drove Zephyrs and obtained gun permits from the administration then governing Los Angeles." The mob had deployed these goons to pulverize studio labor, which in turn had secured muscle from the longshore union. Muir witnessed "one major engagement near the Pico Boulevard gate of the [Fox] studio in which fists put guns to flight. I also saw a platoon of swarthy gents identified as of the Chicago mopper-uppers swagger into a gun store directly across the street from . . . strike headquarters. Word came they were at target practice."[56]

While testifying at the Roselli trial, Herb Sorrell vividly recalled this strike, which lasted for about two months, ending on 10 June 1937. He detailed the melee at the painters' hiring hall on Santa Monica Boulevard, where the studio goons and their opponents broke bones in profusion. The mob also brought some thugs to confront Sorrell directly: the pugnacious pugilist was captain of the picket line at Warner Bros., and he later became captain over the lines at all the studios. One day he received a tip that the goons were about to strike; "we did not wait for them to attack us; we went and attacked them. We went to their hotels when they were having a meeting, and we would catch them coming out and we would slaughter them. . . . [W]e never carried a firearm, we never carried anything but our fists, but we knocked the devil out of them." When the mobsters tried to secure scabs to take the strikers' place, Sorrell and his comrades attacked again "and the ambulance made 19 trips hauling them away."

Sorrell and his co-workers were able to secure support from "liberal actors, writers and sympathetic people" and from the painters' union nationally, not to mention the San Francisco–based longshore union. Bioff fumed at this effort and said he "was going to get" Sorrell; "and in his gutter language [Sorrell] was going to have [Bioff] doing things to him down on Seventh and Broadway that no man should do to another— very bad. And [Bioff] repeated that time and time again." This was not the first—nor last—time that the allusion of homosexual abuse was raised as punishment by the mob and their allies.[57]

What had inflamed the workers' ire was not just the Bioff-Browne levy. Rather, the workers were irate that their 10 percent wage increase was undercut by the use of a double shift; e.g., one six-hour shift at Paramount would be followed by another for RKO—with no overtime pay. Thus, the increase was in effect a wage cut.[58]

Of course, in 1937 "lead property workers, for example, earned two and one half times as much per week as did U.S. manufacturing workers on the average, and over one and one half times as much per week as did traditionally well-paid newspaper, printing and publishing workers." However, despite earning high hourly or weekly rates, film workers often made low annual wages. IATSE "prop makers, electricians, and grips averaged between $1215–1738 for the year 1938. The U.S. Bureau of Labor Statistics estimated that a family of five in [Los Angeles] needed, at the very least, income of $2095 during 1938 to maintain 'minimum health and decency.'" Studios filmed primarily during spring and summer, so employment during the 1930s fluctuated between 19,500 in March to 27,500 in June to 18,500 in November.[59]

However, Hollywood labor could take heart from the obvious upsurge of labor in the region. From 1936 to 1938 "union membership in Los Angeles jumped from less than 20,000 to 125,000 (of about 600,000 workers in all job sectors)."[60] In such an atmosphere, the corruption of IATSE could not stand unchallenged.

IATSE—dissatisfied with the wealth generated by the levy and seemingly oblivious to the changing political dynamics—was in the midst of demanding "full jurisdiction" over "all workers in the production end of motion picture business from porters to stars."[61] An NLRB official, with typical understatement, acknowledged that this maneuver would "bring up a tremendous amount of opposition."[62] Senator Robert LaFollette was told that "the most vicious intimidation is being carried on against union men by the police, who are working closely with the employers in an effort to discredit union members and smash our unions. Gangsters and gunmen have been imported to this area . . . and the police department have issued gun permits to them."[63]

These events were enough to energize the most passive union members; consequently, the Federated Motion Picture Crafts (FMPC), which spearheaded the strike, attracted adherents. Harlan Holmden, an IATSE official, recalled later how Johnny Roselli had brought "five or six of his friends" to Los Angeles, "more or less to maintain order" among the increasingly restive workers. Holmden witnessed the union hall skirmish involving these "friends." There was "some broken [plate glass windows] and some furniture demolished"—along with a few arms and legs.[64]

The mobsters and the moguls directly collaborated to break this strike. Lew Blix, another IATSE official, testified under oath that he was in Bioff's office when Eddie Mannix, a studio executive, made the call to request strikebreakers against FMPC.[65]

Though FMPC waned against superior strength, Sorrell and the painters were big winners; that he had turned down Bioff's bribes in favor of battling the gangsters head-to-head brought new luster to his painters. Soon other crafts wanted to ally with his union, laying the basis for the formation of CSU. Although mob muscle did crush the progressive forces, the lessons learned by Sorrell set the stage for the rise of CSU.

★ The Bioff-Browne administration in IATSE—like many of its AFL counterparts—made no effort to alter the lily-white character of its many locals. In fact, IATSE sent numerous messages affirming racialism. The 1936 national convention in Kansas City was typical, with the event opening to the playing of "Dixie." Constructing whiteness and, more specifically, reconciling the component elements of whiteness on an altar of conservatism and defense of the status quo was a prime object of IATSE.

Naturally Hollywood rampantly discriminated against African Americans.[66] By the time CSU was finally crushed only 10 of the 9,635 weekly studio employees were African Americans, and all of those were actors. There was not "one Negro secretary, cutter, art director, cameramen, grip, reader, prop man, accountant . . . in the motion picture industry." For African Americans the "blacklist" came earlier, hit harder, and lingered longer.[67] Indeed, CSU never came to see that the illiberalism that sustained Jim Crow was the same one that sustained the blacklist.

Nevertheless, the unions' lily-whiteness was not solely due to CSU, since management had the primary role in hiring. Whatever the cause, when Ossie Davis and Ruby Dee came to Los Angeles in the late 1940s to act in a feature film, they "were immediately struck by the fact that we didn't see any black people working anywhere. No technicians, no grips, no electricians, no props people. We didn't see any dark skins in the makeup and wardrobe departments or as hairdressers. From the minute we entered the gate in the morning till the time we left, we were in an all-white world, and that reality was hard for us to ignore." They "once asked a makeup technician why he didn't inquire about the absence of blacks in the unions. . . . [H]e said . . . that he hadn't given it much thought." Unfortunately, this viewpoint was fairly typical, even in CSU.

CSU did not aggressively fight for racial equality, and as African American migration to Los Angeles increased in the 1940s, the union found it difficult to secure the support of blacks, though it was in desperate need of allies. Frances Williams was one of the leading black actresses —and activists—of her generation, going on in the 1980s in the twilight of her varied career to captivate television audiences with her performances in the show *Frank's Place*. She recalled that in the 1940s in Hollywood the black actor John Marriott, who was "extremely well-trained" and "had great dignity," was harassed by film crews who "purposely went out of the way to sabotage his career. . . .[T]he technicians adjusted the blinkers on the lights so that there wasn't one shot you could clearly recognize him." There was a "complete absence of black extras. The Screen Extras Guild had black members who were almost never hired." When the "first black technician [was] hired to work on a picture in Hollywood," she maintained with a lingering scintilla of bitterness, it was for the 1950s classic *Salt of the Earth,* which was produced by "blacklisted" left-wing artists.[68] As the 1990s wound down, Davis and Dee continued to maintain that "unions in the film industry were, and some still are, notoriously racist."[69] Despite its progressive profile, CSU did not forthrightly and rudely challenge this bias when it had the opportunity.

Women of all races within IATSE also suffered. They worked in jobs "traditionally associated with social constructions of femininity such as office work, make-up, hair-styling, costuming, entry-level animation, and screen story analysis."[70] During the war they moved into new jobs "as a result of manpower shortage," as "screenwriters . . . laboratory technicians, film cutters, cartoonists, script clerks and readers."[71] But with the disappearance of CSU, women's already weak position deteriorated further. According to a *Variety* headline, when Soviet film workers toured Hollywood some years after the smashing of CSU, they queried wondrously, "Why are there no women comrades?"[72]

Such matters hardly concerned Bioff and Browne, however, at their 1936 Kansas City convention of 666 locals (with only 27 unrepresented). Browne reported that "non-union [movie] houses" on the West Coast were "a rarity." He was upset, however, by the fact that in many cities nationally "cashiers, doormen and ushers" at movie houses were organized by other unions. He was concerned that the New Deal's Works Progress Administration and its federal theater project might attract patrons who otherwise might go to movie houses and commercial theaters, thus undermining the employers of IATSE members. He objected to the existence of the American Society of Cinematographers, which he considered a "company union" that had "intimidated" and "coerced" workers to join its ranks. He wanted to organize carnival and circus workers, as well as workers in night clubs, supper clubs, cabarets, and summer theaters. If he had succeeded, the mob would have tightened its stranglehold over the leisure time—and consciousness—of a good deal of the public.[73]

This situation explains why the left's challenge during the 1937 strike had been met with such savagery by the mob—much was at stake. When IATSE met in Cleveland in 1938 there was an air of self-congratulation on having beaten back the left; "the ever popular 'Dixie' drew the first burst of applause from the Southern Delegation," signaling that IATSE's conservatism remained hegemonic. However, there were already signs that the comfortable consensus was being challenged. Jeff Kibre, viewed widely as a Communist, presented a report from "IA Progressives" in Hollywood: these locals with membership of about 10,000 had been under a virtual state of emergency for 2.5 years; they were chafing under the 2 percent assessment, which like most union mandates was enforced via "intimidation through gang bosses." There was a "speedup" that led to "accidents to members [as] an almost daily occurrence." Despite hourly wage increases, annual wages continued to fall; craftspeople who made $2,400 in 1929 received only $1,500 in 1937. Half the membership was unemployed, but no effort was made to help them. Studios tended to make films during spring and summer, which left many workers with long stretches of inactivity. IATSE required relatively high fees, dues, and assessments, while studios often hired and fired without regard to seniority. During the 1937 strike the L.A. Central Council had passed a resolution calling IATSE "a company union and a scab-herding agency" and Kibre was hard-pressed to disagree. The "IA Progressives"—who ultimately formed the kernel from which CSU grew—wanted one general studio union in a "single headquarters." Separate crafts should be maintained and should meet monthly, they thought, but each craft should elect delegates to a general administrative council.

Kibre's intervention was not greeted with equanimity. In fact, presenting this report required enormous bravery, for the mob was notorious for murdering union dissidents. Kibre escaped unscathed, however, and the convention proceeded with remarks provided by Mayor—and future U.S. Supreme Court Justice—Harold Burton, Sidney Kent of Fox, and other dignitaries.[74]

However, after the convention, the IATSE leadership did not forget Kibre. Born in Philadelphia in 1906, Kibre came to Los Angeles in 1908. He majored in English at UCLA before gravitating to Hollywood, where his mother worked. In 1934 he joined the Communist Party and became one of Hollywood's leading Reds.[75] Somehow IATSE got hold of a report supposedly written by Kibre and intended for the party leadership. The union circulated the document widely. Here Kibre was said to be seeking a break with IATSE "as the transitional stage towards an Industrial Union affiliated with the CIO." Hollywood, Kibre reportedly said, "probably has the greatest labor ramifications of any major industry in the country. There are more categories of labor and greater variations of income than in any other single industry. On top of this, the contradiction of craft unionism in an economic area demanding industrial action [has] virtually bankrupted trade union morale. Here for the most part is not the problem of organizing the unorganized but the more complex [task] of organizing the disorganized." Kibre was said to be expecting an even larger slash in union wages than had been experienced so far and, thus, "the IA as a company instrument must become industry wide to fulfill its role." In other words, IATSE would not be able to contain workers' anger at this cut unless it encompassed virtually all of studio labor. This could only worsen the horrid conditions in the industry, where seamstresses could earn as little as 35 cents per hour while actors could earn $250,000 working on the same project. Yet like the mob, the Communists were said to be looking ahead to organizing hundreds of thousands of workers in the leisure and amusement industries.[76]

IATSE's wailing publicity over this report indicated not only that Bioff and Browne were becoming increasingly nervous about maintaining their rule, but also they were increasingly resorting to the Red Scare to deflect attention from their own misdeeds. At the 1940 convention in Louisville, the ritualistic playing of "Dixie" seemed to have a desperate air about it. Browne's report hysterically rambled on about the perils of Communism, "the most imminent and dangerous force standing in the path of our continued success." The locus for this pestilence was California; "only recently" did IATSE "succeed in suppressing a Communistic element that was threatening the existence of our West Coast locals." Approvingly, he cited the House Un-American Activities Committee, which had arrived at similar conclusions about the Reds in Los Angeles. "The conditions existing on the West Coast," Browne concluded with dismay, "are entirely different from the rest of the country. Our International being labor's foremost representatives in the Coast's principal industry . . . it is only natural to expect that we would bear the brunt of such attacks."[77] Though Seattle and San Francisco understandably were seen as the vanguard of labor radicalism in the West, given the general strikes that had rocked both cities in previous years, studio labor was beginning to stand out as a similar beacon of militancy in the open-shop haven that was Los Angeles. Browne was worried justifiably about the left's dredging up the tangled legal problems of his comrade Bioff, and about a possible indictment as a result. Browne was even more worried about the challenge of the left-leaning United Studio Technicians Guild to IATSE hegemony. Studio executives, particularly from MGM, had met at length with Bioff and Browne to ensure an IATSE victory, but there were disturbing signs that organized crime's hegemony among studio labor might eventually succumb to the strength of the organized left.[78]

Herb Sorrell argued cogently that "Willie Bioff made more Communists in Hollywood than any other Communist organizer could possibly make. He laid down the racketeering, domineering attitude to the workers, and he made them do things that they did not want to do, and they resented it."[79] Sorrell was right; Bioff and Browne's actions did engender an opposite radical reaction. Even after the 1939 pact between the USSR and Germany, which notoriously drew no loud objection from U.S. Communists, Red prestige continued to grow. This success resulted not because of Moscow gold, but instead because the party seemed to be the only organized force with enough muscle and organizational facility to confront an IATSE leadership backed by the brute strength of organized crime.

★ As World War II approached, the political dynamics within the United States began to change. The impending alliance with the Soviet Union helped to erode the anticommunism that had buoyed Bioff and Browne, just as movies themselves helped to alter the perceptions of Reds.[80] By the spring of 1941 both IATSE leaders had been indicted for their financial miscues.[81] It was in such an environment that Johnny Roselli was put on trial, and Bioff and Browne were ousted from the IATSE leadership—a development that supposedly extinguished mob influence in the union.[82] A "popular front"—a broad array of Communist and other forces united against the ultraright and fascism—was arising.

Similar reverberations were occurring in film industry unions with profiles similar to that of IATSE. In the spring of 1941 Ben Budman, a member of the Teamsters' Hollywood local was expelled for being a Communist. There was nothing extraordinary about his dismissal, except that the union's general counsel, Joseph Padway, intervened, reminding business agent Joseph Tuohy that the firing had violated due process.[83] Violating the rights of a Red would earlier have been a trifling issue, but the political climate was changing. The Teamsters were discovering that "because of the higher wages paid . . . many people who are presently employed in defense industries are attempting to quit their jobs in vital war work to obtain employment in the motion picture industry." This stampede was bringing in added dues, and the new political environment did not allow the unrestrained red-baiting that had previously characterized this union.[84] Particularly after June 1941 when Germany invaded the Soviet Union, and the year after when the United States and the USSR became close allies, assaults on the rights of Communists were seen as untenable. Thus, when the right-leaning Tuohy aligned with conservative forces in Hollywood, he was reproved for joining those "that have nailed us to the cross during all the years in which we were endeavoring to organize."[85]

Even the Screen Actors Guild (SAG), which eventually became a bulwark of opposition against CSU, was showing signs of progressivism as the war was launched. Jimmy Cagney, Edgar Bergen, Roddy McDowall, Jack Benny, Loretta Young, and many others gathered for a birthday bash for President Roosevelt.[86] Cagney, who was close to the left, assumed the leadership of SAG in 1943.[87] SAG worked with the California State

Federation of Labor on basic working-class issues concerning prices and wages.[88] The actor, it was said, must come down from his "ivory" tower and act politically.[89] "Leading actresses of the USSR" were praised and "anti-Negro discrimination" was excoriated.[90] SAG sought to organize film extras, "bit players, stuntmen, etc.," but lost to the competing Screen Players Union. Yet even this defeat showed the changing atmosphere, for not only were unions able to organize, but the campaign was characterized by "mass meetings and underground pulling and hauling for votes."[91] Previously mass meetings in Hollywood to organize a union probably would have been broken up by either the Red Squad or the mobsters.

Writers had long been more militant than actors, and this situation did not change as the war approached. Ella Winter acknowledged that the writers were the "group most feared by Hollywood producers"; they "deal with those uncontrollable entities, 'ideas'; and you don't know where an idea might lead you." Writers were beginning to object to the system whereby "studios own everything a writer creates—plays, novels, radio scripts, poems—if written while he is under contract, and [a] contract for one year calls for three months without pay." With wonder, Winter remarked, "[I]n the last few years there have been great changes in Hollywood. The town has become union-conscious and world-conscious"; writers were "ceasing to be morticians and are becoming doctors."[92]

The mood of progressivism was spreading. In the summer of 1942 office workers in five L.A. film distribution offices went on strike; the action ended after seven days with an agreement by the employer to "grant union shop and job classifications substantially the same as those in Hollywood studios."[93]

The FBI could not help but notice these liberalizing developments, not least because of their reflection on the silver screen. Like meticulous film critics, the FBI minutely analyzed a multitude of films deemed to be pro-Soviet or overly radical, such as *Mission to Moscow, Action in the North Atlantic, Hangmen Also Die, Keeper of the Flame, Edge of Darkness, North Star, For Whom the Bell Tolls, Song of Russia,* and *Seventh Cross.*[94] The FBI kept lists of everyone involved with such films, even though only a few people directly affected the ideological stance taken by this engaged cinema.

However, with the winds blowing so resolutely to the left, intimidating those drifting in that direction was difficult. The United Auto Workers was among the unions producing educational films and contemplating the production of feature-length films, all with a reform-minded touch.[95] The Hollywood Writers Mobilization and the Hollywood Democratic Committee were among the left-leaning organizations that flourished during the early 1940s.[96]

Besides the leavening influences of the war, other developments shaped Hollywood during this time. The struggle of set designers was at the heart of CSU, and unfolding events gave them an advantageous position. Shooting that had formerly been done at remote locations was being moved to "home lots. There will be extensive building of permanent outdoor sets in the heart of Hollywood once more." The impetus for this "re-centralization" was the "increase in planes zooming through [the] San Fernando Valley skies for testing, training and service maneuvers. The valley studios—Warner's, Universal, Republic—are moving all the outdoor sets possible under soundproof stages. Columbia will make less and less use of its 40 acre development of street sets in the valley and find outdoor space nearer home. . . . Script workers are rapidly developing new techniques to keep their characters off the streets. Process work— the use of canned shots of foreign street scenes and scenery racing past the car window—will come into its heyday."[97] By bringing more workers under one roof, this "re-centralization" facilitated worker unity and union organizing while enhancing the role of set designers.

This impetus for set designers simultaneously boosted CSU—and Herb Sorrell. He had already played a leading role in a highly contested strike among cartoonists,[98] and since then he had been regarded as Hollywood's top labor leader. This position gave him the clout needed to form CSU.[99]

By early 1941 *Variety* itself was touting Sorrell as "studio labor's No. 1 leader."[100] Two years later this paper of record concluded that his "Painters Local 644 now is generally recognized as the No. 1 film union. . . . Let a union mention Sorrell and the Producers reach for a pen to sign" a contract.[101] All manner of studio labor flocked to Sorrell and his Painters, because of their supposed ability to deliver sound contracts.

The Communist Party had been accused of paying inordinate attention to Hollywood, but actually the steel and auto industries were more to its taste—and theory. One writer in *New Masses,* an organ that often reflected the party's viewpoint, observed that "it was once the universal custom to dissolve in uncontrollable belly-laughter at the mere mention of the word 'Hollywood,' and it is still the practice among some superannuated esthetes." Yes, "the large majority of films are characterized by bad taste, cardboard characters, artificial plotting, witless wisecracks, slapstick, stale situations, an absence of historical or day-to-day realism and often by themes either dated or distorted." Yet this "young . . . art form" seemed transformed by the war. At a meeting of film unions and guilds, the article continued, "they were making the kind of speeches that I once heard only at the most advanced political gatherings." The author had to "pinch" himself "constantly to make sure it was all happening." [102]

Actually, this was just a bit of condescension from this often "New York–centric" organ, which paid more attention to theater and novels than film. But what could not be ignored was that the left—including the Communists—had been able to develop a foothold in one of the most important and profitable industries in the nation.

REDS

By 1945 the Communist Party in Hollywood was a power to be reckoned with, but the road had been long and rocky. There was the ever-present Red Squad to contend with, not to mention the abject hostility from the captains of industry in Southern California. Though much has been made of the alleged Red influence on the movies' content, anti-Red propaganda is easier to discern. Hollywood waged an "undeclared film war" against any hint of Bolshevism, characterized by a "relentlessness and unequivocal viciousness," which was replicated off-screen.

However, by the time World War II had commenced and the USSR became a "noble ally," this hostility began to soften; Bolshevism itself "received positive treatment in over one hundred feature-length film releases." *Mission to Moscow*, the most oft cited example of this trend was a "two hour long cinematic hagiography of Stalin's regime." But the pro-Sovietism of Hollywood extended much further; "attacks upon domestic radicalism and militant labor"—a staple of prewar cinema—"were basically terminated for the duration of the war."[1] As the documentary film *Red Hollywood* suggests, Communists and leftists in the film industry were able to insert progressive content into films, particularly during the war. Two films by the Communist screen-writer Dalton Trumbo—*Thirty Seconds over Tokyo* and *A Guy Named Joe*—were among the top ten highest-grossing films of 1944; the screenplay for *The Pride of the Marines* was written by Communist Albert Maltz.[2] This cinematic détente also occurred off-screen; for a brief historical moment during the war, the role of Communists in the United States seemed to be normalizing.

If a card-carrying Communist in the 1920s—during the height of the rambunctious Red Squad—had been told that Hollywood would change its tune by the early 1920s, she would have been justifiably skeptical. For the 1920s were a harsh decade indeed for those who proclaimed their allegiance to socialism, working-class radicalism—and Moscow.

The party in Southern California was marked by sharp sociological divisions: some members spoke Spanish, others Hungarian; proletarians coexisted with those mired in the middle class; urbanites read the same party organ as suburbanites; Jews attended meetings with those from Christian backgrounds. Within this diverse world, the Hollywood Left coexisted uneasily. Some leaders, like Nemmy Sparks, felt intensely loyal to the New York City leadership, while others, like Dorothy Healey, exemplified a peculiarly Californian sensibility that often conflicted with Eastern rules, patterns, and even ideology. This diversity was a strength, yes, but it was also a recipe for taut conflict—particularly when external forces were bent on accomplishing this result.

William Ward Kimple of the LAPD spent sixteen years as an undercover agent infiltrating the party, and even served as a local leader until 1939. He was "unit literature agent, unit educational director, unit organizer, the assistant to the Los Angeles County membership department and an alternate on the disciplinary committee on the county level. His wife Clara . . . who also spied on the [CP] was the Los Angeles County dues secretary for the Hollywood subsection . . . [and] secretary of [the L.A. County] disciplinary committee." At this time a vast army of spies operated within political organizations; from 1945 to 1960 the FBI alone employed a reputed 36,000 informants nationally.

Marion Miller, who also infiltrated the party in Los Angeles, conceded that "she was more severe than others in disciplining and expelling recalcitrant members." These spies wreaked havoc on the party and the organizations—like unions—of which they were a part. Burton Levine has wondered if the party "might have developed in some other way" but for spies "pushing it into secrecy, conspiracy, isolation and paranoia." This is a hard question to answer definitively, but agents of disruption did evidently push the party in Los Angeles in unwise directions.[3] Hollywood, which tended to attract the "lumpen"—prostitutes, gangsters, drug dealers, thieves, et al.—was a particular target since the authorities historically had recruited spies from this unstable stratum.[4]

True to its name, the Red Squad kept a close watch on the Communists. Its "weekly intelligence reports" of the 1920s concentrated disproportionately on Communist activities. The squad noticed when the party-influenced Trade Union Education League became "very active," it monitored the *Daily Worker*'s "first appearance" in the city, and watched carefully when the "Walt Whitman School" was opened under the party's auspices. It kept a list of "intellectual radicals" (somehow even obtaining a copy of "Upton Sinclair's confidential list") and attended the exhibitions of "Communist propaganda" films. In a representative maneuver a "confidential informant" told the squad that "there are a great number of communists and their sympathizers who are members of the local Musicians union."[5]

The Red Squad worked closely with local businesspeople in observing Communist activity. Thus, in 1929 a confidential letter by William Hynes of the LAPD told local Standard Oil executives that the CP had established a club in San Pedro, "calculated to appeal to the young worker through his desire for companionship and amiable surroundings. . . . [A] few books, taken from the Los Angeles Communist Party headquarters serve as a nucleus around which a large library will be built. An all-electric radio has been installed, making it possible for many and every taste to be entertained with football games, jazz, operatic music, scientific talks. . . . [T]he club rooms are already becoming a popular rendezvous for the more militant and aggressive seamen. . . . in the short space of one week's time, about fifteen new members have been signed up."[6] LAPD routinely shared such detailed reports with executives, Pinkerton's, other police departments — any with a desire to liquidate the Communist Party. This bilateral cooperation also included the Ku Klux Klan.

The Klan's Exalted Cyclops in Los Angeles offered to share his group's own tidbits on the Communists with the Red Squad and the California Grand Dragon forwarded a resolution to Hynes praising his outstanding work.[7] In 1934 R. C. Flournoy of the Imperial Palace Invisible Knights of the Ku Klux Klan sent a "Dear Bill" missive to Captain Hynes concerning an "important matter to take up with you as soon as possible."[8] Given previous practice, this "important matter" probably concerned harassment of labor and the left.

In a precursor of privatization, when it was not breaking up party meetings,[9] the Red Squad often hired itself out to employers to disrupt strikes. In 1935 the "Furniture Mfg. Assc." gave Hynes $85.50 after he performed an "investigation of violence" by "strikers" and checked the "auto-licenses" of "strikers in and about [the] premises of union headquarters."[10] This service to employers helps explain the curious fact — revealed during his divorce — that Hynes, who did not make more than $200 per week, had $40,000 in the bank.[11]

Despite this repressive atmosphere, the Communist Party — buoyed by its opposition to fascism and its championing of labor and minority rights—was able to make some headway in Los Angeles. This success was partly due to the L.A. CP's early reputation as one of the least sectarian units of the organization nationally. In 1930, dissidents were being ousted from the party but in East Los Angeles, "party policy" was to accommodate "even Lovestoneites"—those viewed as hopeless rightists in other cities—at the party conference at 2704 Brooklyn Avenue; "in carrying out this policy," it was noted, "local conditions must be taken in account when adopting decision[s]."[12]

In 1937 the *Los Angeles Times* reported on a nine-thousand-strong party meeting at the Olympic Auditorium; the party's industrial section provided $1,531 to the party, while the "movie section" was second with $1,000; a "strange woman" gave $1,000 and the African American section chipped in $376.[13] This list of donors represented a rough approximation of party strength, with auto and other industrial workers leading the way and studio labor following right behind. During this era the L.A. County sheriff's office concluded that the "Communist Party leadership and a majority of its rank and file are of the Hebrew race, principally Russian, Polish, Hungarian and Roumanian Jews. . . . [There are] quite a large group of Japanese; the Japanese Communist Party members are particularly cocky and militant, and have distinguished themselves during disorders and riots incident to the quelling of communist demonstrations by their assaults on police officers."[14]

The sheriff's office neglected to mention the African Americans who had flocked to the party's banner in Los Angeles. In 1932 those defending the Scottsboro 9—nine black youths charged falsely with sexually molesting two white women in Alabama—held a rally in Los Angeles that attracted a recent black migrant, Pettis Perry, who went on to play a leading role in the party. In 1938 he became the "first Negro" to run for the State Board of Equalization, polling "better than 65,000 votes." In 1940 he obtained 60,000 votes in a bid for Congress. In 1942 he was the "first Negro" to run for secretary of state, garnering 42,000 votes. These feats were accomplished in the face of a severe assault. The party itself, Perry recalled, was basically "outlawed" until 1934; "all left wing organizations" were "subject to intimidation" by the Red Squad. Many Reds were "beaten, jailed, some maimed for life." Still, Perry and his comrades forced a number of retail establishments to hire numerous "young Negro women" as sales clerks—a major breakthrough during that time—and participated in many struggles on behalf of labor.[15]

By 1934 the party had opened a school at 210 South Spring Street in downtown Los Angeles. Courses were taught in Russian, and included "training for the class struggle,"[16] political economy, "Negro Liberation," trade unionism, and "revolutionary art." An extension branch, the "Hollywood Workers School," operated at 1115 1/2 North Lillian Way. According to one source, this educational enterprise was "reputed to be the second largest of the scores operated by Communists in the United States—surpassed only by the school in New York."[17] The Red Squad reported in detail on who attended these classes, including the number of students present, and even collected the license plate numbers of those who had driven there.[18]

The Red Squad worriedly reported that the "period from June 1933 to June 1934 has witnessed a growth of the revolutionary movement in the United States and particularly in California, the rapidity of which has been almost unbelievable." Two years earlier "the Communist Party in Los Angeles could boast of only a few hundred members, the majority of whom were of foreign birth and whose activities were confined approximately to the environs of Boyle Heights." Although confessing proudly that "avowed enemies of our government are suppressed in Los Angeles," the squad did concede sadly that party "supporters include ministers, doctors, lawyers, teachers, students both of grade school and universities and workers in every industry." The LAPD was "at all times fully informed of the plans and activities" of the party via "under cover operatives," but the organization was unable to halt the increase in Communists.[19] Evidently LAPD had overlooked the ravages of the Great Depression in seeking to comprehend party growth.

Hollywood Communists took advantage of numerous forums to educate the public, some of which came back to haunt them. For example, in March 1935 John Howard Lawson debated Roger Baldwin of the American Civil Liberties Union; the screenwriter took the affirmative on the subject "Are Soviet Methods of Political Justice Defensible[?]"[20] Once the Cold War was launched, some Reds who had defended "Soviet methods" were placed on the defensive.

Still, the biting Depression, which hit California particularly hard, deflected the attention of many Angelenos away from events ten thousand miles away in Moscow. Certainly by the mid-1930s, the Red Squad had its hands full keeping up with the Communists. The group's activities included monitoring individual Reds, like Betty Arden, "a member of the CP," who "is now working as an 'extra' in various studios. She has been very successful for the past few weeks and has the assurance that she will have work the greater part of the time." She was part of the "newly formed MOTION PICTURE SUB SECTION,"[21] which was a constituent element of the CP's concentration in "three major industries[:] . . . studios, airplane and transportation."[22]

The party nationally was moving toward the concept of the "popular front," embracing liberals and centrists; this trend, along with the liberalizing effect brought by Upton Sinclair's strong race for governor, helped widen the party's acceptance.[23] In 1937 L.A. Communist Emil Freed recalled the not-so-distant past, "when we received an address of a meeting, we generally placed it in a gelatin capsule ready to be swallowed in case of arrest," but with the strike in Hollywood, things had changed so much that the party could proffer its support openly.[24]

The Red Squad viewed this development with ever increasing concern. Officers were shocked when in 1937 "Mrs. Alice Eaton, whose husband was Mayor of Los Angeles in the years 1900 to 1904, was introduced [at a Red event] as one of the recent recruits to the Communist Party." Eaton was even active in the conservative Daughters of the American Revolution. The Red Squad was beginning to believe that the party's slogan, that Communism was "20th Century Americanism," may not have been misleading.[25] Squad members viewed with alarm the growing attendance at the workers' school, and seemed particularly concerned over the increasing numbers of Jews in the party's ranks.[26]

Consistent with the theory that the industrial proletariat—factory workers most notably—would play the greatest role in transforming society, the Communist Party in Southern California paid much more attention to the aircraft, oil, auto, and rubber industries and comparatively less attention to the studios. Nonetheless, by 1937 there were reportedly "at least two units in important locals" in Hollywood. However—perhaps tellingly—calls for "at least one Sunday each month" to be devoted to distributing party literature and attaining an L.A. County goal of 2,500 dues-paying members by 1938 did not single out Hollywood for special attention.[27]

Law enforcement officials in the state concluded that by 1937 there were a "total of 226 units and branches in the California district" of the party. "None of these are shop units," although "55 are industrial units and the balance are street units and branches of which some 28 are professional units." If accurate, this assertion suggests that even during the halcyon days of 1937, the party had a surprising inability to establish units on the shop floor. These unit memberships ranged from "3 party members to 50," and the authorities were gravely concerned with their interracial character, particularly when it led to "the mating of Communist white girls with Negro men."[28]

The CP was probably more racially and ethnically diverse than any other party in California at that time. In 1937 the state's registration showed that 194 of the 4,800 members were African American; 174 were Mexican immigrants; 38 were Japanese immigrants; 20 were Chinese immigrants; and 446 were Russian immigrants. The party had grown from 2,500 in 1936 to 6,000 by 1938, and the goal of 10,000 members statewide by 1939 seemed eminently realistic; of that 6,000, about 2,500 were in Los Angeles, and 240 of those were African Americans. The L.A. CP's numbers even seemed to exceed those of the San Francisco Bay area, which had a well-deserved reputation for radicalism—particularly after the tumultuous general strike of 1934. L.A. County's fund-raising quota — $12,500—dwarfed those of San Francisco ($6000) and Alameda ($2500) Counties.[29]

Many factors contributed to the party's growth in the state: the devastation of the Great Depression, the rising specter of fascism, the widely shared perception (particularly among minorities) that other organizations were ill-equipped to combat racism, the upsurge by labor, the defense of immigrants. However, in terms of generating a grassroots response in the state, few events moved Californians as much as the campaign to free labor organizer Tom Mooney (and his comrade Warren Billings). The pair had been jailed after allegedly planting a bomb at a 1916 rally in San Francisco organized by conservative business interests to generate support for the United States' entry into World War I. It was the Mooney case that provided an opening for Communists to work more closely with trade unionists, and this was a major step toward Red influence in Hollywood.[30]

The letterhead of the "Hollywood Committee for the Freedom of Mooney and Billings" included Edward Arnold, Herbert Biberman, Dudley Nicholas, James Cagney, Lester Cole, Melvyn Douglas, Ira Gershwin, Dashiell Hammett, Lillian Hellman, George Kaufman, Boris Karloff, Ring Lardner, Jr., Groucho Marx, Frederic March, Robert Montgomery, Paul Muni, Clifford Odets, Gale Sondergaard, Donald Ogden Stewart, and many more.[31] In 1937 members of this group joined Nathaniel West, Douglas Fairbanks, Frances Farmer, Jerome Kern, Sidney Buchman, and others in filing a petition with Lt. Governor George J. Hatfield of California to demand a "pardon" for Mooney.[32]

The Communist Party played an important role in this "united front" to free Mooney. Party leader William Z. Foster was in frequent contact with "dear friend Tom," reporting to him when "in Los Angeles" for "meetings . . . devoted . . . entirely to your case."[33] At the party's national nominating convention in 1932 at the Chicago Coliseum, "over [a] thousand delegates and . . . fourteen thousand visitors" sent "revolutionary greetings" to Mooney.[34]

The movement that sought to elect the famed writer Upton Sinclair as governor also allied with Mooney. Sinclair promised that "my first action, if I become Governor of California will be to pardon Mooney."[35] He went on to tell President Roosevelt that "we have in California at present one of the worst governments in the history of the United States," and that such malfeasance was what led to Mooney's being "convicted by perjured testimony." Sinclair crusaded avidly for Mooney's freedom, on one occasion providing a list of "ten or eleven thousand names" from his own gubernatorial campaign "to be used for sending a copy of [Mooney's] last pamphlet."[36]

George Bernard Shaw, writing Sinclair from San Simeon, expressed solidarity but still harbored a "fear of associating you with my own political views, which are more extreme than yours."[37] Other celebrities were not as reticent, with Frederic March being foremost among them. With Frank Davis, a "producer at MGM," he helped to make a film on Mooney's case.[38] He collected numerous checks for the campaign. He "distributed quite a bit" of literature on Mooney; in March 1937 at the Screen Actors Guild he was "able to get seven or eight more signatures" on a petition.[39] Robert Montgomery, a future leader of the right in Hollywood, gave $100 to the campaign; March's "Hollywood group" was taking "immediate steps to raise another five hundred dollars" for Mooney.[40]

In many ways, the Mooney campaign was a prelude to the advance of studio labor. Around Mooney gathered Communists, celebrities, and—especially—labor. In a precursor of the rise of "IA Progressives," a number of IATSE officials contributed funds to Mooney,[41] as did the Teamsters[42] and Carpenters.[43]

Herb Sorrell's union, the Painters, was in the vanguard of Mooney's defense. Communist Louis Weinstock played a significant role within this union and this campaign. In 1939 he brought greetings to Mooney "in the name of 15,000 organized painters in the city of New York."[44] In fact, throughout the difficult years of Mooney's imprisonment, the Painters were among the most reliable of donors to his campaign.[45] When Mooney was pardoned, C. E. Ripple, a leader of the Painters in Los Angeles, was among the first to express "gratitude" to Governor Culbert Olson, who made the pardon one of his first official acts after being elected in 1938.[46]

Unions and individuals who played a pivotal role in Hollywood in the 1940s were staunch in their defense of Mooney in the 1930s. The Musicians union donated generously.[47] During this earlier period, Jack Tenney was one of the more reliable progressive voices in the state assembly, before moving to the right and becoming the chief legislative tormenter of CSU. Thus, in 1937 he was claiming credit for being "responsible" for a "resolution to free" Mooney that passed in Sacramento.[48] Sam Yorty, the future conservative mayor of Los Angeles, whose ideological journey was similar to that of Tenney, also was a firm Mooney supporter at this point; Mooney's "appearance before the legislature is an event in my life I shall never forget," he gushed to "my dear Tom."[49]

Soon Tenney, Yorty, and countless others would retreat from their embrace of Mooney. Mooney's identification with labor and the left came to symbolize a progressive era that some would just as soon have forgotten. On the other hand, the Mooney campaign brought closer together various factions within studio labor—painters, carpenters, teamsters, et al.—who were to shake the industry. It was no accident that the 1938 election of Culbert Olson as governor was viewed as an extension of the Mooney campaign, for his release signaled that even in the dankest precincts of California, change was under way.

Ironically, a few years after Mooney's pardon, Assemblyman Jack Tenney was leading the charge in Sacramento against the Communist Party, a crusade that ultimately brought much grief to CSU. In 1943, when many in Hollywood were singing the praises of Moscow, Tenney was holding hearings that heaped scorn on Communists. There was lurid testimony presented about "beach parties in Santa Monica where white girls were used as lures in recruiting Negroes into the Communist Party." Sensational discussion told about the " 'prostitution squad' of the Communist Party, girls who acted as lures in this endeavor." Filipinos, it was reported, were lured into the party "by the use of marijuana."

According to Tenney, an outside force had moved into Hollywood in a big way in 1934, but it was not organized crime—it was the Communist Party. That year, he alleged, "the then Soviet Commisar for heavy industries" sent a "considerable sum of money" to the party in Hollywood "for the purpose of creating an entering wedge into the motion picture industry. . . . Strong Communist factions were implanted and maintained in nearly every Hollywood trade union that had jurisdiction over anything in the motion picture studios." Hollywood had become a "veritable mecca for the Communist cultural clique," and "there is no doubt" about the Reds' "close association" with one "Herbert K. Sorrell." The prominent black architect Paul Williams was listed as a fellow traveler, along with Philip Dunne and Melvyn Douglas.

Yet even before Tenney's legislative crusade against the left and labor, troubling signs of a backlash had arisen against the success of the Mooney campaign. Mooney's lawyer, Leo Gallagher, was viewed as the Communist éminence grise and as a result faced "proceedings to disbar me."[50] The authorities were displeased with Gallagher's view of the Soviet Union as a "a land where conditions grow better from day to day and where every worker enjoys security against every unhappy contingency."[51] Others were unhappy when Gallagher was earlier "called to Nazi Germany to defend the victims of the Reichstag fire frame-up."[52]

The impending war with the Axis powers served to heighten hysteria even more. In the midst of the Pacific War, people feared Japan's plan to "dominate the white races."[53] But this was not the only concern on the ethnic front. Later a legislative committee in Sacramento expressed earnest interest in the "quiet Communist infiltration into the American Jewish Congress." It was noted that "nine out of twenty-one directors of Warner Brothers are Jews; five out of fifteen directors of Paramount Pictures, Inc. . . . Metro-Goldwyn-Mayer, Inc. and Columbia Pictures have a slight majority of Jews in the directorate."[54] The right wing in California had grown deeply suspicious of the Japanese and of leftist Jews. The defeat of Tokyo and the Japanese American internment had helped to assuage the former fear but the latter remained a constant throughout CSU's existence.

Jack Tenney was simply articulating the deep-seated fears felt by many about the Communist Party's apparent strength in Los Angeles generally and Hollywood specifically. The landscape revealed several symbols marking the party's presence. One analyst noted nervously that "in the [L.A.] area as far south as Long Beach, the Communists use wire holders on street corners for distribution of their 'People's Daily World.' This is a more public distribution of Communist papers than in any other city—even New York."[55] The blacklisted screenwriter Abraham Polonksy was being dismissive and impudent when he suggested that the party was like "Sunset Strip. Thousands of people used to go there, hang around a few days and then pass on to some place else."[56] However, Los Angeles housed many streets with hardly any foot traffic, so the party's ability to attract gawkers, if not members, still concerned some.

This concern was not alleviated when Arnaud D'Usseau wrote in *New Masses* that Hollywood "is one of the three great focal points of America and represents the popular drama of this country as Washington represents politics and New York represents finance."[57] The implication was clear: seizing power in Hollywood was important, just as seizing power in New York and Washington was. This was heady talk and could only further stimulate the already raging hysteria about Red designs on the film industry. Yet the Communists nationally and in Hollywood—even during the unique conditions of World War II—were a long way from seizing power and, as Polonksy's comment suggests, constantly battled membership turnover. Marion Miller, who spied on the L.A. CP on behalf of the FBI suggests why: the party lived in a "condition of furious, scrabbling famine as far as money goes"; there were always "major items of overhead—lawyers' fees, the support of Communist-led strikers, reasonably generous contributions to any and every cause that may be linked in some way to the master Communist plan."[58] Kim Chernin, whose mother was local party leader, recalls similar circumstances.[59] The fabled "Moscow gold" failed to materialize in Los Angeles. This environment was hardly designed to retain adherents.

Yet Los Angeles was the epicenter of the equally fabled California Dream: here resided Communists—like John Howard Lawson and Dalton Trumbo—who not only were highly regarded for their screenwriting but whose ample salaries afforded them a lifestyle that was the envy of many. This affluence allowed them to contribute amply to party coffers, while their very existence symbolized that one could be a Communist and still not abjure the California Dream.

Lawson, who was named after a famous eighteenth-century English prison reformer, was born in New York City in 1894. His mother, Belle Hart Lawson, was involved with the Ethical Culture Society but died when he was five. She was the daughter of a well-to-do New York Jewish family. His father, Simeon Lawson, legally changed his name from Levy to Lawson in the late 1880s in a futile effort to escape anti-Semitism. Simeon Lawson was born in the early 1850s of Polish immigrant parents who had come to the United States in the early 1840s to avoid anti-Semitic pogroms. Simeon was also a writer and was close to Baron Julius Reuters, founder of the well-known British news service. Together they founded the *Mexican Financier* journal in Mexico City. Highly affluent, Simeon Lawson provided his son with many creature comforts, and the younger Lawson became a devotee of the theater early in life. This passion continued during his college days at Williams College, where he also joined the Socialist Club. During World War I he served in the ambulance corps of the Red Cross. When just short of thirty, Lawson was injured in an auto accident, which left him lame in one leg.[60]

Some of his early writings did not display the sensitivity of some of his later screenplays. His 1925 play "Processional" featured a "banjo playing, eye-rolling, spook fearing Rastus Jolly"; his 1927 play "Loud Speaker" was similarly marred. His 1928 play "The International" featured a seductive light-skinned "Negro prostitute." But after his involvement in the Scottsboro case, "he became one of the first white American writers in the 20th century to involve himself directly in the actual struggle of American Negroes for legal and political justice." It was during this period that he joined the Communist Party. Thus, when "Processional" was produced in 1937 he renamed "Rastus Jolly" as Joe Green, a "man of dignified deportment." In his 1937 work "Marching Song," Lawson included among his leaders a black worker who "develops from ignorant strike breaker to intelligent striker." In 1953 his play "Thunder Morning" provided one of the most daring portrayals of the black proletariat ever written for the stage.[61]

In 1937, the year of the great strike in Hollywood, Lawson was "preoccupied . . . with the organization of the Communist Party in Hollywood. When the first meeting was held I gave the main report. . . . and I was elected to be chairman of the forty people—actors, writers, directors and their wives—who were present at the first meeting. I continued as the party grew to several hundred members." Initially, the party headquarters in New York City had "discouraged formal organization among film people, considering that it was dangerous, that it was better to proceed informally with classes and discussion groups." Lawson "differed from this view," and ultimately prevailed. The party's reluctance to organize formally was a direct outgrowth of the severe repression generated by the Red Squad and studio spies. In 1934, for example, Lawson's "only contact with the Communist Party in Los Angeles was through a man [who] called on me at the studio. He wore dark glasses and gave me an assumed name. He asked me [for] money, which I gave, and he returned each week for another donation. This procedure was not an affectation. The [party] was condemned to an underground existence in [Los Angeles]; its legality was almost as tenuous as it was in the Deep South." Like Pettis Perry, Lawson ruefully recalled when the party's "meetings were broken up, its [members] were harassed and beaten by the notorious Red Squad." The Sinclair campaign and the city's general labor unrest helped change this situation, but the severe conditions under which the party operated in Hollywood hampered growth, encouraged insularity, and inexorably fomented wrong judgments. Indeed, the Hollywood party operated virtually autonomously in the region; it not only lacked concert with other units but also, because of logistics and telecommunications problems, had a tenuous relationship with the party center in Manhattan. On the one hand, this environment was a poor one for growth and maturity; on the other hand, to the extent that the center misapprehended the peculiar realities of California, this lack of contact could be advantageous.

Yet even after the party became more accepted in Hollywood, it disregarded collectivity, discouraging "detailed discussion of studio assignments, because the writer functioned in a confidential relationship to the producer or director." Contrary to his subsequent reputation, Lawson claimed that he was not "dogmatic" because "I was constantly working with people who were non-Communist and in some instances . . . anticommunist. Since I had respect for other opinions and awareness of the middle-class viewpoint of intellectuals I was not disposed to make excessive demands on non-members. The growing membership was moved by idealism more than by class struggle." Lawson's recollection is contrary to those of some of his contemporaries who portray him as a kind of "Hollywood Stalin." Still, he may have had reason to be suspicious of and haughty toward some of his erstwhile comrades: the Hollywood party "produced a record crop of informers in the period of McCarthyism."[62]

Lawson also lent a hand to some struggling black writers. Though he did not control hiring, it was said that he could have done more in this sphere. Even so, he was miles ahead of most of his non-Communist contemporaries.[63] In 1940 Theodore Ward, one of the most talented playwrights in Black America, thanked him for "having helped me tremendously, for I have read your book on playwrighting, and found your theory of the 'cycle of dramatic action' particularly helpful. It is my idea of the last word in theory. . . . I have not bothered to read anything else." Ward was then leading the Negro Playwrights Company, based in Harlem, which included Langston Hughes, Owen Dodson, Alain Locke, et al.[64]

Lawson came to symbolize Communists' attempt to inject antiracism into movies, a trend that ran counter to the dominant tendency in an industry that was bursting with pride at the mention of *Birth of a Nation, Gone with the Wind,* and *The Jazz Singer,* and other works that many African Americans in particular despised.[65] In *Sahara* Lawson anticipated Afro-centrism when a Nazi soldier objects to being guarded by an African; a character played by the popular Humphrey Bogart tells the Nazi,

"This man's ancestors were men of culture and learning while yours were still crawling in the jungle on all fours."[66] To Joseph Foster in *New Masses,* this "Sudanese Scout, who is meant to represent all Negroes in the United Nations, assumes qualities of leadership never before accorded to a Negro in the films. Not only is he endowed with a knowing ability upon which the expedition depends for its safety, but he demonstrates the discipline of only the most responsible of leaders." Lawson's "purpose" was "to have the Negro serve as the symbol of democracy in the fight with captured Nazis. When the Nazi has to be disarmed, the Negro does it. . . . Again, when the Nazi escapes, the Sudanese goes after him, chokes him with his bare hands, and gives up his life in the effort."[67]

Lawson's reputation as a defender of African Americans was burnished further when the publisher of the local black paper, the *California Eagle,* asked him to join its board.[68] Crusading for jobs for African Americans in Hollywood was one of his pet causes; that CSU did not follow his lead indicates the emptiness of the idea that the party dominated the union.[69] Even after being blacklisted, Lawson continued striving to shape the cinematic image of Africans. Although Alan Paton received the credit, it was Lawson who wrote the screenplay anonymously for one of the early anti-apartheid films, *Cry the Beloved Country.*[70] Paton came to Hollywood to discuss the screenplay with Lawson, and they disagreed significantly about aspects of the screenplay. Although Lawson's words were altered substantially, the shooting script was his handiwork.[71] The film was shot while Lawson was in prison, but he "received a check for final payment, $12,500," when he was freed in April 1951.[72]

Naturally, the portrayal of labor in movies was another of Lawson's passions. Ralph Rogers, Pacific Coast director of the National Maritime Union called *Action in the North Atlantic,* a movie for which Lawson wrote the screenplay, "the finest film about labor any studio has ever put out." This was something to celebrate, not least because in this important year of 1943, "another Hollywood studio has hired a man at $25 a day to act as labor advisor on a series of pictures they have in mind."[73] Lawson, who was grossing more than $1000 per week, was at the heart of this attempt to improve labor's image on-screen.[74]

During the labor unrest of 1945 and 1946, Lawson's positions mirrored those of his party; i.e., he was slow to endorse the strike, then backed CSU relentlessly throughout. Ronald Reagan recalled later how Lawson "was visible at organizational meetings and on picket lines." Lawson's activism was so energetic that the angered Jack Warner "gave HUAC a picture of him with the strikers."[75]

On the other hand, even some of Lawson's staunchest black comrades felt he could have done more to promote black artists in the screenwriters union he had founded. Frances Williams was not only a renowned black actress, she was also a noted activist, having run for office on the Progressive Party ticket in 1948. Yet even this close friend of Lawson was appalled with what she saw as his lassitude in promoting affirmative action in the industry. In her later years, she recalled attending with Paul Robeson a dinner party at Lawson's home: At one point, "Jack said proudly, 'Did you know I was a founder of the [Screen Writers] Guild?'" Williams was dumbfounded. "'You were not!' I was shocked. 'That's impossible because no Blacks can get in it.'" With rancor she noted that "one of the head writers in the Guild said that he'd never met a more knowledgeable man in his field or more qualified as a writer as Countee Cullen. They were no match for him. Yet because he was Black, Countee was not allowed to be a member of the Writers' Guild and therefore could not write for Hollywood." Williams was "so mad especially because these writers were supposed to be the most progressive people. If their attitude was like this, what the hell could you expect from others?" With Hollywood trade unionists' rotten handling of the race question, Reds like Lawson were simply the best of an average lot.

And even when left-wing writers and directors sought to incorporate black writers in meaningful roles, they often did not rise to the standard set by Lawson. The famed chanteuse Billie Holiday was irked with the role left-wing writer Herbert Biberman had created for her in the film *New Orleans.* Lady Day complained to Williams that she was just a "glorified kitchen maid" in this movie: "I have worked all my life singing in nightclubs and dumps so that I wouldn't have to be somebody's servant or cook and that's all that part was about. I was so disgusted." The prospect of a bountiful paycheck caused her to accept this role nonetheless. But again, this disdainful treatment was better than most black actors received, as Williams reminded, for "black actors were held in so little regard that frequently lines for them were not even included in the script. You were told to improvise, and that's what you did."[76] At least Lawson and other left-wingers did seek to include black characters—with lines— in their scripts.

Lawson, however, was neither the highest paid nor, perhaps, the most talented left-wing screenwriter. Donald Ogden Stewart, Sidney Buchman, Ring Lardner Jr., and Abraham Polonsky were likely Hollywood's best leftist writers. However, in some ways Dalton Trumbo stands head and shoulders above the rest not only in terms of income, but also in his ability to add gloss and sheen to what might be called formula dramas. By the year of the 1946 lockout, Trumbo had obtained from MGM the best contract ever held by a writer in the industry to that time: a straight five-year contract, without option on the part of the studio, which gave him the option of a $3000-per-week salary for the length of the job or $75,000 per script. He had complete freedom in selecting or rejecting subject material, a rarity among writers. The amorphous "morality clause," which gave the studios virtual carte blanche to terminate a contract on the flimsiest of grounds was absent from Trumbo's contract. Of French-Swiss origins, Trumbo—who hailed from Colorado—had U.S. roots stretching back to the American Revolution. He was at the peak of his profession, which included 1,200 writers in Hollywood with only permanent year-round labor for 350—with many of the rest working part-time, if at all.[77]

The talented Trumbo—who wrote the passionate antiwar novel *Johnny Got His Gun* and the screenplay for what may have been the most powerful antislavery epic of all time, *Spartacus*—joined the party in 1943.[78] He was not as active in party affairs as Lawson, though he did entertain visiting labor leaders like Harry Bridges when they came to town.[79] Still, he was just as opinionated as his comrade in analyzing intolerance in politics. It was not accidental, he concluded, that of 133 workers purged from the post office, "72 were Negroes and 48 were Jews." Trumbo was instrumental in organizing a 1947 conference at the Hollywood Masonic Temple that lambasted "treatment of minorities in film," particularly Disney's *Song of the South:* "it is wicked," said the conference program, "to lend validity to the Fascist myth of racial superiority."[80] Trumbo argued vehemently that the attack on Communists was a punishing defeat for civil liberties generally: "if a Communist comes first under attack and is overwhelmed, the breach opened by his fall becomes an avenue for the advance of the enemy with all his increased prestige upon you." Los Angeles, a "city overrun with gangsters," was an important front in this battle.[81] Trumbo was vitriolic in his denunciation of the "non-Communist left" for not standing with the party, although contrary to the viewpoint of his comrades, he argued just as heatedly that keeping party membership secret was a "disaster. . . . Either they should have been open Communists, or they should not have been members at all."[82] He dismissed the notion that revealing membership would have made Communists easier to assault.[83]

Along with Lawson and Trumbo, Lester Cole also was part of this Communist screenwriter cadre; as early as 1934—during the height of the Great Depression—he was drawing a salary of $350 per week from Fox.[84]

Here was further proof that living the California Dream was compatible with joining the Communist Party.[85] His screenplay *None Shall Escape*, written as World War II was unfolding, anticipated many of the themes later presented in *Schindler's List;* it visualized the Holocaust for an audience that could only imagine its brutal reality. Likewise, the film *New Orleans,* which the Communist Herbert Biberman played a major role in bringing to the screen, was deemed by "the black press" to be "an astute treatment of blacks," Billie Holiday's reservations not withstanding.[86]

Various intelligence agencies kept a close watch on real and imagined Communists in Hollywood, even during the war when the ostensible basis for anticommunism—the USSR's supposed designs on the United States—had been submerged. Sidney Buchman, "executive producer and assistant to Harry Cohn" of Columbia, was identified by military intelligence as a "strong communist sympathizer; possibly a fellow traveller." Intelligence's "mail cover" on Buchman revealed that he subscribed to a Red newspaper.[87] With precision the military analyst described Buchman as 5′9 1/2″ tall and 165 pounds, with a "freckled scar on right cheek."[88] It was not altogether clear why military intelligence would be so concerned with writers and Hollywood figures—but they were. Theodore Dreiser was described as a "communist fellow traveller or an 'intellectual communist'"; he "has served the cause of the party," it was reported, "as faithfully and probably more effectively than the rank and file of known party members."[89] The screenwriter Sheridan Gibney was deemed a "communist sympathizer."[90]

As this attention to Buchman and these writers suggests, intelligence agents were solemnly concerned over the alleged Red infiltration of the highest ranks of Hollywood. In 1944 the FBI concluded that at RKO there were "four men, including the General Production aide to the Executive Vice President in charge of production, who have Communist affiliations of varying degrees. . . . Of the 30 producers and associate producers of RKO 10 have [CP] affiliations. . . . Of the 183 directors, 15 have Communist affiliations in varying degrees. . . . Of the 53 writers employed by RKO 48 have Communist affiliations of varying degrees. Adding these 8 to the 53 results are 56 out of 61 people who write for RKO have Communist affiliations of varying degrees." Detailed scrutiny was devoted to Trumbo's screenplay for RKO, *Tender Comrade*.[91]

Writers became a topic of intense concern for many reasons, including their attempts to affect the content of movies and their antiracist activism. However, writers were also targeted because of their efforts to receive a larger slice of the wealth they were generating. A pioneer of film noir, James Cain, concocted the idea of an American Authors' Authority (AAA) that would seek to claim more rights—and royalties and profits—for authors; this notion was perceived as a direct challenge to studios and publishers, and was red-baited mercilessly. Meanwhile, the organ of the Screen Writers Guild claimed that this idea was "capitalism, naked and simple. But it is capitalism for writers."[92] The attack on this meritorious idea was yet another example of how anticommunism was deployed demagogically for stark reasons of power and mammon. The mainstream press—which had to be concerned about what its own writers would think of this heretical notion—disagreed.[93] This AAA, one newspaper boomed, "would possess dictatorial power over all screen writers, radio writers, dramatists and authors." It "could organize boycotts against publishers or producers who accept the work of the unorganized."[94] That is precisely the point, countered Trumbo and Lawson, two prime supporters of this concept.

Cain's idea did not take flight, and, deplorably, many other noble notions died prematurely, too. Despite the individual efforts of Lawson, Trumbo, and others, their comrade John Bright recalls that there were "virtually no black people at all in the Hollywood studio section. Hollywood was, and to a great extent today is, Jim Crow." Bright remembers that there was "briefly one black member . . . a black writer." The former Communist Ben Burns, an editor at *Jet, Ebony,* and other leading African American publications recalls a 1945 meeting in Paris where labor leader Sidney Hillman and some of his CP aides made insulting statements about Africans that could have led to a trial for "white chauvinism" if it had occurred a few years earlier—or later—in the United States.[95] Pettis Perry, the black Communist leader in Los Angeles, grumbled that though the war years did bring advance on race, they also brought backsliding; some Communists felt that since blacks would be worse off if Hitler won, they should be quiet and do nothing to detract from efforts against Germany.[96] Jean Rouverol Butler, a progressive woman activist in the film industry, argues that Communists in Hollywood were not much better when it came to women; they were "just as chauvinist as anyone. . . . They didn't think 'the woman question' applied to them," she charges.[97]

These mordant allegations must be kept in perspective. Certainly by the standards of twenty-first-century feminism and antiracism, the Hollywood left was sorely lacking. Yet compared to some of their contemporaneous colleagues and adversaries, who routinely slandered the disenfranchised on- and off-screen, Communists like Lawson and Trumbo sparkled. The director Michael Curtiz, an anticommunist refugee from

Eastern Europe, habitually used the term "niggers," and he was far from being alone in such practices.[98] When President Roosevelt died in the spring of 1945, one military intelligence agent viewed this as an opportunity to strike back against African Americans and others who had been victimized by discrimination—e.g., Jewish Americans. Agent "RHVD" wrote that Roosevelt's death was "the most serious blow that the Jewish element in [the] USA has ever received since the country was set up. . . . The Negroes who have been riding 'high and wide' under the FEPC [Fair Employment Practices Committee] Los Angeles, now have a setback that will bewilder the Negro leaders. . . . Truman was a member of the Klan, make no mistake about this, we read the material on Truman's case. The CIO has received a blow . . . that will make them . . . groggy."[99] A "special report" on this matter monitored reaction to FDR's death and found James Cagney was "the worst of the lot" in his response. "Never in the history of the Jewish groups of this country have they been so stirred up." As for the Communists, their fond hopes were "over in a flash, they have [a] foundation built on sand—the future is dreary . . . a kick in the teeth."[100]

Communists in Hollywood, in other words, had to bear the double burden of existing in an environment that was almost casually anti-black, while seeking to conduct a determined antiracist fight; at times the requirements of the former prevailed over the latter. Yet when the Screen Actors Guild adopted a resolution in 1946 pledging "to use all its power to oppose discrimination against Negroes in the motion picture industry," Communists led the way to ensure passage of this measure that the local black newspaper called "unprecedented."[101] Similarly, when Actors Equity resolved to combat racism, the left blazed the trail.[102] It was the left-led Hollywood Writers Mobilization that joined with like-minded allies in protesting against restrictive covenants that hemmed African Americans into certain neighborhoods in Los Angeles and barred them from others.[103] No doubt left-wing influence helps to explain why African American voters in Los Angeles mostly refused in 1946 to support the black candidate, Fred Roberts—a Republican—in his congressional race against Helen Gahagan Douglas, a white liberal.[104]

The *Daily Worker* conducted a continual protest against the negative portrayal of blacks on the silver screen. The paper's chief film critic, David Platt, joined with the "entire Negro press" in condemning the dearth of blacks in newsreels.[105] However, unlike some in the "Negro press," who felt that employment of blacks was the critical issue—irrespective of the roles they were playing—Platt differed. He argued that "it is time to be stern with Negro artists who accept undignified roles and even more stern with irresponsible newspaper writers who encourage this lowering of standards. I have in mind the Hollywood correspondent of the *Pittsburgh Courier.*"[106] The Communist leader V. J. Jerome was a constant critic of Hollywood portrayals of blacks in such films as *Home of the Brave, Lost Boundaries, Pinky* and *Intruder in the Dust.*[107] In retrospect, his critiques were probably unduly trenchant—perhaps "ultra-leftist"—in that some of the films he assaulted glow with sincerity even today. On the other hand, most African Americans would have enthusiastically chosen extreme antiracists over extreme racists.

Platt found the film *Lifeboat* a "curious study in segregation. . . . The Nazi . . . is far from segregated" while the black character played by Canada Lee was; the Nazi "mixes with everyone and is a vital part of the ship. It is the Negro and not the Nazi who has the shady past."[108] This curious range of activity by Hollywood Communists on the "Negro Question" caught the eye of U.S. military intelligence, which noted carefully the arrival of black Communist leader Harry Haywood in Los Angeles in 1946. Yet such careful monitoring did not prevent the authorities from charging—falsely—that CSU was dominated by Communists.[109]

Communists also paid attention to what was happening with other minorities. The *Daily Worker* admired the Warner Bros. film *In Our Time* because it exposed the "reactionary forces represented by the Polish Government-in-exile," but repudiated its inattention to the plight of Polish Jews.[110] David Platt was "disappointed that James Cagney refuses to use Chinese actors in the major Japanese parts in his new film, *Blood on the Sun.* All the important Japanese characters will be played by Caucasian actors." Curiously, Platt never pointed out that Japanese American actors could be used in the Japanese roles, though to his credit, he did gripe about *Gunga Din* "against which hundreds of thousands have demonstrated in the streets of Calcutta and Bombay."[111]

These Communist initiatives on race were not viewed so benignly by Congressman John Rankin of Mississippi and his Un-American Activities Committee. As the war ended, the party quickly found itself on the defensive, with the anticommunist attack rapidly dissolving into an onslaught on CSU, the union the CP was said to dominate. Simultaneously, a reign of terror targeting African Americans appeared to erupt in California. Referring to San Diego, Margaret E. James of the NAACP asserted "there has been a resurgence of acts of racial violence" in her state. "Negroes have been beaten, fiery crosses have been burned, synagogues have been defaced, signs and symbols of the Klan have appeared in minority group neighborhoods."[112]

NAACP leaders, who had aligned with the Communists during the war, found themselves on the defensive. Thereafter, a full-page advertisement in the *Hollywood Reporter* beseeched black Hollywood stars such as Louise Beavers and Hattie McDaniel to "disavow and repudiate the conference on equal rights for Negroes, planned by the Arts, Sciences and Professions Council. . . . We urge all Negroes not to be deceived by Communist double-talk."[113] Most blacks meekly complied; they saw no alternative. After all, even if they believed in the Reds, said to be local agents of the "evil empire," how could they have faith in CSU when it was so laggard on racial matters? As African American support began to slip away, the party and the union's devastated destinies were settled.

Despite their success at staving off an alliance between blacks and Communists, the authorities continued to worry, perhaps because of guilt over their own horrible treatment of African Americans. Earlier, officials were vexed when Rex Ingram, "prominent Negro screen and stage star was reportedly recruited" into the Hollywood party; since he was a "leader in the Los Angeles Negro colony," this allegation was even more worrisome.[114] Worse, it was said, "many of the leaders in the NAACP are reported to be dominated by the Communist Party."[115] These reputed ties between the NAACP and Communists were increasing the danger of race mixing. Jean Lewin, a member of the Screen Office Employees Guild and "possibly" a Communist, "upon several occasions defended mixed dancing between negroes and white persons at the Canteen."[116]

There were inducements to lure African Americans away from those who only recently had been one of their staunchest supporters. At the 1946 IATSE convention, African Americans—who had been shunted into segregated auxiliary locals and denied delegate privileges while paying full dues in a union that had "Dixie" as a theme song—made advances. They were "given the right to representation at future conventions and the privilege of submitting appeals direct to the general executive board instead of going through their mother locals." At the same time, a resolution was passed urging the leadership to "take immediate steps to rid the International of any subversive, radical or communistic groups."[117] CSU was not sufficiently astute to acknowledge this trade-off, let alone counter it: concessions to blacks and penalties to Reds both undercut the union left.

Likewise, a combination of carrots(e.g., the IATSE reforms) and sticks (e.g., stepped-up racial violence) helped persuade African Americans to loosen their formerly close ties with Communists, particularly in Hollywood. The perception that CSU was in a de facto alliance with the Reds, particularly after the 1946 lockout, weakened black support while hindering the crusade of studio labor.

★ Screenwriters like Lawson and Trumbo were among the staunchest allies of the dispossessed. They backed CSU, particularly after the lockout of 1946. More than actors and directors, these scribes were among the most militant of those toiling in Hollywood, and they were viewed as such by the moguls. They were the most reflective and philosophical about their own role and the medium—or industry—in which they worked. This musing came to a boil early in 1946 when the Communist writer Albert Maltz expressed decidedly non-Communist opinions on critical issues—and the harsh reaction of his comrades was viewed by many as an example of Red squelching of freedom of expression. This controversy came at an inopportune time for the Communists. At that moment, Washington was launching a campaign that would allow, if not encourage, U.S. progressives to attack capitalism in order to contrast "western" diversity with Soviet "totalitarianism." When Reds appeared to be squashing robust and open commentary, many artists concluded that their freedom of expression would be hindered if Communists gained more influence.[118]

As CSU was then being tarred as a "Communist front," this controversy crippled the union's ability to win followers. As evinced by critiques of V. J. Jerome, some comrades could proceed in a sectarian manner, publicly assailing those who should have been provided the warm embrace of the "popular front." The Maltz episode is also suggestive of this trend.

Maltz joined the party in 1935. He "became attached to a party branch in the film section" that included screen story analysts "and some secretaries." There were "weekly meetings" with "serious discussions." Lawson, he felt, commanded "respect that amounted almost to awe and subservience, none of which" was "felt" by Maltz, who thought only slightly better of the Communist leader than he did of the producer Cecil B. DeMille, whom he found "sadistic."[119]

Maltz's tryst with controversy started innocently enough when, in suggesting that an artist can be reactionary and still produce great art, he cited Friedrich Engels' view on writers such as Balzac. The recognition of artists like James Farrell, a Troyskyite, and Richard Wright, who was hostile to the party,[120] drew public and private rebuke from party stalwarts like Joseph North, Howard Fast, et al.[121] Maltz retreated, and party chief William Z. Foster weighed in, warning of "left sectarian" dangers (i.e., all art produced under capitalism is decadent) and "right" dangers (i.e., the artist is free and should have nothing to do with class struggle).[122]

Privately, Bernhard Stern told Maltz that he did not necessarily agree with the critics but didn't like Maltz's original article too much either; Stern felt that James Farrell's work "has deteriorated since *Studs Lonigan* and I attribute it in large part to his Trotskyism; just as Dos Passos has deteriorated because he was infected with that virus. . . . Perhaps what you are now suffering from is an occupational disease of left-wing writers. Other occupational diseases have been controlled. This one can be too."[123]

Millard Lampel told Maltz that "a few of us—Normie Rosten, Art Miller, Walt Bernstein, and a few of the Yank and Stars and Stripes boys are gathering for informal discussions of your article and what lies before and beyond it."[124] Louis Harap moaned to Joseph North that "one of the reasons why the left-wing cultural movement is as weak as it is today, is the crude and obtuse handling of artists at critical stages in their careers."[125] Dismayed by the public rebuking of Maltz, many writers and artists who were contemplating political activism echoed the words of Harap.

Though debating the connection between art and politics was not new, in the overheated atmosphere of a beckoning Red Scare, the Maltz affair was perceived—and constructed—as an example of Communist intolerance toward a creative writer, if not toward creativity itself.[126] This perception was a gigantic step forward in the attempt to suggest that Communist influence in the film industry would also lead to intolerance, perhaps even restriction on the kinds of themes that Hollywood could pursue—a situation that was said to be a radical departure from the status quo.

Contextually, however, this scrap was just a small piece of a larger Communist debate on movies, which Trumbo considered "the most important medium for the communication of ideas in the world today."[127] Norma Barzman has recalled that party life in Hollywood involved complicated discussions of aesthetics and Engels.[128] The party was consumed with divining the proper—or "correct"—theoretical viewpoint and with gaining perspective on Hollywood; the latter's necessary consideration of labor, capital, gangsters, aesthetics, and narrative presented a peculiar challenge.

Early on, the Marxist critic Harry Potamkin philosophized that "most people are eye-minded. The things their eyes see become the things that affect them."[129] This musing was part of the Communist effort to develop an outlook on the powerful medium of film. Thus, in *New Masses,* Archibald MacLeish complained that "movie criticism" carried the flawed "assumption that the moving picture is a dramatic form to be judged by dramatic standards. Actually," he argued, "the moving picture is a fictional form. . . . [T]he construction of the standard Hollywood picture is narrative, not scenic, and its persons are 'characters' rather than 'dramatis personae.'" A movie, he concluded, was like a short story, except that the "reading and . . . visualizing" are done for the reader.[130]

Still, party analyses of Hollywood were not beyond criticism and may have been impacted negatively because of security concerns that hindered collective deliberation and judgments. Louis Harap found it a "sad commentary on the state of Marxist criticism and aesthetics" that the work of Christopher Cauldwell "has never been discussed in any American Marxist publication."[131] If Hollywood Reds had limited their contacts with Manhattan for fear of mail tampering and electronic surveillance, little wonder that they may have overlooked a prominent British theorist.

For his part, Trumbo felt that "the freedom of the artist to express himself decreases in proportion to the increase of capital investment required for the production of the work." Thus, the "freest form is the pamphlet," and it is "not, therefore, difficult to understand why the theater deals less frequently with progressive subject matter than the novel"— and why the movies deal with it least of all. "Hollywood workers speak always of the industry, never of the medium. For motion picture workers are purely industrial workers," which is why they had such a propensity for organizing and striking.[132]

Lawson debated V. J. Jerome—often described as the party's chief "cultural commissar"—on the nature of film.[133] Jerome, also known as Jerome Isaac Romain, was born in Poland in 1896. He graduated from New York University in 1930 after attending the City College of New York. He may have disagreed with Lawson on some points, but they both agreed about troubling trends developing in movies. Writing of *The Song of Bernadette, Going My Way,* and *The Bells of St. Mary's,* Jerome warned of the developing tendency toward "reactionary clericalism." He wrote that there were "1,313 motion pictures released" during 1942–1944, but only "45 or 50 . . . aided significantly . . . in increasing understanding." As the lockout moved into 1947, even this small percentage had shrunk as "today's gangster films" became paradigmatic.[134]

Jerome's critiques of current film fare were mirrored in the party newspaper, the *Daily Worker.* Its film critic, David Platt—who believed that Emile Zola was the "real father of the modern theater and screen"[135] —penned a regular column entitled "Film Front."[136] Platt organized an innovative series of lectures featuring writers like Philip S. Foner and Doxey Wilkerson discussing the themes presented by such films as *Abe Lincoln in Illinois* and *Wells Fargo*.[137] Particularly during the war, Platt was not marginalized, as evidenced by his exchanges on various matters with Bosley Crowther, *New York Times* film critic.[138]

These were intoxicating times for a Communist film critic, when John Carlson's pro-Soviet, anti-right-wing book *Undercover* could be touted by the *Daily Worker* as "the most popular book in army camps according to a recent survey. . . . [I]ncidentally the author . . . is in Hollywood discussing the sale of the movie rights with a couple of interested major studios."[139]

Yet as enthralling as Hollywood was, Communists were not always trooping off there to get films made. Rather, they had encouraged an independent cinema, particularly in the realm of documentaries.[140] As early as 1936 the Communists had helped to organize American Labor Films, a group initiated by Hollywood film workers.[141]

Ten years later the FBI filed a report on the International Film and Radio Guild, which was primed to make 16 mm films "which will portray 'minorities in sympathetic and diversified roles rather than the familiar stereotypes.'" Implicated in this effort were Lena Horne and John Garfield—both hounded subsequently for alleged left-wing tendencies; Nat King Cole and future California Supreme Court justice Stanley Mosk were also involved. One confidential report for the U.S. Senate's Internal Security Subcommittee referred to Mosk as a "CP suspect." The International Film and Radio Guild was seen as part of the Red offensive in Hollywood. Among other things, the FBI report alleged "that the Academy Awards for 1945 were made to many persons, who, if not members of the CP, have engaged in various Communist and Communist-front activities in the past."[142] This fear followed in the wake of concern about left-wingers obtaining radio licenses.[143]

Yet despite this multifaceted activity, David Platt complained in 1944 about the "appalling lack of interest in movies in trade union circles. As a result some of the finest documentary films this country has ever had are not being seen. . . . Only a few CIO locals are using films in their work."[144]

Platt may have been lamenting the failings of the party and unions but the authorities had an opposite concern: the perceived advance of both. A report was filed with the FBI in the fall of 1945 warning that "more and more Hollywood is becoming the center of Communist pressure activity." As the strike was winding down, another report deplored that the Communists had become a "legitimate party. Its influence on public officials has reached an alarming stage."[145] Something had to be done, it was thought, particularly in the crucial film industry, where it appeared to some that Communists had made their most significant leap forward.

★ It was true that the singular conditions of the war had allowed the Communist Party to grow more quickly than it had previously. However, the party's dirty little secret was that its Hollywood organization—which proclaimed vigorously the vanguard role of the proletarians—was disproportionately composed of intellectuals, particularly writers and directors. This situation was a problem, for as the party's theory suggested, painters and carpenters were more likely to lead far-reaching battles against the moguls and to press for democratic gains for society as a whole; the strike of 1937, and that of 1945, suggested this idea. Hence, when the strike of 1945 and the lockout of 1946 occurred, the party did not have as much influence with CSU leaders as the moguls imagined.

To be sure, Communists like Lawson continually sought to bridge this gap between various strata of workers, but CSU leaders like Sorrell had a lingering resentment of Communists because of their reluctance to give immediate support to the 1945 strike. In any event, some CSU leaders felt that expressing resentment toward Communists would save them from being called Red sympathizers: they were wrong.

Moreover, Sorrell thought poorly of the Screen Writers Guild, where left influence was most significant. "Writers," he uttered dismissively, "I consider intellectuals. I consider that most of them can take care of themselves. I am interested more in workers."[146] However, his no doubt sincere interest in advancing the workers could have been vindicated more readily if CSU had united with allies against a common adversary.

It is easy to see why the party attracted proportionately more writers than other sectors of the labor force. Communist writers often contended archly that they joined in greater numbers because they were smarter: however, more mundane forces were at play. Unlike virtually any other work in the industry, writing was done in isolation, with the writer's presence often found undesirable on the movie set; this situation contrasted with the collectivity that characterized the film process as a whole. For the writers, the *party* was the collective. Paradoxically, however, this collectivity was stunted, since security concerns often meant that party writers knew few Reds beyond those who could fit comfortably into a Southern California parlor.

Nancy Lynn Schwartz has pointed out that "in a town of isolated residences and little cultural activity outside movie making, political involvement provided a connection for the Hollywood castaways—not just with the rest of the world but between husbands and wives. . . . [F]or the first time politically aware Hollywood wives had a broad social framework into which they could meaningfully channel their activities." In a world of casual labor and transience, the party was a constant. In a city "without roots, peopled by orphans from urban centers and European refugees, the Party also provided a family of sorts that would not evaporate." This helps to explain, she suggests, why "there were more writers than any other cultural worker in the Hollywood CP." This shallowness of roots may also shed light on why—correspondingly—one of the nation's strongest right-wing movements could arise in Southern California concomitant with the post–World War II boom.[147]

Moreover, the party's politics—which differed sharply from those of a Democratic Party dominated by Dixiecrats and a Republican Party dominated by big business—had appeal. Screenwriters like Lawson, who tried to portray blacks as human beings with the potential for more than menial occupations, attracted those who were disgusted with Jim Crow. The party, as noted, was also concerned with theoretical and ideological issues arising out of this new medium and had a concern with content and craft which placed it among the most reverential practitioners of the movie art. This, too, was appealing.[148]

The "Northwest" section of the party in Los Angeles housed most of the members who worked in Hollywood. According to government records, some of the more important figures in the industry belonged. Again, it cannot be over-emphasized that these reports of informers should not be accepted wholly and literally; informants and their patrons had varying motives and precise accuracy was not necessarily among them. Yet the reports are useful to explore, not least because of what they suggest about anticommunism, gender biases—and anti-Semitism. In short, these reports should be viewed in terms of what they tell us about the authorities' state of mind and should not be accepted in toto as "truth."

According to these sources, the L.A. CP was quite a melange. There was Jack Moscowitz, alias Jack Moss, "an independent movie producer" who was a "close friend" of Lawson and a former "manager for Gary Cooper."[149] There was Frank Tuttle, who in "1925 or thereabouts, rated in the same class as Cecil B. DeMille as [a] director" though as of this 1944 writing he was viewed as "very erratic" but "exceptionally smart." As was said of so many Communists, his party membership was reported to have been directed by his spouse, who happened to be a "Russian born dancer."[150] There was William Dieterle, an "active Communist" in his native Germany prior to his arrival in Hollywood; in the United States he "directed some very successful motion pictures" at Warner Bros. "at an increasingly large salary." He was "naive" and "extremely pro-communist," but like Tuttle, his spouse, Charlotte, was "a very strong willed person" and exercised a "great control" over him—"through astrology" of all things.[151] There were Dave Hilberman and William Foldal, cartoonists who were said to have "led the strike at Disney Studios."[152]

There was Helen Joy Levitt, "personal secretary" to John Garfield and executive secretary of the Actors Laboratory. She was membership and financial director of the L.A. CP's Northwest section in 1944.[153] Garfield in 1945 was "considered to be a key figure" within the party's orbit, though he was not a member—unlike his wife, who was said to be an outspoken Red.[154] Garfield and his spouse were reported to have "been entertained at the Russian Consulate" and then reciprocated "in their home."[155] These activities took place during the war, when the United States and the Soviet Union were supposedly allies against fascism; evidently, however, this factor was seen as an irrelevant consideration. Later, Garfield was listed as a "CP member" in a report that labeled Charles Chaplin as a "CP suspect."[156] After Lena Horne attended a showing of a Soviet film, she was listed as a "CP sympathizer."[157]

This familial tie to the party was also said to have afflicted the Adlers; Lola, along with "Stella, Pearl and Luther," were "all prominent in the theatrical world and reported to be active in the Communist Party."[158] This cabal included Harold Clurman, "producer, director-writer at RKO," the spouse of Stella and reportedly "involved in Communist activities since 1931."[159] These analysts apparently believed that the "personal was political," for they spent a good deal of time detailing intimate connections. In writing of Madeline Ruthven, a former "scenario writer," the analysts noted that she lived with a "lesbian."[160] They wrote in detail of Budd Schulberg, the writer, and his sister Sonya—who was "morally unstable."[161] Jules Carson, alias Julius Karstein, a Communist living in the home of fellow-comrade Paul Jarrico, had been "convicted for robbery" in 1920.[162] With stunning precision, the FBI reports detailed the age, height, weight, hair color, eye color, and other minutiae about Hollywood Reds, though the reported levels of commitment and radicalism of many subjects could be stunningly imprecise.[163] Why such surveillance? Hollywood types were thought to toss aside surnames as casually as they tossed aside lovers, so physical description was deemed a useful way to keep track of them, particularly in the wake of "national emergency." Moreover, there was a haunting fear that the lucre and influence of celebrity could be a powerful tool to advance the causes of minorities, unions, and women; officials believed that tight surveillance—coupled with harassment—could forestall this worrisome trend.

These analysts were particularly interested in racial and ethnic heritage: particularly for Jews, African Americans, and Russian immigrants. A party convention of 1,500 at the L.A. Embassy Auditorium in the fall of 1943 was "composed of about 90% Jews. . . . Most of the men in uniform appeared to be Jews and definitely were with Jewish companions. It was difficult to ascertain approximately the number of Negroes present as they were scattered." [164] In the spring of 1946 a report was filed on a Communist rally of 1,200 in Los Angeles; Trumbo spoke, as did "Lou Harris, a Paramount producer and a slick-tongued jewish [sic] boy." [165] In 1946 another meeting at the Shrine Auditorium, sponsored by the Mobilization for Democracy, was said to have attracted "6000 . . . conservatively speaking 90% Jewish." [166] The report fails to state how Jewish Americans were distinguished from other Euro-Americans. When Meade McClanahan, "13th District Councilman" in Los Angeles and a follower of the fascist Gerald L. K. Smith, was facing recall, military intelligence reported without comment his idea that "Jews and Communists are behind the recall movement." [167]

In the summer of 1946, "RHVD"—who seemed to specialize in this subject—wrote at length on "The Jewish Situation in the East," observing that "in Hollywood, Communism and the Jewish groups seem to play hand in hand. . . . There are hundreds of [Communists] and a great many of the leaders are Jews. They are in the technical department and the script departments are overloaded with them; and among the actors and actresses, there are dozens and even hundreds. . . . [T]ake, for instance the picture *Our Vines Have Tender Grapes*—there is a fine example of a Communist propaganda picture." Such propaganda, he alleged, "is especially [present] where John Garfield, Edward G. Robinson and others of that type are featured." [168]

That "type" presumably included Max Appelman, "formerly" a "stage carpenter" who was said to be "Jewish in appearance." [169] Blandly it was reported that John Wexley, a screenwriter and "CP member," was "beaten and bombarded with anti-Semitic epithets. His assailants are known to the [LAPD]."[170] Special note was taken of Benjamin Goldstein, West Coast representative for Artkino Pictures, who worked on *Mission to Moscow;* he was "formerly a rabbi in Montgomery, Alabama but lost his synagogue because of his efforts on behalf of" the Scottsboro defendants. Born in Oklahoma, he had "blue eyes; blond hair," it was noted with apparent surprise.[171]

The party also had a substantial number of members among publicists, office employees, screen story analysts, and the like. Blanch Cole, a secretary at Columbia, was said to be a Communist and a recording secretary of the Screen Office Employees Guild.[172] A 1945 report stated that David Victor Robison, vice president of the Screen Story Analysts Guild, was "teaching a Communist class in Hollywood." He was a reader at RKO and an "active member" of the party; in 1943 he had transferred from a party unit in Nashville, where he had taught music history at Fisk University.[173] George Hellgren, an auditor at Fox, previously had served in the Swedish military and continued to get "frequent mail from the Swedish Embassy"; he was "possibly . . . a Communist functionary," it was suggested, because his spouse, Nora, was a "prominent CP functionary."[174] Robert Wachman was also said to be a Communist; he was "employed by Steve Hannegan Associates, publicity agents," who were "handling all public relations for Jack Benny."[175]

The Communists did have some influence among CSU's leading unions. Louis Goldblatt, who was of Lithanian Jewish extraction, ultimately served as a leader of the West Coast longshore union, though prior to that he worked in Hollywood as a laborer. He was from a family of Communists. His father worked as a laboratory technician at Fox Technicolor, his brother-in-law John Vigoreaux worked as a painter, and his brother, Saul, was a studio worker. In the mid-1930s his father and brother were "offered jobs in the Soviet Union, where they were setting up their motion picture industry. They wanted them there primarily in conjunction with set construction." The pair worked there for a year.[176]

Carl Head, a Hollywood painter, was supposedly a "strong follower of the Communist Party line" and a "close friend" of Sorrell.[177] The famed cinematographer James Wong Howe was called a "fellow traveller" and the only member of his IATSE local "who seems to have Communist connections."[178] His "connections" included Sanora Babb, "a party member for 11 years" who had "traveled in Russia and boasts of having met Stalin"; she was "single but resides with James Wong Howe, prominent Chinese motion picture cameraman."[179] Alphonse Caya, a truck driver at Warner Bros. in Burbank, was said to be a "communist undercover man in the . . . party effort to penetrate the Teamsters' Union on the West Coast."[180] This list of Communists was said to include Edward Gilbert of the set designers. Russell McKnight, head of the film technicians union, was termed a "CP suspect," while other prominent studio labor leaders like John Martin ("CP suspect"), Matty Mattison ("CP follower"), and Norval Crutcher ("CP suspect"), also were categorized. William Pomerance, business agent for the Cartoonists Guild, was a "close associate of Communist functionaries."[181] Yet what was most striking about this list was that given their elastic requirements for determining party membership, the authorities—even in their internally circulated documents—did not regard the studio labor leadership as Communist Party members.[182]

On the other hand, many CSU leaders were far from being anticommunist, and as the Red Scare got under way, this "lack" was more than enough to discredit them. Some CSU leaders believed that cooperating with the Communists was in their best interest. After all, the party was helping to build class consciousness, which was quite useful in the strikes and lockouts that CSU had become embroiled in. Further, distancing oneself from the Reds apparently would not cause the authorities to halt their anticommunist attack; Sorrell's example suggested that being prolabor was enough for this barrage to ensue.

For example, party-sponsored schools stressed issues like labor history that some CSU leaders felt were necessary for members to know. In 1944 the People's Education Center organized by the party had teachers like Morton Grant, an RKO and Warner Bros. screenwriter; Dwight Houser, a staff writer at CBS; and Augustus Hawkins, a future member of the Congressional Black Caucus.[183] Where else could CSU go to educate its members for struggle?

At this point, the L.A. CP had 2,491 members in the ranks, according to government figures, and the Northwest section was the largest with 443; still, the party's account at Security First National Bank contained only $4,312.44.[184] The FBI concluded that of these members, the bulk— over a thousand—were between 26 and 35, with more than seven hundred having been in the party for 5–10 years. More than five hundred were with the CIO and more than six hundred with the AFL; almost three hundred were with the aviation industry, with Hollywood being next with more than two hundred. More than twelve hundred were Jewish, more than six hundred were "American" (a category that apparently excluded Jews, among others) and seventy-four were Irish.[185] These two hundred Hollywood Communists left a deep impression on government agents. One agent observed that "Hollywood is full of Reds up to its eyebrows and this is no joke." Even in New York City "there are several hundred actors, actresses, singers, radio people" with such ties, with the "'key man' for the Reds" being Paul Robeson.[186]

The party was critical in the formation of the Hollywood Democratic Committee, which had been formed in 1943 to back FDR but in 1945 was reconceptualized as the Hollywood Independent Citizens Council of the Arts, Sciences and Professions and in 1946 as the Progressive Citizens of Southern California. In 1948 the committee took on yet another incarnation, but repeated name-changes could not obscure the fact that it leaned to the left. At various times the committee included Gene Kelly, Duke Ellington, Rita Hayworth, George Gershwin, and Gregory Peck. Like CSU, it did not survive the Red Scare, not least because it was derided as a "Communist front."[187] The Hollywood Writers Mobilization also did not survive, though it appeared to be a permanent part of the industry's makeup when in 1943 it brought together at UCLA Jack Warner, Daryl Zanuck, Walter White of the NAACP, and Walter Huston in a forum that examined the industry critically.[188] These organizations could not survive the pressure and scrutiny that was placed upon them, not least because they were identified as stalking horses for the party. Actually these organizations augured a diminution of the right's strength, and red-baiting them was a fairly blatant way to preclude this eventuality.

A few weeks before the 1946 lockout the party held a meeting in Los Angeles at which its leader, William Z. Foster, spoke. According to the government agent present, "of the some 300 delegates, very few were over the age of 40. Generally speaking, these delegates appeared to be a group of well-dressed, intelligent, young people who spoke well from the floor and discussed things in a very rational way"; over half were women.[189]

As time passed, the stress inflicted on the party began to take its toll, and the comrades found it increasingly difficult to approach matters in a "rational way." Dorothy Healey, the L.A. leader, reportedly had become quite worried about "security." "It was stated there would be no more 'open meetings' and that before an individual may be accepted into the party, he must be approved by the club, the club executive committee and the executive committee and must take a six weeks' orientation class before being recruited or brought into any club."[190] Such stringent measures effectively halted Communist attempts to expand their base. Obviously, word had been leaked about the membership of some prominent party members—particularly in Hollywood—and they in turn were being pressured. Progressives like Bette Davis, E. Y. Harburg, and Dore Schary were being characterized as "CP line follower[s]."[191] Orson Welles had cautioned against succumbing to the "phony fear of Communism," which was "smoke-screening the real menace of renascent Fascism," but his words hardly struck a chord in a public seized by the Red Scare.[192]

With increased stress also came increased squabbling among the membership and a "great turn-over in the Negro membership." At an important party gathering in 1945, Lawson was absent, while other party leaders went for each other's throats. State leader William Schneiderman was deemed "uninterested in the people with whom he works." Max Silver was called "bureaucratic. Nothing in his work is consistent with Marxist concept[s] or leadership." Carl Winter had "poor relations with the trade union functionaries."[193] Later it was reported that Michael Wilson had replaced Lawson as head of the party's "Hollywood Cultural and Professional Groups"; though he was "forceful and convincing," "under stress or direct pressure especially dealing with criticism of the party by opponents," Wilson's "emotions got the best of him."[194]

Yet while they reported on these rifts and weaknesses, intelligence agents were continuing to declare that "there is no doubt that Hollywood and the immediate area now have become one of the main centers of CP propaganda and activity in the United States." The intelligence community apparently thought that heightening apprehension about Communist strength would facilitate the crushing of CSU, which is why these reports have to be used carefully and, equally important, why it is so striking that few CSU leaders were identified as Communist.

The dearth of known Communists in CSU did not halt the constant search for Reds and their sympathizers. Why, it was asked plaintively, were "producers" in the "top executive branches" not moving to squash CSU, unless they themselves were "sympathetic to the Communist cause?" The authorities pointed the finger particularly at Walter Wanger —who had worked closely with Lawson—labeling him a "CP sympathizer." In this report, written in early 1946, the intelligence agent almost wishfully noted that "activities of the CP in the motion picture industry have been so intense during the past few months . . . to the point the producers in Hollywood are considering a shutting down of the industry completely for four months."[195]

Increasingly under siege, the party began to complain about the deficiencies in "political understanding" of its members, a condition which leaders ascribed to a deficit in "study" and misunderstanding of "ideological struggle."[196] These were the pincers—security from the state combined with insecurity of the party—that were to roust the Reds and crush CSU.

Organizations that included Communists—for example, Actors Equity—began to purge them. There was a "long and heated debate" in their highest councils that was characterized by "hysterical, name-slinging brawls. . . ."[197] "Hysterical" was one way to describe the editor of the *San Diego Weekly*, C. Leon De Aryan, when he claimed, "you can tell a Communist by the guttural sound of his voice."[198] In a similar mode, Lela Rogers, mother of Ginger Rogers, complained that Dalton Trumbo tried to put "Communist" propaganda in the script of *Tender Comrade:* for example, lines like "Share and share alike, this is democracy."[199] Continuing this trend, at the California AFL convention in 1947, staff refused to seat a "duly elected delegate" because he was, evidently, a Communist.[200] Lillian Farmer, mother of actress Frances Farmer, ostensibly agreed with this decision when she charged that "Communists in Hollywood and elsewhere caused the mental breakdown of her daughter," which occurred after Farmer's trip to the Soviet Union in the 1930s and her relationship with the left-wing writer Clifford Odets.[201] In response to this delirium, L.A. County was in the process of passing a law that "made it illegal for a [member] of the Communist Party to go from one city in the county to the next without first reporting his first whereabouts to the police."[202] AFL leader Matthew Woll apparently sympathized with the county solons when he suggested that movie houses showing films of "treasonable stars and writers" be picketed.[203] Communists were under fire on all fronts, and bullets aimed at them wounded CSU grievously.

Yet as CSU's opponents surveyed the landscape, they detected several disturbing signals. Not only were the painters in Los Angeles on the march, but the Communist leader of the Painters union in New York, Louis Weinstock, was planning "the biggest demonstration seen yet to pressure the landlords"; the leader of his union was being "bitterly attacked" for "tolerating Communists" while others were concerned about a "small organized gang of hoodlums who are trying to break up" the painters by employing "disruptive underworld tactics."[204]

The Communists had crested during the extraordinary conditions of the war, but afterward that era became a distant, vacant memory. The Communist issue was then used to batter unions like CSU, though that organization was led by Hollywood painters with few Reds at the highest levels. The authorities were bleating about Communist penetration, just as unions were purging their ranks of real and imaginary Reds. Yet mobsters, who continued to enjoy a role in Hollywood, mostly went about their business undisturbed.

PART
3

MOBSTERS
AND STARS

Hysteria spread over the "infiltration" of Hollywood by the organized left, but correspondingly less concern arose about the role of organized crime; this relative acceptance of mobsters was startling, since they casually engaged in violence, introduced a moral corruption in the industry, and artificially inflated prices, while gaining an extraordinary sway over both capital and labor. Perhaps worse, gangsters affected the construction of race, ethnicity—even sexuality. In the period's movies—some of which were produced by gangsters—stars helped to glamorize the image of organized crime, which brought the mob even more influence. Such formidable opposition from mobsters, and the complicity of stars, ensured that CSU would face difficult odds in defeating the moguls.

⭐ Interestingly, though they were sworn enemies, the mob and the Communist Party played similarly crucial roles within the two major classes that confronted each other across the barricades in Hollywood—capital and labor. Both were semisecret, self-selected elite forces within their respective classes, though just as the party was highly conscious of class, the mob was highly conscious of ethnicity. On the other hand, gangsters were not at the apex of capital, though many considered the Communists to be at the top of labor; the mob did not publish a newspaper and pamphlets or otherwise seek to publicize their activity, but the Reds most assuredly did. Indeed, one of the problems in exposing mob influence is its ultrasecrecy, which makes even surreptitious Communists seem wildly open and accessible by comparison. Of course, the historical record contains memoirs and trial transcripts that record mobsters testifying under oath, but the former—and even the latter—have to be read prudently.

The Reds were not prone to violence, unlike the mob. Further, though the mob served the interests of capital, it was also well placed at the highest levels of labor; the Reds, however, were not well placed at all at the highest levels of capital. Still, in the Hollywood context, a telescoped way to understand the mobsters is to view them as "Leninists of the ruling class." Just as the Reds took on difficult assignments for labor, the mob did so for capital. And as the Communists in Eastern Europe were charged later with usurping the role of labor, the same was said at various points about the mob usurping the role of capital.

Yet in discussing the aftermath of CSU's defeat, the Communist screenwriter Lester Cole bewailed that "press coverage . . . minimized . . . mob connections" in Hollywood. The link "should have made headlines," he contended "but the press didn't consider this scandal worthy of investigation. Instead," he groaned, "the focus was on efforts to root out 'subversion'" by Communists.[1]

This oversight was not peculiar to analyses of Hollywood. Stephen Norwood has emphasized the centrality of violence and espionage to management's campaign to disrupt union organizing and break strikes, a process in which the mob was instrumental; yet this glaring fact has not received the attention it deserves.[2]

Mob influence was no fantasy to the Painters, the spearhead of CSU. A number of their locals in New York were controlled by the infamous mobster Louis (Lepke) Buchalter, who was not above using anticommunism to bolster his rule.[3] Lepke and Jacob (Gurrah) Shapiro also sought to control other unions; their battle to seize the Fur and Leather Workers Union also brought them into fierce conflict with Communist labor leaders like Irving Potash and Ben Gold.[4] Lepke and Jacob kept more than two hundred plug-uglies on their payroll "to help run the New York painter's union" alone.[5]

Labor "racketeering" was a major problem in the AFL generally over the years, though it tended to afflict some unions more than others.[6] Legs Diamond, a New York mobster, "got his first job in a labor dispute. He helped 'settle' a strike by using brass knuckles, acid and the butt of his gun." He collaborated with Dutch Schultz and "Lucky" Luciano; the "gang's jobs . . . included . . . working for whatever side hired [Arnold] Rothstein in labor disputes." These mobsters all had friendly relations with certain politicians. George Z. Medalie, Rothstein's attorney and later U.S. attorney in New York and political godfather of the future presidential nominee Thomas Dewey, argued that "gangs are part of the machine for political control and not until politics is divorced from municipal affairs will we get rid of gangsters."[7] In Los Angeles, mobsters like Mickey Cohen had close relations with municipal officials from top to bottom.

One of the key Hollywood unions was the Teamsters, which was saddled with organized criminal gangs within the ranks; their presence could—and did—lead to murder of dissidents. The Teamsters provided a model for how the mob gained a foothold in unions; in 1945, for example, Jimmy "The Weasel" Fratianno was in Los Angeles working with the Teamsters "throwing acid and busting heads at strikes."[8] Business often brought in the mob to maintain "labor peace"—as happened in Hollywood in the 1930s; if union dissidents could not get countervailing aid from other unions—like IA Progressives did with the longshoreman's union—they often felt compelled to ally with their own gangsters to combat those of management. Either way, the mob feasted.[9] As Orson Welles put it, "a group of industrialists finance a group of gangsters to break trade unionism, to check the threat of Socialism, the menace of Communism or the possibility of democracy. . . . When the gangsters succeed at what they were paid to do, they turn on the men who paid them. . . . [The] puppet masters find their creatures taking on a terrible life of their own."[10]

Why did the mob want a "takeover of unions, coast to coast"? Money was one signal reason, but there were others—for "by threatening union members with loss of work, the gangsters could marshal the efforts of husbands, wives, sons, and daughters in support of virtually any scam the gang could dream up, including swinging an election."[11] Moreover, mobsters like Longy Zwillman wanted to dominate unions because this helped him "to find jobs for his army of relatives," not to mention cementing alliances with various other forces by doling out such benefits.[12] As is evident, marshaling and manipulating kinship ties and ethnicity were essential components of this process.

Because of the government's unwillingness—or inability—to root out organized crime, the mob—as investigative journalist Jeff Gerth charged years after CSU's defeat—"has quietly entrenched itself within all levels of the social structure, leading Donald Cressey, consultant to the President's Commission on Violence, to conclude: 'The penetration of business and government by organized crime has been so complete that it is no longer possible to differentiate 'underworld' gangsters from 'upperworld' businessmen and government officials."[13] Decades after CSU's liquidation, an unexpected result became evident: the government's focus on keeping the organized left out of business and government created a limit on the extirpation of organized crime. Not incidentally, organized crime seemed to flourish especially in areas where organized labor was strongest: e.g., Chicago, New York—and Los Angeles.[14]

★ Despite the dastardly role that the mob has played—particularly in unions—gangsters have been often portrayed in films as latter-day Robin Hoods, social rebels, or misunderstood businessmen. Certainly their wide influence in the entertainment industry helps to explain their relatively sanitized image. During the mob's heyday, "the pulp magazines were full of gangster stories; by the early 1930s there were entire magazines devoted to 'Gangster Stories,' 'Racketeer Stories,' and 'Gangland Detective Stories.'" "In 1929," film historian Robert Sklar notes, "the gangster for the first time surpassed the cowboy as a subject for Hollywood filmmakers," and even the "cowboy" movies have focused heavily on the precursors of twentieth-century gangsters—i.e., cutthroats like Jesse James, Cole Younger, and John Wesley Hardin.[15]

Soon life imitated art as these movies became primers instructing would-be gangsters on how to conduct themselves. In 1946 when George Raft, an actor who frequently played gangsters in the movies, came to Florida to spend time with real-life mobsters Meyer Lanksy and Bugsy Siegel, "It was the gangsters who spent their time studying Raft, trying to find out the name of his tailor" and studying his mannerisms, etc.[16] Films like *Scarface* included scenes from real-life—e.g., when Raft and Paul Muni brought flowers to a rival gangster in a hospital, then pulled a pistol out of the bouquet and shot him. Supposedly men from the Capone gang intervened in the editing of this popular movie.[17]

The mob's true role—more often than not—was elided. And even when the movies dealt ostensibly with mob influence within the unions, the force of the message was often subverted. For instance, *On the Waterfront,* which concerned the gangster-dominated longshore union in the New York area, was interpreted widely as a parable depicting the role of Communists.[18] Similarly, Arthur Miller has told of writing a screenplay describing how gangsters murder and threaten union opponents, but studio executives wanted him to change the mobsters into Communists.[19] According to James Agee, John Huston in his screenplay for *Key Largo* "wanted gangsters to represent 'everything that is wrong with postwar America,' but this intent, Agee says, was excised from the final cut."[20]

Coincidentally, the thematic trend toward gangster movies began as mobsters assumed more influence in the industry. Strikingly, according to the Hollywood left, these "gangster pictures played" a major role "in causing legislation against prohibition," enabling an illicit mob-dominated business to become a legitimate mob-dominated business.[21] Another critic has argued that "under the pressure of gangsters, art was being abandoned in favor of fast-buck productions designed to appeal to the lowest common denominator of society."[22]

More than fifty years after the 1945 strike, one study revealed that there had been forty movies about "Billy the Kid" alone.[23] Yet even as CSU was being stamped out, the moguls' representative, Eric Johnston, in a speech at the Waldorf-Astoria to the Protestant Motion Picture Council, decried the proliferation of "gangster pictures." Piously, he proclaimed, "I want to see more films based on the lives of the Disraelis, the Curies, the Pasteurs, the Bells, the Edisons, instead of the Dillingers, the Capones." Worriedly, he remarked, "propaganda forces in anti-democratic countries like to point to gangster pictures as evidence of typical conditions today in America."[24] These alleged "propaganda forces" had a point, as Johnston must have known. The influence of mobsters in the industry inexorably spilled over onto the silver screen, and dramatic portrayals of the Dillingers, the Capones, and Billy the Kid proliferated.

Ironically, even Charles "Lucky" Luciano was heard to complain about how movies glamorized gangsterism. He lamented the involvement of Hollywood in "glorifying brutal crime." This gangster critic was saddened by how "they present murders and robberies . . . and the real hero, the one who gets all the attention, is the biggest criminal." "Dammit!" he exclaimed, "A kid can learn to torture his brother or punch out his father by going to the movies." With confidence, he concluded, "If anybody knows what turns kids into criminals, it's me!"[25]

Yet Luciano's crocodile tears were meaningless, for—as he well knew —Hollywood was an antiunion enclave where the mob had considerable prestige. Gangsters like Benjamin "Bugsy" Siegel dominated unions as they established enduring relationships with mayors and district attorneys in Los Angeles.[26] Outside the city, offshore gambling took place aboard ships—a leisure activity dominated by gangsters. In 1939 state attorney general Earl Warren announced boldly, "I am determined that these ships shall not operate again," but mentioned wanly his concern that accomplishing this goal "will necessarily tie up a considerable part of my staff."[27] Seven years later—as CSU was about to battle gangsters on picket lines once more—Governor Warren was still only *talking* about shutting down the gambling ships. His aide, Warren Olney III, wanted to extend the state's sovereignty beyond the three-mile limit to curb this lucrative business, but scribbled on the margins of his comprehensive memorandum was this notation: "governor states no action to be taken on this."[28] No additional words explained why this decision was made.

One of the governor's rivals, Attorney General Robert Kenny, threatened to arrest Tony Cornero, the "admiral of the faro fleet."[29] Kenny, a member of the leftist National Lawyers Guild who ultimately defended victims of the blacklist, wanted to move aggressively against these mobsters, but he met resistance. Warren's constituents were pressuring him, too; with a modicum of sensitivity one voter demanded that Warren "do something concrete to put this greasy racketeer into his correct place."[30]

But Governor Warren was reluctant to crack down on the mob. One constituent mailed clippings about the infamous gangster Allen Smiley along with a letter asking in stunned amazement, "surely this can't be true that your Crime Commission is apparently doing little or nothing about those underworld leaders already here." He further griped, "Law enforcement agencies have been very lax in their work."

The lack of an indictment understandably baffled Smiley's critics. Born Abraham Smickoff in Russia, Smiley was one of the most powerful gangsters in the state. The columnist Westbrook Pegler charged that Smiley "poses as a producer and director of motion pictures." He was indicted with bandleader Tommy Dorsey in 1944, charged with "amputating part of the nose of Jon Hall, an actor, at a party given by the Dorseys in their home. They all were acquitted." It was Smiley who was "sitting together" with Bugsy Siegel "on a couch" when Siegel was murdered by an unknown assailant. Smiley was not arrested.[31] He was also the key figure in the "organized book making racket"; this questionable business was "able to exist and operate only because" of the "misuse and abuse" of the "communications companies in this state," but somehow Smiley was able to escape unscathed.[32] Smiley was also a pimp of some renown and a rake in the same class as Larry Fay, "then top procurer of Broadway" who "once said . . . that he's had a different virgin every night for six years."[33] Of course, Fay's words should not be necessarily accepted as truth; however, his words reflect the male supremacist state of mind that pervaded the mob.

When the *Los Angeles Daily News* began to expose Smiley's questionable practices, "considerable resentment" was directed "against this newspaper" from "Hollywood and Beverly Hills chumps." Some did not appreciate the paper's assault on characters like "Russian Louie Strauss," a "onetime Siegel bootlicker and practical homicidist" who was instrumental in operating a mob club at Santa Monica and Fairfax.[34]

It was true that gangsters had close connections to members of the elite in Southern California, and this did appear to provide them with some exemption from prosecution. Mickey Cohen, Los Angeles' top mobster, was chummy with Artie Samish—whom he had known since childhood. Samish, a lobbyist, was reputed to be the second most influential man in Sacramento, next to the governor. "See," Cohen explained, "if I had any problems with legislators in Sacramento on things like slot machines on premises, he nipped it in the bud. I was his right hand, and he was my godfather, my senior statesman." Cohen had a "representative in the . . . Police Department" in Burbank, the home of Warner's. "At one point during the 1940s and 1950s," Cohen "had the police commission in Los Angeles going for me. A lot of the commissioners didn't have any choice. Either they would go along with the program, or they would be pushed out of sight. . . . It was all the way up to the top of the box at different police stations. . . . When I was in the mayor's corner, see, a certain amount was put into his campaign each time through my lawyers, Sam Rummel and Vernon Ferguson." Cohen had "the private number" of Mayor Fletcher Bowron "in his office and the private number in his home." He also knew Richard Nixon; they met in 1945 when the future president was considering a congressional race in Orange County, an area which "was important to my bookmaking program." Cohen "put together this dinner at the Knickerbocker when Nixon" was "running for the Senate. . . . It was all gamblers from Vegas, all gambling money, there wasn't a legitimate person in the room." Tens of thousands of dollars were raised, it was said. Cohen "was also involved with setting up . . . [Nixon's L.A.] campaign office—in the Guarantee Finance Building at Ninth and Hill." Cohen also had confidential information about the mishaps of LAPD chief William Parker. "Some gambler" sent the chief "to Miami to one of them police conventions. They catered to him down there and they had these girls waiting for him on this boat. They were half-assed waitresses or hostesses and I guess they'd turn a trick if they had to. One of these girls, Parker pinched her so hard her ass swolled [*sic*] up and was black and blue. She had to go a doctor to get it fixed."[35]

It would be easy to dismiss all of Cohen's words as the ex post facto ramblings of a man in his dotage. However, his claims do help to explain how a man involved in such a wide range of illegitimate activities could escape the hoosegow so consistently, while being featured in newspapers and fan magazines squiring up-and-coming young starlets around town.

In any event, investigative agencies confirmed the broad outlines of Cohen's influence. With subtle understatement, Governor Warren's "Commission on Organized Crime" concluded that Cohen had "effective political connections." When Cohen's bodyguard was slain in his presence, Harry Cooper, "special agent of the attorney general's office," was at the mobster's side. The commission considered this a "curious incident."[36]

Cohen was not the only gangster with ties to the upper echelon of society. Frank Nitti and other mobsters "apparently backed" the "entry" of Joseph Kennedy "into the world of motion pictures."[37] Charles "Lucky" Luciano "even had men in the office of District Attorney Burton Fitts" in Los Angeles.[38] Simultaneously fighting the moguls, the mob, and the state proved difficult for CSU.

★ Organized crime, which was dominated by Italian Americans, suffered a setback when the United States declared war against Italy during World War II. Perhaps unfairly, these mobsters were suspected of being sympathetic toward Rome; in addition, the conditions of war strengthened the natural predators of organized crime—the organized left—which pushed vigorously for prosecution of the mob.

Like many of his colleagues, mobster Jimmy "The Weasel" Fratianno was a fierce anticommunist; Bugsy Siegel was close to a leading anticommunist, Senator Pat McCarran of Nevada.[39] Mob anticommunism did not stop—and probably facilitated—the 1944 conviction of Johnny Roselli, the mob's main liaison on the West Coast.

The prelude to his trial was the ouster of Willie Bioff and George Browne from IATSE, jailed because of their financial shenanigans. As *Variety* observed in 1940, the two were "planning to step out [of the] union limelight, at least temporarily, with the idea of manipulating strings from back stage. A front man would be selected for window dressing, with Willie calling shots from behind the curtain."[40] This plan was complicated by Bioff's graphic testimony against Roselli; Bioff's words were not forgotten by the mob, thus possibly shedding light on why the IATSE leader was subsequently killed by a car bomb in Phoenix in the mid-1950s.[41] What prompted Bioff to testify? He claimed during the trial that a rush of patriotism caused his change of heart: "Pearl Harbor did something to me. I want to cut my prison term down so I can help fight the Axis," he claimed sanctimoniously.[42]

A flood of revelations—based on sworn testimony—emerged from this trial concerning the mob's power in Hollywood. In addition to funding studios and controlling unions, the mob was involved in the basics of the industry—e.g., the buying and selling of millions of feet in film stock. The mob also had influence over trade papers. William Wilkerson of the *Hollywood Reporter,* who often lavished Bioff with gifts, spoke of believing what he wrote—"most of the time." Maybe Wilkerson was referring to his habit of glossing over mob influence in Hollywood.

He was not alone in acting as a shill for the mob. Jimmy Fratianno charged that "this broad at the [L.A.] *Herald,* Aggie Underwood. She's a big editor there . . . prints any shit [Mickey Cohen] gives her."[43] William Randolph Hearst "really had a strong liking" for Cohen too; helpfully Hearst told his reporters to call Cohen a "gambler," not a "hoodlum" and to portray him as "sort of like a Robin Hood."[44] An inspection of Hearst newspapers confirms this insight. In addition, Roselli's insurance business handled the *Reporter's* insurance needs, and the paper's workers were in a union controlled by Bioff.[45]

Roselli—born Filippo Sacco in Esteria, Italy, in 1905—came to the United States in 1911. In addition to serving as a labor racketeer, he also worked in public relations for one of the studios and became a close friend of Pat Casey, the employers' main labor negotiator. The mob in Los Angeles also included Bugsy Siegel (de facto boss of the "vital movie extras union"), Mickey Cohen, Jack Dragna, "the Capone of Los Angeles," who also happened to be a leader of the Italian American community in Southern California. Typically, this gangster was also an ethnocentrist.[46] The mob also had inroads within the Teamsters, a union that refused to observe CSU picket lines in 1945.[47] Of course, there were factions—ethnic and otherwise—within organized crime; the ouster of Browne and Bioff proved to be a "godsend" for crime boss Sam Giancana of Chicago, for example, allowing him to increase his influence in IATSE to the detriment of his competitors.[48]

Convicting Roselli and his comrades was no easy task. Key witnesses were afraid to testify for fear of bodily harm,[49] and these fears were not misguided.[50] Even so, in 1944 the defendants were convicted. In 1947, however, in the midst of the lockout and weeks before proclamation of the blacklist, Roselli was paroled—a maneuver which "provoked a national scandal." Eyebrows had been raised earlier when Bioff and Browne were freed in 1945, before one-third of their sentences had been completed; income tax violations were dropped against Bioff.[51]

The mob had been politically well connected for some time. Bioff had charged that in 1937 when the California legislature began an investigation of him, he gave $5,000 to the right person and the inquiry fizzled. The Republican Party charged that President Truman and his attorney general, Tom Clark, "refused to help the inquiry into the paroles" of Roselli and his confederates.[52] The mob had provided a generous retainer to Paul Dillon, a St. Louis lawyer and former campaign manager for Truman, a move that apparently did not hurt the mobsters.[53] Perhaps this arrangement is why Giancana, later accused of helping to swing the presidential election in Illinois in 1960, called FDR's successor "their boy."[54] Likewise, Longy Zwillman had charged that he helped to swing the 1932 election to FDR through the influence he wielded in New York and New Jersey.[55] Before the reign of the Democrats, mobster Diamond Joe Esposito "routinely boasted of meeting with Calvin Coolidge and dispensing votes and favors at the President's request."[56] Even accounting for some mobsters' tendency to inflate their accomplishments, it was evident—as Governor Warren's crime commission suggested—that the mob was not without friends in high places.

The changed political atmosphere brought by the transition from the war to the Red Scare boosted organized crime—a force that preyed upon militant unions. Soon organized-crime figures were controlling the installation of jukeboxes, which gave them enormous influence over the direction of popular music. As was typical, L.A. mobster Mickey Cohen "had a club called 'The Rhum Boogie' on Highland Avenue. It was a black-and-tan joint where the Treniers broke in their act. Many of the great black acts broke in at this 'Rhum Boogie.'"[57] The mob also gained hegemony within the pornography industry and came to control gay clubs arising in urban areas.[58] As George Chauncey has written, "columnists occasionally commented on the presence of gay men in the social milieu of the gangsters." Dutch Schultz was "harbored and nursed by a whole colony of nice boys, whose ministrations were more tender than those of the most tender female nurse."[59]

Hyper-masculinity was a critical aspect of mob culture; this culture was shaped profoundly by prison experiences that further inflated the "ordinary" subordination practiced by gangsters. Certainly, homosexual abuse of enemies was a mob specialty,[60] just as the mobsters' robust attitude toward sexuality generally attracted them to a Hollywood that often was perceived as dissolute.

As Roselli's biographers observe: "The sudden and enormous success of the movies spawned an orgy of vice that threatened to shatter the industry. Drug use was widespread, including cocaine, heroin and illegal alcohol. Sexual favors were demanded by casting directors and became a sort of alternative currency. Mack Sennett's Keystone Studios had to be tented and fumigated for infestations of venereal crabs."[61]

Moreover, sexuality may have been defined more expansively in Hollywood than in any other part of the United States. Such a scene was made to order for the mob, which could supply all of the illegal substances and prostitutes that Hollywood could handle.

It was not accidental that the modern gay rights movement was initiated in Los Angeles by a former Communist who had worked as a screen extra (in the union dominated by Bugsy Siegel) "often as a stunt rider for Republic and Monogram westerns." Harry Hay, a lover of the popular actor Will Geer, admitted to having two or three "affairs a day between 1932 and 1936."[62] Hay deployed the skills he had obtained in the party in order to advance the cause of the despised gay minority. That the party had substantial experience in confronting the mob, which sought to control gay clubs and other "sexual venues" beyond the mainstream, gave radical gay Angelenos the edge needed to challenge this experienced and unscrupulously crafty foe, and thus sharpen their skills even further.

These varied linkages, in particular mob influence on the entertainment industry, helped to make organized crime one of the most powerful—albeit hidden—shapers of postwar culture in the United States. The mob's 1930s vision of organizing the entire amusement industry never occurred, but the mobsters' influence was no less for that.

★ These events do not fully depict the extent of the mob's influence. In Hollywood, as elsewhere, organized crime was predominantly an amalgam of Jewish- and Italian American thugs. Their lack of principle, along with ethnocentrism, helped to complicate ethnic relations and the construction of a synthetic "whiteness," whereby racial identification took precedence over ethnic or ethnoreligious affiliation. An essential part of this construction of whiteness was antiblackness; the absence of blacks from the ranks of mob families was at once suggestive of ethnocentrism—and racism—and sheds light on the relative absence of African Americans in Hollywood during this period.[63]

Anti-Semitism seemed to be a more salient factor among the ultra-right in Los Angeles than did anti-Italian sentiment. Thus, as moguls were accused of being soft on their co-religionists in unions, and as trade unionists were being accused of being no more than a bunch of "Jewish Communists," Italian American mobsters had the chance to erode the power of their Jewish American counterparts. Hatred between these two influential ethnic groups was colored indelibly by gangland relations.

Of course, Jewish- and Italian Americans were not alone in emphasizing their ethnic backgrounds. The "Westies," an Irish American gang in New York City, were not above "using their ethnic heritage as a framework for their criminal deeds."[64] African American gangs in Los Angeles also leaned toward nationalism.[65]

Of course, all mobsters were not strict ethnocentrists. Daniel Bell notes that Frank Costello had a good deal of "ethnic pride," as did most gangsters; consequently, he helped a "substantial number of Italian judges sitting on the bench in New York" to obtain their posts, along with "many Italian district leaders." But he also aided some "Jewish and Irish politicians."[66]

While the racial umbrella of "whiteness" tended to curb ethnic tensions among Americans of European descent, it did not erase such tensions within organized crime. The biographer of Longy Zwillman, a Jewish mobster with some authority in show business, has remarked that "most of the Italian gangsters in New York were anti-Semites. . . . Vito Genovese was also a bigot."[67] The biographer of Bugsy Siegel's paramour, Virginia Hill, concurs, adding, "Italians and Jews often did not mix well in the Mafia."[68] Jimmy "The Weasel" Fratianno, on the other hand, said ruefully, "[Y]ou've got to give the Jews credit . . . they started out as fronts for the Italians and now they've got millions they made through Italians."[69] Self-proclaimed mob lawyer Frank Ragano conceded that "Sicilian-Americans of my generation were brought up by our fathers to believe that we must instinctively trust our countrymen. We were inculcated to band together because of the biased attitudes of the Anglo establishment."[70] Seen from varying perspectives, the point becomes clear: mobsters frequently carried an ethnic and ethnoreligious consciousness.

"The Weasel" may have had Meyer Lansky in mind when he conceded the Jewish mobsters' skill at laundering money. Lansky was a Zionist and widely viewed as the mob's top money man. As early as the age of fifty he wanted to be buried, "like his grandfather" in Israel. Eventually, he came to distrust his Italian American colleagues and decided to live in Israel. His critics charged that he was simply trying to elude the long arm of the law, but Lansky had contributed to the Israel Emergency Fund prior to his departure. Interestingly, within Israel only the most right-wing, ethnocentrist forces backed Lansky.

Suspicion of Italian Americans was not the only ethnic grudge held by Lansky; like Ragano he was hostile toward those he thought were the true ethnic elite. "The Wasps couldn't have it . . . that a bunch of Jewish and Italian street boys could make so much money in Vegas and other places. They wanted to drive us out—and finally they succeeded."[71]

La Cosa Nostra, as it was called, was a "secret society with fewer than 5,000 . . . formally initiated male members of Italian heritage, operating out of twenty-four select cities."[72] Many of its prime rituals excluded non-Italians and, at times, non-Sicilians. Ethnic conflict seemed more pronounced in Los Angeles—with its less settled hierarchy and its more rapid economic and population growth rates—than in mob citadels like Chicago and New York. The opportunities opening up as a result of the post–World War II boom only heightened the tensions. Even Governor Warren's commission was struck by the conflict between Mickey Cohen and Jack Dragna.[73] Some of this squabbling was over who would appropriate the riches of the new gambling mecca, Las Vegas. This conflict eventually led to the murder of Bugsy Siegel.[74]

Years later Cohen—who clashed repeatedly with Roselli—remained bitter about what he perceived as anti-Jewish discrimination within the mob. "Being Jews," he remarked caustically, "Benny [Siegel] and me, even Meyer [Lansky] couldn't be a real part and parcel" of the top ranks of the mob. Jack Dragna, he felt, "was of the old school where only Italians ran things, and certainly not like Benny with his Eastern ways." Siegel, to his ultimate detriment, did not care: " 'Fuck Dragna' was his attitude—and he did"—an approach that led to Siegel's premature death.

Cohen thought he faced a major barrier that his Italian American comrades did not have to contend with: he had to "fight the coppers too, because a lot of the coppers were Nazis themselves in those days." Thus, the extremely powerful Red Squad could be more prone to harass Jewish-rather than Italian American mobsters, thus hampering their activity and heightening their ethnoreligious consciousness.

Like Lansky and Dragna (who in addition to his mob leadership also was viewed as a leader of the entire Italian American community in Southern California), Cohen too was ethnocentric. He tried to help Jewish businessmen and raised funds for the Irgun (a right-leaning political movement) when they were fighting for Palestine. While Italian American mobsters were suspected of being sympathetic to Rome and the Axis powers, Cohen spent time during the war seeking out presumed Nazis and beating them up. He "got so engrossed with Israel" that he "actually pushed aside a lot of . . . activities and [did] nothing but what was involved with this Irgun war." Thus, he "got involved with this goddamn

Israel war for three years and . . . started to have relationships with Irgun members back in Israel."[75]

Cohen, who often referred to Italian Americans as "wops," was stunned by the murder of Siegel. This slaying "signaled a takeover of the 'rich harvest field' [that] Los Angeles" and Las Vegas "had become. . . . [This] movement was well under way by Frank Costello and the Italian mob to move in on the West Coast."[76] Unfortunately for CSU, this complex maneuvering came during its major life-and-death struggle. Coming as it did in 1947, Siegel's murder also served as an intimidating signal to the mostly Jewish American moguls, who were under pressure in Hollywood and who feared that their enemies might maneuver to eliminate them too—albeit in a more civilized manner than that used on Siegel. These moguls had been accused repeatedly of failing to corral the Jewish radicals who presumably controlled the Communist Party and, it was thought, CSU.

The growth in anti-Semitism following the war was not reassuring either. Squashing the Communists and, consequently, CSU seemed a small price to pay for the moguls and, in any case, was consistent with their perceived class—and perhaps ethnoreligious—interests. The fact that the moguls would smash with barely concealed relish their presumed co-religionists demonstrated both their fealty to class concerns and their suitability for admittance into—if not promotion within—the hallowed halls of whiteness.[77] By smashing CSU, these Jewish moguls could also demonstrate their "American-ness." Jewish American moguls retained their posts, though their co-religionists in organized crime were forced to retreat in the face of a determined offensive by their Italian American counterparts. Jewish American radicals like Lawson were jailed because of their refusal to accept the postwar dispensation.

★ An intimate relationship existed between mobsters and some stars. They enjoyed each other's company; the former often employed the latter in clubs and elsewhere, while the latter returned the favor by portraying the former favorably in the movies. On the other hand, the mob also policed and disciplined recalcitrant stars. Many stars thus had objective reasons for crossing CSU picket lines and, indeed, for becoming some of the union's more implacable foes.

George Raft had friendships with many mobsters, including Siegel and Owney Madden, the baron of Hot Springs, Arkansas. Raft referred more than once to his "long time friend"—one of his "two special friends"

—the erstwhile mob lawyer Sidney Korshak.[78] Raft was not alone in forging such ties. Sam and Chuck Giancana alleged that the mob sponsored numerous stars, including "the Marx brothers, George Raft, Jimmy Durante, Marie McDonald, Clark Gable, Gary Cooper, Jean Harlow, Cary Grant and Wendy Barrie." The mob in Chicago "used its money and influence to try and get close to everybody from Ronald Reagan to Ed Sullivan."[79] "The Weasel," like Roselli, a former producer, claimed that he "knew half the movie people in [Hollywood] on a first-name basis. Jack Warner, Harry Cohn, Sam Goldwyn, Joe Schenck, Clark Gable, George Raft, Jean Harlow, Gary Cooper."[80] Longy Zwillman was a lover of the star Jean Harlow.[81] Frank Sinatra's relationship with organized crime figures is well known. Mob lawyer Frank Ragano quotes him as declaring, "[T]hey helped me become what I am today." Like "many show business and sports personalities," Rocky Marciano was drawn to the gangster Santo Trafficante.[82]

Mickey Cohen called Sinatra "his best friend. When Frank was going pretty bad, when he was getting kind of discouraged, I had this testimonial dinner for him at the Beverly Hills Hotel." Sinatra, who had been associated with the left during the war, felt obligated to make a forced march to the right, a journey that left him in the embrace of the mob.[83] One of Cohen's men, Johnny Stompanato, like a number of other mobsters before him, dated stars: in his case, Lana Turner—whose daughter was accused of stabbing him to death—Ava Gardner, and Janet Leigh. Both Robert Mitchum and Sammy Davis, Jr., acted as "character" witnesses for Cohen during his numerous trials.[84] Mobsters, like most Americans, longed for the glitter and prestige that stars were thought to bring, a fact that may cast some doubt on their stories. However, as major investors in the entertainment industry, mobsters definitely had reason, incentive, and opportunity to consort with the exemplars of the glamour industry.

Mobsters attended the leading Hollywood parties and the most sophisticated soirees, often with glamorous actresses in tow. In 1947 the *Washington Times-Herald* observed with wonder that "California gangsters" had "social entree among the parvenus" and "themselves rank as the Astors and Vanderbilts of their time and place."[85] The mob was riding high, and its ability to deliver muscle to squash CSU was a large factor.

The leading actors—the stars—also felt compelled to turn against CSU. Those crossing CSU picket lines included the brightest celestial bodies in the firmament of Hollywood, even some who had been scorned previously as acolytes of the left. Ray Milland, Lucille Ball, Olivia De

Havilland, Judy Garland, Clark Gable—even the Three Stooges—did not stand with CSU.[86] CSU was livid; "what you make-up toters need," the union sputtered, "is to come to our Open Mass Meetings on Sunday evenings and find out the kind of world you really live in."[87] CSU urged its allies in the labor movement to pressure the stars with boycotts and other tactics. The Pomona Valley Central Labor Council reprimanded Ingrid Bergman. "We cannot call you 'sister' in this letter," the council members said with anger, "as we do not believe union sisters pass picket lines." "By unanimous" vote the council insisted "that the finger of scorn should be pointed at each of you. . . . [Y]our name has been placed on our 'unfair list' and we shall instruct our people to avoid patronizing pictures where your name appears."[88]

Bing Crosby supposedly "apologized to pickets" after crossing their line "on the basis that the line wasn't there when he went" to see a movie at a Paramount theater. "But we wonder," said a CSU missive, "who [*sic*] he apologizes to at Paramount when he goes through that picket line every day" in order to work? The velvet crooner was contrasted with Edgar Bergen who "received a round of applause from the pickets as he turned away from the box office when he saw the picket line."[89] CSU was especially frustrated with the stars' impact; because of their notoriety, their failure to back CSU effectively isolated the labor federation.

Of course, the Screen Actors Guild as a union had its own grievances with the moguls. Despite the life of luxury that stars were presumed to enjoy, "between 1937 and 1946 the number of players under long-term contracts to Hollywood studios varied between six hundred and eight hundred." This meant that a significant percentage of the union was perpetually unemployed, and even the lucky hundreds had to endure one-sided adhesion contracts that neither stipulated the length of the working day nor included payment for rehearsals. Despite this rigorous existence, a congressional report in 1922 captured the persistent image of the actor's life with references to "debauchery, riotous living, drunkenness, ribaldry, dissipation, free love"—all "conspicuous." Some of these alleged rogues were making "something like $5000 a month or more," which was "extracted from poor people in large part."[90]

The always insecure actors tended to feel that they had much to lose by aligning themselves with a supposedly "Communist" CSU, particularly when their own alleged luxurious existences were viewed as largely undeserved. Moreover, not all actors were closet leftists straining to reveal their revolutionary colors. Gary Cooper had visited "Albert Goering, in-

Pickets confront "scabs" and police at
Warner Bros., 27 September 1946.
Photo from *Los Angeles Examiner* courtesy
Hearst Newspaper Collection, Dept. of
Special Collections, University of Southern
California Libraries.

Jack Warner of Warner Bros.
This mogul headed what was
regarded as one of the more "socially
conscious" studios, and during the
war he produced pro-Soviet films.
Yet the mass picketing of his studio
caused him to reconsider previous
political commitments.
Photo courtesy of Herald Examiner Collection,
HE-001-571, Los Angeles Public Library.

Mickey Cohen, right, key chieftain in the ranks of organized crime in Los Angeles. Like many mobsters, he was involved heavily in the entertainment industry and was quite ethnocentric. Frequently mobsters supplied moguls with "muscle" to crush strikes.

Photo courtesy of Herald Examiner Collection, HE-001-574, Los Angeles Public Library.

Katharine Hepburn, actress and union supporter, with Robert Kenny, lawyer and leader of the California left, at a rally at Gilmore Stadium, Los Angeles, 19 May 1947. The moguls and the GOP feared the influence of progressives like Hepburn and Kenny in city hall, Sacramento, and Washington, D.C.

Photo courtesy of UCLA Special Collections.

In the fall of 1946, Ronald Reagan (center, at microphone) was not yet the right-wing Republican he was to become. Here he appears in an anti-racist radio play sponsored by the "Mobilization for Democracy," a so-called Communist front.

Photo by Ben Polin, courtesy of Southern California Library for Social Studies and Research, Los Angeles.

On various occasions, Reagan impressed many with his contradictory ability to speak rapidly and fluently— or, if the situation demanded it, to baffle listeners with non sequiturs.

Photo by Ben Polin, courtesy of Southern California Library for Social Studies and Research, Los Angeles.

John Howard Lawson, leader of Hollywood Communists. That he was Jewish, like many of the moguls, alarmed anti-Semites, who worried about this minority's alleged undue influence on the powerful medium that was film and who fretted about these executives' supposed reluctance to crack down on their coreligionists.

Photo courtesy of *People's Weekly World*, New York.

Disney workers picket a theater during their 1941 strike. The draconian working conditions at this studio radicalized many workers, turning some toward the Communist Party.

Photo courtesy of Southern California Library for Social Studies and Research, Los Angeles.

The 1941 cartoonists' strike at Disney catapulted Hollywood labor leader Herb Sorrell to prominence.

Photo courtesy of Southern California Library for Social Studies and Research, Los Angeles.

This labor unrest at Warner Bros. was part of a postwar upsurge by unions that was foiled by the dawning of the Red Scare.

Photo courtesy of Regional History Collection, UCLA Libraries.

*For a while, a powerful union of extras
was controlled by mobster "Bugsy" Siegel.
Stars, many of whom were insecure
about their lofty status, were often
reluctant—with notable exceptions—to
support the demands of their co-workers.*

Photo from *Los Angeles Examiner* courtesy
Hearst Newspaper Collection, Dept. of
Special Collections, University of Southern
California Libraries.

*Pickets mass at Paramount Studios,
23 October 1945. The quality of
movies was impacted as skilled workers
went on strike and "scabs"—who often
were not as talented—took their places.*

Photo from *Los Angeles Examiner* courtesy
Hearst Newspaper Collection, Dept. of
Special Collections, University of Southern
California Libraries.

UCLA students join in CSU picketing. Politicians, furious at student support for labor demands, launched an investigation of this school in the aftermath of the strike.

Photo from *Los Angeles Examiner* courtesy Hearst Newspaper Collection, Dept. of Special Collections, University of Southern California Libraries.

CSU members and their families picket Columbia Studios, 20 October 1946. Though militant, CSU was slow to reach out to African Americans and other communities of color during their confrontations with the moguls and mobsters. This was a major reason for their downfall.

Photo from *Los Angeles Examiner* courtesy Hearst Newspaper Collection, Dept. of Special Collections, University of Southern California Libraries.

After battling with demonstrators at Warner Bros., police officers salute them when they unfurl the U.S. flag. Throughout this period of labor unrest, CSU maintained a naïve faith in the idea that the government was on their side.

Photo courtesy of Herald Examiner Collection, HE-001-573, Los Angeles Public Library.

A sheriff's car burns at MGM Studios, 4 October 1946. Through their influence with government, the moguls were able to maneuver local police departments against studio labor.

Photo from *Los Angeles Examiner* courtesy Hearst Newspaper Collection, Dept. of Special Collections, University of Southern California Libraries.

Opening of the trial of 208 pickets fighting four misdemeanor charges, 12 December 1946. As the 1946 lockout unfolded, labor was hamstrung when it had to spend considerable time in the courtroom defending itself rather than on the picket line.

Photo from *Los Angeles Examiner* courtesy Hearst Newspaper Collection, Dept. of Special Collections, University of Southern California Libraries.

The Hollywood Ten, screenwriters and directors, await imprisonment. The weakening of progressive forces in Hollywood allowed the moguls to gain more control over the production process and facilitated the reduction in the number of "socially conscious" films.

Photo courtesy of the Southern California Library for Social Studies and Research, Los Angeles.

Herbert Sorrell, leader of the
Conference of Studio Unions, prepares
to be jailed. This pugnacious former
pugilist was accused repeatedly of
being a Communist. He was not,
but this charge was instrumental
in derailing his union.

dustrialist brother of Herman Goering" in Germany.[91] Maurice Chevalier, the French actor who became a star in Hollywood, collaborated with Germany during the war by "performing for Nazi troops in Paris and Berlin."[92] Ginger Rogers' collaboration with fervent anticommunists was well known.

Still, there were leftist SAG members whose livelihoods were imperiled as the war ended and the political climate changed. On 16 November 1943 in Los Angeles, there was a gala event celebrating the tenth anniversary of U.S.-Soviet "diplomatic relations." On the program was a shining roster of Hollywood's finest: Edward G. Robinson and Walter Huston were featured, along with Dooley Wilson. Jean Renoir arranged the staging for this event, which was sponsored by the National Council of American-Soviet Friendship; patrons included Charles Chaplin, James Wong Howe, Paul Robeson, Leopold Stokowski, Walter Wanger, Orson Welles, Paul Henreid, Robert Rossen, and Upton Sinclair.[93]

This leftward trend continued after the war—for a while. Another gala event in early 1945 featured the premier of a work adapted for the screen by Ring Lardner, Jr., entitled *Tomorrow the World,* which concerned the re-education of Nazi youth. Charles Boyer, Fred MacMurray, Dick Powell, and Lena Horne were among those present. Paul Henreid captured the feelings of many when he warned, "neutrals are either killed or they become traitors. In either case they die. I think it is worthwhile remembering this."[94]

Days before the lockout, *Time* magazine tackled Hollywood's Independent Citizens Committee of the Arts, Sciences and Professions (ICCASP), a premier left-leaning group. "It can call on Gypsie Rose Lee to bare her navel and William Rose Benet to write a script." With amazement, if not awe, *Time* said that "Lena Horne will sing at any rally and Walter Huston will recite the Gettysburg Address. Frederic March belongs and so do Eddie Cantor, Charles Boyer, Humphrey Bogart, Edward G. Robinson, Charles Laughton and Robert Young"; this allegiance, it was concluded, "gives ICCASP a unique leverage on thousands of U.S. voters."[95] ICCASP opposed the Red Scare and the Cold War, supported more sympathetic portrayals of minorities on-screen, and generally sympathized with CSU. This type of agenda was seen as dangerously provocative by leading anticommunists, who determined that this leftist trend should be confronted, if not conquered. Because numerous stars who stood by the progressive banner were non-Communists, the wail of anticommunism was useful in stampeding many of them to the right. The leftists' retreat hampered SAG's ability to address the staggering unemployment in their ranks, and the already powerful moguls simply acquired more strength.

The bold Edward G. Robinson, one of the more vocal members of ICCASP and SAG, encouraged Robert Kenny to challenge Warren for the governorship, since the future chief justice "has been tops in doing nothing for the state." Robinson told the left-leaning Kenny, "I think you should listen to the voices that ask you to run for Governor in 1946 and decide to let us put your name in nomination. . . . Count me," he said with confidence, "as one of your many, many supporters."[96] This act was a continuation of the actor's leading role as a booster of the left. In 1943 he warmly informed Jessica Smith, editor of *Soviet Russia Today,* that he had just "made a recording to be broadcast from Moscow" providing aid and comfort to the Red Army, which he praised for its "courage, valor and achievements." He was able to "talk in Russian," for he had been studying the language.[97] A few months later he praised the land of Stalin as "a land where anti-Semitism is a high crime against the state! No—there are no wailing walls in the length and breadth of the Soviet Union." He deemed performing in Maxim Gorki's *The Lower Depths* "one of the most significant experiences in my career . . ."[98] But it was not long before the barrel-chested actor issued a groveling apology for his pro-Soviet gumption.[99]

No doubt Robinson felt that he *had* to retreat from the left, for he might otherwise have had difficulty securing another acting job— or like John Garfield, he may have been pushed to an early death. As early as December 1946 one journal named the former " 'Little Caesar' a Little Red." Robinson supposedly sponsored a number of organizations deemed less than worthy, including the Hollywood Democratic Committee, the American Committee for the Protection of the Foreign Born, the National Council of American-Soviet Friendship, and other so-called "Communist fronts."[100]

Robinson was also said to be a member of the notorious "Stalin's Stars." Other supposed members of this ignominious band were Katharine Hepburn, Groucho Marx, and Charles Chaplin.[101] Bette Davis was not in this supposed hall of shame, although military intelligence had alleged that she was a "Communist sympathizer and fellow-traveller. The original meeting for the organization of the communist infiltrated Hollywood Canteen was held at subject's home and she was elected president."[102] A key Canteen goal was to uplift the armed forces' morale, an ostensibly favorable purpose from any perspective, but in this case especially so, for Davis—like many other liberals—had become tangentially involved with the Communist Party at a time when the United States itself was in an alliance with the USSR.

The actor Melvyn Douglas was a staunch anticommunist, though a liberal. Yet his opposition to the Reds was not sufficient to save him from harassment, in part because the Red Scare in Hollywood was aimed as much at progressivism as Communism. Indeed, this fact was the ultimate lesson of CSU's destruction. In early 1946 as the great strike wave accelerated, Walter Reuther of the auto workers' union gave "thanks" to Douglas for coming to Detroit to speak at a rally as "200,000 GM strikers" walked the picket lines.[103] Yet Douglas disdained the Progressive Citizens of America, the left-leaning organization that was seen as a forerunner for a challenge to President Harry S. Truman, protesting that his "nomination to the executive board was without my knowledge."[104] Douglas' protestations did not spare him a blistering anti-Semitic assault from Congressman John Rankin, who referred to this friend of Eleanor Roosevelt and Hubert Humphrey by his birth name, Melvyn Hesselberg, and suggested that he was one among many Jews hiding behind Anglo-Saxon names, to Hollywood's detriment.[105]

The right-wing storming of Hollywood followed the war so quickly that it caught many stars unprepared and unable to fight back effectively. However, the fury and rapidity of the offensive were somewhat foreseeable. In retrospect, the wartime détente was an exception, and the resumption of the status quo ante was, perhaps, predictable.

After all, stars were accused of being dupes of Reds before the war, too. As early as 1934 James Cagney was accused of aiding the Communists through his links with Lincoln Steffens, Ella Winter, "and a mysterious woman named 'Mary.'" The same accusation was leveled at Dolores Del Rio, Lupe Velez, and Ramon Navarro; there was fear that stars who, in any case, belonged to a union—SAG—would throw their considerable magnetism and incomes behind strikes and strikers.[106] The star system had been enormously profitable for the moguls, but it seemed that in lining the pockets of so many who—after all—were members of a union, studio executives may have been sustaining their own grave diggers.

Even during the war, a Red Scare seemed to loom. In 1944 Ginger Rogers' mother warned against Red infiltration of Hollywood and the injection of "communistic propaganda" into movies.[107] A few days earlier, perhaps naively, John Garfield described his joy in encountering some of Tito's partisans in Yugoslavia; he "lacked words," said the *Daily Worker*, "to describe his emotions on 'seeing these heroes who have already become a world legend.'"[108] Tito eventually became a foe of Stalin—but he was still a Communist, and that, along with Garfield's support of CSU,[109] was enough to raise questions about the actor's reliability.

During the strike and lockout, the studios placed considerable pressure on the stars to back away from CSU. Since CSU had clashed with SAG over who was to represent extras, many stars were not inclined to resist that pressure and back the union federation. Still, IATSE singled out Garfield's alleged radical credentials in one of their many flyers raising the question of CSU's supposed Communism.[110] Another flyer pointed the finger of accusation at Lionel Stander, Artie Shaw, and Dalton Trumbo.[111] But it was Garfield—perhaps because of his stardom and his spouse and secretary, who were presumed Reds—who seemed to arouse the most hostile sentiment. One of his last films, the boxing drama *Body and Soul,* was denounced by the columnist Westbrook Pegler as a celluloid "Communist front." Pegler noted with suspicion that the production company was headed by the son of FDR aide Harry Hopkins. Worse, Garfield "used to be" known as "Jacob Garfinckle, also Jules," and his "parents [were] born in Russia." These statements were code language stating that the actor was a "Jewish radical."[112]

Edward Dymtryk, who directed *Crossfire*—a rare cinematic attack on anti-Semitism—argued that actors, being creative, leaned toward the left since they were thinking "in terms of new things all the time, not in terms of set things." Dymtryk, who eventually became a "friendly witness" before congressional committees investigating the left in Hollywood, suggested further that as actors become stars—affluent and popular—they begin to lean toward the right, fearing that what they possess may be taken. The tensions between and among Hollywood's creative and "noncreative" forces spurred contradictions and temblors that pushed stars particularly from left to right, besides sparking tremendous insecurity among them.[113]

Like Frank Sinatra, Ronald Reagan could be regarded as suggestive of the above paradigm. At first, the future president denied that he was involved in making accusations of Communism. As late as June 1947 he asserted vehemently that he was "not only misquoted" but "smeared"; "I am a trifle surprised," he said self-righteously, that anyone "should place any credence in anything the professional red-baiting section of the press says" about his alleged anticommunist statements.[114] This statement was a bit disingenuous, for during the same year he began "providing information about . . . ICCASP and other Hollywood activities" to state authorities, "had received the code name T-10," and had begun to carry a gun for fear of alleged retribution from CSU supporters.[115]

After the dust had settled and years had passed, Reagan dropped his prior reticence and blasted CSU with both barrels. "The strikes," he charged, "contributed substantially . . . to the final disintegration of Hollywood as the key movie manufacturer of the world." Reagan's meaning here is unclear, for at the time, Hollywood films were still the premier revenue earners in the global market. He also blamed the Reds for the strike and lockout: "their aim was to gain economic control of the motion picture industry in order to finance their activities and subvert the screen for their propaganda." Happily, he concluded, "the picket lines that spring [of 1947] dropped almost to nothing."[116]

Reagan's critics were disgusted with his performance. Philip Dunne, the Oscar-winning screenwriter of the moving *How Green Was My Valley,* maintained that the actor "postured all over the place" during the labor unrest. He "talked about going through the picket lines and people threatening to throw acid in his face. Actually," says Dunne, "all the goon stuff was on his side." Still, Dunne recognized with clarity that the performance he gave during the travails of CSU "launched Reagan on his political career."[117]

Contrarily, Charles Chaplin's refusal to follow the path trod by Reagan accelerated his estrangement from his adopted homeland. He knew Sorrell and, as a result, became friendly with Father George Dunne, one of the first to expose the machinations of IATSE.[118] Early in 1947 CSU *News* happily quoted Chaplin as saying, "I never walk through picket lines myself, and I don't wish anybody to do so while working for me."[119] This kind of association, along with his own personal peccadilloes, brought the British-born comedian a plethora of troubles.[120] As early as 1944 the *Daily Worker* expressed concern that Chaplin was becoming "the first victim of the small minority of red-baiters in the movie industry."[121] Chaplin was showing up at venues—e.g., serving with John Howard Lawson as a pallbearer at Theodore Dreiser's funeral—where the "red-baiters" were not exactly welcome.[122] His personal problems entered this political realm when his first wife complained after their divorce in 1920 that his "socialist theories" had done much to wreck their marriage. "He brought his radical friends to the house," she said, "and I didn't like them. I wouldn't eat with them."[123] Eventually, Chaplin's infatuation with "socialist theories" so displeased his enemies that he felt compelled to abandon the United States for exile in Europe.[124] Sorrell and CSU had lost yet another ally.

Other friends of CSU were not so lucky and were unable to escape into exile. Sterling Hayden had joined the party in mid-1946. He "was told it would be helpful if the Screen Actors Guild could be swung into line in support of a strike." So he "went to a cocktail party and began to meet actors and actresses who felt the same way."[125] This activity, which at the time seemed rather innocent, contributed to his being called before a congressional committee in 1951. The same happened to Lionel Stander, the actor whose whistling of the Communist anthem, "The Internationale" in a movie was often cited as evidence of Red subversion in Hollywood. Speaking before the Un-American Activities Committee, he declared that when he "exposed the criminal records of Browne and Bioff, the racketeer gangster officials who later went to jail," he was blacklisted.[126]

The calamity of blacklisting bedeviled many stars who stood with CSU. The screenwriter, Walter Bernstein, whose screenplay for *The Front* later satirized this practice, has argued that the moguls were reluctant to implement blacklisting since "they always wanted to be able to have access to as big a pool of talent as they could." But the sound business practice of nondiscriminatory hiring could easily be interpreted as being soft on Communists or "Jewish radicals," so the moguls quickly "folded."[127]

Blacklisting was not all externally induced. Previously, "most cases of blacklisting . . . were imposed for alleged drunkenness, unreliability and capers of that sort." However, said the *Daily Worker* in 1939, "with the advance of union organization in the film business, the blacklist was hauled out again to be used against actors and writers who joined their craft unions."[128]

★ There was an uncanny parallel between the decline of CSU and the reassertion of mob influence in the entertainment industry. Perhaps coincidentally, of the eleven killings that Jimmy "The Weasel" Fratianno participated in, nine took place between 1947 and 1953, the period when CSU was undergoing a lingering death.[129] Though facing congressional investigation, leading mob figures—like Johnny Roselli— were leaving prison and reasserting authority in Hollywood during this same period.

Moguls, mobsters, and stars had numerous opportunities to encounter each other. There were the racetracks, like Santa Anita. There were the mobster-run gambling ships, where stars often performed and moguls lost huge bankrolls. Meyer Lansky says the ships "offered America's entertainers their most remunerative live venues."[130] And after the ships were shut down, the entire operation simply moved inland to Las Vegas, where there was even more money to be made.

The crossroads where mobsters, moguls and stars met were often charged with tension, not least because moguls liked to enlist mobsters to discipline stars and others. Mickey Cohen tells of the time when Harry Cohn wanted mobsters to murder Sammy Davis, Jr., because of his affair with the actress Kim Novak, fearing that an interracial relationship would harm her marketability. Cohen met with Cohn about the matter and the mogul referred to the charismatic entertainer as "that fucking nigger bastard." Cohen claims that this slur upset him and that although the star was not murdered, Cohn allegedly threatened Davis with the loss of his one good eye if he continued the relationship.[131] However, Novak did recall being called into Cohn's office "where she found him 'surrounded by all these men, including people in the mob.' "[132] Though Cohen was quite self-righteous about his alleged antiracism, mobsters were generally conspicuous racists, as demonstrated by their enterprises in Jim Crow Las Vegas.[133] Yet this episode does provide a glimpse of the mob's social utility in Hollywood as a freelance agent for policing the industry generally and keeping stars in line specifically. This episode also provides insight into the folkways of the moguls and how—and why—they moved with such vigor to hammer CSU.

MOGULS

A thin line often separated those who became mobsters from those who became "legitimate" businessmen. Often both grew up in the same neighborhoods and had intimate associations. Some of those who became legitimate businessmen began their economic endeavors on the illicit side of the street.

That some could escape negative branding irked Meyer Lansky to no end. "Why is Lansky a 'gangster,'" he lamented "and not the Bronfman and Rosensteil families?" Like this mobster, they too had been involved in bootlegging and other unsavory practices, so why did he alone have to bear the stain of gangsterism?[1]

Mobsters were silent partners of the movie moguls, too, but the latter did not seem to suffer obloquy as a result. The bankrolling of Harry Cohn and Columbia Pictures by Longy Zwillman was well known, as were his business dealings with Joseph Schenck of MGM.[2] Allegedly, Sam Giancana "often conducted business with producer Harry Cohn" as well.[3] The moguls' esteem in the public eye did not seem to suffer from such unpleasant associations.

Relations between mobsters and moguls were quite intimate. Carl Laemmle, Jr., fell in love with Virginia Hill, despite the fact that she was the paramour of Bugsy Siegel.[4] Top studio executive Eddie Mannix "had made friends with a number of gangsters when he was just a kid working construction at New Jersey's Palisades Park. He liked the company of bookmakers, bootleggers, prize fight promoters and talent agents, in that order." He was "good friends" with Mickey Cohen and through the famed L.A. hoodlum "knew some pretty nasty people who knew even nastier people," including "policemen who weren't getting by on the money they'd saved up for retirement."[5] Such associations helped Cohen to place his associates in jobs at studios like Warner's.[6]

Joseph Schenck, head of production and then board chairman at Fox—as well as president of United Artists theaters—was quite friendly with Willie Bioff during his tenure at IATSE. Schenck entertained the corrupt labor leader in his home and gave him an inscribed photograph. He bought Bioff 1,000 shares of Fox stock, 1,000 shares of Consolidated Oil, and 500 shares of Continental Can and provided him with $95,000 for the purchase of his sprawling Southern California ranch.[7] At Roselli's trial, Schenck argued that these gifts were just extortion, remuneration provided out of fear; others saw them as bribes to buy labor peace.

This trial also revealed that Roselli was a "confidential investigator" for Pat Casey, the studio's leading labor negotiator. Labor disruption was particularly troublesome during the shooting of films—a time-sensitive process in which elongated schedules were the rule and not the exception; a "confidential investigator" like Roselli could be quite helpful in ferreting out the reason for such disruption and helping to "eliminate" it. The moguls relied not only on outlaws but also on those who apprehended them, too. Roselli's lawyer, Otto Christensen, contended that "there must be and is a closer allegiance and alliance between the police authorities [and the studios] in a producing area than there is between any other group in the country, because these pictures in cans are vulnerable every minute until they are finally sold and have brought in the box office receipts."[8] This "alliance" between the police and studios worked to CSU's detriment when the various Southern California police departments routinely bashed the federation's picket lines.

One reason the moguls moved to dominate IATSE was that they believed the theater projectionists were becoming unruly and using labor disputes as an excuse not to do their jobs, thus costing revenue. By coming to rely on the "police authorities" while maintaining ties with mobsters, the moguls created a combustible process rife with the possibility for corruption and wrongdoing on all sides. These possibilities were realized in 1946 when the strike wave in Los Angeles prompted the Merchants and Manufacturers Association to form a "Citizens Law and Order Committee" to supplement LAPD's assault on labor. This tactic, which created a wide opening for mobsters, was endorsed by Mayor Fletcher Bowron.[9]

★ Though moguls like Louis B. Mayer, Harry Cohn, and Jack Warner willingly carried out their perceived class responsibilities—e.g., breaking unions—some viewed the moguls solely as Jews, an apparent liability. The ultraright, which was growing rapidly worldwide as the movies were rising as a preeminent industry, repeatedly pointed to the Jewishness of several of the moguls as an explanation for the radicalism of studio labor and the morally corrupt themes these studios were accused of propagating.

Though these Jewish moguls were not known for producing movies with Jewish themes, anti-Semitism was a theme in the movies from their beginnings. For example, in 1908 a U.S. producer made a film *Leah the Forsaken,* a story of how anti-Semitic persecution in nineteenth-century Germany wrecked a "love affair of a young Jewish woman and her Gentile lover."[10] Yet despite such efforts, Budd Schulberg is probably correct when he suggests that from the industry's inception, "to be anti-Hollywood was, in a sense, to be anti-Semitic."[11]

Early on some insisted that "the motion picture industry has become a Jew industry run by and for Jews." "Jewish culture," it was stated, "has seized the American cinema and is substituting Jewishness for Christianity."[12]

This message was repeatedly stated by the ultraright; however, some on the left were also unable to resist the fools' gold of anti-Semitism. Theodore Dreiser, the famed novelist, was compelled to apologize for saying "if you [listened] to the Jews discuss Jews you will find that they are money-minded, very pagan, very sharp in practice. . . . Left to sheer liberalism as you interpret it, they could possess America by sheer numbers, their cohesion, and their race tastes, and, as in the case of the Negro in South Africa, really overrun the land." John Howard Lawson and Michael Gold, two leading Jewish Communists, met with Dreiser for an explanation, and to highlight his failure to see "class distinctions."[13] A point worthy of further exploration is how the prominence of Jewish-Americans like Lawson within the party may have helped to exacerbate pre-existing anti-Semitic biases and thus further inflame anti-communism.[14]

During an age marked by the rise of Hitler, the most virulent anti-Semitism was predominantly a phenomenon associated with the ultraright. According to Steven Alan Carr, "[A]s a group Jews were considered to be particularly sympathetic to Communism. The appearance of *The Protocols of the Elders of Zion*"—a fabled anti-Semitic concoction about a plot of Jewish Communists and capitalists to seize global control—was a setback to the campaign for religious equality.[15] This obnoxious bigotry found fertile ground in Los Angeles—a city that prided itself on its Christian roots. Jews were barred from the Lawn Tennis Club—so they founded the Hollywood Lawn Tennis Club.[16] Harry Hay, an Angeleno and founder of the modern gay rights movement, has recalled that in the 1920s "anti-Semitism was widespread in Los Angeles . . . as the very name of the Social Purity of Pasadena attests. Restrictive covenants in sales agreements often prevented Jews from owning property in many parts of the city."[17]

In this era, anti-Jewish fervor was far from being localized in Los Angeles: it was a global phenomenon. The rising Nazis in Germany used the movie industry to set the stage for the Holocaust. The chillingly entitled film *Unworthy Lives* "triggered the full-scale implementation of the first mass-extermination program." The 1936 film *I Accuse* "contributed substantially to the popular acceptance of 'mercy killings.'"[18] Some in Hollywood felt an intense responsibility to counter this propaganda—which in turn caused anti-Semites to charge that this concern illustrated the supposed perils of having powerful Jewish moguls in Hollywood.

However, not all the Jewish moguls consistently opposed fascism. Harry Cohn, the mogul with probably the closest connections to mobsters, admired Benito Mussolini. Non-Jewish powers in Hollywood, such as Walt Disney and the industry's prime funder, A. P. Giannini of the Bank of America, also looked fondly on Il Duce. In 1936 Giannini welcomed Carolo Roncoroni, president of Italy's Fascist National Confederation of Business and a member of the Joint Executive of the Fascist Confederation of Industrials, to Hollywood to discuss cooperative filmmaking with Rome. The following year, during the making of *Snow White,* Disney visited Italy and was entertained by Mussolini himself in his private villa. Hal Roach, another mogul, became friendly with Vittorio Mussolini, the dictator's son, and formed a joint venture with him, backed by MGM. Roach was furious when the war interrupted this grand alliance, arguing angrily that it failed because the "Jewish people in the picture business didn't like it."[19] Joseph Breen, one of the more influential forces in the movie industry, was another of the numerous anti-Semites populating an industry that was said to be dominated by Jews.[20]

Such biases were challenged aggressively by the Hollywood Anti-Nazi League, which, at least before the German-Soviet Non-Aggression Pact of 1939, was a powerful force that incorporated leading actors and directors. Their ranks were replenished regularly due to the Nazis' intolerance, which continually drove leading German artists such as Bertold

Brecht into the arms of Hollywood, where their reflections on their strange, new homeland led to conceptual breakthroughs like the evolution of film noir.[21]

The Nazis and their friends did not accept these developments passively. Fritz Kuhn of the German American Bund popularized the charge that "Jewish Hollywood" was the "Reds' chief base of operations." This distorted observation was made after the release of Warner Bros. *Confessions of a Nazi Spy* and was repeated by the reactionary priest Father Charles Coughlin and his soulmate, Gerald L. K. Smith. Ultimately, this opinion was adopted by some members of the House Un-American Activities Committee, which investigated Hollywood.[22]

The Hollywood left hotly denied that there was either Jewish—or Communist—control of the industry. As early as 1941 one left-wing news service contradicted Charles Lindbergh when the aviation hero complained of supposed "Jewish control of the press, radio and movies"; actually, it was countered, "Jews number only a bare 33% among film executives. The movie moneybags are entirely Wall Street-controlled, and as un-Jewish as can be. Even under the most Jew-conscious interpretation, not more than 10% of financial control (the control which really fixes policies) of the movies can be said to be in Jewish hands." As a congressional committee was launching yet another investigation of Hollywood, the Federated Press blamed the intrusion on "one G. Allison Phelps, rabid anti-Jewish and anti-alien radio commentator in Los Angeles, [who] now takes credit for having started the investigation. Behind him . . . is a certain Russell Mack, disgruntled ex-scenario writer, with contacts in Nazi Germany." Included in this unpalatable alliance was Winfield Sheehan, a former producer whose spouse hosted the Nazi filmmaker Leni Riefenstahl—"Hitler's pet"—when she visited Hollywood.[23]

In the United States generally and Los Angeles specifically, a powerful isolationist bloc had developed that at times linked opposition to antifascism with anti-Semitism. Among these forces was America First, which was irate about the anti-Nazi films emerging from Hollywood—or so contended its critics.[24] Subsequently it was revealed that Hans Thomsen, charge d'affaires at the German Embassy in Washington, "asked Berlin for $3000 to help a Republican Congressman take about 50 isolationist members of his party to Philadelphia to push for an antiwar platform."[25] Chair of the organization in Los Angeles was the attorney John Wheeler, son of the powerful Senator Burton Wheeler. When they sought to raise funds from "wealthy men in Los Angeles" the group contacted Walter Braunschwiger, vice president of the Bank of America.[26] Solicited also were Harry Chandler of the *Los Angeles Times,* Cecil B. DeMille, and several oil and real estate barons.

The perception that Jewish elites, notably the moguls, were bolstering the opposition to fascism enraged many isolationists; that Communists also opposed fascism solidified the idea in the isolationists' minds that the moguls too were ultimately subversives. These sentiments spread to neighboring Mexico, where bitter protests featuring tossed stench bombs erupted at theaters in Mexico City showing films by "Jewish American producers."[27] Back in the United States, Allan W. "Bill" Wells assailed Joseph Schenck for allegedly blacklisting him. Schenck, he said, was a "Russian born Jew" while, he—Wells—was "a native born citizen." He accused Schenck of making "anti-Christian movies" and of meeting with Soviet representatives in 1922; a "handful of Jew Communists in Hollywood" did not escape his reproach either.[28]

Unfortunately such explosive charges did not emerge solely from an easily dismissed fringe. Senator Gerald Nye, who had established credibility with the left during the 1930s because of his investigations of the "merchants of death" (arms manufacturers), claimed in 1941 that a small group of Eastern European Jews and a few Englishmen controlled movie production in Hollywood. Many of these suspects were hauled before his congressional committee in September 1941 to explain their "premature anti-Nazi" stance.[29] In the run-up to these controversial hearings, witnesses before HUAC spoke of Hollywood being the main source of funds for the Communist Party and "raised the specter of an international conspiracy involving the Jews and . . . Communism."[30]

Inflammatory charges about "Jewish control" of Hollywood subsided somewhat after the United States entered the war against fascism, but even before this conflict ended the charges were revived. These concerns congealed with the formation of the Motion Picture Alliance for the Preservation of American Ideals. One of the "ideals" the group wanted to preserve was inferentially revealed when an Alliance leader in 1944 told a Hollywood audience they "all looked as though they had the same father and mother"—i.e., that they were all Jews.[31]

The moguls, whose patriotism fused with their revulsion at the Holocaust, generally did strive to assist the battle against fascism. Robert Kane supervised Fox's operations in Europe, which included theaters in "occupied regions." He offered to "furnish" Washington "systematic and regular reports." Said an investigator for a congressional committee, "Mr. Kane has and will have a great deal to do with molding public opinion in England and in the United States."[32] Likewise, during the war

William Cline, who worked for Paramount, reported regularly to Washington from his vantage point in Mexico about the activities of Germans and Japanese.[33]

The conflicting pressures of bigotry and anti-fascism created a dilemma for Jewish studio executives. They faced anti-Semitism at the same time that Jews in Europe were being slaughtered. Expressing concern about their co-religionists inevitably engendered the bigoted idea that they were engaged in special pleading, just as their inability to exterminate unions fueled the wrongheaded notion that they were soft on "Jewish radicals." The moguls' opponents also believed it dangerous for non-Christians to influence this powerful medium; as a result some Jewish executives felt compelled to distance themselves from their co-religionists.

Walter Wanger — one of John Howard Lawson's favorite producers — took the opposite tack. As his aide informed Dr. Israel Goldstein of the Synagogue Council of America, "Mr. Wanger makes a very large annual donation to the American Jewish Committee."[34] Wanger was a dues-paying member of the Beverly Hills lodge of B'nai B'rith. He contributed to the United Jewish Appeal, whose grateful leader commented on Wanger's "profound concern with Jewish problems."[35] In 1943 as the Holocaust was unfolding, even Harry Cohn forgot his previous support for fascists as he spoke of how "every Jew in Hollywood" should "drop everything else you are doing and tell this story to every Jewish leader in the industry."[36] Shortly thereafter Louis B. Mayer held a dinner meeting focused on Jewish issues that included many top executives and stars, such as Samuel Goldwyn, John Garfield, Ernst Lubitsch, Dore Schary, David O. Selznick, Hal Wallis, Jack Benny, and Jack Warner.[37] After this gathering, Wanger worked closely with Congressman Will Rogers, Jr., who in the fall of 1943 flew to Europe to investigate the rescuing of Jews.[38] Then Wanger and Cohn got together with Mendel Silberberg to announce a meeting at the Hillcrest Country Club on the "continuing problem of anti-Semitism and the broad field of Jewish public relations." The Communist screenwriter Lester Cole was invited to this meeting.[39] Perhaps the moguls could have done more in fighting anti-Jewish fervor globally during the war, but they certainly were not silent.

Like Jewish American elites before him, Wanger acknowledged that reducing bigotry against African Americans helped reduce bigotry against Jewish Americans. He worked closely with Walter White of the NAACP, who continually sought Wanger out for intelligence about antiracism. Speaking of Bette Davis, White remarked, "I understand [she] is very militant in her friendship for a colored girl with whom she went to school in Kansas City"; "James Cagney, Jean Muir, Frances Lederer and Lionel Stander were interested in the Scottsboro case," he added.[40] White had sought out the right man. Wanger—the Oscar-winning producer of *I Want to Live! The Invasion of the Body Snatchers, Cleopatra,* the antifascist classic *Gabriel over the White House, Blockade, Foreign Correspondent, Stagecoach,* and other popular movies—happened to be one of the leading executives fighting bigotry.

Unfortunately, Wanger's open-minded attitudes about race were not reciprocated by other moguls during this period. David O. Selznick debated whether the African American cast members of his questionable epic *Gone With the Wind* should be invited to its Atlanta premier for fear of offending racists.[41] Aware of the negative images he was propagating, he worried that the film's racial depictions might harm relations between African Americans and the "Jews of America," and considered hiring a black college president or editor for a meager $2,000 to defend his movie.[42] Rabbi Barnett Brickner counseled him that "since individuals, who are Jews, are charged with the production of films, they must make the supreme effort to provide the best type of film."[43] Val Lewton warned him not to use the epithet "nigger" in the film, reminding him how the "rank and file . . . threw bricks at the screen" nationally when "inadvertently" Lionel Barrymore used the slur in one of his movies.[44] These cautionary words did not prevent Selznick from making a film that was protested against by numerous African Americans; Selznick even contemplated suing one of his more vociferous critics, the African American Communist Ben Davis.[45]

Though the moguls spared no expense in producing extravaganzas such as *Gone With the Wind* that were criticized as racially insensitive, the presentation of contrary messages was seen as more problematic. The black actor Canada Lee grumbled about the "southern white supremacists" who dominated the mass media and the "pre-censorship" that stifled the production of more progressive images.[46] In the early 1940s the black writer Chester Himes "went from studio to studio with his stories but was turned down everywhere. At one point he was on the verge of being hired as a reader for screenplays but was afterward told that Jack Warner 'didn't want any niggers on his lot.' At another where he was being considered for a publicity position, he learned that the all Negro cast of *Cabin in the Sky* was excluded from the whites-only commissary."[47]

Reducing the overall level of bigotry was hard when anti-Negro racism was blithely tolerated. This casual racism helped to create an atmosphere where hatreds of all kinds could flourish. Ironically, the illiberal antilabor fervor that the moguls so freely exhibited during the strike and lockout helped fuel an equally illiberal anti-Semitism.

Moreover, the fact that some of the most insistent investigators of Hollywood also happened to be stolid conservatives—and anti-Semites —was difficult to ignore. The California legislator Jack Tenney had served as the running mate of Gerald L. K. Smith in the ominously named Christian Nationalist Party. HUAC's counsel, Robert Stripling, "was a southern white supremacist who had previously assisted Ernest Sullivan, a former publicist for the Bund."[48] Such affiliations clearly colored the perceptions of those who were scrutinizing Hollywood.

A report from the FBI, issued as pickets were still encircling the studios in 1946, nervously pointed to "several outside organizations financed by large contributions from the Hollywood industry which cooperate in this support and protection" of the Communist Party. This list included the "Southland Jewish Organization, B'nai B'rith . . . Jewish Worker Council." There were, warned the FBI, "also other smaller groups of the same nature and controlled by the same types of persons."[49] Another FBI agent had a more sinister analysis: "The feeling seems to be growing in many quarters that the industry itself is not averse to being used by this movement because of the intense penetration of the industry by European refugees."[50] The agent was reflecting the broadly held perception that—as one anonymous though well-circulated flyer put it— a "Jewish monopoly" over the industry "brazenly discharges non-Jewish men and women and replaces them with refugee Jews from Europe." Why would these studios, the flyer asked, make anti-Nazi films that are boycotted in Germany, thus causing a fall in profits? Why make *Blockade, Life of Emile Zola,* or *Confessions of a Nazi Spy?*[51]

As the lockout proceeded, some sensed that affluent moguls were still acting as if the popular front of World War II's zenith—when Communists and antifascists freely cooperated—was still in place. These moguls did not seem to understand, it was thought, that the winding down of the war put an end to this unity and that a new order required not an embrace but a punishing of Communists and left-leaning trade unionists. This perception that the moguls were out of touch with newer realities did not erode in March 1945 when the *Los Angeles Times* reported that Walter Wanger had joined with Dalton Trumbo in a "fete" for Harry Bridges, a labor leader who was widely believed to be a Communist.[52]

The American Jewish Labor Council took this situation quite seriously. In June 1946 Max Steinberg recalled with disappointment a controversial incident involving a HUAC investigator who informed Professor Clyde Miller of Columbia University, "you should tell your Jewish friends that the Jews in Germany stuck their necks out too far and Hitler took good care of them and that the same thing will happen here unless they watch their steps."[53]

This was not an isolated incident. Virtually to the day that the 1945 strike broke out, Dr. John Lechner—"famed for his self declared war on American-born Japanese"—joined "the Motion Picture Alliance's Howard Emmett Rogers" in a conservative rant on a local L.A. radio station. "The program ended with Lechner-Rogers partisans shouting, 'Tell about the Jews! Tell about the Jews! They're worse than the Communists even!'"[54] Early in 1946 the organ of "We, The Mothers Mobilize for America" cited Adelle Cox of their Los Angeles unit, who argued that the figures given for the "exterminated Jew" during the recently concluded Holocaust were "like FDR's lies: Super colossal."[55]

Just in case the Jewish community failed to get the message, an eruption of anti-Semitism broke out in Los Angeles at the conclusion of the war. In mid-1946 Temple Israel at 1704 North Ivor Street in Hollywood was desecrated; this act was attributed initially to the Ku Klux Klan, but there were even more baleful suspects. There were German slogans scrawled on the walls, and the synagogue had "received more threatening letters . . . some of them have been written in German." Moreover, "the Rabbi stated that the only person who might be looked upon with some suspicion who was in the church that day while the janitor was gone was a man in the uniform of a captain of the U.S. Army."[56] At the same time, a cross was burned in front of a "Jewish Fraternity House" in Los Angeles.[57]

Instead of arousing concern among the intelligence agents infesting Los Angeles, these incidents seemed to embolden them to be more explicit in expressing their anxieties about the direction of the Jewish community. A few days after the temple desecration, one agent warned that "organized Jewry is out to control organized labor either by the liberals or the Communists. . . . [O]ut in Hollywood, Communism and the Jewish group seem to play hand in hand." Outlined was a remarkable scenario uncannily similar to *The Protocols of the Elders of Zion:* "the Jewish real estate agents are coming out and buying property at unheard of prices. . . . The Jewish people are slowly but surely securing a stranglehold on the poultry and egg business. . . . The Jews are setting up cooperatives and they are joining up with the radical National Farmers Union. . . . [T]here [are] rumors making the rounds . . . to the effect that the Jewish race had set a program in this country whereby they were to bankrupt the country and create such a chaotic condition from black-market activities that the people would be willing to accept any sort of a program advanced by a progressive group. . . . [T]here are no less than 175 to 300 Jewish attorneys in [New York City] who are playing the Communist game from start to finish."[58]

To be sure, there was a disproportionately high number of Jewish moguls—just as there was an over-representation of those with roots in northwest Europe in the U.S. elite generally—a ratio that somehow failed to ignite a furor. And, as Arthur Liebman has written, "the Jewish contribution to the Left in the United States during the twentieth century ranks the highest of any immigrant or ethnic group."[59] There was no mystery to this phenomenon either. Those who feel the most pain often scream the loudest; the victims of bias often feel driven into protest movements. This explains why African Americans also have been disproportionately represented in protest movements during the second half of the twentieth century.[60] But this intelligence agent was suggesting something far more treacherous and menacing. He seemed to be harking back to a classical anti-Semitism and the canard that there was a conspiracy to establish hegemony by Jews of all classes.

Dore Schary, an executive at RKO, provides a useful case study of the impact of these negative trends. In a congressional appearance in the fall of 1947, he boldly announced that he would continue to hire screenwriters who were Communists. Schary, who had served on the executive body of ICCASP, was slow to recognize that the political climate had changed, and he was quickly bombarded with a hailstorm of criticism. At the Disabled Veterans state convention in Long Beach, a resolution was adopted unanimously condemning this production head for his "unharmonious Marxian policies disguised as an expression of liberalism."[61] This resolution, which literally equated Marxism with liberalism, neatly encapsulated the essence of the rising anticommunism; by tarring liberalism with the brush of Communism, all of progressivism was scuttled while all of conservatism was neatly boosted.

Schary, who was Jewish, inevitably faced allegations that he was soft on Communism because he was supposedly reluctant to rout his co-religionists in the party and CSU. The L.A. Jewish Community Relations Committee, in a statement drafted by Schary, deplored "the attempt now being made by anti-democratic forces to group all Jewish organizations and individuals with Communism and Communistic activity."[62] This protest did not save Schary; when Howard Hughes took over the studio, Schary's post at RKO became untenable, though he was able to move on to MGM.

Partial responsibility for these anti-Semitic attacks lay with an industry downturn that led some to conclude that their economic position was eroding because of alleged Jewish—and leftist—domination. This explanation seemed plausible to Myron Fagan, who was Jewish, but aligned with Gerald L. K. Smith, Wesley Swift, Salem Bader (a right-wing Arab trained in Great Britain), and other leading anti-Semites. Fagan, author of the well-circulated work *Moscow over Hollywood,* was a screenwriter who had fallen on hard times.[63] Yet despite the Red Scare, he could see Jewish Communists like John Howard Lawson still living relatively well, despite the harassment they faced; he simply concluded that this must have been due to a religious cum political conspiracy. One of Fagan's chief allies was Duncan Spencer, "a leading figure in The Great Pyramids which is the hot-house organization for the KKK"; he was a bodyguard for Gerald L. K. Smith "and is very, very violent in his denunciation of the Jewish tycoons who run the movie industry. He was a member of Local Union #644, but was expelled for non-payment of dues and does not have a good record with that union."[64] He too could easily blame his plight on the alleged hegemony of "Jewish radicals."

Hollywood's response to this challenge was varied. It was apparent that if the moguls had not followed their class instincts and wiped out CSU, they may have been wiped out themselves. Simultaneously, the incipient civil rights movement—which boosted the fortunes of African Americans—eroded bias generally, notably anti-Semitism. The crippling of the union movement as the civil rights movement rose was the signature trend of the postwar era. This contradictory shift to the right on class but to the left on race and ethnicity proved to be a boon for the moguls; in fact, it seemed designed with them in mind. However, the trend contained the seeds of its own demise, for without the kind of mass base that the union movement represented, a turn to the left was not sustainable.

A cinematic response also ensued. Despite the hue and cry of the anti-Semites, the moguls had included Jewish themes in movies less often than some had imagined. However, concomitant with the liquidation of CSU, Daryl Zanuck moved to produce a lavishly funded attack on anti-Semitism, *Gentleman's Agreement,* featuring the captivating new star Gregory Peck. As Zanuck told writer Laura Z. Hobson, the studio "budgeted two million two hundred thousand dollars for the picture which is a considerable amount considering the fact that we have very few sets or technical expenses connected with the production and this means the majority of our money is going into an attempt for perfection."[65] Of course, the film quickly drew comments from anti-Semites; Hobson, who had written the story on which the film was based, was derided as "Laura (Zingleman?) Hobson" after excerpts of her narrative had appeared in *Cosmopolitan*. "It would take more than your magazine or Hobson," raged this L.A. critic, "to make me love a Jew. I've had too many personal contacts."[66]

But Zanuck also articulated forceful opinions that were echoed by his fellow moguls. "If we do not succeed in showing to the world the advantages of the American way of life," he reasoned, "then somebody else will probably come forth with another way of life that may impress the peoples of all countries more, and then all that we have fought for in this war will have been lost." By his own admission, Zanuck proceeded to produce films "inspired" by J. Edgar Hoover, including the tellingly entitled *The Iron Curtain*, designed to besmirch the "life" of that unnamed "somebody else."

Gentleman's Agreement and *The Iron Curtain* represent the two trends of an era—a leftist lurch forward against bigotry with a rightist bow to the FBI. The problem, again, was that the blow against bigotry was not sustainable, as long as the price paid was strengthening of the right. Still, through this tormented process, Hollywood moguls were able to reassure doubters—in the short term—that, noxious propaganda notwithstanding, they were not all closet leftists yearning to impose socialism in league with their co-religionists in the unions. Simultaneously the moguls were able to use cinema to erode skepticism about the idea of Jewish men in powerful positions. This was good for the moguls, of course; it did not, however, bode well for CSU.[67]

★ Albert Warner, vice president and treasurer of the studio that carried his name, testified at the trial of Johnny Roselli. He was asked about *Scarface*, but replied that it was not a Warner's film, though *Public Enemy* and *Little Caesar* were. Then the examining attorney asked whether he believed in these movies' theme that "crime does not pay," and if so, why did he pay off IATSE leaders? Warner was then asked why, if he was so frightened of Bioff, did he discharge an employee seeking to dislodge the union boss from the IATSE leadership.[68] The flummoxed Warner dribbled out an inadequate response, exposing himself as yet another mogul who collaborated with mob puppets.

That Warner Bros., widely viewed as the most socially conscious studio, also collaborated with mobsters highlighted the importance of the mob's relationship to Hollywood. This revelation also suggested that the studio—contrary to the admonitions of the anti-Semites—was willing to carry out its perceived class responsibilities, even if these actions harmed the interests of unions and Communists.

Nevertheless, besides producing some of the era's more insightful films about fascism, Warner's also did some good deeds in Southern California. In 1938, for example, Jack Warner "generously gave an anti-fascist theater group in Hollywood free time on the Warner Brothers radio station." Moreover, said the left-wing journal *New Masses* in an "open letter" to Jack Warner, "your company has, in addition, compiled as good a record as any in the production of progressive topical films." [69] Five years later, the *Daily Worker* film critic, David Platt, could continue to refer to Warner Bros. as "the most progressive studio in the country." He rhapsodized about this "tremendous film factory" in Burbank that included a "plaster shop, plumbing shop, carpenter, machine and paint shops." [70]

The Warners had supported FDR, just as many on the left did. In 1944, days before FDR's re-election, Jack Warner joined Walter Wanger, Katharine Hepburn, Humphrey Bogart, Charles Boyer, James Cagney, Lester Cole, Bette Davis, Judy Garland, Gene Kelly, and Edward G. Robinson as they expressed "support for our President" by hosting an "informal dinner party" featuring "entertainment unique in Hollywood history" at Los Angeles' Ambassador Hotel. [71] With the moguls backing Roosevelt, others could more easily express support for this popular president. Earlier, Robinson, Bogart, Schary, Wanger, Leo Carrillo, Dorothy Lamour, and a host of other stars had endorsed Roosevelt. [72] Merle Oberson, Claudette Colbert, Bob Hope, Joan Bennett, Desi Arnaz, and other stars were accorded a "reception and tea at the White House," evidence of Roosevelt's largely successful effort to bask in the glow of celebrity. [73] After the 1944 re-election, Warner modestly stated that he was "happy to have had the opportunity to be a spearhead which I honestly felt I was, in the motion picture colony" on behalf of FDR; Warner believed that there was "little being done . . . at the time I took over." [74]

Warner Bros. established a richly deserved reputation as one of the more socially conscious studios. It was called "in fact the only studio with a Jewish identity. . . . It maintained a heavy complement of Jewish stars . . . and fiercely defied anti-Semitism in its films. . . . Moreover, Warner Brothers was one of the few studios to cut Nazi Germany out of its foreign market—most of the other lots, though run by Jewish producers, had to be banned by the Nazis before they would [relinquish the] lucrative arena."[75]

The Warners epitomized the popular front in Hollywood, not least in their collaboration with Communists like Lester Cole. In 1944 *Daily Worker* film critic Platt visited the studio in Burbank, where he conferred with Robert Buckner, producer of *Mission to Moscow*. The producer confided to the critic that "Jack Warner was deeply concerned over the growth of anti-Semitism and was looking for a suitable story for a film about Jewish life in America."[76] Platt—though he wanted a film on the Warsaw Ghetto uprising—recommended filming the Ben Field novel *The Outside Leaf*. This was not the first time that the left felt sufficiently confident to make recommendations about films Hollywood should be making. In mid-1942 a *New Masses* writer requested that the industry make a "*Mrs. Miniver* of Russia and China."[77]

That a Communist film critic could advise a studio on projects indicated how much the war had changed things. For it was not the party that had instructed Warner Bros. to produce the passionate love letter to Stalin's Soviet Union, *Mission to Moscow;* it was, according to some sources, the president himself. This film stirred controversy later because it portrayed the Soviet leader as a benevolent man much loved by his people and because it depicted the Moscow Trials of the 1930s as a justifiable jettisoning of internal enemies. This was not the only film that consciously attempted to shape wartime consciousness. *Mrs. Miniver, A Yank in the RAF,* and *The White Cliffs of Dover* were consciously pro-British, though for obvious reasons these films did not stir as much concern about Hollywood's producing of "propaganda." Nor was *Mission to Moscow* the only high-profile film that raised concern about Communist influence on the cinema. IATSE leader Roy Brewer later bitterly recalled a scene he had noticed in the award-winning drama *The Best Years of Our Lives,* in which a character who makes a comment perceived as anti-Soviet is clubbed; this event "wasn't in the original script," he moaned, but was slipped in as a result of a devious Red plot.[78]

The screenwriter Howard Koch did not want to write the *Mission to Moscow* script, but received a personal request from Harry Warner asking him to do so; Koch met with both him and Jack Warner, which was odd, since the mogul traditionally met only with bankers and stars—not lowly writers. At the meeting Koch was instructed that the White House wanted this film made; Koch, who was of the left but not a Communist, proceeded to do his duty.[79]

Joseph Davies, the former U.S. ambassador to the Soviet Union, who wrote the memoir upon which the film was based, later denied that the film was made at FDR's behest. His book was a best-seller, and he maintained, there was a clamor at the time to turn it into a movie. He did call Warner Bros., however, and offer to sell the film rights.

The two stories are not necessarily inconsistent: the Warners could have called the White House and could have been instructed that the story was worth filming, independent of whatever Davies may have done. In any event, Davies told this version in 1947, when those who had appeared to be naive in dealings with Communists were coming under fire and there was an interest in revising history.[80] Alternatively, Warner Bros. could have simply noticed how well the book sold and, as so often happens, assumed that a film would do just as well. A studio that collaborated with mobsters to destroy militant trade unions was hardly the best candidate for being painted a Communist dupe.

Though it may have been in accord with the ideological zeitgeist, the movie was not a raging success at the box office.[81] Later Warner Bros. miscalculated again: In the fall of 1945 the studio, "figuring pro-Russian sentiment has increased," decided to "try to salvage some dough from *Mission to Moscow,* which lost a barrel of coin when it was originally released."[82] The film was rereleased and again failed to capture public imagination.

This film, perhaps more than any other, was used as evidence that having Jewish moguls was dangerous, because they were supposedly susceptible to the entreaties of Jewish trade unionists and Jewish Communists. This theory was simply not true. It was apparently the White House, concerned about how an antifascist alliance could be maintained with Moscow when anticommunism was so widespread in the United States, that persuaded Warner Bros. to make this film—not the film critic of the *Daily Worker* or John Howard Lawson.

Still, the incendiary charge of being "soft on Communism" toughened Warner Bros. and helped create a dynamic that ensured that the studio would be a major battleground during the strike and lockout. Meanwhile, many in CSU felt that focusing their pickets at Warner Bros. would be most effective, not least because past actions seemed to demonstrate that this studio was more progressive—relatively—than its counterparts. Hence, CSU hoped to break the weak "progressive" link in the studio chain by pressuring it to cut a deal that could be duplicated by other studios. This strategy may have been just another miscalculation by CSU's leader, Herb Sorrell, for the recent accusations against Warner's gave the studio a need to demonstrate its mettle. Besides, did it really make sense to focus union ire on the most progressive studios? Wouldn't such a move play into the hands of the ultraright? Wouldn't the predictable result be to drive Warner Bros. to the right?

Stephen Vaughn has written that Warner Bros. "fired more than any other studio" after the labor unrest. "Jack Warner," he says, "was among those who retreated from liberalism. He began to reassess his politics soon after the war. After strikers picketed his studio, he claimed that he was the 'victim of a gigantic communist conspiracy' and vowed never to make another 'liberal' movie. From then on, he said, he would vote for Republicans."[83] Politically minded screenwriter John Wexley recalls running into Jack Warner "that day after a lot of fighting took place" at his studio; the two were "in a steam bath, by chance. He said, 'I saw you on that goddamn picket line. Stop striking. Fuck off!' He was angry. I was just a yapping dog annoying him."[84] Like a number of other moguls, Jack Warner was under grave stress, faced as he was with unhappy workers, unforgiving anti-Semites, and an uncertain economy at home and abroad.

Warner, perhaps feeling the need to undermine allegations raised about his wartime dalliance with Communism, took one of the hardest lines against labor of any mogul. His studio hired several former police officers and detectives, including Blaney Matthews, a former FBI agent: these men rapidly gained a merited reputation for unrelenting violence against strikers. Warner also tightened links with military intelligence, whose interest in Hollywood was long-standing.[85]

★ Contrary to the beliefs of the anti-Semites, all of the moguls were not Jewish, although Jews were under more pressure than Christians to display their class fortitude. Howard Hughes, who took over RKO, was not Jewish; in fact he was a known bigot.[86] Walt Disney may have been worse. He was one of the Hollywood leaders who wined and dined Leni Riefenstahl during the Nazi-era filmmaker's U.S. tour.[87] According to his biographer, Disney too had "connections to organized crime"; as a "domestic spy for the United States government," he believed fervently in the so-called "Jewish-Marxist conspiracy." His *Three Little Pigs* included a scene in which the "Big Bad Wolf disguised himself as a Hebrew peddler to trick one of the pigs into opening his door." Disney conceded that this was a spoof of Carl Laemmle's effort to take over the Disney studio. Though much was made of Lionel Stander's whistling of "The Internationale" on-screen as an example of alleged Red subversion, Disney's featuring of swastikas in its cartoons drew relatively few comments. Disney's only full-time black employee shined shoes and "in his lifetime, no female studio employee ever reached the executive level." [88] CSU had its genesis in a tussle with Disney's studio concerning wages and working conditions for cartoonists. When labor revolted in 1945, Disney was one of the moguls most eager to see CSU eliminated.

Referring to his battle with this studio, Herb Sorrell contended that "Mr. Disney had more Communists than any other . . . studio at the time this strike took place." Why? Sorrell replied that "Mr. Disney created more Communists with his substandard wage scales and the way he handled his people." [89] This comment reveals the secret of the Reds' success in Hollywood: the enforcement of draconian labor policies while the studios were obviously generating obscene amounts of wealth made it easier for radicals to make inroads among workers.

To an extent, Cecil B. DeMille fit the Hughes-Disney profile. Because he was not Jewish and not a Democrat, this powerful filmmaker did not face challenges about his ultimate allegiances. He was a loyal Republican, having been a delegate to party conventions in 1936 and 1944. [90] He lent a hand to up-and-coming conservatives like Ayn Rand, who in 1934 expressed her "gratitude" to DeMille after he had helped this self-avowed "very inexperienced, very bewildered and frightened little immigrant from Russia." "If I have achieved any success," she told him in a note attached to her latest screenplay, *Red Pawn*, "I owe it to your instructions." [91] He was a friend of the military before the launching of the Cold War made the practice de rigueur. [92] As early as 1937 DeMille was sharing intelligence with the local Chamber of Commerce about Communist rallies, particularly those involving the participation of studio labor. [93] Likewise, he collaborated with the FBI, including lobbying for legislation mandating "liberalized retirement benefits for Special Agents." [94] The FBI office in Los Angeles, as a result, often did favors for him—and vice versa. [95] In 1942, through the good offices of DeMille, the FBI found out about Joseph Hoffman, a pianist "who lives at Vista and Franklin Avenue," a home where "German is spoken continually." A painter who had done work in this home was "astonished at the wealth of radio material [there,] some of it built in behind panels." [96]

DeMille was a fervent opponent of unions and worked closely with other employers in advocating "right-to-work" laws. [97] In the strike year of 1945 he established a foundation to fight for this kind of legislation. DeMille had been "forced off the air for refusing to pay a one-dollar union assessment to support a political measure to which he was conscientiously opposed," and this incident, it was said, sparked his political activism. [98]

DeMille was in close touch with the L.A. Merchants and Manufacturers Association, the historic voice of antiunionism, on right-to-work and other crusades.[99] Of course, he was a diehard anticommunist, once averring that "western civilization is at war right now with an utterly ruthless and implacable enemy. Until our enemy learns to fear God, we shall do well to keep our powder dry"; he disdained "more pathetic propaganda for peace when there is no peace."[100] DeMille collaborated with the ultraright Dallas oilman H. L. Hunt, in seeking "to set up . . . a large national organization" that might include "Bing Crosby, Bob Hope and Miss Pickford" and other "Hollywood people whose past records would indicate their adherence to the conservative side."[101]

The congressional committee that formulated the Taft-Hartley legislation heard early and often from Mr. DeMille. Well aware of union activity at the studios, he called specifically for laws to ban mass picketing: "the right of free speech is not an unqualified right," was his opinion. Taft-Hartley was a "magnificent piece of work," DeMille thought, but it did not go far enough. He was fed up with the jurisdictional disputes that consumed CSU and IATSE: whether "greenhouse men" or "property men" should move a bale of alfalfa, for example. "I have been through a very long strike," he recalled, the pain still echoing in his voice; "we had to smuggle people into our plant to get them to work. It was like a besieged army."[102]

DeMille was feeling besieged for other reasons too. Though the postwar era witnessed the growth of independent film production companies, Cecil B. DeMille Productions was liquidated in 1946.[103] The company's problems stemmed in no small part from difficulty in the all-important European market but DeMille seemed to feel that labor troubles were the real culprit. One of his responses was to lend a hand to dissident union members who wanted to challenge the concept of the union shop.[104]

As DeMille's economic troubles mounted, he seemed to become more involved in politics. In 1944 Earl Warren was effusive about the producer's "unselfish service" to the GOP.[105] Herbert Brownell was ecstatic about DeMille's "splendid help" to the GOP ticket that year.[106] Just as many of the Jewish moguls were organizing for FDR, DeMille was doing the same on behalf of the President's opponents.

Backing political candidates was a long-standing practice of the moguls who recognized that it paid to have friends in Sacramento and Washington, D.C. Officials could be helpful in appointing friendly judges, passing antiunion bills, or knocking down tariff walls overseas. As early as 1926 Warner Bros. provided the U.S. senator from California Hiram

Johnson with a pass granting him admittance to the studio's movies; "this little courtesy is the least we can do for one who is infinitely interested in our business," he was told.[107] Louis B. Mayer wanted the senator to attend the Oscar ceremony of 1931; "I will [consider] it a personal favor," he said.[108] Mayer energetically extended favors to politicians and bureaucrats. He was especially generous toward James F. T. O'Connor, the comptroller of the currency during the Great Depression; "your friends, myself included," began Mayer in a typical effusion, "get more pleasure in extending courtesies to you than you do in receiving them."[109]

California politicians like Earl Warren became deeply involved in all manner of "motion picture controversies," including mundane disputes between actors and employment agencies.[110] In turn, politicians kept a close eye on their antagonists—who also happened to be the enemies of the moguls. Warren kept an extensive file on Robert Kenny—who was simultaneously both a top challenger in the governor's race and an attorney for studio labor.[111] Johnson and Warren communicated about "the CIO and radical elements" and the "left-wing."[112]

Franklin Roosevelt had quite cordial relations with the industry's de facto "censor," Will Hays—a Republican. Roosevelt's son James sat on the board of United Artists. His son Elliott married the actress Faye Emerson. His daughter, Ann, married John Boettiger, who in 1934 was awarded a high position in the "Hays Office." Leading Democrats from Joseph Kennedy on down maintained intimate ties with Hollywood. These political contacts did not guarantee a totally smooth ride in Washington for the moguls. Consider, for example, the antitrust suit brought against Hollywood in the 1930s that culminated in 1948 with a decision severing the tie between studios and theaters. Yet even this sign of the moguls' difficulty in dictating to Washington carried a troubling message for labor. For this momentous litigation accelerated the anxiety of the moguls, making them less prone to compromise with CSU.[113]

Hollywood was bipartisan. David O. Selznick, who produced *Gone With the Wind,* was a member of the Executive Committee of the GOP's Finance Committee in Southern California. In the fall of 1946 he told Governor Earl Warren that he had "finally sold my long-standing idea of a permanent Hollywood Republican Committee to a number of prominent Republicans in the industry. . . . [A]t the second meeting we had about two hundred present and we expect to have between one and two thousand at the next meeting." He wanted his "good friend Earl" to address this powerful group.[114]

The moguls' catering to the politicians paid off during the strike of 1945. Governor Warren kept in close touch with the sheriff of L.A. County, receiving reports and forwarding recommendations about how to best handle this unrest. It did appear that the future chief justice seemed more solicitous toward the needs of capital than those of labor; after all, he was a Republican, the party most vigorous in its defense of big business. Yet despite his friendliness toward management, one friend of capital warned Warren that he too was soft on labor. "Frank Murphy lost the re-election to the governorship of the state of Michigan," the future chief justice was advised, "because he handled the strikes in Flint and Detroit as you are handling them in Burbank and Hollywood."[115]

Capital proved a difficult client to please. The incessant pressure from the moguls obligated politicians to favor the studios more than they might ordinarily have done; this favoritism only increased when unions were coming to be stigmatized as sites of strength for Communists.

★ Moguls were generous sources of campaign funds for politicians, some of whom had to run for office every two years. As Warner and Mayer had demonstrated, moguls could also be exquisitely courteous in inviting politicians to premiers and parties, replete with tables groaning with the best food and drink, ringed with glamorous faces of all kinds. These fetes provided an extraordinary opportunity for various forms of corruption to take root, for, axiomatically, labor could not match the munificence of capital—which inexorably came to be favored.

William Randolph Hearst, the chief magnate of the press, had a soft spot for gangsters like Mickey Cohen and starlets like his spouse, Marion Davies—whom he promoted shamelessly and without ethics.[116] His gossip columnist, Louella Parsons, who once remarked in passing about the "seventeen . . . daily columns which go out of Hollywood," made sure that her own never favored unions over moguls.[117]

Those who administered an industry based on glamour had exceptional assets that could influence the press as well as politicians. Bosley Crowther, film critic of the all-powerful *New York Times,* often drew upon the generosity of Arthur Lubin of Universal Pictures during his trips to Los Angeles, at times residing in his "spare room."[118] CSU could hardly expect even neutrality from the press, when the journalists who monitored the industry were so susceptible to the niceties of the moguls.

Government influenced the critics as well. Just as Warner Bros. was apparently encouraged to produce *Mission to Moscow,* Clifton Fadiman— acting chairman of the "Writers' War Board"—instructed Crowther about the need of "damning all or perhaps merely not noticing those [films] which unconsciously create a favorable impression in people's minds of any section of the German people."[119] Bureaucrats who could instruct journalists on how certain films should be covered could certainly instruct them on how the film industry itself should be covered.

Such pressing concerns brought the Hollywood progressives together for a conference in mid-1947—a time when it was evident that CSU had suffered a stinging defeat and a blacklist might be on the way. Darr Smith, former city editor of the *Los Angeles Daily News,* recounted a "frank admission" he had heard "from three prominent and respected newspapermen that they'd like to make a fair representation of the CSU case, but that they couldn't." The "drama sections carried much advertising from the studios—and at a rate of pay higher than, for example, a department store." The studios, he was informed, "would prefer to have everybody forget about the lockout-strike–jurisdictional dispute so that it would die quietly. The studios had passed the word around that the strike [*sic*] was dead, that production was back up and that really there was no sense in giving space to a lost cause." This, said Smith, was a "conspiracy of silence and . . . thought control." There were "two papers in town," he said, "which consistently print nothing or one paragraph accounts, or, if there is no opportunity, extremely nasty, half-truthful stories, about the CSU."

Many factors contributed to this state of affairs. "One publisher had a deep hatred of Herb Sorrell for many years because Sorrell and some other painters appeared on a Newspaper Guild picket line in front of the publisher's plant. The other paper strongly dislikes Sorrell because he recently filed a $1,225,000 libel suit against it for attempting to discredit him."[120] A few days after the 1945 strike commenced, the front page of the *Los Angeles Examiner* illustrated the insuperable obstacles faced by CSU. Just above an article on the strike was the headline, "Disney Premier to Aid Examiner War Wounded."[121] The studios' relatively unhindered ability to contribute to the press's pet causes dwarfed whatever support CSU may have considered. It was difficult for CSU to fight the moguls and the mobsters and the state and the press.

★ Making movies was not a consistently profitable business. From the depths of the early 1930s to the heights of the early 1940s, the industry was often on a roller coaster from the red to the black and back again. This fact was a commonality of the studios, though distinc-

tions existed between and among them. MGM, for example, was cele-
brated for its polish; that its chief, Louis B. Mayer, was once the nation's
highest-paid executive was suggestive of this studio's polished profitability as well. Paramount was noted for its often clumsy editing, though
since it controlled more theaters than its competitors, its films could
be more daring in subject matter. Paramount suffered grievously when
antitrust litigation forced the studios to divest their theaters. MGM was
known as the producer's studio and Paramount as the director's. Universal
was one of the few studios to routinely employ women directors, which
may be why the cliffhanger as "feminist fantasy"—with the "heroine very
energetically routing the villains and saving some bumbling boyfriend"—
flourished there.[122]

More often than not, however, the studios' class predilections were
uniform both off-screen and on. Will Hays and Joseph Breen, the official "censors" designated to ensure that sexual and other ostensibly offensive subjects did not make their way into movies, "intervened to have
the studio change dialogue" so one movie "would show miners' condition[s] improving and imply that workers had little to complain about."
Breen, fearing encouragement of labor unrest, was reluctant to approve
films that showed company property destroyed. Hays was part owner of
a coal mine in southern Indiana, and Breen once handled public relations
for the Peabody Coal Company; these experiences were thought to influence their ideas about how mines and miners should be portrayed in the
movies. Both men were hesitant, in any case, to pass favorably on films
that seemed to speak positively about unions.[123] In fact, the "Hays Office"
was established after World War I in partial response to growing concern
about the proliferation of progressive themes in movies.

As World War II was ending, the cudgels of Hays and Breen were
taken up by the Motion Picture Alliance for the Preservation of American Ideals (MPAPAI). Formed in February 1944 at a meeting at the Beverly
Wilshire Hotel, the MPAPAI was consciously designed to combat the
growing influence of CSU and the left in Hollywood; Walt Disney served
as vice president and DeMille's old friend Ayn Rand also worked with the
group.[124] Years later Robert Vogel, an executive with MGM, conceded that
"the excitement of the war caused you to lose your balance" and "we created things that didn't exist." Hence, "we went overboard in creating this
organization," this MPAPAI.[125] But that view was far from the consensus
in studio suites in the 1940s.

The left was enraged by the coming of the MPAPAI, which it saw—
correctly—as a conscious rejection of the popular front. The members

were "brain storm troopers" and a "Motion Picture Bund" chortled one *New Masses* writer. Presciently it was added that MPAPAI was "attempting to terrify producers and writers with the threat of a blacklist of progressives." The alliance, which included the director King Vidor, was deemed "violently anti-Semitic"; these "boys," it was noted with contempt, "are frankly out to 'drive the Reds out of Hollywood.' "[126]

MPAPAI was not welcomed warmly by liberals either. Roger Baldwin, the avidly anticommunist leader of the American Civil Liberties Union, wanted to speak with the industry's trade association about issues that MPAPAI would have opposed. He wanted to "abolish the state censorship boards" and "lessen the stranglehold which the Legion of Decency and other sectarian organizations have" on the industry. He wanted more "freedom of expression on the screen" and an "improvement of the status of the screen writer, especially in the direction of giving him a greater control over what he writes."[127] Baldwin's concerns reminded MPAPAI of the distinct danger that the wartime antifascist alliance and popular front would continue after the shooting stopped.

Still, Hollywood did have to make serious adjustments as a result of the war; these changes favored the conservative bent of MPAPAI. Box-office returns from the European and South American markets contributed heavily to Hollywood's gross income in 1938, and provided almost all of the actual profit. This lucre from overseas was a partial result of Hollywood's unscrupulous tactics against foreign, particularly European, moviemakers, including the manipulation of tariff barriers and the Production Code on "morality to 'show' people that foreign films were simply not American." In search of capital during the war, many of the studios were driven further to deepen their relationship with "large investment banks."[128]

As the war approached, Hollywood had discovered that its overseas market was disappearing. The mogul Samuel Goldwyn recommended reducing annual output from 500 films to 150, an idea *New Masses* castigated as akin to "crop limitation" or "plowing under every second and third row of B pictures."[129] What would a reduction in output mean for the jobs of CSU members, and would the studios simply be willing to absorb a strike since they wanted to reduce output anyway?

This was not the only financial upset that the war brought to Hollywood. Due to military demand, the supply of film stock was "drastically smaller in 1945 than it was in 1944." This could mean postponing thirty features and even sacrificing the quality of movies, as directors might be forced to do scenes in one take, or lengthening the workday with rehearsals to ensure that this one take was done as perfectly as possible. The dearth of film stock could also help make the studios willing to absorb a strike in 1945.[130]

Indicative of the seriousness with which Hollywood faced this new economic landscape was the appointment of Eric Johnston to head the Motion Picture Producers and Distributors Association. Hailing from eastern Washington—though born in Washington, D.C., in 1895—the boyish-looking Johnston had formerly headed the U.S. Chamber of Commerce and had run for the U.S. Senate in 1940; some were touting him as presidential timber by 1948. His campaign literature in 1940 underlined the fact that he "practiced . . . collective bargaining" in "his own business." He employed four hundred in three companies: Columbia Electric, Brown Johnston Company, and Washington Brick and Lime.[131] He emerged from a working-class background, was once employed as a docker, and served as an intelligence officer with the U.S. Marine Corps in China, where he resided in the early 1920s. In the spring of 1944 he visited with "Premier Stalin." At that point he professed belief "in Russia's right to her social, economic and political system without outside interference."

Johnston was cut from the same cloth as Wendell Wilkie. He had been mentioned prominently for the post of commissioner of baseball and was viewed widely as the preeminent, enlightened popular-front businessman. In 1945 "[a]s soon as" he arrived in Washington, D.C., as head of the Chamber of Commerce, "he sought out William Green of the AFL and Phil Murray of the CIO."[132] Variety viewed the "$100,000 a year prexy" as a "student of modern labor relations."[133]

Johnston's experiences abroad, including his relationship with Stalin, were seen as a prime plus in his new post. In 1946 he was contemplating another trip to Moscow; on his last trip there he had an unprecedented four-hour conversation with the Georgian Communist, and, said Variety, "he apparently got along very well with the Soviet chief of state," with whom he hoped to conclude a "film accord."[134] As late as the fall of 1946, this trade paper was saying Johnston "feels that much of the bogeyman that has been built up around the European communists is propaganda and poppycock"; rather, these Reds were "hardheaded businessmen."[135] "European communists"—no doubt—would have considered Johnston at that juncture a leading member of the "realistic wing" of the "bourgeoisie."

His relations with Stalin were as varied and deep as those of any other U.S. citizen, including leaders of the U.S. Communist Party. His wife, Ina

Johnston, later recalled that Averell Harriman, who had served as U.S. ambassador and was heir to a major fortune, "didn't meet Stalin personally until Eric introduced him." [136] Johnston was expected to use his vast global experience to knock down protectionist walls keeping Hollywood movies out of foreign markets, including those zones of Europe where Moscow was thought to wield influence. *Variety* concluded in September 1945 that he would "spend most of his time in Washington looking after the foreign situation by working with the State Department." [137]

Johnston was waging a two-front war. Penetrating the markets of Eastern Europe was a priority. However, his "free screen" policy was aimed not only at "totalitarian" nations but also at those that were "nominally democratic." He felt that Hollywood "shouldn't overload the foreign market merely because we have a heavy backlog of pictures produced during the war"; on the other hand, the industry shouldn't simply acquiesce to the desires of its war-devastated competitors either. The problem for CSU was that this backlog could allow the moguls to absorb with equanimity a lengthy strike.

By November 1946 Johnston was in London, negotiating with leaders of the U.K. film industry and renewing old acquaintances with friends like Harold Laski, who brought Johnston "a book which he autographed and a story of his encounter with Stalin this past August." [138] This meeting may have been the most pleasant part of Johnston's dreary journey. He found "conditions all over Europe . . . depressing"; what was "most discouraging" was the "attitude of the Europeans toward America. The majority have little or no respect for either America or its people. Here in England the feeling is even worse. . . . There is an organized campaign on in the newspapers against America," though the "average American is totally unaware of the anti-American feeling here. . . . [E]ven our London MPA secretary in the office, though she works for an American concern and is well paid, has little or no use for Americans or their pictures."

France was worse. It was "shocking. The communists have infiltrated everywhere except the high position in the government. The newspapers are completely controlled by the communists." [139]

Suggestive of Hollywood's importance was the fact that Johnston met in London with the U.K. foreign minister, Ernest Bevin; the chancellor of the exchequer, Sir Stafford Cripps; and the president of the board of trade (and future prime minister), Harold Wilson. The British were "tough traders, but on the whole . . . fair." Teaming up with Allen Dulles, a future CIA leader, Johnston was able to get an "agreement." Yet there was "constant suspense and nervous tension" during these meetings; "we were brutally frank with each other, and there were times when not only diplomacies were cast to the wind, but tempers as well." Hollywood did not get all that it wanted; the studios were able to get half their "earnings" out of the nation in dollars and half "through the making of motion pictures in England or the purchase of property such as theaters." Johnston's talks in Moscow with "Molotov and others" were also "extremely frank—to the point of brusqueness" though the agreement was not as favorable to Hollywood.[140] Yet the question for CSU was equally blunt: would the agreement to make more films in the United Kingdom mean a cutback in Hollywood production, and even if the Communists abroad and their allies realized their dream of eroding Hollywood's hegemony, what would that mean for the future of CSU?

In September 1946 the Screen Writers Guild, which had yet to be purged of the left, requested renegotiation of the accord between the United States and France on movies; among other things, this accord had restricted the showing of French films in the United States to Hollywood's advantage.[141] The Guild was concerned about democracy and intellectual exchange, while the moguls were concerned with market share. If the moguls could oust those who stood in their way—like the guild—they could better reach their goal.

Johnston had other problems. He was not pleased with the incessant attention the industry received; there were "500" reporters who spent "all their time just covering the motion picture studios." "I don't believe," said Johnston, "there are that many people covering any other big industry." [142]

He didn't "like the Hollywood side" of his job at all. He had little love for Jack Warner, who had "achieved those pinnacles simply because" he was "void of compassion." He didn't get along with Spyrous Skouras of Fox either. A central problem was that the moguls were bound together in a marriage of convenience—a trade association—but they "couldn't get along [among] themselves"; Johnston thus had to spend considerable time as a "mediator" to keep them from sabotaging each other.[143] Then there were men like David O. Selznick: independent producers, who—according to *Variety*—were reluctant to join Johnston's "complete united front" among moguls, on the assumption that the trade association was tilted toward the interests of the major studios.[144] Nor did Johnston appreciate it when his aide Edward Cheyfitz was hounded after confessing to be a former member of the Young Communist League.[145]

Yet looking back, Johnston recognized that he had provided a boost to the industry at a critical moment. His global perspective proved crucial in helping Hollywood survive antitrust litigation and troublesome labor problems. In 1959 he declared that "if it weren't for the increase in foreign revenue, we would really be almost out of business, probably *would* be out of business. But the foreign revenue has increased, quadrupled, in the last fourteen years." [146] [emphasis his]

Europe was not only important as a market for films, it also enabled the movie moguls to branch off into other lucrative areas, as well as providing opportunities for laundering huge amounts of cash—an area always of interest to organized crime. John Ruffato, one of Johnston's aides, later recalled that his boss "did such a good job" of marketing U.S. films abroad that incredible amounts of cash were produced that could not be "exchanged for American dollars." Thus, in Italy, Ruffato's job was "more of negotiating the transfer of funds than it was of marketing American films." One time the studios used the lira they had accumulated to build a ship in Italy, sold it to Swedish interests, and used the krona to buy Irish whiskey, which was shipped to Argentina, which had an "excess of American dollars" because of the "beef they sold." In this way, $18 million were safely transferred into the studios' coffers in the United States. [147]

These difficulties in foreign markets led to a major concession that directly impacted CSU: the moguls began to make more films abroad— e.g., in Western Europe—in order to escape currency fluctuations, protectionism, and the like.

The problem was that CSU proceeded as if it were merrily unaware of the larger context of movie production and assumed that militancy alone was sufficient to bring gains. At times the federation seemed not to recognize Hollywood's importance to the nation's overall export earnings, balance of trade—and ideological arsenal. Johnston's trip to London, despite the anti-American feeling he encountered, was a step toward the Cold War, because binding the United States and its erstwhile allies against a common foe—Moscow—would necessarily lead to diminished tensions among Washington, London, and other important capitals. Likewise, targeting and isolating Communists would allow anti-American sentiment to seem the sole province of this increasingly scorned force of Reds, thus sapping the venom from anti-Americanism. Hollywood inevitably became a major force in preparing the way for both the Cold War and the Red Scare. Hollywood helped to produce leaders like Ronald Reagan who were essential in constructing the Red Scare and propelling the Cold War—while CSU often seemed cheerfully oblivious to these larger historical forces that were shaping the terrain on which it fought.

★ Even as the war plodded on, it was apparent that Hollywood was entering a brave new world of production. Mexico had emerged as the second-most-fecund moviemaking nation in the hemisphere, surging from one feature in 1931 to eighty in 1944. Both United Artists and RKO had begun building studios south of the border with Mexican partners.[148] With such facilities up and running, both studios could avoid employing the often obstreperous CSU members.

The war's conclusion revived once dormant conflicts between U.S. and European filmmakers—conflicts in which the Hollywood left often adopted stances opposite those of the moguls.[149] This rift only reinforced the moguls' predisposition to rid themselves of the left, for this question of global competition was serious business. David O. Selznick may have been hesitant about joining Eric Johnston's "united front," but he realized that the linked questions of foreign markets and Communists were also central to independent producers.

As the war was ending in 1945, Selznick wanted to move rapidly to increase exports before the major studios could "cut each others' throats, to [say] nothing of cutting ours." He asked Morris Ernst, the influential attorney and "fixer," what he thought of employing as foreign emissaries former FDR appointee Sumner Welles and his chief at the State Department, former secretary of state Cordell Hull; Selznick mused that Hull might be available "if the old boy is able to get around . . . [he] needs a little dough, as I gather is the case from his recent application for a pension."[150]

Selznick's advisor, Morris Ernst, was equally concerned that the "entire motion picture industry is in a perilous position" because of "foreign business"; worse, there was hardly any "semblance of leadership with ingenuity" within the industry.[151] But Selznick was more worried about the majors elbowing independents like him out of the global marketplace. He was concerned that the big studios would export collectively, further squeezing companies like Selznick's. "The majors," he concluded glumly, "can afford to have a substantial portion of their product unreleased in one country or another. . . . [A]n independent cannot afford to do without his foreign market [on] even one picture."[152]

From worrying about capturing foreign markets, Selznick turned to the content of the films he was sending abroad. Weeks before the war in Europe ended, he was already expressing unease about the left's ideological offensive in Europe, abetted by its Moscow allies. "We [should] not send film abroad that can be used against us," he admonished; "no Russian film is made that is not designed either blatantly or subtly to ad-

vance communistic ideals," and Hollywood should act similarly to promote its ideals, he advised. Though he thought his side "naive," Selznick
displayed more prescience than his opponents within the Hollywood left
when he foresaw that the moguls would "be faced with ideological warfare in Europe, regardless of Dumbarton Oaks, San Francisco and all the
good will in the world." Mournfully, he added, "Communists will therefore start with a big edge."[153]

What was infecting Selznick's concern about Communists abroad
was his growing rage about the activities of their presumed comrades in
Hollywood. The strike of 1945 had barely been under way before Selznick
was telling Governor Warren that "many small industries may be driven
out of business"; "we have had to shut down production and suspend
hundreds of employees," he added dismally. Again, he distinguished his
competitors: "the strike is not affecting the big studios in the fashion
that it is us . . . because of the large pools of manpower they have to
draw upon . . . and because they have huge backlogs of finished films."
He wanted Sacramento to intervene or at least for the governor to lean
on prominent southern Democrat Jimmy Byrnes—who "perhaps needs
a little personal income"—and coax him into intervening.[154] Yet another
advantage the moguls held over CSU was their ability to guarantee a better
life for erstwhile public servants, like Byrnes, Welles, and Hull.

The usually confident Selznick was floundering about, considering
throwing money at any leading Democrat who might accept his offer and
who might be able to talk CSU into returning to work. CSU, which was
far from being a master of tactics, often acted unconcerned about the conflicts between the major studios and the independents. The moguls themselves were not united, torn by tensions between Jews and anti-Semites,
Democrats and Republicans, major studios and minor. Yet these moguls
had advantages: notably their class consciousness and their ties to mobsters, politicians, and the press. These advantages proved decisive when
the time arrived to confront CSU.

PART
4

STRIKE

Though "detailed studies of long-term trends of strike activity are surprisingly rare," it is evident that in the United States "the rate of strike activity has always been high compared with that in other countries": "strikes [here] have at times involved massive, bitter, and violent struggles between workers and employers." U.S. strikes often have involved struggles for control of the workplace, while in "other countries the struggle has been politicized or brought under institutional control"—e.g., powerful political parties that avowed to represent the interests of unions and the working class. In Europe during the 1930s "Social Democratic governments in several countries began to take over many functions which had previously been left to market forces. Many key battles were thus moved from the economic to the political arena, and the nature of strike activity changed as a result." Paradoxically, despite the high rate and bitterness of strikes, the labor movement in the United States has been "among the least radical in political terms."[1]

The CSU strike was a prototype of this pattern. A "Social Democratic" government in Sacramento or, especially, Washington could have sought to resolve the jurisdictional issue that drove CSU to the picket lines, rather than to collaborate with moguls to drive CSU from the industry. Sorrell alluded to this point when he was asked by a congressman why he seemed to rely more on strikes than law. He responded simply, "[Y]ou can't do that . . . [P]eople who tried to go to the law for relief . . . are eliminated. It is impossible. I can give you one example after another."[2]

Of course, strikes were not a purely twentieth-century phenomenon. From the rebellion of Greek silver miners at Laurium in 413 B.C., to the builders' strikes of the temple and palace at Jerusalem in 29 B.C., to the strikes of English journeymen shoemakers and weavers in the fourteenth-century, to the great U.S. strikes in 1877, the ability of organized workers to withdraw their labor has been a crucial and potent weapon to be wielded by subalterns.[3]

However, Communist leaders like William Z. Foster studied strikes systematically, viewing this weapon as one of the sharpest arrows in the quiver of the labor movement; the connection between Communists and labor activism was so strong that some automatically associated strikes with Reds. Strikers, said Foster, were more susceptible to "revolutionary ideas" during strikes. Before striking, he recommended, unions must "survey" the "state of the industry," "the strength and disposition of the enemy's forces," and the "general political situation." Employers wanted strikes to take place during the "slack season"; Foster counseled that, instead, strikes must "be waged at periods of the greatest industrial activity." Search out interlocking directorates—e.g., the ties of moguls with bankers—and press those pressure points, he advised. "National election periods" present "favorable opportunities" for striking, since during this time the public is often more alert to social and political concerns.[4]

Correspondingly, John Steuben, a leader of the Little Steel strike in 1937, asked: "[I]s it possible to apply to the battle of social forces basic ideas of military strategy—fighting on the offensive; importance of morale; element of surprise; discipline; mobilization of reserves; capturing the initiative?"[5] The answer was yes.

Sorrell, who was not exactly a master of tactics, violated virtually every one of Foster's and Steuben's simple points when he ordered the 1945 strike. Most of all, he (and, to be fair, many others) did not anticipate that the war's end would bring a sharp turn to the right that would disembowel the popular front that studios like Warner Bros. had joined. The studios shifted sharply to the right and seized the opportunity to rid themselves of a troublesome force—Sorrell's csu.

★ World War II, by some estimates, was as much of a watershed in the history of U.S. labor as the 1930s had been.[6] The National Defense Mediation Board and its successor, the National War Labor Board, were as important as the Wagner Act in molding the contours of industrial relations in the United States. According to Howell Harris, "[M]any of the distinguishing features of the contemporary American labor movement emerged" during the war and early postwar years.[7] Typically, California was a site of contestation as these national trends were being shaped. The state had seen an explosion in growth of the labor movement; between 1931 and 1938 the AFL there had grown from 100,000 to 291,000, while by 1950 there were 1.354 million union members making up 43 percent of the nonagricultural workforce. Southern California, the heart of the arsenal of democracy, had witnessed a dynamic growth with the working population of L.A. County alone increasing by 400,000 from 1940 to 1944.[8]

Despite the no-strike pledge, one analyst has written that strikes actually increased during the war, from an average of 2,000–2,750 between 1935 and 1940 to 4,956 in 1944. "The average duration of strikes doubled in 1945 to ten days, then doubled again in 1946 to twenty-four days." Jurisdictional disputes were a major issue before and during the war, as unions often fought among themselves as much as they squabbled with management.[9] Some unions found it easier to poach in areas ostensibly beyond their own perceived organizing mandate rather than to organize within their own realm.

Again, California was a leader in jurisdictional disputes, and not only those involving CSU and IATSE. A particularly acerbic fracas engulfed the International Longshoremen's and Warehousemen's Union and the International Association of Machinists, while others raged between unions in the CIO and those in the AFL.[10]

In this turbulent atmosphere, CSU was aware of certain advantages it held over management, and this knowledge may have given the leadership a false sense of security. Y. Frank Freeman, a vice president at Paramount, conceded that his "industry is one that does not have tremendous reserves in dollars to carry on a long labor fight. It needs the money that is taken in at the theaters from day to day to come to Hollywood to make the pictures, which remains invested for a long period of time before it can be recovered." This situation favored unions, he acknowledged, and led to "appeasement" of them.[11]

Studios were hardly bereft of weapons, however. Pat Casey, their chief negotiator with labor, recalled lovingly those days before union strength when "there were thousands of fellows hanging around those gates trying to get jobs in the studios";[12] this "reserve army of labor" remained a strong deterrent against unionization and strikes.

Still, workers did have countervailing power that could neutralize— if not negate—management strengths. Nicholas Schenck, the president of Loew's—which included MGM and which maintained facilities "in practically every country"—admitted under oath that carpenters particularly had a stranglehold over film production, for "if you cannot have any carpenters and you cannot build [sets], you cannot make pictures. . . . That applies practically to all the main crafts. You could not do without spotlight men, you could not do without electricians."[13] Even IATSE admitted that "in the early days of the strike there was a real need for scenic artists—they being members of a highly skilled craft."[14]

Roy Brewer of IATSE scornfully dismissed the importance of painters, concluding that "in an emergency anybody can use a brush," but this was an exaggeration at best.[15] However, his brash estimate was indicative of the point that all studio labor was not indispensable. The studios were surprised pleasantly, for example, when they discovered the "ability of Technicolor to continue operations without the services of 87 machinists" who struck. "Predictions had been made that [the] company could not continue operation for two weeks. It is understood that temporary repairs are being handled by plant superintendents who do not belong to [a] union, with studio heads of photography giving once over to cameras."[16]

Of course, the studios depended on labor differently. "The studios are not all built the same," explained Pat Casey. At Warner Bros. they "have a tremendous amount of staging. If something had to be retaken of this thing 2 weeks from now on the Warner lot, they would not have to take it down." The same was true for Fox but the opposite held for RKO and Paramount, whose strength was in owning theaters, not in maintaining sprawling sound stages.[17]

★ For various reasons Hollywood was gripped with ferocious jurisdictional combat. A Paramount executive after the war counted "28 combinations of local unions between whom jurisdictional differences existed or still exist." Even within units of CSU and IATSE acrid disputes arose. Sorrell's Painters Local 644 had internal differences between sign writers and scenic artists. There were conflicts between IATSE's Machinists Local 789 and IBEW Local 40; the former did machinists' work and the latter did electrical generator work on the same job, providing management an opportunity to stir up trouble between the two. Within IATSE Local 44, disputes arose between property makers and property men over whether to place a rattan box or baskets in a scene. Conflicts took place between plumbing Local 78 and Local 44, and between IATSE Local 727 and Local 724.

Though management often used the tried-and-true tactic of "divide and conquer" to worsen—if not foment—conflict within and among locals, the studios increasingly viewed jurisdictional warfare as draining. While making a film after the war, Columbia directed Local 44 to build a fuselage onto a large airplane. The union wanted to paste or glue unbleached muslin over the entire surface of the plane, but due to jurisdictional tensions between Local 44, Local 644, and another local, the studio was "at a loss": if glue were required, grips would claim jurisdiction; if wallpaper paste were involved, the painters would claim jurisdiction. To "avoid arguments and possible work stoppage," the studio "accepted a less satisfactory finish in order to keep peace."

Some studio executives considered jurisdictional snarls simply inefficient. IATSE 727, for example, accepted orders only from 727 foremen, "yet a grip foreman must be in charge of the scene dock, who in turn can issue orders only to the No. 727 foreman. One foreman is all that is required."[18]

As is apparent, IATSE itself was bedeviled with internal jurisdictional disputes between and among its locals. Bickering seemed part of the culture, and IATSE members and locals could easily have concluded that this kind of wrangling was a normal part of trade unionism—perhaps the central part.[19] This kind of internal contention was possibly a safety valve that exhausted militant anger and energy that otherwise might have been directed—perhaps futilely and dangerously, it was thought—toward the studios.

Ruefully, Frank Freeman of Paramount recalled fiery jurisdictional conflicts—about water. "The water bottle was empty on the set and one fellow started to put the filled water bottle into the empty stand. They called a stoppage because he didn't have jurisdiction over the water bottle. They had to send out for a laborer somewhere out on the back lot for the laborer to put in the water bottle. They were all thirsty and couldn't work until they got a drink." Not only was this setup inherently conflictual, he thought, it was also featherbedding, pure and simple—with layers of unnecessary labor.[20]

The unions had good reason to contest jurisdiction during the war; business was booming and the possibility of incorporating new duespaying members was a prize too rich to resist. "All during the war," Sorrell recalled with approval, "we had a 6 hour day in most of the crafts. All crafts worked 8 hours for 9 hours' pay. They worked 6 days a week and they worked continuously. . . . The studios [ran] full blast. They did not have a foreign market then," he noted, not altogether accurately, "they did not need it."[21] The effervescent Sorrell may not have recognized that this breakneck shooting schedule may have been the studios' way to accumu-

late a backlog so as to better absorb the kind of lengthy strike that would
be needed to subdue CSU in the near future.

The set decorators were essential to the making of movies. As Sorrell put it, "[A] set decorator is a man who studies periods of furniture,
periods of architecture, knows what kinds of rugs [to place] into certain
castles, what kinds of furnishings to [place] in certain kinds of homes. . . .
He is in a way an artist."

The set decorator might have to find these materials or sketch them
for others to construct, and to work with other "artists, draftsmen," et al.
to complete the process. Thus, said Sorrell, it made sense for set decorators to join Local 1421 rather than IATSE's "propmen," who "handle all
the furniture" but don't design it.[22]

Historically painters in Hollywood had been paid more than painters
in other industries; because of severe work fluctuation, the studios had
to "pay a higher rate of pay in order [to] keep a pool of people available to meet these terrific . . . peaks of production." Painters often had
to be on call to respond to ongoing script rewrites.[23] Even publicists had
unique requirements. "Distant location work" required "long and arduous hours." They had to "write . . . articles" and "entertain the press and
important visitors to the sets and do this work at all hours."[24] These often
adverse working conditions fueled the rise of CSU.

Management, in short, was no innocent in this process. By not bargaining with CSU's Screen Set Designers, Illustrators and Decorators
Local 1421 in mid-1944 because of a representational counterclaim by
IATSE, the studios helped to set the strike of 1945 in motion. Local 1421
had given the producers an appropriate number of authorization cards
from its members, signifying that it was indeed a proper bargaining agent
for the decorators but the producers insisted that the local file a certifica-
tion petition with the National Labor Relations Board. The local complied, but IATSE intervened, claiming that the decorators' work placed
them within the jurisdiction of the IATSE's property department. At that
time the National Labor Relations Board (NLRB) office in Los Angeles would not accept petitions in which jurisdiction was contested by a
competing union; the office deemed these jurisdictional disputes to be
internal problems for the AFL to settle, so 1421 withdrew the petition. A
few set decorators then struck to force recognition. This two-day strike
brought the War Labor Board into the picture. Sorrell maintained stoutly
that the studios could have stepped in at that juncture to request an election, but declined, arguing that they were trapped between IATSE and
CSU: "That is what created the strike of [March] 1945," he contended.

In February 1945 arbitrator Thomas Tongue ruled that the producers should recognize Local 1421's claim, but the producers refused, even after the set decorators—including both strikers and their replacements—voted on 24 May 1945 that this local was their proper bargaining agent. The studios' refusal is what extended—and, in a sense, created—the strike of 1945.[25] After the March 1945 strike, the studios sacked the strikers, then insisted that any representation election for set decorators could not include the walkouts but must include the scabs who had replaced them. All the while, the studios devoutly maintained that they were innocents caught in a tug-of-war between CSU and IATSE.

In March 1945 William Hutcheson, leader of the carpenters nation-wide, met with Richard Walsh of IATSE and Pat Casey of the studios to discuss this job action and the possibility of a grand settlement that would divide—presumably for all time—jurisdiction between CSU and IATSE. But during the meeting a vexatious issue arose that was to lead directly to the 1946 lockout: Hutcheson and Walsh clashed over the issue of set erectors and the carpenters' fervent desire to control all moviemaking jobs that involved the use of wood. Carpenters did not control all jobs involving wood in breweries, mines, and CIO factories, so why should they control such in the studios? asked Walsh. Pat Casey, who was integrally involved in this meeting at Manhattan's Hotel Commodore, recalled that the two men met with hundreds of photographs of movie sets spread before them. When Hutcheson demanded suzerainty over anything containing wood—even microphones—the meeting collapsed.[26]

For their part, the carpenters—and the CSU of which they were a part—had good reason to believe that Walsh was working covertly with the producers to squash CSU.[27] Walsh had served during the Bioff-Browne regime, and CSU still viewed him as their puppet. As Sorrell put it at a Screen Actors Guild meeting of 1,200, "Walsh was vice-president under Browne—if he was a good vice-president he knew what was going on, and if he wasn't a good vice-president he wouldn't have gotten to be President."[28] Walsh, a former stage electrician from Brooklyn initially defended Bioff and Browne when they came under attack, which only served to fuel suspicion of this latest IATSE leader.[29]

Pre-existing tensions existed between IATSE and other unions. The Red screenwriter Lester Cole acknowledged that IATSE "control meant the death of democratic unionism; its constitution stated that only the national president has the right to order a strike regardless of any membership vote."[30] Only 16 of IATSE's 950 locals were in Los Angeles, but those in Hollywood were the most powerful, with the rest comprising mostly projectionists in far-flung localities. By vesting so much power in the union president, IATSE effectively had weakened the strength of studio labor.

The Hutcheson-Walsh meeting was thus destined to flop, though this fact did not bar AFL brass from straining to stifle the strike. AFL chief William Green, immediately after the walkout, fired off a telegram of protest to Sorrell and added for good measure, "I officially disavow your strike" and it "ought to be terminated at once."[31]

He was ignored.

Hence, CSU went on strike as the studios and IATSE continued trying to produce movies. The latter two recognized that if they could hold off CSU, they could divide the industry between themselves. Both would be rid of a pesky ideological foe; both would be spared certain jurisdictional disputes. The two had an objective reason to collude against CSU, and according to Zach Cobb, the Carpenters' attorney, they did precisely that.[32] Afterward, Walsh confessed unashamedly that he had collaborated with the moguls to break the strike.[33]

★ An estimated 10,500 CSU workers went on strike in March 1945—and the conflict lasted until October.[34] The painter Hans Burkhardt—who once studied with Arshile Gorky and created a painting, *Protest,* depicting the conflict—recalled it as a "bloody fight, it was terrible."[35] Cecil B. DeMille spoke sadly of "men who had worked for me 25 or more years, walked off the studio lot when the strike was called—tears streaming down their faces. These men were friends of mine since they worked . . . [on] the production of *The Ten Commandments* and *The King of Kings.* One day I walked in the picket line with these men, carrying a banner—not that I was in sympathy with the strike but I was in sympathy with the men."[36]

This episode left DeMille with a lingering anger. Preparing later to testify before Congress, he noted in reference to CSU leaders—whom he contemptuously referred to as "labor czars"—that a "decision made by 8 or 10 more men could do more damage to this country than 8 or 10 atomic bombs dropped at the same moment." Vowing to curb this power by dint of legislation, he grumbled that labor "may want the right to strike. That I don't know. But I do know they want the right to work." DeMille then pledged to push for a bill that would restrain the power of unions—a bill that came to be known as the Taft-Hartley legislation.[37]

From the strike's beginnings, CSU opponents had emphasized that legislative steps needed to be taken to restrain such militant activity. In April 1945 Karl Struss denounced "Madam Frances Perkins," the secretary of labor: "You have done nothing to settle this senseless, stupid but expensive strike"; "this strike is . . . a crime as well as treason," he fumed, referring to the context of the war. "If you do not intend doing anything about this strike you should resign"; after all, he continued, "the government is losing millions of dollars from not receiving the twenty percent withholding tax, the social security tax, the unemployment tax."[38]

Undaunted, workers continued to pound the pavement, encircling the studios, carrying signs and chanting slogans, seeking to discourage other employees from going to work, and thus seeking to bring production to a halt. This was an era of pent-up labor demand when numerous unions found themselves on strike. Courts in California generally disfavored picketing. In 1937 Judge Hartley Shaw had tried to bar "any loud noise or cry" on the picket line while other courts retained a residual resentment toward the very idea of picketing itself.[39] In 1940 the U.S. Supreme Court protected picketing but later that decade began to retreat.

Though many workers were motivated to picket, some craftsmen could have found construction work, rather than walking in a circle carrying a sign while shouting. During a strike of Southern California's United Auto Workers, Local 216, for example, strikers were tempted by outside employment. Hence, like many other unions, Local 216 imposed a dollar fine for "every picket assignment missed. There was also voted a work penalty of $5.00 per week for all members who took other jobs and asked to be excused from their picket duty." CSU attempted similar measures with mixed results.[40]

Roger McDonald, a CSU member sent to New York City to organize the picketing of theaters, was told by his wife that "the strategy committee" was "trying to find a means of making every union member responsible for picketing at least one night a week—and for those getting strike benefit pay—every night for 3 solid hours." This was hard work that required extreme dedication, particularly when compensation was virtually nil. CSU sought to extend picketing to "17 first run houses and 15 neighborhood theatres," besides the studios.[41]

Initially, McDonald was "assigned picket duty" at Fox; he had to report to his "picket captain on arriving for duty" and had to have his "card punched when leaving, so as to carry a record of time spent on picket line." Picketers were instructed not to "make any reference to race, color or creed"—although the last was violated freely.[42]

This was the adverse atmosphere that confronted CSU. The strikers tried to moderate potentially harsh responses by lightening the usually glum picket line. Once a group of extras, perhaps insensitively, "supplied several pickets in costume, one group depicting Indians bearing banners declaring themselves original Americans and demanding recognition of their stand in the strike."[43]

Seeking to slow the flow of revenue to the studios, CSU also picketed theaters, which the studios had acknowledged more than once as their ne plus ultra. These pickets at theaters became a favored CSU tactic—they were described as the " 'atom bomb' of the present struggle"; this strategy allowed CSU to harm the box office, while involving whole communities across the nation in its crusade.[44] One group picketing the thriller *Lady on a Train* told potential customers: "Save your money. We'll tell you all about it. Don't be fooled by Dan Duryea—Ralph Bellamy did it. He's the killer. And David Bruce gets the girl!"[45] Soon two L.A. theaters agreed to drop any movies made at "unfair" studios until the strike was settled. When "pioneer movie producer D. W. Griffith refused to pass the Paramount theater picket line," CSU knew that it had devised a sound tactic that could potentially drain the all-important box office receipts.[46] CSU began to develop its own blacklist of stars who crossed its picket lines, a growing roster that came to include Rosalind Russell, Robert Montgomery, John Wayne, Leo Carrillo, Humphrey Bogart, Susan Hayward—and many more.[47]

Exemplifying their continuing devotion to the antifascist alliance, picketers chanted and carried signs proclaiming, "Labor continues the fight for democracy"; "Labor produced for victory. Now let's produce victory for Labor"; "Warners have millions of dollars! But we have the United States Government Behind Us!" (This latter slogan was suggestive of the strikers' naïveté and of their failure to recognize that the antifascist alliance of the war was ephemeral.) "Remember Willie Bioff? The [studios] are trying to force us into company dominated racketeer unions."[48]

A "Ten Commandments of the Pickets" was issued by CSU: "Always be Ladies and Gentlemen." "Participate in no Violence on the Picket Line and do not use Obscene Language." "You must picket in a single line or circle." "You must not walk two abreast." "It is your right to use such terms as 'Rats,' 'Fink,' 'Scabs' and 'Scalie' as this is not Obscene Language."[49] Pickets were warned not to "become embroiled in a discussion of the pros and cons of the strike. Even if the person to whom you are speaking is violently opposed to the strike, it is still possible to get a donation from him on the grounds that workers' families need food and shelter. . . . Speak as though you are proud of the job you have undertaken."

There were also "song suggestions": "to tune of 'East Side, West Side,'" sing, "Inside, outside, all around the town, folks will never forget the names of Walsh, Bioff and Browne, Browne, Bioff and Walshie, Pals through thick and thin. Cut your throat with a smile and whisper, 'Anything to win.'"[50]

The strikers' definition of obscenity was quite flexible. The least problem that those crossing the picket lines encountered was a blizzard of slurs. Frank Freeman of Paramount contended that the verbal abuse was startling. Still shaken, he confided to Congress, "I have seen women in the picketlines, when people would come through, using epithets that I never knew a woman could express or could use until I came to Hollywood and found that situation. I tell you it just shakes you from the bottom right on up."[51]

Warner Bros. accused picketers of a theater at 6425 Hollywood Boulevard of actually striking ushers; they "argued and remonstrated with customers who had purchased tickets," too. Provocatively, "a large number of the members of the picketing group has been girls scantily dressed who specialized in efforts to get service men and men in uniform into the picket line."[52]

It did not take long before workers fighting for their livelihoods began to up the ante. They were attacked, but were also accused of retaliating—and more. Roy Brewer of IATSE claimed later that strikers bombed the homes of those who crossed picket lines—i.e., his members. "There were a series of such incidents—five bombings in all—and there were some severe beatings." They "seemed to concentrate on the men that were employed in Technicolor." A conflict had raged within IATSE Local 683 between those sympathetic to CSU and those who were not, and Sorrell's strikers were trying to resolve this dispute with violence, Brewer contended.

Sorrell denied strongly that his members were bombers. In fact, he recalled visiting the lobby of the Hotel Roosevelt and encountering Willie Bioff there, along with "four or five 'torpedoes'" who specialize in bombings. Arguing that these were self-inflicted wounds, most likely perpetrated by Bioff's men, Sorrell pointed out that no one was hurt in these bombings. In addition, the studios replaced the damaged homes with brand-new ones.[53]

Brewer's comments were probably exaggerations, but even so, the strike was clearly hitting home. Weeks after it had begun, one trade paper was griping that the strike "is costing many an independent practically his business."[54] Before that the *Motion Picture Herald* warned that "it could turn out to be Mr. Exhibitor, the innocent bystander, who gets hurt most by the strike against the major studios." IATSE was threatening to compel projectionists to go on strike if the studios caved in to CSU demands, while Sorrell's troops vowed to boycott any films made during the strike. Meanwhile, the studios—which actually conspired with IATSE to squeeze CSU—acted as if they were the injured parties standing between two warring unions.[55]

The *Motion Picture Herald* had raised by inference a good point: CSU could have channeled workers' anger more fruitfully by being more sensitive to tactics—particularly the age-old ruse of "divide and conquer." For the independents—like David O. Selznick, for example—were not as gung ho about this strike as the major studios. The independents had their own trade association—the Society of Independent Motion Picture Producers—and had different interests and slimmer profit margins: they were also less capable of absorbing lengthy strikes.

After a month, one of Selznick's colleagues was outraged when he heard that the majors were saying that the strike was "progressing satisfactorily." He, instead, worried that the "very existence of independent producers will be at stake" if the strike continued.[56] Selznick often worked on RKO and Pathe sets, and he feared that these studios were not strong enough to survive either; such a result could force him into an unsatisfying relationship with Warner Bros. or another major—or into liquidation. The majors understood this peril, realizing that the strike could injure independents like Selznick, whose *Gone With the Wind* had been one of the most profitable movies of all time.

CSU itself grasped this problem. Selznick filed away one of the federation's newsletters showing Walsh of IATSE holding a balloon labeled "major studios," while floating away into the stratosphere was a balloon labeled "Selznick": beneath this cartoon was the caption "Gone With the Wind."[57] Yet CSU failed to devise a strategy for taking advantage of this schism between the studios and the independents.

Selznick's company also complained about IATSE and collected literature about the alliance's gangster connections and its attempts to cover them up.[58] Yet Selznick had other problems similar to those of the majors. He worried about the "odd chance that one of the girls in [the] stenographic has an Uncle or an Aunt on the picket line." Fearful, the executives started typing their own documents, which—given their lack of practice—slowed the work process considerably.

Selznick had good reason to be suspicious. CSU joked about its intelligence-gathering capabilities within studio suites: "Take the case of Producer 'A': He raves and rants and hatches a move against us and dictates it to his sec, Miss 'B' . . . 'A' leaves, convinced we're cooked . . . 'B' grabs the phone and dials us and . . . well, it works as smooth as that! Sister of Exec 'F' is a strong union minded gal . . . but he doesn't know! Exec 'J' wines his Sec at Mocambo, dines her at LaRue's and reveals all in his ap't! . . . Sort of a very direct wire service." [59]

Yet Selznick's possible problem paled into insignificance when compared with others. His company surveyed Paramount, Fox, and other studios and discovered that all "were working under difficulties but working nevertheless and getting pictures made. The sets at Goldwyn were spotty. In some instances the work was excellent and in others from fair to poor." This survey, spurred by Selznick's concern about his impending production of the much criticized *Duel in the Sun,* was sobering.[60] For if the strike decisively harmed the quality of movies, attendance could plummet and the steady stream of revenues to studio coffers—and those of independents, too—could slow to a trickle.

Even Jack Warner himself was not immune from CSU desperados. He "did not dare go into his own studio," said Brewer, "and if I had gone near Warner Brothers Studio during that period when they [CSU] actually controlled it, I would have had to have at least 250 men to protect me." [61]

Warner was being pressured from all sides; not only did he have to contend with striking workers and balking stars, but the age-old problem of anti-Semitism also arose. L. T. Sheppard signed his name to an insulting letter to the "two Warner Brothers"; "you are a pack of real kikes . . . real dirt Jews and . . . cheap Jew B——rds, you know just what I mean." For good measure, he added, "It would give me the greatest pleasure to crack your worthless skulls together." [62] Warner was receiving anti-Semitic assaults from all sides, but he took the tirades from the right much more seriously, which did not bode well for CSU.

Jack Warner had absorbed the brunt of the strike, which did not improve his usually volcanic temperament. Angrily, he demanded that the Screen Directors Guild provide an "apology" for "accusing us of engaging thugs to combat the pickets at our studios." [63] Alternatively, he could not have been pleased when Ross F. Walker of Glendale chided him for having "contributed heavily to the stinking 'New Deal' campaign. I am wondering how you like it now?"[64]

Some supposed CSU supporters resorted to raw bigotry in expressing their frustration with Warner Bros. Others were irate that the "local hammer and sickle-ites" were tossing the "charge" of anti-Semitism.[65] Jacob Solomon, in contrast, warned the studio that "fascism in Europe begun [sic] in the same manner as it now takes place in the movie industry. . . . As a Jew, a progressive, a citizen, [I] do implore you for the good name of the Jewish people . . . to stop this horrible crime. . . . Recognize the Local union 1421."[66] Warner refused to budge: some were accusing him of philo-Semitism, while others charged him with creating the climate for a resurgence of anti-Semitism. From his point of view, paying more attention to what the surging right was saying made more sense.

CSU was adept neither at exploiting rifts between independents and major studios nor at fighting anti-Jewish bigotry—nor was it particularly nimble in handling relations with fellow unions. Screen extras disaffiliated from SAG in December 1944 to form the Screen Players Union (SPU). The extras' disaffection was fueled by many problems, e.g., irregular employment, poor working conditions, and fierce job competition. When SPU allied with CSU, SAG responded not only by supporting the formation of the Screen Extras Guild, but also by voting in March 1945—with an overwhelming margin of 3,298 to 96—to cross CSU picket lines. Retaliating, CSU persuaded Golden Pictures to use only SPU members, even though the new union was not part of the AFL, whereas SAG was. This move further alienated the stars, among the most important allies to have in any conflict with the studios.[67]

The strike did present other problems for the majors. Peter Lorre was among the stars feeling that "their careers are being damaged" because they are "branded as scabs" for not observing picket lines. Steve Trilling of Warner Bros. soothingly reassured Jack Dales of SAG that because actors "work only occasionally," they may overestimate the trauma and damage associated with crossing the line—still, a number of actors continued to balk.[68] At the height of the strike, Lorre "shut down The Verdict[,] the last production on the lot. Frightened of the violence but even more of being called a scab, Lorre refused to continue."[69]

Other actors were influenced by the "definite pattern of threats of violence and intimidation . . . at all the studios." Fred Meyer, director of industrial relations at Fox, informed Jack Warner that "men are being met at their cars and told not to come back tomorrow. Others are being called at their homes, while still others are being stopped on their way to work."[70] However, despite the discomfort that stars like Peter Lorre may have felt about crossing picket lines, movies continued to be made throughout the seven-month strike—and they featured some of Hollywood's biggest stars.[71]

★ By mid-March 1945 the studios had a weekly payroll of $2.5 million and 130 films on the shelves—a nine-month supply. This was not necessarily the most fortuitous moment for a studio strike.

Still, shortly after the strike was launched, "business offices were in a snarl" and "without electricians to operate generators, no current was available to shoot scenes on prepared sets." Disney, Monogram, and some independents were unaffected by the strike because they had bargained with Local 1421.[72] Columbia, RKO, Universal, Warner Bros., and Fox were affected most severely, with MGM and Paramount right behind.

The Communists were no less displeased with the strike. Sorrell and CSU had "fallen into a trap" they contended. Hutcheson, the "reactionary Republican labor boss of the Carpenters Union and close ally of John L. Lewis," was a culprit, along with the moguls, they argued; Sorrell's actions were deemed "highly individualistic and irresponsible." The Communists claimed that "production" was "virtually unimpaired" by the strike.[73] The strike was antidemocratic, they claimed, since CSU as a whole never voted. It simply had backed the "unilateral action" of six hundred Local 1421 members who walked out: "that is the total number of workers in the movie industry who have officially voted to strike."[74]

Organizations believed to be close to the party agreed with the Reds. As late as September 1945 the Hollywood Democratic Committee was reviewing its earlier refusal to take a position on the strike.[75]

The Reds' criticisms were not going unanswered. At a mass meeting at Hollywood's American Legion Stadium, Edward Boyle—a set decorator—assailed the Screen Writers Guild for not backing the strike, and added that the group's failure was due to the influence of "leftwingers." These "leftwingers" and "capitalists" made "strange bedfellows," it was said.[76]

The Communists did blast the producers who canceled union contracts and discharged workers who walked out: "[T]his amounts to a virtual lockout. . . . Its obvious intent is to initiate jurisdictional war. . . . This has been a cardinal aim of the producers from the very beginning," and CSU had fallen willingly into this trap.[77] Still, the Communists could not have been pleased when their presumed ideological polar opposite—the

Los Angeles Times—agreed with their viewpoint, declaring that the strike "takes the blue ribbon for asininity in wartime labor relations disputes."[78]

The Communist critique was echoed among some studio unions. The Screen Publicists Guild, the Teamsters, and the Screen Story Analysts were among those that voted initially not to back the strike.[79] Yet CSU had struck a nerve among workers with its audacious action. The climate was redolent with criticisms of big capital and its role in plunging Germany, Japan, and other nations into war; inevitably, these comments made U.S. workers more skeptical about big capital's intentions in the United States itself. Thus, "picket lines [did] grow" during the first two weeks of the strike. Warner Bros. was the "hottest spot," not only because it had been targeted by CSU but also because some members of IATSE Local 44 at this studio were sympathetic to CSU.[80] As *Variety* reported, "[D]espite a wire from Dick Walsh, the IATSE prexy, thousands of IA workers refused to cross picket lines, even in the face of threats of fines and having cards revoked."[81] Days later at a "rebel meeting of some 1500 IATSE members at Hollywood Legion Stadium . . . Eugene Mailes and Erwin [*sic*] Hentschel, leaders of this rebellion, were suspended from membership by [the] board because of their actions."[82] Members of IATSE's property men's union walked out at Warner Bros. after forty-eight of their number refused to do the work of striking CSU members.[83] Nevertheless, IATSE continued seeking to organize its own locals of painters and carpenters—in league with the moguls—to replace CSU permanently.

Vanguard, an independent studio, was forced by the strike to suspend production on a film starring Gregory Peck, Jennifer Jones, Joseph Cotten, Lillian Gish, and Walter Huston.[84] This stoppage seemed like good news to CSU, demonstrating that its muscle flexing had impact. Yet weakening smaller studios could only strengthen CSU's primary antagonist—the big studios. The majors, however, were affected also. MGM's location unit of *She Went to the Races* was forced to "vacate shooting at the Hollywood Park race track. . . . [T]rack management was notified the carpenters and building service employees would walk out if the company was allowed to shoot."[85] The makers of *Night and Day*, the story of Cole Porter, starring Cary Grant and Alexis Smith, failed to do retakes because of the strike. "A screen test was also cancelled when Eleanor Parker failed to appear."[86]

Selznick's *Duel in the Sun* had problems, too. "The all-star cast . . . refused to work when mass picketing began" at RKO, where it was being filmed. "Jennifer Jones, leading lady in the $4,000,000 spectacle, walked out when she saw the pickets. Lillian Gish walked past the studio waving to the pickets when she saw the line. Other players—Gregory Peck, Lionel Barrymore, Walter Huston, Charles Bickford . . . did not show up at all."[87]

Moguls were resorting to clandestine maneuvers to get movies made, trying to avoid heavy impact on the filmmaking process. CSU asserted that "Russia's racy raconteur, Prince Alexander Golitzen, Universal art director on *Scarlett Street* under supervising art director John B. Goodman, was having his drawings made in a vacant hideaway house at 10950 Landale in North Hollywood. . . . 'Prince' Golitzen and his boss . . . lured several yellow members of [Local] 1421 into 'sneak scabbing' in the hideaway."[88] Picketing the studios led to a fragmenting of the filmmaking process and a decline in the centralization that had been Hollywood's hallmark; like independent production, this fragmentation accelerated after the strike.

These forced changes were also having impact on the quality of movies. "Hollywood is talking," said one reporter, "about the beautiful door built by a scab carpenter for a set at Paramount. Nobody could open it because the knob and the hinges were all on the same side."[89]

The Screen Directors Guild had taken note "of the fact that quite recently many employees have been set upon and badly beaten"; thus the guild's leader John Cromwell "instructed our members that they need not risk physical violence in attempting to enter or leave" the studios. Someone other than skilled and experienced auteurs would have to be found to direct films, again with a dramatic impact on film quality.[90]

By mid-June CSU was claiming that not one film had been completed since the strike; the studios disagreed. Press reports indicated that there would be a movie "shortage in [the] fall" with a "60%" drop in output. The "usefulness of old sets, which the producers have been revamping and re-using for various pictures, has been about exhausted. Independent producers, caught without stockpiles of sets such as are to be found on major lots, have been hit hardest. . . . Production of around 15 independent pictures has been held up as a result of the studio strike. . . . If the strike continues into July, it is contended, the shortage will be felt into December or later."[91] Other sources dissented from this view, with one alleging that movie production was "up" since the strike, with thirteen films being started during one week alone in August and with forty others in various stages of production.[92]

The strike did, however, lead to changes in how films were made. There was a "tremendous increase in the use of process shots. In every major studio and some of the independents, process units are busier than at any previous time in film history. Outdoor and indoor footage, stowed away in vaults for years, is being dragged out to form backgrounds for new pictures, obviating the necessity of new sets and thereby saving labor and money. Process photography also does away with time and expense of location trips."[93] Viewers might groan when seeing, in the midst of their favorite western, an obviously phony background scene supposedly depicting a saloon, but the strike allowed few alternatives to such process shooting.

Process shooting also required less CSU labor; this was among the disquieting signals that CSU could ignore only at its peril. Concomitant with the strike, for example, the studios began hiring IATSE members to take the place of CSU members; this development would not only complicate the settlement of the strike, it would also deepen the objective alliance between the studios and IATSE.[94] More ominously, reports began to circulate about "private police forces" entering the fray. Soon there were stories about painters "beaten," and others "knocked unconscious with a blunt instrument" and "severely pummeled with fists"; still others were injured "seriously enough to be treated at a hospital."[95] Such assaults on strikers were fraying relations—perhaps intentionally—between CSU and IATSE, whose members had expressed much sympathy for their fellow unionists. "Civil war" was now being threatened between the two as clashes escalated.[96] At the same time there was a growing fear that the CIO would snatch the opportunity presented by strike turmoil to oust the AFL from Hollywood.[97]

Unions, too, have been known to use strong-arm tactics during strikes, and CSU—led by the combative Sorrell—was no exception to this brutish rule. In late May 1945 John A. Van Meter, 43, a member of a non-striking AFL union, was on his way to work in the studio when he was approached by two "roughly dressed men." One said, "[Y]ou're a rat if you go through that picket line," and then proceeded to knock Van Meter down and kick him in the face.[98] Extra police and sheriff's officers were alerted for duty as the picket lines grew. Reputedly, workers had received instructions to "cut out the politeness and get tough."[99] A "small fire" that broke out at Samuel Goldwyn's studio may have been a direct response to this environment.[100]

As the war in Europe concluded and the no-strike pledge lost its urgency, the Communist Party became more favorable to the strike. Not coincidentally, more unions did, too. By late July the Screen Cartoonists Guild at Warner Bros. and MGM had joined the strike, and the studios seemed to be getting more desperate as CSU accused them of recruiting schoolteachers, off for the summer, for labor.[101]

The executive committee of the Screen Office Employees Guild voted 46–2 to recommend that "3000 white collarites stay outside the picket lines"; though this mandate was not observed universally, it was a sign that CSU was gathering momentum. The Screen Analysts Guild voted to observe the picket lines, as did the Screen Publicists Guild.[102] Then the CIO's executive board gave another boost to CSU when it voted unanimously in August to boycott "theaters showing 'hot' films"—i.e., those being made during the strike. This was a direct reversal of a statement by CIO council president Kenneth C. Beight, who had said weeks earlier that "under no circumstances" would his organization take a position on this "unfortunate jurisdictional difference."[103] The Newspaper Guild emulated this move by voting unanimously not to permit their members to handle publicity material from picketed studios.[104]

This coming together of labor led ineluctably to charges of devious Communist plotting. Certainly over time the strike's image had improved among the Reds. More positive words about CSU were no doubt heard when Bette Davis, Joseph Cotten, Edward Dmytryk, and James Wong Howe spoke at the "People's Educational Center" at 1717 Vine Street in Los Angeles—during a session touted prominently in the party newspaper.[105] Suddenly, charming stories began to appear in the party press about the joys of picketing theaters controlled by the studios. "Service men, alone or in groups, often respect the picket line," the intrepid reporter discovered. "The Marines have the best record and air force officers the worst. Soldiers with girls are more likely to go through [the lines] than soldiers by themselves." Why? "I think they don't understand, and they don't want to look cheap to their girls," said one observer. "That's why it helps to have girls on the picket lines," the writer concluded.[106]

When CSU altered its tactics and began amassing its own pickets at one or two studios rather than dispersing them, the federation was able to put enormous pressure on the affected studios. In response the studios obtained an injunction barring the stationing of more than six pickets in the vicinity of a "motion picture plant." The order specified that not more than four such pickets could be stationed within twenty-five feet of the vehicle entrance of the studio and not more than two within twenty-five feet of the pedestrian entrance. The order prohibited any attempt to obstruct delivery of supplies into a studio, the use of sound trucks or any other sound-magnifying devices and any yelling at studio employees, tenants, or customers of the studio. From Sacramento came word that the State Employment Stabilization Commission had upheld a ruling of the local office that studio employees who refused to work during strike were not entitled to unemployment insurance.[107] Later the Screen Office Employees Guild was restrained by a court order from disciplining members who crossed the picket lines.[108]

These injunctions and rulings indicated that CSU's strike was influencing the studios' fortunes, protestations to the contrary notwithstanding. Even before the Communists fully supported the strike, bringing along other fence-sitters, CSU was not doing badly. In mid-April 1945 Sorrell had been crowing, "[W]e haven't lost one man from our ranks since the strike started, but we have on our records the names of more than 1000 members of IATSE who quit their studio jobs and refused to work while the strike was on."[109] By early June he was still boasting that he had Hollywood "by the throat, and if they don't give up, we'll throttle the industry."[110]

The strike had divided studio labor, not only between CSU and IATSE but also within the two organizations. Like other unions, the Screen Publicists went back and forth on support of the strike—opposing, then supporting; supporting, then opposing. Cracked one observer, "[T]he flacks couldn't make up their minds."[111] In mid-August the Screen Office Employees Guild voted 894 to 666 to keep working after a "secret ballot" and after "bitter verbal battles until the early morning."[112]

The Teamsters, who delivered supplies to the "dream factories" in Burbank and Culver City, were an important segment of the labor force, and they were hostile to CSU, too. Their Hollywood representative, Joe Tuohy—who eventually took a lucrative position with the studios—explained to Teamsters boss Daniel Tobin that the "strike is in its seventh week and while the picket line is still strong, Sorrell is getting no place. The IA are in complete control with the Producers standing pat and determined to rid the industry of this constant menace regardless of the price." Proudly, he announced, "[O]ur men [are] all going through the lines. There isn't much work but they all get a full week's pay anyway." There were problems, though, for "our men have had to haul the men signed up by the IA to replace the strikers, and this they rebelled against at first." This was "very embarrassing," he said.[113]

It was not only embarrassing, it was tense and "a little rugged for a while because the strikers really tried to win over the sympathy of the Teamsters, telling them if they refused to deliver, the strike could be won in a few days. Now they are very bitter toward us and make it as uncomfortable as possible for our members. In any case," he said with resignation, "where we found that men were afraid to go through, we escorted them in, which made us very unpopular . . ." There were glimmers of hope, however: "As I see it," said Tuohy, "the IA are in complete control and the strike is practically over." His opinion was that CSU had miscalculated completely since "the studios are learning that with a little more efficiency they can cut down their forces about [one third] and in the future will call for less men." [114]

For his part, Tobin, the leader of what was to become the nation's largest union, was not happy with IATSE for issuing charters for the formation of painters and carpenters locals during the midst of the strike, a move that was bound to ignite future turmoil. He reminded Tuohy that the Teamsters were crossing picket lines not because they disliked CSU but because the no-strike pledge demanded no less. In a curious message sent hours before the bombing of Nagasaki, Japan, he reminded Tuohy that "someday we may get more radical . . . depending upon the change in world conditions." [115] The meaning of these words was unclear. Did he mean that the ending of the no-strike pledge would result in more strikes by Teamsters? Or did he mean that the end of antifascist unity would mean the Teamsters could become more "radical"—i.e., radically conservative? In retrospect, the latter seems closer to the truth.

What did come with the victory over Japan and the conclusion of the war was a sharper focus on the role of Communists in the labor movement. CSU apparently did not recognize that with the end of the war would come an end to any sympathy with the ideal that the USSR purported to represent—the organization of workers.

Hours before the war's end, Tuohy was reporting about a Central Labor Council meeting where members voted 290 to 164 "condemning Communistic activities in the labor movement." [116] IATSE was quick to capitalize on this sentiment. With barely concealed glee, the union alliance quoted a member of the Screen Cartoonists Guild who reputedly proclaimed that "Communism has outgrown New York as its headquarters. Henceforth, our activities will evolve in Hollywood, where the prestige, influence and support of our comrades in the film industry will strengthen our ranks and carry our fight to people from every walk of life." [117]

★ This idea of a "Red CSU" became the IATSE motto, one that it intended to ride to victory. IATSE even published a flood of anticommunist propaganda targeting CSU. [118] At IATSE's convention in

Chicago, the usual "Dixie" was played to greet the delegates, but another theme accompanied the union's favorite song. Prominent California legislator Jack Tenney asked plaintively, "[W]hy does the Communist Party want to control Hollywood?" His answer was simple: "California has been an important concentration point for Communism in America. It has been important because in Hollywood we have the greatest medium of propaganda that has ever been conceived in the world."[119]

Tenney's stark and gripping words exemplified the frenetic haste with which CSU opponents rushed to tag the union federation as "Communist." This was nothing new for Sorrell. During a congressional hearing John R. Robinson of Compton, former president of District Council Number 4 of the Maritime Federation of the Pacific, charged that Sorrell had tried to recruit him into the Communist Party in 1937 and had even flashed his membership card. Sorrell also discussed sabotage, Tenney said.[120]

This question of Communism was the reason IATSE provided for removing local autonomy from many of its locals and investing so much power in the union president; this distribution, it was said, hindered Red infiltration at the grassroots. This possibility was an "extreme emergency," Walsh recalled. While serving in the George Browne administration, Walsh had been informed about the "Communistic element" in Hollywood, and, consequently, he backed the extreme measures that were necessary to root the Reds out.[121]

Walsh's top lieutenant in Hollywood, Roy Brewer, continued this theme, sending a steady stream of relevant material to Daniel Tobin of the Teamsters, including an alleged summary of Sorrell's Red affiliations.[122] Brewer, the former campaign manager for Senator George Norris, demanded that the FBI investigate this question—and the bureau was all too eager to comply. Brewer "further stated that the Communists had complete control of the representatives in Congress from Southern California and had similar control over the National Labor Relations Board." Brewer advised that "if necessary" he would willingly "turn in politics and become a Republican" rather than see this steady left upsurge.[123] The left was shattered, but Brewer nonetheless became an official in the presidential administration of his friend Ronald Reagan. He prepared for this role by berating Helen Gahagan Douglas, a politician and the spouse of actor Melvyn Douglas, for backing the "pro-Communist clique" conducting the strike.[124]

At the various investigative hearings where the CSU leader was questioned, repeatedly he was confronted with "photostatic copies of Communist Party documents and exemplars of the handwriting of Herbert K. Sorrell" purporting to show his membership card and party record.[125] Sorrell in turn repeatedly charged that these documents were fakes, a mob ploy invented during the 1937 strike and burnished during his confrontation with Disney a few years later. With his typically indelicate verbiage, Sorrell countered, "We were lily white [AFL] people, but the minute that Bioff stepped in, the cry of communism comes in. It is always that way. It has been that way; it continues to be that way." [126]

Sorrell was not off the mark. In my opinion, he was no Communist, nor were most of his fellow CSU leaders. The party had criticized the strike and came onboard only later. However, a larger agenda was involved in this red-baiting; it was designed to discredit CSU, paving the way for IATSE's control over studio labor and the moguls' control over the entire production process. That this might mean an increase of mobster influence in the industry was viewed as an irrelevant detail or a necessary price to pay.

When the strike erupted, Hollywood Communist leader John Howard Lawson was working at Columbia. Every morning at seven o'clock, he would participate in the picket line at Warner Bros., then go home at nine; this support came after the party had placed its imprimatur on the strike. Warner Bros. did not appreciate Lawson's picketing in Burbank, so the studio snapped his current picture and sent it to Harry Cohn. Lawson then had a seven-year contract at the studio, but Cohn was infuriated with him and threatened his future tenure at the studio. Lawson threatened to quit in a heated telephone conversation with Cohn. The studio boss got his revenge by giving Lawson only half credit for a film that he claimed to have written in toto, except for a bit by Sidney Buchman. Lawson was so angry that he refused credit altogether.[127]

Lawson's loss of credit for his film distortedly mirrors the Communists' receipt of credit for the CSU strike. The chief of the Hollywood party was nowhere to be found when this strike was devised or when it got under way, yet his party was given credit for the monumental effort.

This inattention came at an inopportune time, for the party itself was undergoing a wrenching change wrought by the ouster of its leader, Earl Browder, and a turn away from his own wartime popular-front policies, which included an embrace of big business. This position was now viewed as inappropriate for the coming Red Scare.[128] Emil Freed of the CP's 59th Assembly District associated the party's lethargy in supporting the strike not with the no-strike pledge of antifascist unity but with the "revisionist policies" of Browder. Freed found preposterous Browder's idea that just as Moscow and Washington could unite during the war, labor and capital could unite in the United States.[129]

Linking the strike to the Communists required a great leap in logic—and in evidence—though the party's flap over Browder contributed to a confused atmosphere that allowed all manner of distorted ideas to take root. Still, even Pat Casey, the studio's chief negotiator with CSU, denied that the conflict was "communistic inspired."[130] He denied further that Sorrell was a Communist, but linking CSU with the Reds was much too attractive a proposition to allow mere lack of evidence to derail it. Thus, the strategy continued to be used to discredit the strike wave, which was coursing across the nation. An investigator for the Senate Internal Security Subcommittee found contrarily that "in no sense can it be said that the recent strike wave in key industries was the result of a 'Communist plot'. . . . Communists were involved," it conceded, "but there are many other factors in the recent strike flare-up; post-war economic problems, shifting labor-political alliances following FDR's death, cost of living pay demands, efforts to keep war take-home pay, AFL-CIO battles, bad management public relations, labor's desire to strike at an effective moment to hold war-time gains, and in some cases business desire to select an equally effective moment to weaken unionization."[131] The latter factor was especially apropos in explicating the Hollywood strike, but this insight was lost in a tidal wave of red-baiting.

One CSU supporter felt that IATSE's escalation of red-baiting was just another way to bail out the studios. "If I read it right," he said, "[IATSE] says the workers shouldn't hit the producers for raises because the poor producers are soon going to be in a bad economic position because the Russians are holding up foreign export of American films. That's really going to bat for the bosses."[132] This worker had stumbled onto a raw reality. Because Moscow was viewed as such a fundamental threat to Hollywood's profit cushion abroad, CSU carried a burden that other unions did not, thus giving added resonance to red-baiting in Los Angeles. Moreover, according to CSU, Brewer and Walsh were doing precisely what they accused "red revolutionists" of doing: they were trying to "wreck" labor in order to "preserve the status quo."[133]

★ In one week in September 1945 about 37,000 workers were laid off in Los Angeles. "The War Manpower Commission estimated over 100,000 production workers had been idled since V-J Day. Still ahead were 45,000 layoffs in aircraft and 10,000 more in shipbuilding and repair. Los Angeles manufacturing jobs declined to the prewar total of 152,000."[134] For CSU these layoffs raised the specter of an increase in the "reserve army of labor" that might try to take members' jobs and through competition might drive down wages. For the labor movement this competition was more than a hint that the new postwar arrangements would be determined by capital. In this context the CSU strike took on further meaning as a test case to ascertain which class would have the upper hand in the immediate future. Thus prompted, CSU sought to expand the reach of its pickets.

Roger McDonald, born in 1905, began work at Selznick Pictures in Culver City in 1938. This illustrator worked on *Gone With the Wind, Rebecca,* and *Intermezzo,* then worked for the British producer Alexander Korda before moving on to Goldwyn, RKO, and Universal. As a "production story illustrator," he used his "imaginative capabilities" as an artist to interpret with "illustrations, the continuity, the mood, the action, the visual tempo, the characterization, the drama, as designated to him by the producer, and/or the director and/or the writer."[135] In 1943 he began working for Fox, where he joined the Society of Motion Picture Artists and Illustrators, which was affiliated with the Painters as the Screen Set Designers, Illustrators and Decorators. By 1944 he was on the latter's executive board and found himself in the midst of the tumult that led to the 1945 strike.

In September 1945, at Sorrell's behest, McDonald was dispatched to New York City to work with unions there on picketing theaters and raising funds. He checked into the Hotel Roosevelt and immediately contacted the business agent of United Scenic Artists, Local 829 of the Painters, for assistance, but he "appeared unenthusiastic."[136] Sorrell told McDonald to collaborate with Louis Weinstock, the Communist painter, and the International Workers Order (IWO)—a fraternal organization derided by some as little more than a "Communist front." They have "given us great cooperation financially and with pickets," Sorrell said enthusiastically. "Louis knows these men and can give you the necessary entré [*sic*] to them."[137]

In this political climate, McDonald's overtures to Weinstock and the IWO raised questions about him in others' eyes. "Many of the AFL unions were suspicious that I was Communist," he recalled while "most of the Communists were afraid I was a 'plant' or an undercover agent"; of course, "they were both wrong."

Yet this occurrence illustrated the cruel dilemma CSU faced as the Red Scare lurked: the Communists were not fervently ardent about Sorrell's leadership, whereas the anticommunists suspected him because of his willingness to work with Communists. These mutual doubts tempered devotion on all sides.

Weinstock proved helpful, but he too had his qualms about the CSU leader; he "criticized Sorrell," said McDonald. Yet Lawrence Lindelof, the none-too-progressive president of the painters, was not fond of the CSU leader either; "he spat on [the] carpet of the hotel room. Then he chewed his cigar and spat right on the wallpaper. 'Sorrell,' [Lindelof] said to me, 'doesn't know what he's doing out there in Hollywood. He's always doing something crazy.'"

From the Communists' point of view, Sorrell violated a cardinal principle of trade unionism with his cozy relationships with management. This, in their mind, vitiated his admirable militancy. When McDonald was sent to Manhattan, strangely his ticket was paid for by Pat Casey, the studios' chief labor negotiator and a former close colleague of leading mobster Johnny Roselli. McDonald, who was no friend of the Communists, subsequently wrote an apologia disclaiming any affection for them and emphasizing that "to my knowledge there was not a single Communist in Local 1421." Yet even the decidedly nonradical McDonald was puzzled by Sorrell's friendship with Casey. They "were friends of some kind," he observed. "Some said Casey helped place Sorrell in control," McDonald added suspiciously, and "helped him organize" CSU "in order to control the unions through Sorrell. Some said Casey tolerated Sorrell for the information he could bleed out of him. Some said Sorrell controlled Casey."[138] This latter suggestion was highly unlikely. Either way, though, for all of his militancy, Sorrell in many ways had not broken with the model of "business unionism"—including intimate friendships with management—that characterized many of his fellow AFL leaders. Yet his militancy prevented him from enjoying these leaders' full support. It was inevitable that Sorrell would get squeezed by all sides—and would be forced to disappear.

As it turned out, McDonald's effort to organize the picketing of theaters in New York City—which could have been a powerful weapon—fizzled. Suggestive of the tough times McDonald faced in Manhattan was the fact that he felt compelled to change "the word [']workers[']" on the leaflet "as it doesn't get such a good reaction from many people."[139] McDonald's symbolic annihilation of *workers* was a precursor of the day when the term *working class* itself would become passé and was supplanted by the all-encompassing phrase, "middle class." When Sorrell asked McDonald to use "paid pickets if necessary," it was apparent that the project was in trouble.[140] Privately Sorrell called his ambassador in Manhattan "a nice boy but a square peg does not fit in a round hole."[141] Days after McDonald's arrival in New York, Sorrell told him that because of the need to "reduce overall expenditures due to heavy disbursements for NLRB hearing attorney fees and increased strike benefits," he had to end this once hopeful Manhattan mission.[142]

This brusque setback may help to explain why as the strike entered its nerve-racking sixth month, tensions flared and rifts increased. Members of the Screen Publicists Guild began returning to work in defiance of their leadership.[143] A newly organized Motion Picture Studio Publicists Association notified major studios that it represented a majority of the working press agents and warned them not to negotiate with the SPG.[144] A rebel faction of the Screen Office Employees Guild broke away to form its own union. At a meeting of Painters Local 644, Sorrell got into a scuffle with one of his members. "He put his finger under my nose," said the feisty CSU leader "and I slapped him." IATSE projectionists picketed Williams Film Laboratory, forcing it to shut down; the union wanted the employer to hire more workers but he denied having enough work to justify such a move.[145]

Irma Mae Ross, a script clerk with Warner Bros., cozily praised her boss: "you have fed me, clothed me, for sixteen years . . . and made it possible for me to buy my home." With evident sincerity, she concluded, "I love Warner Brothers."[146] She was not alone in these sentiments. During the height of the unrest, scores of workers at Warner Bros. sent their employer a petition proclaiming similar sentiments.[147] Many workers feared alienating their employers by striking when there was a surplus of labor.

Simultaneously, though CSU and IATSE were clawing desperately at one another, their bosses were displaying an exemplary class solidarity. At an October 1945 meeting of the moguls, "Joe Schenck . . . said that on behalf of 20th Century Fox he would be glad to pay his pro rata share with all members of the Producers Association of any losses Warner's might incur for having borne the brunt of the strike alone." Harry Cohn of Columbia offered to let Warner Bros. use "all his sets."[148] This solidarity occurred at a time when labor was busily cannibalizing itself.

All of these developments were a reflection of the negative situation CSU faced as a result of the strike and the increasingly perilous plight of militant labor in Los Angeles generally. In early October 1945, in a tense three-hour argument, IATSE and CSU squared off at the NLRB (National Labor Relations Board) on the issue of whether the "strikers were legally fired." This determination was relevant in determining whether these

Local 1421 members were eligible to vote in the election for representation of the Set Decorators. If the strikers were "legally fired," an election could be held without them, which could have led to an IATSE victory and a maiming defeat for CSU. Still, CSU lawyer Abe Isserman called IATSE a scarecrow, deflecting attention from the producers who were seeking to erode Sorrell's federation.[149] Ultimately CSU prevailed and its ability to continue pressuring the studios—and movie houses—with pickets was no small reason why.

As summer turned to fall and the strike dragged on, it was evident that something had to give. Loud and rowdy pickets remained at the studio gates and their compatriots gathered at theaters in various locales. At the "gala Hollywood premiere of Paramount's $2,000,000 production of *Duffy's Tavern* . . . only 300 people crossed the picket lines"; the "average for a first performance is 3000 admissions." Edgar Bergen was "cheered and applauded by the spectators for refusing to cross the picket lines" while Paramount actor Eddie Bracken "had no such scruples."[150] Smugly the studios claimed that the strike was not hurting them at all, but fewer were believing them.

CSU was hurting, too.

★ By October 1945 CSU was not just running out of money, it was running out of patience. Temperatures were at record highs and nerves were frazzled. Anger rose further when word was leaked that "two members of the [NLRB]" hearing Local 1421's case had a financial "interest in theatre chains."[151] Roger McDonald's spouse was telling him that the "fellows have lost the strike, or at least concede that it is probably lost, and are meeting to find the best way out of the whole thing." Picketing had failed to close theaters in other cities. "There have been vague rather conversational mentions of pickets in Seattle and Portland, nothing about lines being established in Chicago or Cleveland." She was told that there were "80,000 unionists ready to picket theatres" in Detroit; "however since that time there has been no further word about it and today when someone asked Herb about it he said they might actually get 8 pickets if they were lucky."[152]

This was the calm before the storm.

At one of CSU's many meetings at Hollywood's Legion Stadium, a member suggested closing down MGM in Culver City. Sorrell demurred since the "chief of police at MGM" was a "pretty good guy and MGM is [a] big studio" and those wanting to go to work "could go in at the other gates." From his 1937 experience, Sorrell felt that Warner Bros. would make a better target, for it would overreact—and it did.[153] Beginning in early October and continuing for the next few weeks, a chaotic jumble of events gripped Hollywood.

Strikers had begun massing at 4 A.M. on a typically warm day during this pivotal month;[154] shortly thereafter, "strikebreakers, goons and county police" attacked those picketing in Burbank. They were "armed with chains, bolts, hammers, six inch pipes, brass knuckles, wooden mallets and battery cables."[155] Blaney Matthews, "head of [Warner Bros.] private gestapo," gave the orders to the county sheriff, whose men "marched two and three abreast. . . . Steel-helmeted and reinforced with tear gas masks, night-sticks, some carried 30–30 Garrand rifles and two were weighted down with an arsenal of tear gas bombs."[156] CSU pickets had their own "white-painted air-raid warden helmets" that "shone eerily in the predawn gloom."[157] These helmets and weapons added to the perception that this strike had become a pitched battle, a war.

What had incurred the ire of the studio was that mass picketing had virtually shut down the studio. What had irked CSU was the attempt to get injunctive relief to reduce sharply the size of its effective force. There were an estimated 300 pickets at the main gate and several "roving squads of huskier pickets . . . stopping cars and preventing any from getting near the studio. Squads also spotted 15 or 20 non-strikers," contended *Variety,* "who were seen inside the studio yesterday standing among onlookers and gave them a heavy battering."[158]

As Sorrell recalled it, "[F]irst, they drove through the picket lines at a high rate of speed, several cars. I think we took four people to the hospital." "Now, I wasn't there at that time that happened," he reminded, but he did recall when the "fire hose" was "dragged out"; "they turned it on the people's feet and just swept them right out from under . . . they threw tear gas bombs . . . there were women knocked down. . . . It was a slaughter."[159]

Elaine Spiro, an ingenue of an actress, recalled that "studio police lobbed canisters of tear-gas from the roofs of the one-story buildings forming the entranceway."[160] Some of these bombs detonated, releasing noxious fumes.

One reporter saw "fists fly" as "four automobiles were overturned"; "scores of men were beaten" and "several women hurt." Warner Bros. guards hurled "gas bombs." There were two police officers and forty-three strikers hurt. "The replacement workers stormed the picket line at 6 A.M. swinging chains . . . and fists. . . . [A] pitched battle broke out. . . . Forty deputy sheriffs and 160 police from Burbank, Glendale, San Fernando and Pasadena" intervened."[161] Photographs showed hundreds of nonstrikers charging the picket line; "many had armed themselves with lengths of chain, auto battery cables, sticks and other implements."[162] Warner Bros. resembled a "feudal castle of old" besieged by strikers, but protected by scabs, "goons," and police.[163]

A contemporaneous CSU source saw "police hitting the pickets from the inside and the spearhead of scabs hitting it from the outside"; thus, the line was "pierced." "A picket dropped to the sidewalk from a blow on the head from a monkey wrench."[164]

Macklin (Porky) Hall, Jr., "one time 'fat boy' in Hal Roach comedies and now a special effects man," was "beaten so severely by pickets that . . . he was reported in critical condition." The *Los Angeles Times* pointedly noted the presence of a leaflet from the "North Hollywood Communists' Club." The picketers were not just studio labor, they averred; "only about 50 per cent of the men and women in the picket line . . . were actually film studio workers"; the rest were from the longshore union, aircraft union, other unions, and possibly the Communist Party.[165]

Referring to that awful day in Burbank, one woman picketer said, "[F]ascism [ran] wild." Scabs and police "held lead pipes" and "monkey wrenches." One picket "sidestepped a blow aimed at his throat by a man wielding a screw driver. He felled the man with his fist, then stamped on the wrist of his assailant." Still, "strike breakers ducked through, running inside the studio. . . . [T]hey ran, arms interlocked, heads down."[166]

It all seemed "very rugged" to Joe Tuohy of the Teamsters. He realized that CSU was "prepared to put up a fight." It was not just goons and police but the IATSE itself which "massed all of their strength and broke the picket line and got their people through but only after they were stoned and clubbed; many of the men were badly cut up." His Teamsters "had refused to go through under these conditions and I don't blame them because I had a lot of trouble ducking the flying missiles even from my vantage point across the street."[167]

Edward Mussa of Local 1421 also found the experience quite "rugged." There was a high pressure fire hose being used and "tear gas, then goons with pieces of chain and black jacks."[168] These were "professional thugs . . . paid $50 each." It was such a massacre that a "big deputy sheriff walked away from [the] mass slugging and wept."[169] This could only have been perpetrated by organized crime, it was thought.

Jack Cooper, a publicist, and his wife were "peacefully, though not blissfully, walking up and down in front of the Warner studio" that fateful morning when "suddenly" their "grief was broken in on by a division or battalion . . . of deputy sheriffs. Some had sub-machine guns. All had sidearms, clubs and teargas bombs." The couple were arrested and held incommunicado.[170]

Arthur Silver of the trailer department at Warner Bros. found the entrance to the studio blocked by three overturned cars. He then saw a "huge truck, open in back. There must have been fifty goons in it, stripped to the waist, with leather bands; I had never seen anything like it in my life. These men were monsters! And they were ready to go in to bust the strike." Quickly, Silver departed for the safety of home but then he got an anxious call from an executive. "Mr. Warner wants you to come to the studio," he said. "How are we going to win the strike if everybody stays out?" Convinced, Silver "came in and . . . stayed at the studio. . . . It was a wild two weeks. Nothing but crap games and card games at night, and the best of food. Every night the police at the auto gate would tell us when the pickets left so we could drive home and see our families. Then we'd come back at twelve o'clock and the parties would be going on. Some of the guys would get girls in there and some of the actresses would come in. Those parties were wild!" he noted lasciviously and longingly.[171]

The tumult continued. Elaine Spiro was so nervous she "slept [only] a few hours"; she was plagued with "excitement" and "mild anxiety." She had an "excess of nervous energy" that she could only release by doing some ironing; but being so excited, accidentally "the hot iron brushed my left forearm giving me a burn that left a permanent mark."

The events that unfolded on 8 October also left a "permanent mark" on the region and the industry. Spiro saw a thousand picketers confronted by police "armed with automatic rifles." Then she saw a "large open cattle truck" that "pulled up nearby and about 50 tall, muscular men emerged from the rear" with "chains." Across the street "Artie Shaw, the musician and Marsha Hunt, a well-known young actress" were worriedly watching the escalating confrontation.

Then Spiro spied "perhaps 100 helmeted L.A. County Deputy Sheriffs and lots of studio cops . . . running with batons at the ready." She was immobilized as she "watched the scene a few feet away: goons and replacements smashing people's heads, faces, bodies; deputy sheriffs and cops knocking down men; a girl wearing a white hard-hat and Red Cross arm band pushed down on to the pavement" by a scab; "the cops dragging people to the Paddy Wagon; three cops beating up a bleeding man lying on the ground."[172]

Many of Governor Earl Warren's angry constituents were not as shaken or disturbed by these events as was Ms. Spiro. Al Matthews, an attorney representing the "plate window insurers," had a particular concern as he witnessed the shards of broken glass littering the landscape. He wanted to know if the governor knew that "2500 pickets have surrounded" Warner Bros.; "they molested all persons seeking entry" and "overturned police autos."[173] Quickly, Warren's aide contacted "Colonel Mitchell, Adjutant General's Office" who reassured him that the "situation at Burbank is well in hand."[174] But unbeknownst to the press and others, Mitchell sent a "state guardsman to the scene" in "civilian clothes" though the "sheriff's office did not wish to bring unfavorable comments upon" itself by revealing this detail.[175]

The guardsman may have felt the situation was "well in hand," but he would have had a hard time convincing others of this. One angry woman complained to Warren that "my husband hasn't been home for three days and nights now—why? Because of these communistic loving maniacs who threaten to get even with all the fellows who broke through the picket line."[176]

That random leaflet from the North Hollywood club of the Communist Party was coming to dominate subsequent interpretations of the Warner Bros. riot. This theme took strange twists. Alfred Haddock, a self-proclaimed "Republican," told Warren that the head of the painters and carpenters "both backed the Republican candidate for the presidency of this nation in the last November election and therefore are hardly red." No, he was more worried about the Warners themselves, who had put "red propaganda into their pictures," such as *Mission to Moscow.*[177] Could it be that such a film revealed a pro-Communist bias on the part of these moguls—a bias they shared with their co-religionist, the alleged "Stalin of Hollywood," John Howard Lawson? Would this explain why these strikers thought they could strike militantly with impunity? Was this a conspiracy so immense that it implicated capital and labor alike?

Most analysts, however, were not looking for Reds in the executive suites, but in the halls of labor. One friend of MGM Studios was "very anxious" for Warren to meet with Roy Brewer of IATSE, for "this man has information that the strike and pickets are dominated by Communists to a greater extent than any strike he has ever known."[178] This was no longer a "jurisdictional dispute" said William Wilkerson of the *Hollywood Reporter,* but a fight against Reds.[179]

The riot at Warner Bros. hit Hollywood—and the nation—like a thunderclap. The cult of celebrity meant that the public had a ravenous hunger for the most inane details of this star-dominated industry. Thus, when news emerged from Hollywood about Reds and labor strife, it was bound to grab national attention. George Pepper, a stalwart of the Hollywood left, told a member of the Democratic National Committee that the strike was leading to "resentment against [the] Democratic Administration" and has "profoundly affected our power to mobilize this community behind progressive legislation." [180] He, too, had miscalculated. The White House was worried more about being associated in the public mind with Reds than in getting left-wing votes.

Still, this riot in early October was simply the beginning of a chaotic period of disorder. Days later strikers were picketing Paramount on "Van Ness Street at [the] Lemon Grove intersection. Assembling across the street opposite the picketers were 'IA workers.' At a prearranged time officers started clearing the way for the line 'crashers' who started their spearhead simultaneously with the officers maneuvering of picketers to clear a path. The officers used their clubs to force pickets back." [181] RKO and Columbia were closed down by pickets, some of whom adopted the tactic of "sit-down picketing" forcing mass arrests.[182] Mass picketing closed down Universal; the strikers' ranks were "swelled by the addition of nearly 500 machinist union members from Lockheed." [183] At a Paramount theater there was "a regular free for all. . . . The fellow who started the fight was carrying a white handed gun." "Evidently," it was said, "the producers aren't above getting hoodlums planted around a picket line." [184]

Things had calmed down a bit at Warner Bros. It was so "relatively peaceful that the studios called back Dance Director Leroy Prinz—who had been twice slugged by pickets last week—and 20 dancing girls"; he could now continue working on *Night and Day*.[185]

There were reasons for this relative quiet. One CSU supporter went to Warner Bros. at noon on 10 October and "was astounded to find only four pickets at [the] main gate two at [the] side gates." "Everyone arrested was carted off to jail, after being held in [the] studio sound stage for 2 hours sans bathroom facilities and without food and having been fingerprinted there." Some of the "goons" were those "gangster scab replacements the IA had fixed up various studios with." The "most incredible thing about the riot was that the firemen and guards who held the firehoses belong to a union affiliated with our group and the brothers wanted to throw the local out of the Conference but were told that the men would be kicked out as of yesterday. A fireman wanted to quit because he refused to turn the hoses on the crowd."

"Everyone directly in the path of the hoses was knocked down and rolled around in the broken glass that littered the street and at the same time gas bombs exploded in the midst of things," it was said. Cappy Duval of IATSE had provided his men with "canes," "blue in color" with "two narrow metal bands around them"; they were for beating pick-eters.[186] Some "of those monkeys—about 25 men up on the parapet which towers over the sidewalk 50 or 60 feet, dropped tear gas bombs down on the pickets just before opening up with the fire hoses. It was a state of siege."[187]

Sorrell, who was no stranger to violence, was not discouraged by the riot. "If they want it bloody, let's make it bloody!" he cried.[188] A studio worker who claimed that Sorrell had broken his jaw and ribs as he sought to enter Warner Bros. realized the CSU leader was not engag-ing in puffery.[189] CSU itself was clearly not an organization of pacifists. Juliette Carr, arrested at Columbia for spitting in the eye of a police offi-cer, claimed, "I had bronchitis . . . and how did I know anyone would be in the way?"[190] Another militant woman striker, Bernice M. Lesher, a thirty-five-year-old office worker, was accused—then convicted—of toss-ing coffee on police officers at RKO.[191]

Because of assistance from other unions and students from UCLA and other colleges, CSU was able to amass hundreds of pickets at a number of studios. "Heavy lines formed again at Warners, Paramount, RKO and Republic" in late October. At RKO, the studio resorted to using buses to "transport workers through picket lines, after picking them up outside the lot at a prearranged point." Still, because of the strike only half of the studios' scheduled films were shooting.

The events of early October tarnished the already fading glitter of Tinseltown. Bette Davis continued refusing to cross the lines, thus help-ing disrupt production. Director Lewis Milestone did not find all quiet on this western front; unable to make it to the studio to continue work on *Love Lies Bleeding,* he had his apparently fungible "chores" taken over by Byron Haskins. The Screen Publicists Guild and Screen Office Employees Guild panicked, fearing that the studios would move their offices to Man-hattan and fire their members in anticipation of falling revenues. Mayor Paul Brown of Burbank wanted martial law imposed, which would have meant a suspension of constitutional guarantees.[192] Monogram Pictures, soon to be extinct, revealed sharply declining profits.[193]

"Even executives failed to show up at Universal," the Communists proclaimed with joy, as they scored the moguls for their "switch to gang-ster tactics."[194] In a surreal scene "several hundred cowboys" and stunt men were sent home by Republic Studio since picketing had shut down production.[195] An acute sign of the times materialized when a CSU supporter not known previously as a supporter of Reds felt compelled to say she was "beginning to see why" the Communist Louis Weinstock —"whatever his weaknesses"—"is a very important [leader]."[196] More scribes were beginning to agree. By mid-October, "all of the writers employed" at Warner Bros. had "either been laid off or discharged."[197] It seemed like Hollywood was falling apart—or being radicalized.

Pressure was building for a settlement.

More than 4,000 attended a mass rally sponsored by the Hollywood left and its allies at Legion Stadium. Two resolutions were adopted, one condemning police violence and the other demanding that Truman's Department of Labor and NLRB move to address the underlying issues of the conflict. A "surprise speaker," Russell McKnight, president of IATSE Local 683, indicated that if Walsh's union did not push for a settlement it could face further fragmenting.[198]

Celebrities raised their voices. John Garfield, Rex Ingram, Dalton Trumbo, and John Howard Lawson volunteered to act as observers at the picketing of the studios. They professed to be "deeply shocked at the violation of American civil liberties in the breaking up of picket lines."[199] Aldous Huxley escaped from his writer's warren long enough to join Lockheed workers on the CSU picket line.[200]

Meanwhile, capital was waging its own offensive. Joseph Schenck and "13 top flight producers" met with the L.A. district attorney to demand "mass arrests" and vigorous prosecutions of the picketers.[201] A temporary restraining order was obtained to bar CSU, inter alia, from picketing and "intimidating plaintiffs" with "vile names or words or ridicule" or "cursing at, swearing at, shouting at . . . or making . . . opprobrious, insulting" remarks toward the studios—particularly with "loud speakers."[202] The chastened Jack Warner, who had loosened ties to the trade association of moguls, now saw the need for class solidarity and hastened to tighten this relationship.[203]

It seemed that CSU was not the only one that could miscalculate. The vicious brutality practiced against the strikers had soured a sector of public opinion which at this early date had not been sold completely on the idea that the unrest was all due to Communist machinations. The violence caused more to examine the issues of the strike, and when they discovered that the strike resulted primarily from the moguls' thwarting the will of Local 1421 members, they were prone to sympathize with CSU. Many in the public began to agree that CSU was the appropriate bargaining agent for Local 1421, that the strikers should be reinstated (which, it was felt, would ensure implementation of the first demand), and that existing union contracts should be respected.[204]

By 29 October the strike was settled. It was "nobody's victory," said the *Los Angeles Times* since many issues were to be fully negotiated over the next thirty days and those not settled were to be arbitrated. Agreement could have happened in March, the paper said with exasperation.[205] Perhaps. But their editorial did not acknowledge that the moguls were bent on ousting CSU—and they had failed. Hence, the returning CSU strikers could justifiably see their resumption of work as a victory.

It was a mixed victory, however. Yes, CSU was to be deemed the bargaining agent for set decorators, but IATSE could still confound the issue by encroaching on the federation's jurisdiction over various studio tasks; and a three-person panel was to decide any jurisdictional issues that the two could not work out themselves. The strikers' replacements were to receive severance pay when released and strikers were to return to their jobs. However, IATSE argued, no final determination was made to fire the replacements, only to prevent them from doing the work of the former strikers.[206] The stage had been set for Act Two: driving CSU out of the studios with eager replacements waiting in the wings to take the members' place on stage.

Still, this had been a costly battle for the moguls. They had lost millions during the strike, and at a time of pressing foreign competition, this loss was no wee matter. The virus of unionism had seemed to spread; RKO became alarmed as movie-house managers sought to organize.[207] There were pleasant problems, too. The former scabs were "reporting every morning" to the studios "with nothing to do but hang around and exchange dirty looks, harsh words and threats with their old enemies of the picket lines."[208] As a dress rehearsal for dealing with CSU, the moguls "prevented" those IATSE members who had supported the strike from returning to work. They were "locked out," charged CSU; yet little did the federation know that a similar fate awaited its members in 1946.[209]

The L.A. Police Department had learned a lesson too: it adopted a new training film entitled *Riot Control* in preparation for future emergencies.[210] The FBI also had taken worried note of these events; its local agent was troubled by the "extreme violence, mob riots and . . . general situation of anarchy. . . . [T]he law enforcement authorities seemed to be unable to cope with the situation." Continuing its idea that the walkout was not misfeasance but nonfeasance, the FBI wondered why "the authorities for some unknown reason appeared to be unwilling to make the attempt" to crush CSU and the strike. Perhaps the Jewish moguls were not the only force sympathetic to the Reds; perhaps this infection had spread to the state. Frankly, the bureau was "amazed at the influence of the Communists on the public officials of [Los Angeles]."[211]

As for Sorrell, he had other rivers to cross. A few days after the strike ended, he narrowly escaped what was thought to be a murder attempt.[212] He claimed that he was fired on while pulling out of his driveway in Glendale.[213] He explained that he had been on his way to the airport to catch a plane: "I backed out of my garage," he recalled later, "and when I backed out, a car drove across and filled my car full of slugs. They shot it up." Sorrell called the police, but no culprits were apprehended.[214] He had received anonymous death threats before, but this was the first time "anyone took a shot at him."[215]

Sorrell had other worries also. How CSU workers were being treated after the strike was not "something to brag about. They herded them onto stages and they practically put them in concentration camps."[216] Faced with scabs and moguls still ill-tempered about the strike, CSU members had returned to an unpleasant environment. The Teamsters leader, Joe Tuohy, felt that—despite their sullen reception—the returning CSU members were not "belligerent." They set up "stewards' meetings" and asked for "unity." This cooperative atmosphere had "quite an appeal to the workers and would have led to a strong united rank and file group, but the IA officials stepped in and demanded that such meetings be discontinued." Tuohy, as well, was enduring "more trouble in the last few months than we have ever had," which he blamed on Communist agitation. "We are trying the ring-leader who starts all the trouble on a number of charges. . . . He is the only member who refused to work during the strike. . . . [H]e fraternized with the pickets and was carrying information to the strike committee from our meetings."[217]

This purge was a mere hint of what CSU was to suffer. Yet when the members held their "gala rodeo and all nations show at Wrigley Field" in early November, further troubles seemed like a faraway prospect, for set to join them there were Joe Louis, Eddie "Rochester" Anderson, Roy Rogers, and Dale Evans.[218] These entertainers were on CSU's list of heroes. But the federation had little admiration for Charles Laughton, Nigel Bruce, Basil Rathbone, Donald Meek, and Sabu, who were "not required to enter any studio where there was mass picketing" during the last ten days before the strike's end but did so anyway.[219]

These line crossings were just an indication of a deluge of bad news for CSU. That these actors could turn their back on the federation with little apparent fear of retribution was an indication of things to come. The state legislature decided to investigate those UCLA students who had joined the picket line. Meeting on campus, a state investigative committee was met with cries of "fascists" and "suckers," but it was not deterred.[220] University regents were asked to investigate the students and faculty. "Whether rightly or wrongly," said the *Los Angeles Times,* "UCLA has come to be known during the last 10 years as a hotbed of foreign-type radicalism, a vociferous center for Communist-front organizations."[221] So prompted, the regents voted to "demand loyalty" to the United States, which—presumably—did not encompass support for strikers.[222]

In addition to being painted as Red, CSU was also being portrayed as violence prone. At the trials of those arrested at the studios, testimony was so lurid about "women pickets using filthy language and obscene phrases" that women with more tender dispositions were removed from the room. The brawling CSU was said to have marched at the studio gates in an oval four-hundred strong with four abreast; inside the oval were "goons," and when nonstrikers tried to pass through to get to work, they faced the "other side of the oval." This strategy was employed with "military precision."[223] Sorrell tried to explain the oval: when the police and their helpers "hit the line, they hit it with vengeance . . . so we put the women inside where they wouldn't be hurt, and we put the older men outside of them and the younger men outside of them. . . . So when they hit us, they hit a wall." This defensive tactic, he concluded mournfully, was portrayed instead as a fiendish maneuver.[224]

Pickets were carrying "8 to 10 inch pieces of rubber hose filled with lead and pipe, 6 inch iron bolts, 2 × 4 pieces of concrete, bits of bricks and bottles," it was said in reply.[225] This picketing was led by an ex-convict, Anthony Schiavone, a painter with a San Quentin pedigree, it was maintained.[226] A cry erupted to punish severely those arrested, and a Burbank judge was censured by legislators for not doing so.[227]

Nineteen forty-five was ending on a dismal note for CSU. War veterans were picketing CSU headquarters at Fifth and Western, "some of them in uniform." These picketers were against Communism, they said.[228] CSU's old nemesis Jack Tenney proclaimed that the strike was little more than a "small but full dress rehearsal" of the Communists' "new strategy."[229] Increasingly, millions across the nation were coming to agree with him.

LOCKOUT

The conclusion of the strike did not bring a respite for an increasingly beleaguered CSU. The tagging of its leaders as Reds reached a new level of intensity. Yet CSU's head, Herb Sorrell, continued to maintain a touchingly naive faith in the good intentions of studio executives like Pat Casey and even Eric Johnston; Sorrell even confessed that he had "come to like" the moguls' chief representative, the head of their trade association.[1]

To his credit, Sorrell led a union that—relatively speaking—was a model of democratic unionism. In the leading body of CSU were representatives of the various crafts represented in the federation. Meetings at their headquarters at Fifth and Western were frequent and spirited. This was a major reason why CSU could not be underestimated: it had broad-based strength. But organizations are often the lengthened shadow of one individual, and so it was with CSU and Sorrell's dominating presence. Though outsiders charged shrilly that Communists dominated the union, this concept was laughable. The Communist foundation in the union movement was within the industrially based CIO, not in the crafts, which resisted the idea of socialism and even collectivity. But this plain fact was ignored as the moguls moved to oust CSU from the studios—for all time.

★ It was agonizingly clear that the settlement of the 1945 strike was a mere interlude before the real fight resumed. The FBI office in Los Angeles told J. Edgar Hoover as early as November 1945 that the strike was over but "it now appears that a new strike is underway."[2]

The bureau may have been referring to a series of brushfires that broke out as soon as the strike ended. Initially the AFL threatened that unless the studios got rid of the Film Office Workers Guild, which was chartered when the Screen Office Employees Guild (SOEG) walked out, there would be another strike.[3] A few weeks later SOEG backed up this threat by engaging in a "20 minute work stoppage at Universal" after the studio ignored the union's ultimatum that two hundred workers who had formerly been within CSU—but had departed during the strike—be allowed to rejoin.[4]

CSU was demanding a sizable wage increase, because a planned drop in film production would mean a drop in pay that members simply could not afford; the federation demanded forty-eight hours pay for thirty-six hours work.[5] But then the AFL refused to back a strike over this demand, and three key CSU affiliates declared that they would "not honor . . . picket lines" if the walkout were called.[6]

If CSU leaders had been paying careful attention, they may have noticed the need for an adjustment of tactics. A seven-month strike—during which workers are paid only nominal strike benefits—is extremely burdensome. CSU was spent—in more ways than one—by this strike. A few months after the conflict concluded, a CSU member was killed while trying to burglarize a store, an indication of growing desperation.[7] Another prominent CSU member was arrested "on charges of burglary and receiving stolen goods."[8] A screen extra "turned to safecracking because he was not making enough money as an actor"; this former card dealer had committed "70 burglaries" during an eight-month period.[9] Later Paul Kittrelle, a "film studio worker" was exposed as the "nude burglar."[10] A painter and his film-tech wife were arrested for burglarizing $35,000 worth of loot from the homes of Hollywood socialites: working so closely with the wealthy was difficult without getting the urge to unburden them of their belongings—particularly after suffering through a lengthy and costly strike.[11]

Workers were also facing court dates because of mass arrests, and some were facing convictions. Disunity still plagued the torturous relations between the CSU-connected Screen Players Union and the SAG-affiliated Screen Extras Guild; failure to work out a modus vivendi with the stars no doubt extended the strike, and CSU might have faced a more successful future had it accommodated this key sector.[12]

Local elites, feasting on a steady diet proclaiming Red perfidy abroad and at home, had developed little tolerance for trade union militancy. Los

Angeles, beamed the *Los Angeles Times,* had "the fewest strikes during the war and during 1945 of any large manufacturing center in the nation." The only haze that blurred this bright rainbow of good news was CSU's "jurisdictional film strike," which "was the longest, the most bitter and the most costly of the 35 strikes of 1945. It cost 1,500,000 man-hours of productive time." Though many were aroused with urgency about the rise of the CIO, the *Times* noted soberly that "of the remaining 34 strikes, 20 were called by AFL unions and 14 by the CIO." Over 75 percent of these strikes had begun after V-J day, but the energetic CSU, of course, had struck even before V-E day.[13] The consensus was that there was a chafing problem in Hollywood, and that problem was CSU.

IATSE had its problems too. Richard Walsh was facing considerable opposition in his locals, some of which were planning to unseat him at their next convention.[14] But it was CSU that faced the most jeopardy in 1946. Some CSU workers were disgusted with the AFL's stand-pat attitude and were considering "going CIO or forming 'one big independent union.'"[15] They were not pleased when Sorrell countered that he was "fighting for preservation of trade or craft unions as against . . . an industrial union."[16] At a time when maximum unity was needed by all of studio labor, the opposite reigned. When Sorrell collapsed in his office due to high blood pressure—following an eighteen-day jail term after the Burbank riot—his "very serious" condition appeared to be a metaphor for what was happening to CSU.[17]

"Unhealthy," however, would not be the term used to describe the labor movement in Los Angeles in early 1946. These unions—like their counterparts nationally—were gearing up for a monumental strike wave that was to increase calls for restraints on labor. The CIO in Los Angeles played no small role in planning this wave. By January "every international union" in the CIO central council had formed a "joint strike strategy committee, a central finance committee and a central publicity committee. . . . The finance committee has set a goal of one hour's pay each week from workers who are not on strike and it will also stage giant collection drives in churches, clubs and other groups as well as from progressive businessmen and other individuals."[18] The L.A. CIO set a goal of organizing 500,000 workers in 1946, "its biggest sustained organizing effort since the union boom days of 1937."[19] Communists had significant influence within CIO unions, particularly longshore. But Local 576 of the United Furniture Workers was not atypical either; organized in 1938, half its members were Chicano, and the rest were Jewish- and African American. This 3000-strong local was accused of being a "Red union" and came under assault as it was planning to participate in this massive union push.[20]

The CIO also had developed a political analysis that CSU could well have studied. Big business, CIO leaders warned, is trying to "capture full control of the government." Getting "tough with labor and with our wartime allies has created business 'confidence' in the future. This confidence is based on the hope of keeping labor costs down while prices go up—and securing flush markets both here and abroad." There was "every reason to expect a relatively early collapse of this boom." Consequently, *"every channel of public information will be utilized*—newspapers, radio, movies, public forums, attack on labor, especially the CIO, will be stepped up. A Moscow plot will be discovered behind every economic demand of the unions."[21] [emphasis CIO]

The CIO's sharp analysis often was not mirrored in the rank and file; this divergence sheds light on the concomitant failures of CSU. The General Motors (GM) plant at South Gate, a CIO bulwark, like IATSE, seemed to prefer workers from the South. Though the UAW nationally was known for antiracism, at this shop "racial tolerance stopped . . . at the factory gate. Most autoworkers who accepted blacks as co-workers did not accept them as neighbors." Further, "as some local industrial workers began to feel the benefits of unionization—in higher wages and better job security—they drifted beyond the sympathy of non-union workers." Thus, GM went on strike from the winter of 1945 to the spring of 1946, but at this plant "the enthusiasm dwindled" by the second week of the strike.[22] It was hard to maintain the consciousness and bellicosity so necessary for the successful prosecution of a strike when illiberal forces like racism and a dearth of class solidarity were so pervasive. This was no less true for CSU.

★ As the spring of 1946 approached, CSU continued to be plagued with divisiveness. A CSU rally at Hollywood's Legion Stadium was not only boycotted by IATSE but also by SAG, its Extras Guild, and a number of other AFL unions.[23] When Sorrell said he might call a strike "within 48 hours" about half the unions in his federation dissented.[24] Other AFL unions were putting Sorrell on trial for "pro-Communism"; this contention led to a floor fight at the AFL convention in San Francisco.[25] The International Association of Machinists was splitting irrevocably between pro- and anti-CSU factions.[26] The studios did their part by firing and laying off machinists with CSU ties and by throwing out some

CSU carpenters and painters, too; immediately, remaining CSU members declared they would not work on sets handled by the replacement machinists.[27] The publicists were splitting too.[28] By June CSU, undeterred by this unraveling of the ranks, was predicting that soon all the major studios would be "inoperative."[29]

By July CSU was back on strike. This moment did not appear to be opportune for such a dramatic maneuver. The commotion surrounding Winston Churchill's "Iron Curtain" speech in Fulton, Missouri, had indicated that "Communism" was going to be even more of an issue than it had been in the recent past—and CSU was allegedly "Communist." Yet, despite labor disunity and other impediments, CSU prevailed.

IATSE refused to cross the lines—as did prominent actors like William Powell[30]—and within hours CSU had won a stunning 25 percent wage increase, along with a thirty-six-hour workweek with time-and-a-half pay for any overtime. These "new wage increases," the *Los Angeles Times* announced ominously, placed studio labor "considerably above the wages paid to comparable workers in other Los Angeles industries."[31] Was the seditious message being sent that labor militancy paid dividends?

The oft-criticized Sorrell also managed to broker the "treaty of Beverly Hills," which was thought to have brought a rapprochement with the studios. The agreement was made with his typical élan. While pickets were still marching, he drove past Paramount to see how his forces were doing; he heard that Teamsters were calling a meeting to force their men to go through the lines. One worker asked Sorrell to go to the meeting but he was reluctant; however, after someone insinuated that he was frightened to attend, he went. "When anybody dares me I go," said the bold and sneering Sorrell. Joe Tuohy, the Teamsters' leader, didn't want to let him in, but was forced to do so after some members demanded Sorrell's presence. Tuohy was booed. Sorrell, on the other hand, spoke for over two hours to the attentive audience. Then in walked Roy Brewer and Cappy Duval of IATSE, Sorrell's intractable enemies. The leaders talked and decided to meet with studio executives, which led to the treaty that was designed to resolve lingering disputes.[32]

The good news continued for CSU. Its Screen Publicists Guild won a representation election over competitors.[33] NLRB issued an unfair labor practices complaint against ten studios as an outgrowth of the 1945 strike.[34] Earlier a compromise had led to the cessation of the mass trials stemming from the 1945 strike: of the 1,100 defendants, 300 pleaded guilty and the rest were freed.[35] Later the judge, under pressure, scuttled the deal, but the case against the defendants was evidently not very strong.

At the IATSE convention a formidable opponent of the leadership—who had only lost a board position by a six to four vote—backed CSU and "asserted that Browne-Bioff men still hold power in the union."[36] Another important player, the Screen Writers Guild, was engaged in a raucous debate as to whether it should alter its official position of not joining in strikes; this shift too was good news for CSU.[37]

But in some ways this good news was a "false positive," suggesting that CSU faced a situation more rosy than the actual circumstances warranted. For rumbling in the foreground could be distinctly heard the none-too-distant roar of anticommunism. Though Walsh had only narrowly won re-election, he was given the right to expel Communists from the ranks when he saw fit—without any appeal.[38] Matthew Woll, a top leader of CSU's own AFL, warned that his organization would lead boycotts of any films featuring Reds.[39] Increasingly, protest was being associated with Communists—and both were discredited.

The popular columnist Victor Riesel exclaimed, "[S]how me a mass picket line and I'll show you Communists trying to get into the act." Seeking to turn CSU's strength with women trade unionists into a liability, he added, "[S]ometimes the comrades dispatch their be-sweatered cigarette girls with hot coffee and glamour to approach the pickets. . . . Sometimes the leftwingers use a slick jive band and female hep-cat comrades to attract the strikers to regular Communist dances."[40]

A military intelligence operative derided the Communists' "$5000 a week radicals," an obvious threat to CSU's more affluent allies. The "combined beauty and genius" of these stars had "become an important part of the Communists' propaganda machinery."[41] Included among this crew, it was said, were Talli Wyler (wife of director William Wyler), Gene Kelly, Vincent Price, Sterling Hayden, and others.[42] "The Communists have dug into the movie industry like ticks," yelped a local newspaper; the party, it was alleged, "gets more money from Hollywood salary and wage earners than any other source, including Moscow." The press warned of the making of another *Mission to Moscow* by these "Hollywood Fat Cats."[43] When Norval Crutcher, a key IATSE operative, tightened his ties with CSU in early 1946, many felt threatened.[44] CSU was collaborating with the Emma Lazarus Club, the steamfitters, the jewelry workers, and others, but what seemed to attract attention was the Communist connection.[45]

There were other troublesome signs. When redwood lumber workers went on strike in July 1946, "strike-breakers" were recruited from the "skidrows of San Francisco, Sacramento, etc."[46] Carpenters and their allies in response decided not to touch "hot lumber"; at the same time carpenters were becoming intensely worried about the trend toward "prefabrication of housing," feeling that this practice might cut into their employment prospects.[47] The carpenter question was to be the crux of the 1946 lockout, and these workers were obviously in a jittery state about their future.

Weeks after this contretemps involving redwood workers, "three masked men broke into the strike headquarters of the printing trade unions. . . . Don Steep, the lone occupant at the time was said to have been beaten into a state of unconsciousness and securely tied." The office was wrecked. After that an oil workers' strike reached "violent heights." World War II veterans—an increasingly conservative force—formed the "Yardbird Veterans' Political Association" and offered to recruit scabs. A GI trucking company was formed to cross picket lines that Teamsters would not violate. In turn, when the CIO Brewers Union went on strike, "truckloads of scabs, herded by Los Angeles police and by the Teamsters, daily rushed the . . . workers' picket line." Teamsters clashed with electrical workers; machinists crossed swords with carpenters; the Brotherhood of Railway Trainmen fought the Amalgamated Association of Street, Electrical Railway, and Motor Coach Employees; the welders battled the machinists. The war's end ushered in a disordered, often violent scene in labor—frequently involving the kind of jurisdictional disputes that had become de rigueur in Hollywood; this pandemonium was not conducive to trade union unity.[48]

Disturbing signals proliferated as the moment approached for the lockout. In late August 1946 longtime CSU ally Jeff Kibre was indicted; he had become an organizer for the International Fishermen and Allied Workers and had been charged with violating antitrust laws after he organized boycotts and picketing to improve his members' livelihood.[49] The Hearst-owned *Los Angeles Herald-Express* was on strike, which meant that once work resumed this press mogul would be even more ardent about the need to weaken or eliminate unions.[50] A nationwide musicians' strike was threatened, which reminded the public of the volatility in the entertainment industry that CSU had come to symbolize.[51]

There were technological developments that did not augur well for studio labor either. Fred Pelton, a "producers' labor administrator," had devised a "system of studio design" that could reduce the need for workers. It involved a "number of stages nestled close to each other. A power center is located at [the] most convenient point, thus requiring a minimum amount of electrical cable. Various types of studio workshops are compactly laid out adjacent to the stages. The entire industrial area of the studio is serviced by rail streets with huge railroad turntables located where needed." It could "result in a 30% saving in costs of set construction and operation." RKO and Columbia were among the studios that had "evinced deep interest in the new studio design."[52]

Thus, despite the July 1946 victory, CSU was not in a position to take on a life-or-death struggle in September 1946; but that was precisely the position it found itself in.

At a meeting of "major CIO and independent unions" it was noted that "management has devised a new, powerful strategy to smash unions. This new strategy is . . . to force a lockout with impossible demands and widely publicize the lockout as a 'strike,' then bargain unions down to the lowest possible minimum and stall final settlement to starve out the union members and their families."[53]

This "new strategy" was precisely what was deployed against CSU.

Obviously, this development was anticipated; yet the cascading whirl of events that accompanied the turn from the popular front to the Red Scare often interfered with foresight.

Still, all along came indications that something big was afoot.

★ It was hard for CSU to focus on structural and strategic changes in the industry—no matter how far-reaching—when the federation was bogged down in jurisdictional contests with IATSE. These confrontations led directly to a lockout of CSU by the studios in September 1946.

This dispute had emerged as a result of the 1945 strike. The conflict concerned whether CSU carpenters or IATSE grips would have control over "set erection." When this task was awarded to the latter, the stage was set for the liquidation of the former.

As a result of the 1945 strike and the subsequent messy working situation, in which the studios had replacements doing CSU functions, a three-man team from the AFL was established to arbitrate disputes. Unfortunately, none on the team knew much about the bizarre intricacies of studio labor, and besides, recent indications suggested that the AFL brass was not exactly enamored of CSU. So in December 1945 the team awarded "set construction" to IATSE, sending CSU into conniptions. Then in August 1946 the three AFL men reversed field, but IATSE declared their reversal null and void. Weeks later CSU proclaimed that unless erection was done by the carpenters, they—and other CSU members—would not handle these "hot" sets. Producers, naturally, sided with IATSE, stating that the December 1945 decision was binding.[54]

The three-man panel that had made the initial decision included three AFL vice presidents: postal worker William Doherty, barber Felix Knight, and railway worker William Birthright. The men had only thirty days to investigate this issue of jurisdictional conflict, which had stumped experts for decades; and they visited only one studio. By suggesting that carpenters would control "all trim and millwork" while IATSE would have "erection of sets," the team injected a new level of complexity in an already complicated workplace.[55] The men's leader, William Green, "was in a state of general confusion himself about the situation in Hollywood." Apparently he "had been told that the [CSU] people were all Communists," and he was "reluctant to make a clear-cut statement in which he would be taking sides with a group of people who had been described to him as Communists."[56]

B. B. Kahane, a vice president at Columbia, conceded that an AFL arbitration decision in December 1945 granting "set construction" work to IATSE "changed the practice that had been going on in the studios for many years." The Jesuitical distinction between "erection" and "construction" was deemed critical, though it was evident that before the strike, set building was a carpenters' function and this classification changed only when they walked out. This dispute was not at issue during the July 1946 strike, nor was it addressed in the treaty of Beverly Hills.[57] For years, as Sorrell noted correctly, carpenters had built sets while grips had taken them apart, put them away, brought them back, and set them up or erected them. Grips used hammer and nails, but they always erected what had been already constructed by carpenters.[58] Pat Casey agreed that the "grip handles the sets after they are made. He ties them up, and fixes them and braces them and then takes them down and puts them away and stores them and brings them back to be used again."[59]

There was much at stake. If Carpenters Local 946 won "set erection work," it would have had "additional employment for 500 men, with another 250 jobs depending on interpretations of property work and the term 'miniature sets.' Many lucrative jobs were at stake"—and increased dues payments to the local's coffers besides.[60]

Andrew Mackay, a carpenter with Scottish roots, told Congress that after he went to the studio that momentous day in September 1946 he was ordered to leave before he even had the opportunity to declare whether he would work on a "hot" set. Harry Beal, a carpenter foreman at Columbia, was dismissive of his IATSE counterparts. "These men are not carpenters," he declared. "I can state that, because I have had those men under me at the Sunset lot. When you give them plans, I have to discuss the plans and bring the foreman back several times to show him with reference to it and he has not completed his work properly and the men, it is pitiful that is all there is to it. It takes three or four of these men to do one man's work, and it isn't half done."[61] Beal's words fell on unconcerned ears: this jurisdictional dispute over set erection had been constructed to oust CSU from the studios for all time.

By the "24th or 25th of September," in 1946 said carpenter James Skelton, "all of our men had been locked out by the major studios." They were "not asked to work on hot sets"; they were simply "fired." "We never called a strike," he protested. Repeatedly in the ensuing months the carpenters had requested a meeting with the studios but were rebuffed.[62]

This development was not accidental. In September 1946 Roy Brewer confessed that he met with studio executives, SAG leader Robert Montgomery, and other actors at Hollywood and Western. They discussed the suggestion that theaters and studios be closed down nationally. A plot was hatched to create "hot" sets that would presumably force carpenters, painters, and other CSU workers to walk out. As it turned out, those who did not leave were asked to do so.[63] At a congressional hearing in 1947 Y. Frank Freeman of Paramount was confronted with notes from these secret meetings. IATSE had denied the notes' validity, but Freeman conceded their "integrity," as they were taken down by Victor Clark, an aide to Pat Casey.[64] The guilt-ridden Casey himself confessed to Father George Dunne, a CSU ally, that he had leaked these notes which showed clearly that the lockout had been "deliberately promoted, manipulated by the producers, together with the IATSE leadership." Why did Casey admit to his action? It was a form of "[Catholic] confession" said Dunne.[65]

Charles Boren, a vice president at Paramount acknowledged that the CSU carpenters' final checks had been made out before the unionists were asked to work on "hot" sets, further confirming that the lockout was no accident: it was a well-defined plan designed to oust CSU from the studios.[66]

"Those carpenters were removed, some by being told to leave the studio and some by being physically removed from the studio," said Zach Cobb, the carpenters' attorney. After their ouster, they could return only to an open shop—in violation of the agreement ending the July 1946 strike and in conflict with IATSE's closed shop policy. Such a situation would have created an even more conflict-ridden "dual system of operation."[67]

In the midst of the lockout *Variety* reported that "curbed by strike-bound Hollywood studios, high domestic production costs and foreign quotas on U.S. pix imports, an increasing number of American films are being diverted to production in studios of other countries." This trend was to continue. The studios were also "striving to wrap up lensing on as many pix as possible in view of the current labor strife"; thus, "Fox has brought into the cutting room all eight films slated for release during the first quarter of 1947." This hurried filmmaking's impact on quality was undetermined.[68] Inside the studios there was worry about a work slowdown in sympathy with those being locked out.[69] This was no trivial matter since the "studios were bulging with new story acquisitions."[70] Yet with 130 unrelated films in the can or in the cutting room and with a "minimum number of pictures in production, the studios apparently were not caught napping by the strike [*sic*]."[71]

Nevertheless, the studios were damaged by the lockout. SAG was informed that "over twenty-five productions have been postponed or abandoned for the duration of this controversy; shooting and processing of color film has been discontinued; 'dailies' are being delayed and inexperienced workmanship retards current production to a snail's pace. As a result, more and more actors are unemployed every week."[72]

SAG, still smarting over its disputes with CSU about jurisdiction over extras, had voted 2,748 to 509 to cross the picket lines.[73] But SAG voted "overwhelmingly" to defeat a motion by Ward Bond requesting more "police protection" at the studio gates so that he and others could more easily cross the picket line. Gene Kelly led the fight against this motion. Ronald Reagan, who was in the midst of a political metamorphosis, revealed that his transformation was almost complete since he "previously had favored the board of directors order for actors to go to work rather than respect the lines." Reagan's comrade Frank Sinatra—the "bobby-sox idol"—who too was undergoing a conversion from left to right, but was "generally considered liberal" at that point, "spoke sharply in favor of going through the lines." Karen Morley's effort to defeat the motion to cross the lines was turned back[74] at this gathering that produced "one of the largest attendance records in the organization's history" and included all of the "big-name film stars."[75]

Actors were not as bad off as screenwriters, who had been handed a ukase by the moguls demanding that scripts henceforth stress "positively the ideas of free enterprise."[76] Their guild resolved to aid any member who refused to cross the lines and as a result was victimized by a producer. Many reclusive writers were not accustomed to the "firearms" that had been "used in the vicinity of at least one of the studios."[77] They were unsettled by the presence at studio gates of police officers with no badges or badge numbers who felt free to bash picketers with impunity.[78] During the 1945 strike, their guild was subjected to "disruptive tactics" and worse to keep members from backing CSU; some members were worried about harsher tactics in 1946.[79]

★ The peremptory manner in which CSU was ejected from the studios led to discord that rivaled the Burbank riot of 1945. Painters were beaten as they tried to enter Warner's.[80] Picketers hurled "rocks through buses carrying workers" across picket lines. Selznick had to stop production on *Little Women* and *The Paradine Case* due to this strife.[81] Other studios were filming on location—and discovering valuable lessons in the process—as they sought to escape the unrest. From a height of 1,000 feet, Sorrell—an accomplished pilot—directed his troops and thereby avoided a court order barring him from the picket lines.[82] Undeterred, the studios chased him with their own airplanes; "in order to duck" them, he recalled, "I would have to fly way out in the ocean until I got clear out to where [they] thought I was going to China, then I would come back and land at a different airport." Another time Sorrell "landed in a berry patch, due to the fact that someone fixed the plane on me"— i.e., sabotaged it.[83]

Meanwhile, there was a "near riot" at MGM as 500 pickets confronted scabs.[84] Taking careful note, Joan Crawford refused to cross the picket lines, while IATSE members were threatened with dismissal if they emulated her.[85] All the while, cameras recorded this real-life drama for possible use in subsequent court cases.[86] In response, wily picketers "used mirrors to slant sunlight into the lens of cameras that were being used by the studios to make a record."[87]

At first Sorrell was tactful, reminding his troops that he didn't "want anyone doing anything to those who cross picket lines, especially actors." He personally "stymied an acid throwing plot." But that attitude quickly changed. Because of expected violence, the ultra-chivalrous Sorrell conceded that he would "rather not see any women pickets." Being behind bars did not frighten this macho leader either: "Jail isn't so bad," he declared, "I had some of it. You get a nice rest."[88]

Soon Sorrell's soothing rhetoric changed and he began spouting words of fire. "There may be men hurt," he warned, and "there may be men killed before this is over but we're in no mood to be pushed around any more!" Sorrell brought to the picket lines a "newly developed far-sounding megaphone with electric power from a battery" that boomed his voice far and wide. However, his words did not influence Raoul Walsh, Mickey Rooney, Greer Garson, Esther Williams, Red Skelton, Clark Gable, and legions of others who steadily crossed CSU picket lines.[89]

By the second or third week of the lockout, CSU recognized that this was not just a battle to return to the studios—it was a battle for survival. Newsreels with overheated narration brought to a larger public the story of this conflict, which had reached "new heights of bitterness."[90] New picketing tactics were deployed at MGM to block entrances to the studio. Limited to eight pickets in a line at any one time, CSU members kept up what was termed a "shuttle" system of picketing, whereby eight were on the line, eight leaving it, and another eight going in every minute. This meant that CSU could amass more picketers while technically not violating the court order limiting its numbers.

Pickets not on the line stalled their automobiles at the main labor entrance, blocking the gate for minutes at a time. Still, three buses cracked the line with the aid of several hundred law officers. The motorcade's exit was blocked by a sit-down, which delayed departure until officers had arrested twelve of the pickets. Buses were bombarded with bricks and other missiles, causing significant damage. About fifteen people, both pickets and police, were taken to hospitals, suffering from heavy clubbing.[91]

There was open fighting with fists, clubs, stones, and bottles at MGM, involving CSU members—many in WW II uniforms and some wearing battle ribbons—and their opponents.[92] "We fought for our country" one CSU member proclaimed, "now we are fighting for our jobs. Our late president, Franklin D. Roosevelt said this was right."[93] Some of these uniformed veterans carried a U.S. flag and sang the "Beer Barrel Polka." Others carried banners calling for "upholding the ideals of Franklin Roosevelt."[94] "One minute," said one reporter, "deputies fought demonstrators . . . the next minute the officers stood at attention as marchers paraded past with the American flag."[95] This invocation of Roosevelt and the flag was poignant, revealing a perhaps sophomoric faith that elected officials were on CSU's side and not on the side of those who raised funds for their political campaigns. Yet the blows from police batons and the ensuing silence from the White House quickly disabused many about which side the government was on.

When this realization began to dawn, trade unionists reacted with even more uncontrolled fury. CSU members at MGM smashed windows of vehicles seeking to cross the lines, yanked hoods open, and ripped out engine wires and radio antennae, and even attempted to overturn six of the fifteen cars headed through the lines. As a bus at 6472 Santa Monica Boulevard was filling with IATSE members, twelve rushed them, ripped open their pockets with knives, seized their wallets—and a fight was on.[96] Protesters scattered tacks in the path of movie stars' automobiles.[97] Thousands of onlookers shouted jeers, booing and uttering foul language. CSU members mocked police, goose-stepping and crying, "Heil Hitler." Another bus carrying IATSE members had its leather seats slashed with knives; nearly every window was broken, sugar was deposited in its tank and the wiring system was torn out. One deputy, who had been knocked down, was kicked into unconsciousness before fellow officers with drawn, cocked guns rescued him, while picketers cried, "[K]ill him! kill him!"

Father George Dunne, a CSU sympathizer, recalled "a man being carried across the street by four policemen. Two of them were holding his arms, one each, and two carrying his feet, one each. They were carrying him like a sack of wheat along the street. A fifth policeman was going along with them and smashing his fist down into the defenseless face of this man."[98]

Inside the studios Roy Brewer reported that his IATSE members were being attacked by CSU members who had yet to be locked out. They were "badly beaten" and "threatened," he charged, and their tools were stolen. Simultaneously Brewer was asserting that "the morale of the picketers is breaking" and that the "picket lines are weakening daily and that picketers in conversation . . . indicate that they are disillusioned."[99]

"Mrs. Madelyn Thomas, wife of Julius Thomas, Carpenters Local 946," was not "disillusioned." She was in charge of first aid for film victims of goon and police violence. Bearing a "French accent," she had "two sons with the heroic French who fought Hitler" and saw her work on the picket line as an extension of their labor.[100] "Hungry pickets" were consuming "100 pounds of coffee, 200 dozen doughnuts and twice as many sandwiches—every day." This feast was organized by CSU's "women auxiliary."[101]

Madelyn Thomas was kept quite busy, since the tumult of the picket lines continued throughout October 1946. At one point three thousand pickets paraded the streets of Los Angeles armed with loudspeakers, banners and placards. The marchers started in front of Columbia where police ordered the demonstrators to break up on the grounds that they had no marching permit. Instead the marchers toured the town, making stops at Paramount, RKO, and the Technicolor film laboratory. Along the route, marchers were jerked out of line and herded into waiting patrol wagons for transport to the Lincoln Heights jail.[102] Later stink bombs were released at seven first-run movie houses at the "peak of Saturday night business."[103]

A turning point during the lockout came in mid-October when IATSE members who worked at film laboratories went on strike in solidarity with CSU. These workers were "very key," said Roy Brewer; "before a set can be torn down they require that they be able to see the set on film." The workers "shut down" the lab while there were "20 million unprinted negatives in their plant at that time." "It was really a crisis," he sighed. But Brewer was up to the challenge: "we moved in . . . and took charge of the laboratory local." The "most noted violence took place" then "in the form of five bombings. Five of the homes of our members who broke with the pro-Communist membership were bombed."[104] IATSE tried sixteen elected officers of Local 683 and declared them "former officers."

Though Brewer did not admit it, his takeover was touch-and-go for a while. At the local's office at 6461 Sunset, preparations were made to resist, including men on the roof twenty-four hours a day. When Brewer and his invaders first arrived at the headquarters, they were met by several dozen husky men with baseball bats. After a heated argument, Brewer and company left.[105] At Technicolor Film Corporation, 38 were arrested in a two-hour period shortly after dawn, while an angry throng of 2,000 objected. One woman threw a cup of coffee into the face of an officer, another smacked an officer on the head with her handbag.[106]

The studios were hurting. *Sinbad the Sailor,* a color film originally scheduled for a holiday showing was replaced by *It's a Wonderful Life,* a black-and-white feature; inside sources claimed that the switch was due to "technicolor print difficulty" brought by the IATSE job action.[107] John Martin of Local 683 boasted that "technicolor is completely shut down, black and white is barely struggling. 27 productions are held up, 8000 feet of film was burned by a scab chemist."[108]

Fifty years later, fifty men recalled that as rookie LAPD officers they never made it to their graduation because they were sent hurriedly to battle protesters at Technicolor Motion Pictures, the *L.A. Times* reported on 23 September 1996. "They spit at us and yelled at us," said Bill Johnson of Burbank. "They had a lot of females in the front row to buffer the males from the police," said another officer. "The crowd started calling us 'black shirts,' 'Gestapo,'" as the officers drew their batons.

The officers were angered by these women. One officer was supposed to return to work at Douglas Aircraft after the war, but refused because he could not handle the fact that women "he had trained were now his superiors." Now he was fighting women toe-to-toe. Just as with race, CSU was subject to criticism because of the dearth of women in its leading ranks; however, it is striking that any residual male supremacist ideas among CSU leadership did not bar them from placing women in the front line, a tactic that often disoriented adversaries.[109]

The press charged that CSU was embarked on a "reign of terror."[110] Mildred Schellenberger, wife of a studio worker who crossed the picket lines, said that she was awakened in the middle of night by a four-pound rock crashing through the front screen door of her home at 6018 Carpenter Street in North Hollywood. Then she received an anonymous telephone call saying, "If your husband doesn't quit his job you're going to be a widow."[111] A Molotov cocktail was tossed at the home of one studio worker who did not respect the picket lines.[112] An IATSE property man was struck in the face with a blackjack as he answered the doorbell at his home. Arson was attempted at the home of one of his colleagues.[113] Subsequently John Darby, a movie extra, was beaten to death.[114] When fire destroyed $50,000 in props at Universal, the finger of suspicion was pointed at CSU;[115] the same happened when electricity at the Consolidated Film laboratory was cut.[116]

Violence, editorialized the *Los Angeles Times,* had given CSU a "black eye"; "bad as the 1945 strike was, the 1946 one is worse for this element of underhanded terrorism and the state must act," the paper demanded.[117] The *Times* worried that mass arrests would be insufficient to halt the picketing since "cases were dismissed both here and in Burbank in wholesale fashion, simply because there were too many of them." Responding, Governor Warren denounced the violence. Later top CSU leaders were indicted for "criminal conspiracy" as a result of the bombings of IATSE workers' homes.[118]

Sorrell was enraged. At a meeting of 7,000 he insisted that the studios were doing the bombings and were the central culprits in the wave of violence. The moguls had imported "known Chicago and Detroit gangsters," he bellowed. Few were listening, however. The joyous page-one banner headline of a local newspaper, "GOP landslide sweeps nation" was the public's response.[119] A few days later the state responded to this clear electoral message and ignored concerns about the inefficiency of mass arrests when 700 were corralled at Columbia in one of "the largest mass arrests ever made in California."[120] After two months of the lockout, more than 1,300 had been arrested.[121]

Sorrell had his own complaints about violence. During the lockout he received a threatening phone call. "I laughed," he recalled, "because I get a lot of calls like that from a lot of crackpots. They do all kinds of things to intimidate me and my wife." Shortly thereafter an officer—or someone in a police officer's uniform—pulled him over as he was driving, handcuffed him, then bopped him on the head. "When I woke up," said the dazed Sorrell, "I had my hands tied behind me and my feet tied up to my hands." Sorrell claimed that he had been beaten and dumped in the desert, fifty miles north of the Mojave.[122] Luckily, he recounted, he was found in a ditch by a "passing motorist." He escaped with a "battered eye and friction burns" on his "abdomen."[123]

The press had no sympathy. A biting editorial hailed the studios for not meeting with CSU until it renounced "violence." Sorrell, the press chided, "seems to [have] no face-saving exit from an impossible situation." He had to "admit he called a strike [*sic*] he can't win, and reporting to hungry members he has got nothing for them. . . . [H]e seems to have no alternative."[124] CSU's "hungry members" were indeed suffering; one stressed film worker even killed himself, his spouse, and his rival for her affections.[125] Meanwhile, the studios rewarded IATSE with 25 percent wage increases.[126] This message was difficult for studio labor to ignore.

IATSE reciprocated by taking an ever harder line against CSU. Paul Perlin, a member of IATSE Local 80 went to his union meeting in October 1946 at 6472 Santa Monica Boulevard. He objected to a point on the floor and his business agent, William Barrett, accused him of being a spy for painters and carpenters. Said Perlin, "approximately a dozen people whose faces were unfamiliar . . . started shouting simultaneously, 'throw the bastard out' . . . then they made menacing moves in my direction." The very next day his supervisor informed him of Barrett's command that he be refused further employment at Enterprise Studio, though he had worked a decade in the industry and was a combat veteran. "It is imperative," pleaded Perlin, "for my living and that of my family and for the safe delivery of my unborn child that I be permitted to earn a living. . . . I have no other source of income than my work at the studios," he implored futilely.[127] The poor unionist must have confused IATSE with CSU, where freewheeling debate in meetings was the norm. With the departure of the "Communist" CSU, free-speech limitations became rampant among studio labor.

There was another difficult directive to ignore: quite simply, the moguls were able to use their influence with the courts and police to overcome CSU. Police brutality toward picketers was par for the course in Los Angeles.[128] The Merchants and Manufacturers Association, founded in

1896, "commanded the allegiance of 80 to 85 percent of the city's large firms." These connections between the police and "the large employers in Los Angeles became so lucrative for the former that after a subsequent maritime strike, a police official recommended that 'each executive from each oil company in the harbor district should be invited and entertained at our police range for lunch.'"[129]

The moguls' affection for the police was no less intense. Rex Zimmerman, an officer with the police department of Culver City, claimed that "the entire Culver City Hall were placed on the Metro-Goldwyn-Mayer studio's payroll"—including himself. He was paid in cash at the rate of $1.50 per hour, in addition to his regular salary. There were "no records kept and no receipts." Funds were also provided to "police who came from El Segundo, Manhattan Beach, Palos Verdes Estates, Redondo Beach, Hermosa Beach, Inglewood, Santa Monica, Maywood, Southgate and Huntington Park." These officers, who appeared in and out of uniform, were paid to do the studios' dirty work. As the lockout was reaching a crescendo, Zimmerman spied the "running down of a picket by a truck owned by the Brittingham Catering Company." After the driver was booked, William Walsh—the MGM personnel director—asked him to drop the charges; he balked and Walsh "became very angry." Zimmerman was suspended and almost lost his job.[130]

This police assistance to the studios irked CSU and its allies to no end. "Traffic accidents and deaths in [Los Angeles] are highest in the world," huffed the film technicians, "but movie producers have hundreds of police officers diverted from traffic to strikebreaking duty."[131]

As a result of this aggressive policing, hundreds of CSU members saw the inside of jails. They attempted to counter this misery by breaking out in song. Here they were aided by Pete Seeger and other members of People's Songs, a left-wing group that contributed their musical skills to protesting workers. Robert Minkus had been jailed after picketing Columbia in mid-November. He faced "four days of indignities and unspeakable crowding, food and filth." Yet he departed with his "spirits high" after "singing . . . songs and composing new verses."[132]

The same thing happened at the Lincoln Heights jail. "Girls who thought they would be depressed, found comfort and a spirit of unity through singing. We wrote our own verses to familiar tunes and used them to communicate between cells."[133] There was singing not only in jail, but on picket lines as well. At Columbia on the day of mass arrests, there were "14 gals" present "with fine, clear voices. . . . This attracted many more guys to the picket lines." After being imprisoned, they decided to start a "hunger strike. This decision was reached by having the word spread via the grapevine and voted on in each cell, which was now organized in true union fashion, with a steward and a committee." Again, "song was the solution" as they communicated through ditties. "We had set up a beautiful and novel communication system," and even the "drunks and prostitutes" responded favorably.[134]

The "drunks and prostitutes," however, must have recognized that their left-wing cellmates lacked influence with the police. This was the province of the moguls.

⭐ csu's relationship with sag was, well, star-crossed. The presence of stars guaranteed that this labor conflict would attract more attention than others then raging nationally, and exposure was good for csu. However, the possibility that stars might use their celebrity on behalf of militant trade unionists filled the moguls and their allies with grave apprehension, thus ensuring that csu would face an extraordinarily determined opponent across the barricades.

The star system had made the Screen Actors Guild essential to the continued health of Hollywood, and if csu had been able to win over the group, it would have gained a major key to success. "You could always get finks to wield a paint brush or hammer," said csu ally Father George Dunne, exaggerating slightly, but the star system made actors harder to replace.[135] In addition, the imbroglio that engulfed csu and sag over who would control screen extras soured their relationship.

Hence, csu members might not have been surprised if they had been allowed to read an internal sag document in the fall of 1946. Pat Somerset of the actors' guild had "talked to Dave Beck of the Teamsters"; he "re-iterated what Dan Tobin had told Edward Arnold and myself a couple of days before, viz.: that the strike [sic] had gone too far to be compromised in any way . . . there were too many complications for permanent peace, and that as far as he was concerned, he was tired of having his members in the middle of constant turmoil, and that the only solution would be to beat the [csu] once and for all, and that although he did not condone the settlement of a strike by physical force, he could see no other way out in this case."[136] The "only solution" rapidly was implemented.

Even studio labor was subject to the magnetism of the stars who had served Hollywood so well. sag helped organize a 24 October 1946 conference call featuring Sorrell, Reagan, Gene Kelly, and the three arbitrators of the December 1945 decision. The purpose was to clarify what the team had meant in its decision and subsequent August 1946 clarification. Kelly, one of the more consistent progressives in Hollywood, still castigated Sorrell, telling him he was "being shortsighted"—"you are going to risk suicide," he warned. Sorrell adamantly disagreed, insisting that "if it is a long strike [*sic*] we can exist. We have a lot of backing. There are many members behind CSU. They may be small here but we belong to big internationals. As you know, we can go out and work. . . . [W]e don't have to go to studios to work." These three arbitrators were disingenuous, he declared firmly to Kelly: "when they talked to you, they talked one language and I know they talked another language when they talked to me."

That evening at 8:30 at Hollywood's Knickerbocker Hotel, SAG met with its erstwhile co-workers from CSU and IATSE. Not surprisingly, it was the "star system" that had brought all of studio labor—including sworn enemies—together. Ronald Reagan wanted the press barred from the gathering since it was "anti-labor." The still liberal actor was evocative as he remarked, "every one of us here realizes that the one hope for progress and a liberal outlook in America and social gains and social welfare depends on organized labor." With passion he declared, "right here in this room for the first time is the one thing that the employers have feared most in Hollywood . . . here is all of labor shoulder to shoulder and side by side exactly the way it should be." He detailed his extensive meetings with AFL boss William Green—who at one time cried from the stress of it all. The pair met with the three arbitrators whose December 1945 decision awarding "set erection" to IATSE had set the current uproar in motion. Amazingly, with Sorrell sitting in the meeting, Edward Arnold declared that William Hutcheson of the carpenters had proposed accepting the December 1945 decision if Walsh of IATSE "would help . . . clean out Sorrell from Hollywood." Reagan also reflected IATSE's viewpoint when he argued that at one time or another all studio unions had scabbed, so why simply act as if IATSE were the sole transgressor?

The CSU leader typically declared once again, "I'm just a dumb painter from Hollywood." Truthfully, he added, "I go off salary when the men go off. I am not one of those stuffed shirts that sit back and draws pay while my men work half time and picket half time, and get by in that way. . . . [P]retty soon I have to borrow money to live." But he was a painter and like his men, he could still work in the construction industry—California was in the midst of one of its periodic building booms. Thus, the painters were in no hurry to return to the studios without a valid contract. He disputed the idea that IATSE and CSU could not work together, a notion that prompted a demand for the latter's liquidation; the two groups were working together right that minute with some "independent[s]" who had been "very good to us."

Future Republican senator George Murphy of SAG objected. Maybe painters could work somewhere else but "actors can't work on the outside." Reagan tellingly agreed: "I am one of those that if people get the idea and stay away from the box office, I may find myself out of work." However, the future U.S. President seemed angrier at CSU than those who had control over his livelihood. "I know I have made a lot of enemies. . . . I have had to have guards for my kids because I got telephone warnings about what would happen to me. . . . Now smile," continued the charming actor, "I don't know where the telephone calls came from." Turning to Sorrell, he declared, "I know I took them seriously and I have been looking over my shoulder when I go down the street." In case Sorrell failed to grasp his intimation that CSU was threatening him, Reagan told him directly, "[Y]ou do not want peace in the motion picture industry."

The dumbfounded Sorrell quickly replied, "Nobody is threatened more than I am. My telephone rings all day long. . . . [W]hen I come up to the house I have all kinds of stumble-bums waiting around the house wanting jobs." He not only had to deal with gangsters threatening him but also moguls who had undue influence on fellow labor leaders.

The studios, he continued, called the three arbitrators who made the December 1945 decision and "told them what to do." Regaining his thread of thought, he told Reagan, "[S]ome of you I like very much, including you, Ronnie, and [I] was very much surprised at that outburst." Gene Kelly interjected forcefully, "[I]f Mr. Reagan attacks Mr. Sorrell, I want it understood that is not the official feeling of this body."

Roy Brewer was angry about the talk he had heard of basically splitting up IATSE by sending cameramen to IBEW, costumers to the International Ladies Garment Workers Union, and laboratory workers to IBEW. The IATSE unions, he proudly proclaimed, "have contributed more leaders to the AF of L in state and federated bodies and central bodies than any other union of our size in this country," and now some louses were talking loosely about dismantling his union. Hutcheson of the carpenters had the nerve to say, "God made the trees, but the wood belongs to us!" A representative from the musicians union reminded him that some of these jurisdictional battles had lasted "35 and 40 years." The unavoidable conclusion, Brewer thought, was that all should expect more conflict.

The most surprising thing about the evening meeting was that even as midnight approached, the attendees were still discussing things amiably—and with no overt red-baiting. Admittedly, this occurred before the November 1946 election, which firmly indicated a new departure in U.S. politics. Finally, at 1:30 A.M. the meeting adjourned. Matty Mattison of CSU thanked SAG, "particularly . . . Miss [Anne] Revere, and Gene Kelly and John Garfield. I think they kind of steered us in the right direction tonight." This event was the high watermark for union cooperation in Hollywood; soon thereafter red-baiting accelerated with breathtaking speed, and purges became virtually compulsory.[137]

As time passed, for example, the mood within SAG changed. President Robert Montgomery was told by one of his Beverly Hills members that the union could "live, I'm quite sure, without them, let us see if they can live without us. I'm quite sure carpenters, painters and set decorators will be thoroughly helpless without someone to act in their sets."[138]

This unforgiving mood had not yet completely blanketed SAG when a special December 1946 meeting was called by 350 of the guild's "Class A members." Reagan, who described himself here as a "New Deal Democrat," spoke fluently, impressing some with his acumen, if not his articulation. Even Edward G. Robinson "absolutely marveled at [Reagan's] clear and sequential presentation." Reagan did not, however, impress Hume Cronyn, who spoke against the future president's viewpoint, which was now less favorable to CSU. Paul Henreid was concerned that "a great many of our fellow actors have become innocent victims of this strike. . . . [Q]uite a number of actors have been unemployed for that reason." Alexander Knox was worried about the quality of the films that were being made: "[S]cripts are being rewritten to eliminate large sets. [T]his also eliminates small parts. . . . [S]tudios are cutting down their list of [contract] players." Some jurisdictional fights had lasted "40 years," he mused, "if we wait that long Van Johnson will be playing the parts now played by Mr. Lionel Barrymore." If CSU was broken, then SAG would be bruised, he counseled. This meeting, which began at 8:30 in the evening, lasted almost four hours. Again, there was hardly any red-baiting. Reagan and Knox were clearly the most effective speakers, and even the former was not that hostile to CSU. Adolph Menjou, who became a premier anticommunist, made the motion to support the SAG board, which was amended to include a call for negotiations between CSU and the studios; the motion passed. Considering that the moguls had sworn off talking to CSU, this vote could be deemed a victory for Sorrell—and a victory for pro-CSU forces within SAG.[139] What was striking about this meeting was that as late as mid-December 1946, anticommunism was not as hegemonic in Hollywood as it was to become a few months later.

What had happened in between to change the environment so decisively? The hearings on Taft-Hartley legislation had sent a clear signal that militant trade unionism would henceforth be viewed as equivalent to Communism. Momentum gathered for a blacklist of those unwilling to observe this edict. Then came the coup de grâce: the smashing of CSU.

Jack Dales, longtime executive secretary of SAG, remarked later that Reagan's performance that mid-December evening propelled him into the presidency of SAG five months later—and arguably, from there, to the White House. Edward G. Robinson opposed him (as did Katharine Hepburn) but he was still impressed by Reagan's presentation.[140] Alexander Knox was less impressed; he remembered that Reagan "spoke very fast. He always did, so that he could talk out of both sides of his mouth at once."[141]

But whatever pro-CSU sentiment existed in the upper echelons of SAG withered in the heat of the postelection offensive against real and imagined Reds. Duke Wales of the Association of Motion Picture Producers shared with Buck Harris of SAG a list of "foreign labor organizations to which CSU sent its appeal for support"; "keep both this information and its source confidential," he advised.[142] Quickly Dales wrote various unions in France, Mexico, Sweden, Australia, and elsewhere, seeking to undermine the CSU initiative.[143] When the supposedly Communist-dominated World Federation of Trade Unions (WFTU) wrote its "dear comrades" at SAG to "agree that inter-union quarrels should and can be settled by peaceful negotiations and arbitration at the various levels of the Trade Union Organization," it was evident that the dirge for CSU could begin.[144] The "Kinematograph Society" of Britain concurred with WFTU—despite a "lengthy communication" from CSU.[145]

Reagan, who later claimed—falsely—that he was a fierce antagonist of CSU in 1946, became exactly that by the time of the blacklist in 1947. If the subsequent recollections of CSU supporters can be believed, his opportunism was egged on by CSU harassment. George Kuvakus recalls that Reagan "had a limousine pick him up at his house, take him to work and they were all armed . . . and they brought him home at night under cover." Kuvakus was a CSU operative, helping the federation out with a "little sabotage work against the movie industry and so forth"; thus, when production moved to Tarzana or the Valley to do westerns, "they had armed guards on all the buses and they armed guards in cars following the buses and so forth. There was talk about blowing up the buses, if possible." Kuvakus and his fellow saboteurs even "approached Reagan's house . . . one morning, waiting for him to come out in his limousine, and most of us were armed, and we confronted Reagan when he [came] out and his body guards pulled out shotguns on us . . . he was lucky to be president I should say because one of the guys says 'Jesus Christ don't kill him!' He come that close[,] let's put it that way. . . . Then the cops chased us. . . . They arrested two guys." [146]

Thus, by the time Congress came to Hollywood in 1947 to investigate jurisdictional disputes, Reagan was in no mood to praise CSU. On the other hand, he had not expressed the relentless anticommunism that marked a good deal of his public life. He did, however, exhibit tendencies that marked his presidency: though he had impressed even opponents like Edward G. Robinson with his fluent presentations, at this hearing Reagan seemed confused. However, he almost seemed to use this confusion as a tactic: he had converted bafflement into an art form. Reagan obliquely referred to having been in "the Army"; he also misstated dates and events at meetings. At one point he said jokingly, "Pat [Somerset] says I am mixed up." Reagan, who had been intimately involved in CSU and IATSE's negotiations with the studios, displayed his storied talent for invention during sensitive moments.

On the other hand, Reagan's testimony in this crowded hearing room may have been affected by the conditions there. At one point, a congressman asked that those who "have come into this hearing with firearms on them" should "hide them behind the door some place because I don't want to issue any order here that people would be searched before they come in here." [147]

★ CSU members soldiered on gamely, claiming that gangsterlike tactics were used not by them, but against them. They were the "victim of gangsterism"; "the list could go endlessly—of injured vets slung into patrol cars; of innocent bystanders brutally beaten; of pickets followed home and sapped by goons." [148] Even a high-level official in city government admitted that "Eastern gangsters . . . are all over the place, attracted by the easy pickings. . . . The truth is, our law enforcers are virtually impotent in coping with the gangster influx or with carefully planned crime." [149] CSU echoed this statement, declaring that the studios themselves were trying to impose a "gangster-controlled government." The district attorney, Fred Howser, was to be replaced by William Simpson, who was "sponsored by Mendel Silberberg"—a Republican and attorney for the moguls—and by Bob Gans, who was known as the " 'Slot Machine King' during the infamous Shaw regime" in Los Angeles. There was an

"alliance of Simpson with the underworld and the motion picture producers," just as "Warner Brothers now controls Burbank and MGM controls Culver City."[150] This effrontery was to be duplicated on the screen,
CSU sniffed, as Warner Bros. was planning to supplement gangster films
with "Russian spy pictures," thus glorifying its mobster ally while de-
faming its labor opponents.[151]

CSU played up the good news: MGM had made only six movies in six
months. This was "less than normal production," and "costs have jumped
to five times what they were." "Re-issues" like *The Bowery* and *Sun Valley
Serenade* had a "bad reception," CSU gloated. With amusement the federation noted that bankers were sweating.[152]

Sorrell was upbeat. CSU was "in much better condition" in mid-
December 1946 after eighty-eight days than after a comparable period
during the 1945 strike. "Scarcely any prints are being made at all," he insisted, due to the "splendid support" of Local 683 of IATSE. Box office
had "dropped 15 per cent."[153] Hal Roach "deserted the Motion Picture
Producers Association," CSU said, "because it is reported he completely
disapproves of the labor policy."[154] "Scab set designers" at work for Fox
at Granada Studios at 672 Lafayette Park were found and routed by CSU's
"mobile pickets."[155] When CSU appeared, construction work was halted
on a number of quonset huts being erected on the RKO ranch in Encino.
The same thing happened at a Warner Bros. unit filming atop Bunker
Hill at Third and Olive streets: about fifty picketing members of Local
683 arrived on the scene and made so much noise that the sound effects
men could not drown them out.[156] An RKO unit shooting outdoors at
Chatsworth had to fold up its tent and steal quietly away when efforts to
"bribe" pickets to stop singing songs out of tune came to nought.[157]

Vincente Lombardo Toledano, the Mexican labor leader, told CSU
that there would be no outsourcing of developing and processing of film
to his country during the lockout.[158] Toledano came to Los Angeles in
February 1947 to address CSU workers and promised—according to the
watchful FBI agent present—to "shut down every motion picture theater
in Mexico for one day in sympathy with the . . . Hollywood unions." Days
later a CSU rally featured John Garfield, Harpo Marx, Eve Arden, and
other stars; $6,000 was raised.[159] Though CSU was in the process of being
purged from Hollywood, with chutzpah they called for "the blacklisting
of those stars who have worked so actively against us."[160]

But upbeat news coverage full of official optimism could not obscure grim reality. By mid-December 1946, charges were being prepared
against 1,300 who allegedly violated a court order by continuing to picket

studios.[161] Deputy City Attorney Roland Wilson said he was preparing for the "biggest mass trial in the history of the United States." A trial of almost seven hundred was planned for February. CSU was beginning to reflect the anxiety as police had to be called to its 5165 Santa Monica Boulevard meeting due to "threats of physical clashes," with Sorrell—predictably—at the center of the dispute.[162]

Ralph Peckham, a CSU member, expressed the sentiments of many when he exclaimed, "I'm tired of dealing with lawyers. I want to go back to painting."[163] Happily, it was reported, the "first break in the solidarity of the defendants" came as five decided to plead guilty and were fined a meager $25 each. This ruling was an invitation to break ranks with CSU—and the invitation was accepted. For those not interested, the city offered another disincentive: all defendants had to attend all court sessions, including the picking of a jury. This decision effectively demobilized CSU, which had to shift from picketing to sitting in uncomfortable, makeshift courtrooms jammed with hundreds.[164]

Assistant City Attorney Don Redwine energetically "spiked" the "rumor" that prosecutions would be dropped if the lockout was settled: this story provided further incentive for CSU to see through the legal hearings to their distasteful end.[165] These proceedings culminated with the jailing of CSU's attorney, Leo Gallagher, because of his vigorous advocacy.[166]

The imprisonment of CSU's attorney signaled that those he was defending faced an uncertain fate at best. For those who were wondering whether they had made the proper decision by aligning with CSU, the studios helped in formulating an answer by "distributing $9,941,000 in back pay" to "members of 12 studio nonstriking [sic] unions."[167] SAG's Screen Extras Guild was to receive a cool $1 million in back pay.[168]

Thus, Joe Tuohy of the Teamsters was able to maintain that the preceding bedlam had "quieted down to routine picketing." Tuohy, like the moguls, felt that "the only real solution to peace in the industry is to lock out the groups that precipitate all the trouble and eventually replace them."[169] Though Tuohy remained worried about the "top goons" of longshore's "Harry Bridges" and their ability to assist CSU, he was elated that by December 1946 the "meetings Sorrell's group calls are poorly attended and the excuses threadbare." Studio executive Eddie Mannix "told" Tuohy that "Sorrell was ready to quit too."[170] Certainly the pair hoped this rumor was true, since the Oakland General Strike, which showed no sign of abating, already was feeding apprehension that the contagion of labor strife could spread.[171]

This fear did not abate when it was revealed that Oakland's painters had participated in the "violent actions" of the dramatic "two-day" episode.[172] Nonetheless, despite the perception that the labor unrest in Hollywood could spread statewide and thus reinforce CSU, by as early as December 1946, the federation had been defeated—decisively.

⭐ However, the reality of this defeat had not dawned in December 1946, and in any event, Hollywood had its own problems. The weakening of CSU, contrary to the opinion of some, had done little to eliminate pressing difficulties.

CSU claimed that by February 1947 "upwards of 35% of studio personnel throughout the industry have been laid off without regard for seniority, speedups have been instituted in all crafts. . . . [P]eople are scared."[173] Hollywood was in the midst of a cutback, pressed as it was by challenges in overseas markets, the impending threat of television, and an antitrust lawsuit. Pat Casey argued that because, among other reasons, "England has shut off their money, . . . the studios have gotten down to probably the lowest ebb that they have been in 20 years, to my knowledge." Thus, he suggested, even if they wanted to welcome CSU's return, they could not, since "the jobs are not there for them to go back to."[174] The smaller studios and independents, scheduled to make 150 fewer films in 1947 than in the preceding year, were scarcely doing better.[175] Films were moving steadily out of Los Angeles with "nine top features . . . to be produced in New York and . . . others will be filmed in Mexico and elsewhere."[176]

This trend accelerated. Mayor William O'Dwyer of New York City produced a five-year "no jurisdictional strike pledge from 12 AFL unions . . . in an open bid to make New York the movie capital of the world." Ironically among the unions representing 20,000 members signing this vow were IATSE, painters, carpenters, Teamsters, and others who had been waging war against each other in Hollywood.[177] Five years later the AFL in Los Angeles had organized a "campaign to halt what it calls the 'runaway' production of films by Hollywood producers in foreign countries," a clear sign that—contrary to certain opinion—the crushing of CSU had done little to resolve the underlying problems in the film industry.[178]

In fact, CSU's demise may have worsened things for the industry. According to a vice president of Loew's, since the release of so many talented CSU craft laborers, "the efficiency of labor has dropped considerably." Though the studios paid carpenters $2.50 per hour and the construction industry generally paid up to $1.95, California was undergoing the "greatest building program we have had for 20 years," thus carpenters—often intimidated by Hollywood's frightful reputation in labor-management relations—could find work outside of the movie industry, albeit at lower wages.[179] Sorrell had predicted this movement; the ability of carpenters and painters to find work outside of Hollywood helps to explain the intransigence of many CSU leaders.

Still, the studios were not exactly hurting either. In 1947 Fox, a key participant in the lockout, revealed a net profit of $22.6 million for 1946, almost double that of the previous year's profit of $12.74 million. Average salaries of executives in the industry amounted to $215,000, while those unlucky enough to be working outside of Hollywood brought home a mere $104,000. Some in the Hollywood suites were garnering almost $1 million in yearly salary.[180] This largesse had escaped studio labor. By 1950, profits had been "far higher than anticipated," but no wage increase was in the works: "1947 wage scales still prevail and will continue under contract until October 1951."[181]

Ousting CSU had done little to calm the troubled waters of the entertainment industry. By September 1947 the CIO was groaning about "reported scabs going through picket lines of [a] strike at Capitol Records."[182] Red-baiting had not halted either. Roy Brewer of IATSE dramatically informed the House Un-American Activities Committee that the disturbances in Hollywood were caused "by Communists"; the 1945 decision by NLRB on CSU was "evidence of Communist influence" on this august body.[183] At first, Eric Johnston—head of the trade association in Hollywood—railed against this approach. He "lashed out" against HUAC, reasoning that if some nations believed that Hollywood was infested with Reds, they could likely boycott the industry.[184]

But a month later he had retreated swiftly. In late November 1947 the moguls, through Johnston's trade association, announced that they would suspend the screenwriters and directors who came to be called the Hollywood Ten until they declared "under oath" that they were not Reds; the industry, it was reported, would "not knowingly employ a Communist."[185] There was dissent at first. John Huston, George Stevens, John Ford, William Wyler, and other leading directors told Speaker of the House Joseph Martin and the HUAC chairman that they were "opposed to communism" but wanted "guarantees of the Constitution," too.[186] But with the decimation of CSU and its progressive voice, picking off writers, directors, and actors became easier. The blacklist had begun.

The practice was endorsed quickly by IATSE, the Teamsters, and most of the Hollywood unions. It was enforced, too. This exclusionary practice, contrary to popular opinion, did not affect writers, directors and actors alone.[187]

The Screen Writers Guild immediately charged into court. Its lawyer, the well-known barrister Thurman Arnold—along with lead plaintiffs that included Oscar Hammerstein II and Richard Rodgers—said, inter alia, that the blacklist was a restraint of trade and an antitrust violation. The organization's journal announced that the effort "to end the blacklist is the most important action writers have had to take in the United States. Either all of us are free to write as we believe or none of us is free."[188]

The Communist screenwriter Lester Cole insisted that there was even more at stake. The industry's "1948 product is the least distinguished in film history," he alleged. Why was this? According to Cole, it was "the result of the sickening spreading plague of the blacklist." With more regret than anger, Cole lamented that "as the subject matter of films becomes more and more limited, it follows inevitably that the number of writers incapable of dealing successfully with the decreasing number of permissible themes will increase."[189] When Daryl Zanuck announced the production of *The Iron Curtain*—which preliminary indication suggested would be not just an anticommunist movie but a bad movie—Cole's warning appeared vindicated.[190]

SAG had been instrumental in the evisceration of CSU, but its rewards for this chore did not seem immediately apparent. The representation of actors was already fragmented among unions—including Actors Equity and the American Federation of Radio Artists, which was soon to encompass television performers—and many feared SAG's share of this pie would shrink. Jack Dales of SAG warned rivals that his union refused to "commit organizational suicide"; SAG did not want a "nationwide merger of all actors' unions." He wondered, "Why should an actor have to belong to two unions and pay dues to both, depending not upon his work but upon the proposed disposition of the film?" Why should "live unions . . . control the live field and the film unions, the film field?"[191] In other words, SAG wanted its rivals to commit "organizational suicide" but SAG itself was unwilling to swallow this hemlock. Thus, there was fear that jurisdictional wrangling could sweep through the field of acting. Ronald Reagan hoped for a "peaceful resolution" of the "television problem," but optimism was waning at SAG headquarters.[192]

CSU spent the years following 1946 enduring the death of a million cuts, though in the months following this pivotal year, Sorrell carried on as if the heady days of the war were still in place.

In January 1947 Pepe Ruiz, the Screen Cartoonists' business agent, voted to give CSU "one half our monthly strike assessment" to "fight against IATSE producer gangsterism."[193] CSU assured him that this gesture was not an unwise investment; the federation's "people" were "holding solid. The Painters have not lost more than 15 men and most of them were not good union men to begin with. The Carpenters likewise have been holding and Herb feels that as long as the men stay out, everything is safe."[194] Sorrell was similarly confident; picketing can "get awful tiresome after the first six months," he confided. But "the hell of it is we have them over a barrel, and they don't have sense enough to realize it yet. They will come to one of these days and then we will settle."[195]

This guileless faith would have been endearing and enchanting if it had not been so misguided. He never lost his faith in the AFL either; yes, the group "stinks," he declared, but of the rival CIO—where some of his Communist enemies had more influence—he said, "when you find you are in it, also stinks in places too."[196] The tragedy of Sorrell was that he was like a man without a country: too much to the left for the rigid "business unionism" that characterized too many in the AFL and not enough to the left to feel comfortable with his natural allies, the Communists and the CIO.

Surely and steadily CSU was dismembered. The studios and IATSE combined to form a rival machinists local, leaving CSU machinists on the outside looking in.[197] That same year, 1947, also saw George Mulkey "a self confessed former Communist" withdraw his electricians from CSU because "too many people in that organization 'supported the Communist party line.'"[198] To be sure, CSU ally Darr Smith was correct when he observed that the electricians and Building Service Employees Local 278 left CSU only after being ordered out by their internationals: their departure was not a desertion. And when the Screen Story Analysts left CSU, it was a result of members' "effort to save the remnants of a weak and staggering local."[199] But motivation—pure or impure—could not obscure the simple fact that CSU was slowly perishing.

CSU Local 1421 in the spring of 1947 moaned, "[W]e are low on funds, members are doing all sorts of unpleasant jobs, sitting in court is anything but fun, assessments are heavy and the cost of living is high. . . . Are we ready to surrender? Let's be clear about it; that is our only alternative."[200] Months later the set designers voted to follow the painters and "permit long-unemployed, impoverished members to go back to work even if it involves crossing the 13-month-old picket lines"; this was approved by a vote of 88–23. Even Sorrell himself approved.[201]

There were still 3,000 workers locked out then, though CSU claimed a figure of 5,000—with 4,000 more, including quite a few in IATSE Local 683—out of work for varying periods. There had been a loss of at least $17 million in wages.[202] The workers' plight was symbolized by Elmer Rusk, a painter in Hollywood since 1903, who now found himself with no income, along with "several operations and a lot of hospital bills." Charles Albright, a carpenter, had been treated for a severe case of ulcers since the lockout. Thomas Hill, another carpenter, had to "build myself a smaller place to keep going."[203] CSU members had been denied unemployment compensation to assist them in overcoming their financial setback, which only added pain to penalty.[204]

The number of CSU adherents was dwindling, not least because of hard times and harassment. Despite this, military intelligence operatives continued to maintain a keen interest in CSU. They had a "complete check" on hundreds of CSU members, including "description, residence, previous arrests."[205] Later they reported that CSU members were "transferring" to IATSE; the former was "slowly becoming a defunct organization."[206]

Predictably, it was the CIO, not the AFL, that lent a hand to struggling CSU members. The organization contacted its affiliates in Los Angeles in an effort to "find jobs" for CSU members who wished to work in "CIO industries"; CSU and Local 683 of IATSE, CIO leaders said earnestly, had "made a big sacrifice for the progressive union cause in Hollywood." CSU members were still "hanging tough"; nevertheless, the "desire" was to "get them placed in decent jobs and to keep track of them—not to force them to scatter to the four winds and be lost to the major movement." There were three groups to attend to: "older men," "women workers," and the "bulk" who were "younger well trained [male] workers in film laboratory techniques but most of whom have some other skill also." CIO unions—auto workers, longshoremen, steel workers, electrical workers—all recommended openings for these castaways.[207]

The painters nationally were helpful—for a while. In 1947 the "Executive Board" met in Manhattan "for the purpose of showing movies of the Hollywood [lockout] of our Sister Local 644." Generously, a vote was taken to determine "whether or not to assess the membership to further help" Sorrell's members.[208] But this aid proved to be too little, too tardy.

The 1947–1948 congressional hearings in Hollywood, however, were a more telling signal of what was happening to CSU. Congressman Carroll Kearns, the former railway worker and teacher who chaired the sessions, was friendly with arch CSU supporter, Father George Dunne.[209] However, Kearns quickly became comfortable with the California lifestyle, riding to the hearings in a "sleek 1947 Cadillac sedan assigned to him by a Metro-Goldwyn-Mayer limousine dispatcher."[210] Particularly in 1948 these hearings became a venue for venting bizarre accusations about Sorrell's alleged Communist Party membership. A metaphor for these sessions was committee counsel Irving McCann's physical assault of AFL attorney Joseph Padway: the spilling over of their heated exchange symbolized the committee's excesses.[211]

Kearns voted for the Taft-Hartley bill, whose passage was prompted in part by the disorder in Hollywood. A poor seer, Sorrell predicted in 1948 that in "the next two years the Supreme Court will annihilate many sections of the bill."[212] Roy Brewer of IATSE also disliked the bill. The anticommunist provisions were not what bothered him; rather, he considered the secondary boycott provisions worrisome. An independent could do a film with "nonunion cameramen. . . . He can hire his whole crew, if he can get them nonunion . . . and that we will be precluded from using our economic strength to protect the wage scales of our members."[213] In short, he feared that someone could undercut his union just as IATSE had coldly undercut CSU. In the end, Sorrell was wrong: Taft-Hartley was not "annihilated." Brewer, however, was right: it did weaken IATSE.

CSU was weakened, then obliterated, by the lockout. CSU member Roger McDonald noted dolefully that by 1947 the organization "began to disintegrate." Contrary to the critics, CSU had been a heterogeneous organization, which soon began to splinter into its constituent elements; "there were so many colors and shadings" by 1947 "that no one could tell who was who. There were right wing Socialists, left wing Republicans and middle of the road Communists." These forces, disgruntled and dismayed by what had befallen them, often assailed one another vigorously—which in turn diluted morale and heightened the devolutionary spiral that had afflicted CSU.[214]

Sorrell told Congress that CSU had been "on strike for 8 months," then "locked out for a year or a year and a half now, we had 1000 to start with, we call a meeting, and we get 600 or 700 or 800 to the meeting. . . . And that is the reason they are not racing back to the studios," he insisted, "and they are not Communists."[215] Was CSU a "lost cause" it was asked in the spring of 1948? "Hell, no," replied Sorrell. "The unions . . . are still in pretty good shape after 18 months on the bricks," he contended. "The majority of our members still belong. On the other hand, the studios haven't made a picture worth seeing since we've been out, and they won't." There was more unemployment among studio labor than at any time since the Great Depression, he maintained. "It took 25 years for most of those skilled craftsmen to get where they were . . . not 18 months." The hiring of unskilled replacements was increasing the cost of labor, contrary to the studios' expectations when they sacked CSU.[216] These contentions may have all been true, but the studios believed that in the long run they were better off without CSU.

By December 1948 "the book finally was closed" on the lockout, with the levying of fines totaling $9,650 on thirty-two of the picketers and jail sentences for five others. In October 1949 the "last victim" of the lockout, Emil Freed—a Communist—was released after serving a one-year jail term; he had been selling party newspapers across the street from the picket lines when arrested. By November 1950 there was "no picketline for the first time in almost five years: the United Brotherhood of Carpenters has called off the token picket line it had maintained ever since the so-called jurisdictional fight that started in 1946."[217] Toward the end, Edmond DePatie, a vice president at Warner Bros., recalled that many were feeling sorry for CSU: at times there was only a solitary picket marching resolutely in front of the studio.[218]

The independents and IATSE leaders did not fare too well either after the defeat of CSU. By 1950 a lawsuit was alleging that the major studios had sought to pound not only CSU but also the independents like Monogram and Chadwick as well.[219] Four years later Roy Brewer was running against his colleague Richard Walsh to determine who was to head IATSE. Brewer, who went on to work closely with future U.S. president Reagan, spoke of the "almost unanimous dissatisfaction with the Walsh administration."[220] Astonishingly, he charged that the Walsh administration was too close to employers; worse, Walsh and his team used "terroristic tactics."[221]

In 1952 the painters union in Hollywood was notified that its charter had been revoked; the union advised its members—all three hundred of them—to seek a new affiliation with another union. This notification followed the Hollywood local's refusal to oust Sorrell as business agent in accordance with the international's wishes.[222] That same year Howard Hughes was so "afraid of 'red' taint" that he closed down RKO. Production had been at a standstill for years, ever since he insisted on scrupulous screening of employees for supposed radical tendencies.[223]

The Communists themselves were the ostensible target of such measures and they indeed were suffering. Admittedly Louis Weinstock, the Communist leader of the painters, was re-elected in 1948—though by a slim margin.[224] Two years later a Communist, Bernadette Doyle, obtained 500,000 votes in California in her race for state superintendent of public instruction.[225] Yet, despite their mutual pain, the Reds and Sorrell were still not getting along. They accused him of "playing along" with Congressman Kearns' committee in a vain effort to cut a separate deal against the Communists' interests—and his own too, they suggested.[226]

At the end, CSU became important as a litigant—albeit a losing one—as the lawsuits it pursued established important precedents in fields like antitrust, along with oil, sports, music, and other fields of law.[227]

CSU sued the major studios and IATSE, charging a joint conspiracy to destroy the federation and independent producers. CSU's claim was that IATSE agreed not to provide labor to the independents in order to curb their output of movies, thereby increasing the value of the majors' product and guaranteeing longer runs of their movies. In return, the studios agreed to smash CSU, thereby increasing the value of IATSE. Independents produced about 15 percent of Hollywood's output, but its products were "far less expensive," averaging 20 percent of the majors' costs. Sorrell's lawyers pointed out that as soon as the affiliates left CSU, the majors would negotiate with them about returning to work. Moreover, the lawyers said, IATSE charged independents more than they charged the majors.[228] Evidence showed that IATSE's Roy Brewer had demanded that independents "discharge all CSU members on pain of losing services of IATSE cameramen, soundmen, props, grips, etc." Monogram Pictures was "told to fire CSU employees at its ranch or the [latest] Johnny Mack Brown would not start."[229] CSU lost this suit, although its claim had undeniable merit. By 1956 Sorrell had lost the court case challenging his dismissal as business agent of Local 644 of the painters, for whom he had served from 1937 to 1952.[230] In a sense, this loss marked the official end of CSU.

★ Besides the obvious factor—the onset of the Cold War and its handmaiden, the Red Scare—there are other reasons that shed light on why CSU, this once powerful labor federation, could collapse, then disappear.

There was the strange relationship between Sorrell and the studios' Pat Casey. As explained by a correspondent of Dalton Trumbo, Casey was an "elderly" man of "considerable personal wealth." He had been a "confidante" of Sorrell for a "great many years." The CSU leader was convinced that he was "shrewder than Casey" and that he got more out of the relationship than his interlocutor. "It is believed, however, that Casey is so shrewd that in the course of these confidential conversations with Sorrell, he actually shapes CSU policy without Sorrell realizing it. Casey is an Irish-Catholic, a Jew-baiter in private conversations (which may be a tactic he pursues in Jew-baiting leading figures in the industry to show Sorrell that he is on the side of the unions)." Glenn Pratt, a CSU leader and "an almost constant associate" of Sorrell, later went into business with Casey. The woman with whom Pratt was "very much in love," Flo Contini, was also the CSU secretary and both were Irish-Catholic—like Casey.[231]

Frank Pestana, who "unsuccessfully attempted to seize control of the CSU from Sorrell in 1947," said that Sorrell was "suckered into putting up picket lines" in 1946 by "assurances from Casey that the producers would fold up in a matter of weeks," though Pestana was "unable to furnish any proof of this allegation." However, "as late as the 1950s" Sorrell was "playing golf with Casey who according to MGM President William R. Walsh loaned Sorrell $5000 when he went into the paint contracting business in the 1950s."[232]

By his own admission, Sorrell thought highly of the moguls' representatives, even though they were the ones who destroyed CSU. This fact was curious at best.

Still, not all of the vast blame must rest upon the broad shoulders of Sorrell. The three-man AFL committee that made the December 1945 decision awarding set erection to IATSE and then reversed field in August 1946 deserves some responsibility. Later the committee muddied the waters even more when in November 1946 two of the three—Felix Knight and William Birthright—"denied authorship of the August 16" clarification; later, "Birthright . . . added to the confusion by" changing his mind and claiming authorship once more.[233] This Keystone Kops routine kept studio labor on edge at a time when confusion was least wanted.

Sorrell's parent painters union was not that helpful either. The painters were past masters at fomenting jurisdictional battles, having waged these internecine struggles with roofers, bricklayers, blacksmiths, and plasterers, to name a few; it was no mischance that their Local 644 in Hollywood was bogged down in similar disputes. Worse, in 1946 as pressure on CSU was mounting in—and by—California, Governor Earl Warren was invited to address the painters' national convention. Of course, he did not offer support to those locked out; instead, he made a veiled though pointed red-baiting attack, which did no good for CSU.[234] Why the painters would provide a platform to a chief antagonist of CSU was hard to understand.

In fact, the AFL was wary of CSU, feeling that it carried the contagion of radicalism internally that it was busily fighting externally.

To win a labor battle against the major studios, CSU would have had to mobilize broad sectors from a wider community. Many of its labor allies were engaged in their own strikes and job actions during this year of agitation, a fact that should have pushed CSU to become more involved in reaching out to an increasingly diverse Los Angeles. The African American community, for example, was growing by leaps and bounds, but CSU's approach to them was clumsy at best. A moving moment occurred during the July 1946 strike. William Riddle, a "Negro janitor," started through the picket line and was seized. The visibly angered Riddle told his captors, "'I ain't white enough to get into your union. Your picket line ain't good enough for me!' The captors released Riddle and he went on in to his work."[235] CSU did not recognize that just as the popular front was being overthrown, elites were changing their line on African Americans, embracing them so as to more effectively charge Communist regimes with human rights violations. That the *Los Angeles Times,* which so often mangled stories about African Americans, would portray them compassionately in this vignette, should have sent an advance warning to CSU. The old AFL policies of racial exclusion—which should have been opposed in principle anyway—became a weighty albatross after the war.

Certainly, there were African Americans within CSU—but they were few and far between; CSU would no more have considered affirmative action to increase its African American membership than it would have thought of trying to colonize Pluto. To be fair, the Screen Office Employees Guild complained that the film industry had only six blacks in its Manhattan offices.[236] During the 1945 strike when "five Negro members of Building Service Employees at Walt Disney's were on the picketline"— with "their wives"—the Communist press blared the story as if it were a huge triumph.[237]

Building Service Employees Local 278 had "50 per cent Negro membership," and many of these workers stood with CSU, though not necessarily on the picket line. There was a "tacit agreement between producers and IATSE" mandating that the "only work available to Negroes in the industry is janitor work"—and a bit of acting in stereotyped roles.[238] CSU was not energetic in attacking such calcified biases, a failure which redounded to its own detriment.

Strikingly, CSU often resorted to racist iconography in its literature. The federation used stereotypical images of Africans, for example.[239] Still, CSU was not in charge of hiring practices in the industry, nor was it in charge of Jim Crow. It simply did not do much to oppose discrimination, even though strong efforts could have helped it. Thus, CSU was in a poor position to win over allies, like the NAACP, which were desperately interested in Hollywood.

The NAACP and CSU could have united in protest against the Selznick production *Duel in the Sun*. This mogul, who was responsible for *Gone With the Wind*, was not an NAACP favorite. CSU was picketing as this movie was being made. When the movie was released, Roy Wilkins of the NAACP called it "colossal trash." Members objected both to the role played by Butterfly McQueen and to the stereotyped portrayals of Native Americans. A confidante told the NAACP that it "strikes a telling blow at any program attempting to better race relations through the medium of the motion picture." Because *Duel in the Sun* was a movie with a substantial budget, its faults were even more glaring.[240]

At first when the Red Scare arose in Hollywood, the NAACP was resolute; the " 'communist' issue," roared leader Walter White, was used as a means of expressing "vicious anti-Semitism." But within months White was restraining Thurgood Marshall from filing an amicus brief in the Hollywood Ten case, although these men "were among the writers in Hollywood who had been most friendly to Negroes." Marshall knew that liberals like Walter Wanger and Bette Davis claimed to be in the same camp, though he had "yet to see anything that any of them have done for Negroes." Consequently, though he desperately wanted to do so, Marshall was prevented from coming to the defense of the left in Hollywood for fear that such an action would taint the NAACP's cause as it jockeyed to gain civil rights concessions.[241] A subtle message was sent to the NAACP leadership when Frank Barnes, a postal worker who headed the Santa Monica chapter and who had been leading the picketing at Sears Roebuck on the issue of job discrimination, was brought up on "loyalty charges"; he had been charged with consorting with "subversive groups" like the Communists and the "American Jewish Congress."[242] This maneuver effectively throttled any possibility that the NAACP in Southern California would rise to the defense of CSU. Though the CSU leadership failed to fully recognize the fact, the garotte was tightening around its collective neck.[243]

CSU was not terribly advanced on gender questions either. Its literature often featured scantily clad women picketers who were referred to as "glamorous piquettes."[244] As the political environment changed from the popular front to the Red Scare, CSU was unable to adapt its tactics to incorporate newer allies—allies that should have been incorporated all along.

There were, of course, factors beyond CSU's control that led to its defeat. Not only was the national political spectrum shifting to the right[245] as CSU took to the streets, but so was the labor movement itself.[246] In such an environment, it was more than difficult for a union that tolerated Communists to any degree to survive. The terminal decline of CSU was part of a larger national trend of vibrant local unions being overrun by larger national entities—like IATSE—with the ample assistance of national elites.[247]

EPILOGUE

Though the labor militance epitomized by CSU has become a distant memory as the new millennium dawns, episodes of labor unrest continue to hit Hollywood.

Nonetheless, unions seem unable to curtail the power of management, though the industry itself is growing—and becoming ever more profitable. Indeed, the trends that had emerged in the 1940s—particularly the influence of organized crime—have become all too real a half-century later and have spread across the globe.

★ In the 1990s Hollywood contained "more than 4,400 firms that made their living from the film business and 100,000 freelancers who labour in the industry."[1] Though aerospace continues to dominate the Southern California economy, Disney alone has 11,000 employees and MCA-Universal has 8,000.[2] Hollywood still remains essential to the financial health of leading banks. Movies rank "as one of the most profitable areas of banking and with the right understanding of the business" are deemed "extraordinarily safe." An executive of the Imperial Bank described "the film business the way he does it, as the 'safest and most lucrative' area of banking, similar in many respects to real estate lending. . . . [He] said experience is crucial to knowing the producer and what kind of stars and creative talent are behind a film." John Miller of Chase Securities said that his parent bank—Chase of Manhattan—"has been in the entertainment business for 50 plus years and hasn't backed out"—and has no intention of doing so.[3]

In 1997 "movie ticket sales set another record" as the industry appeared to be recession-proof.[4] Box-office receipts that year were a hefty $6.42 billion, compared to $5.7 billion in 1996; movie attendance in 1997 was a record 1.4 billion, a 7 percent increase over the previous year. In that same year, 413 films were released in the U.S., 125 more than were released ten years earlier.[5] A report by Los Angeles' Economic Development Corporation revealed that 96,000 jobs were added to the movie-industry between 1990 and 1997; total movie related employment in L.A. County stood at 500,000, generating $25.6 billion in economic activity there. Though studios like Disney played a sizable role in this economy, the long-term growth of independents and the relative decline of studio employment had continued: a "whopping 78 percent of jobs" in this industry "came from companies with one to four employees."[6] Foreign revenues in the 1990s accounted for about 42 percent of a film's total revenue, and "those percentages are expected to grow." The nagging worry that foreign films would erode Hollywood's market share persists; the current perception is that French movies in France, Spanish movies in Spain, etc., are pushing U.S. movies out of the market. Jack Valenti, the former aide to President Lyndon B. Johnson, replaced Eric Johnston as head of the industry trade association, which still has as a central purpose knocking down protectionist barriers. Valenti claimed to be the highest-paid executive of such an association, which is somehow fitting given Hollywood's outsized share of the nation's export earnings.[7]

Studio labor continues to be concerned about the "runaway" production from Southern California to friendlier climates abroad. Tax breaks and the weak Canadian dollar lured more productions north of the border; Australia also was attracting more and more Hollywood filmmakers. The Screen Actors Guild charged that in recent years 11,000 acting roles have been lost to Canada alone; permits for feature film shooting in L.A. County fell 13 percent in 1998.[8] Just as in the 1940s, automation and related trends continue to devour jobs in Hollywood. Between 1989 and 1999 the industry hemorrhaged a stunning 125,000 jobs. By way of comparison, when the Berlin Wall fell and the defense industry, the other pillar of the region's economy, lost 75,000 jobs over the next few years, this was seen as a national catastrophe.[9] Still, the ripple effect of this development is not negligible, given Southern California's role as the locomotive of the nation's economy.

The influence of the industry on management practices could be gleaned further when prominent consultants began recommending film production techniques as a model for industry generally. "Why have corporations in the first place? Why not make things the way independent films get made? That is, someone writes a script, someone agrees to direct, they get financing, choose actors and a production crew, make the film, get someone to distribute it, and then all those involved disband, perhaps never to see one another again."[10] Such thinking helped to drive a wave of "downsizing" that imposed the traditional insecurity of film workers onto the labor force generally. As manufacturers making other products moved vigorously to incorporate Hollywood's production techniques, workers were initiated into what some termed a "virtual corporation." With militant unions like CSU out of the way, management found it easier to exercise its prerogatives unilaterally.

Other industries apparently had not considered fully the implications of utilizing this "Hollywood Mode of Production." Elmer Bernstein, a composer for the movies for almost five decades, noted recently that nowadays he was taking less time to create musical scores than he had at the beginning of his career. "In the old days, with the studios," he recalled, "they didn't worry so much about time and how long you took, because everybody was on salary. Now that everybody is working week to week, time is very important."[11] He did not comment on what impact this new mode of production has had on the quality of Hollywood music, though it is easy to infer that quality has been affected.

Stars, some of whom have grown accustomed to receiving $20 million per film, also have reason to be concerned. A "computer graphics revolution" is in the works that would create "synthetic stars" who look human but are actually the creation of a technician at a keyboard; these "stars" would not make ungainly demands, would not join SAG, and would be endlessly replicable.[12] On the other hand, the passing of time has not eroded the perception that writers remain the indispensable element in the production of movies. This notion was confirmed when Columbia capitulated and agreed to "share a portion of the profits of successful movies with them in addition to paying their usual fees."[13] Writers were finally beginning to get a first-class seat on this gravy train.

The entertainment industry, said *Business Week,* was now "the driving force for new technology, as defense used to be."[14] Yet as one study puts it, although "a voluminous bibliography could be constructed of books, articles and popular press devoted to the artistic side of this industry, almost no attention has been paid to the people who work in it, finance it, and profit from it. We know very little about the union-management relationships in this industry."[15] It is as if the conflict involving CSU had been so traumatic that an unconscious effort has taken place to repress, then erase, the memory of what having a strong union could mean in this crucial industry.

Of course, labor-management conflict itself has not been eliminated. In mid-1998 a familiar scene greeted motorists in Burbank: placard-carrying picketers from Local 839 of the Motion Picture Screen Cartoonists were protesting the policies of Nickelodeon, which increasingly had shifted production abroad and hired nonunion labor at home.[16]

★ In the fall of 1946, workers at Toho Studio in Japan went on strike; the union split as the strike spread to other studios. The union, inter alia, was seeking more influence over film content: "the contract with the union specified that the company only make films that had been approved by a committee including union members. This gave some filmmakers undreamed of control over the content, style, casting and budget of their films. Many directors, communist and noncommunist alike, appreciated this new freedom." The modest budgets of independent films led to more location shooting, lending the films a heightened sense of realism that mirrored Italian neorealism and Brazilian cinema novo. Ultimately the strike was squashed with the aid of the U.S. occupation authorities.[17]

These events in Japan, which eerily mirrored similar developments in the United States, suggest that there may be transnational trends within the entertainment industry that may shed light on Hollywood.

In Japan, for example, the yakuza—organized crime—also established a foothold in movies, strip shows, and entertainment generally.[18] From there the yazuka expanded and developed close ties with banks.[19] Organized crime was becoming transnational and using its ill-gotten gains from the entertainment industry as a launching pad from which it could expand into other sectors.

This extended reach of organized crime seems to be a common feature of many nations. Former mayor Cuauhtémoc Cárdenas of Mexico City charged that "organized crime . . . is now [responsible] for more than three-quarters of the crime committed in the city."[20] In Moscow, "50 or more members" of the 450-member Duma, or Parliament, "and their assistants [are] said by the interior ministry to be 'linked to the criminal world.'"[21] In Italy, former prime minister Giulio Andreotti was put on trial for alleged ties to the Mafia.[22] In Turkey a "public opinion survey taken . . . under the auspices of a member of Parliament found that . . .

two-thirds of Turks believe 'a politics-mafia-police triangle really exists' ";
some alleged further that " 'state gangs' may be behind many of the thousands of unsolved killings over the last decade."[23]

In Taiwan Justice Minister Liao Cheng-Hao said that about 10 percent of the "elected officials in the legislature and National Assembly—
the latter Taiwan's standing constitutional convention—had gang affiliations of some kind. . . . [T]he real figure is higher." The rebel province's
"most prominent gang-connected politician, Luo Fu-tsu . . . has identified himself as the 'spiritual leader' of one of Taiwan's largest gangs,
the Heavenly Way Alliance." He was also—appropriately—"chairman of
the legislature's judiciary committee."[24] In neighboring Hong Kong, the
"Hollywood of Asia, the world's second largest exporter of films after the
United States," the industry was dominated by organized crime in what
was fast becoming a "gangster society."[25]

These Chinese developments reflected the legacy of the mainland.
There in the 1920s Chiang Kai-shek collaborated with racketeers, such as
Green Gang leader Du Yuesheng; they acted as labor bosses, labor recruit-
ers, and plant managers. They helped Chiang break unions.[26]

In Jamaica, gangsters learned their "bad-boy style from Hollywood."
The "evanescent way that Kingston's familiar mercilessness meshed with
the Hollywood imagery [that gangsters] cut their teeth on as youth" was
striking to many. These hoodlums "worshipped the gunfighters in Hollywood westerns"; they were in the "time honored tradition of gunmen
modeling themselves on Hollywood desperadoes."[27]

In India the "underworld finances part of Bombay's movie industry,
the police say, and use extortion to squeeze producers of box-office suc-
cesses."[28] There "actors travel with armed escorts. Directors have gone
into hiding. Producers are removing their names from the credit lines of
films. . . . Police and industry insiders say mobsters have long acted as
godfathers to India's movie business, financing producers shunned by the
country's banks."[29]

In sum, Hollywood is not sui generis in attracting mobsters—though
Southern California, particularly in the 1930s and 1940s, seems to have
provided a template for others to follow. Nor is the United States unique
in reflecting the pervasive influence of gangsters—from rap music to dress
to mannerisms. This seeming universality suggests that there may be
something about the entertainment industry that attracts mobsters and
that we must deepen our analysis of gangsters as a class, or at least a stratum, with its own interests and transnational presence—à la capital and

labor. Whatever the case, in an evident continuation of developments noticed when CSU was under siege, Southern California—as the example of "gangsta rap" exemplifies—has been a hotbed of these trends.

Sidney Korshak died in 1996 after almost sixty years of legal practice; one of his earliest clients was the Chicago mob. The producer of the *Godfather,* Robert Evans—who himself was involved in questionable activities surrounding his movie *Cotton Club*—called Korshak "my consigliere . . . my godfather and my closest friend." He had good contacts, said Evans, with the "heavy muscle."[30] Yet he brokered many deals with industry behemoths like the late Charles Bludhorn of Gulf and Western, Lew Wasserman of MCA, and Kirk Kekorian of MGM. He worked closely with Jimmy Hoffa as the "overseer" of the Teamsters' investments in hotels.[31] Korshak, a resident of Southern California, was not the only figure in the orbit of the entertainment industry who was accused of having mob connections. In 1978 Warner Communications was on trial for having similar arrangements.[32]

The omnipresence of organized crime was made clear when Chicago began providing a bus tour of gangland spots from the 1930s: "the saloons, gambling dens, shops, brothels, breweries, where" Capone and his comrades did business. "This bus is a theater on wheels with Chicago actors dressed in baggy pants and wide-brimmed hats, who know their parts—and their history—well."[33]

The mob was not just a sideshow for tourists. Mobsters have expanded into money laundering, large-scale drug dealing, and more legitimate businesses.[34] Wall Street has been invaded by gangsters.[35] Small-scale mobsters are involved in more prosaic activity. In New York City "legitimate tenants were driven from their apartments by gangsters and other low-lifes brought in by unscrupulous landlords . . . an organized ring of tenant terrorists." They "hired themselves out to landlords from 1978 to 1984" and "installed drug addicts, prostitutes, thieves and other criminals in vacant apartments to commit burglaries and assaults against tenants, and to cause floods, set fires, strew garbage and otherwise terrorize the tenants."[36] Most of all, mobsters still maintain control over many unions, particularly the painters who had once embraced Herb Sorrell.[37] This barbaric grip has been sustained with a kind of violence that made what happened in Los Angeles in 1945–1946 seem mild by comparison.[38]

African Americans could not and have not remained oblivious to these developments. The Black Panther Party (BPP), which was born in California, consciously grounded itself among and within the "lumpen"; in fact, the party organized a singing group with this generic name, signifying a belief in the transforming role of pimps, prostitutes, gangsters.[39] The BPP was walking in the footsteps of the 1930s Harlem and Chicago "policy kings" and gamblers who emerged as "race leaders" and who, like Jack Dragna and Meyer Lansky, were ethnocentric.[40]

Nowadays these trends arise almost informally. In 1997 filmmaker Spike Lee "took some of his friends, 'muscle,' he calls them, to 125th Street with baseball bats to clean the bootleg copies [of his latest movie] off the street."[41] Rap music impresario Marion "Suge" Knight, a member of the L.A. gang the Bloods, allegedly formed his firm—Death Row Records—from drug money.[42]

In short, the tentacles of organized crime have extended their reach sensationally, even in comparison to the admittedly halcyon days of the 1940s. Strikingly, movies that glamorize the most banal and quotidian details of the gangsters' existence often provide a manual for those across the globe who seek to emulate them—as the example of Jamaica suggests. CSU's ouster from influence removed a troublesome barrier in the path of this development.

The Communist Party has faded in Hollywood, along with febrile hysteria about alleged Jewish influence in the movies. As a new century opens, there is little question that the formerly obstreperous screenwriters have been eclipsed—their new deal with Columbia notwithstanding; film is a "director's medium," it is said, and the director is the "auteur" of the film. One thing has not changed, however: organized crime's influence in the entertainment industry has not disappeared.

★ By 1958 Communist leader Pettis Perry claimed, "[W]e hear that in L.A., as in Philadelphia, that when Negro people move into an area, that white Left and Communists, immediately flee to other areas, that are still lily white."[43] By the early 1960s, resistance to racial integration remained just as obdurate in the neighborhood as in the workplace, so much so that Reds—who prided themselves on their avant-garde attitudes on race—were affected.

Hollywood was not unaffected by these regressive trends. The NAACP said "many" unions there had "no Negroes."[44] Spike Lee, one of the few African Americans working regularly as an actor-screenwriter-director, is bitter about this. "There is no high-ranking African-American," he said ruefully, "who can green-light a picture. But I can always count on my brother-man security guard to wave me through the studio gates. In my meetings with various departments—distribution, marketing, publicity, 20 people in the room—I rarely see anybody who looks like me. That's the case throughout the industry—from the studios to the agencies, the management companies, the publicists, the craft unions and the critics." The eminent black actress Frances Williams—who appeared in more than fifty films, twenty television series, and seventy-five theater productions—agreed with the diminutive artist, one of the few true auteurs in the business. She was a leading member of SAG for decades and to her dying day continued to resent Ronald Reagan, who—she charged— "immediately dissolved" the "Minority Committee" of the union upon his ascension to leadership in the wake of CSU's demise. Not surprisingly, minority clout in the industry fell correspondingly with this maneuver.[45] Though the numbers of Latinos, Native Americans, and Asian Americans in the United States has increased dramatically since the heyday of CSU, their representation at all levels within this industry—in a region where they reside in great abundance—is also problematic.

The role of women of all races and ethnicities has not improved dramatically either. CSU, which was heavily dependent on the militance and toil of women workers, nearly excluded them from the higher ranks of leadership; CSU tactics—e.g., having women picket in bathing suits— were questionable also. This pig-headedness obtained despite the fact that Local 683 of IATSE, whose solidarity with CSU in 1946 almost tipped things in the federation's favor, had many women in its ranks. Yet almost fifty years after the dissolution of CSU, the situation of women workers in the industry seems little improved.

The Teamsters still have mob—and entertainment—connections. Their leader of long-standing, Jackie Presser, had a "rolodex" that "bulged with the names and numbers of television and movie celebrities. . . . [M]any of these luminaries also had long time Reagan connections." "One of his principal contacts" was "Marty Bacow" who was a "bagman for film producers who wanted to buy labor peace." Teamster officials "were receiving kickbacks in return for labor peace—a practice that was prevalent throughout the film industry."[46]

As in the 1940s, Hollywood remains a relatively high-paying industry. In the late 1990s, the union minimum for camera operators was $1,583.20 per week; costume designers, $1,583; set decorators, $1,706.14; grips, $24 per hour; extras, $79 per diem.[47] Yet unions remain weak, and in 1987 one perceptive writer asked, "[C]an the Hollywood unions survive?"[48]

This question was asked because IATSE had lost tremendous strength since 1946 and was barely in a position to protect the interests of its members. IATSE's triumph in 1946 had not necessarily been a boon for studio labor.

In the spring of 1997 Brent Hershman, thirty-five, fell asleep while driving home after working nineteen hours on the set of a New Line Cinema film; this exhausted father of two small children drove his car into a utility pole; he was killed instantly. Such extraordinarily long working days had become common in Hollywood.[49] At Universal "union readers" were being "replaced by nonunion readers who were, among other things, younger than their terminated predecessors." What these displaced workers called the "Mother's Day Massacre" demonstrated "the inability of their union to protect their jobs."[50] Meanwhile in Burbank, Warner Bros. was "downsizing, re-engineering, outsourcing." This would include "possibly . . . the mail room, security, the fire department and maintenance/janitorial. . . . [A] few weeks ago Warner shuttered its 18 month old in-house digital effects division."[51]

A "stunt performer and extras on *Titanic*—co-financed by 20th-Century Fox and Paramount Pictures—say they were subjected to appalling work conditions and a significant number of mishaps"; these incidents were "symptomatic of an even bigger safety problem in the film industry."

More than a decade after director John Landis was acquitted of involuntary manslaughter charges stemming from the deaths of actor Vic Morrow and two children on the set of *Twilight Zone—The Movie,* there remains a shocking lack of accountability for on-set accidents. This fact may be tied to the allegation that "some crew personnel who testified against John Landis reportedly had trouble finding work after the trial." The blacklist continues, albeit in other forms.

On-set tragedies are on the rise. Safety problems are rife throughout the film industry, afflicting nonstunt people as well as the professional risk takers. In 1995 no fewer than four people were killed on U.S. film sets, though reliable figures for the motion picture and television industry do not exist. In fact, these figures aren't even included in the data collected by the California Occupational Safety and Health Administration. Cal-OSHA also lacks any authority to adequately punish either production companies or distributors when performers get hurt. Spokespeople for the seven majors claim that they don't even keep track of production injuries.[52]

All the while, IATSE has not mounted the sort of vigorous protest one would expect from a union whose members are under siege.[53] Of course, nonunion productions—which have proliferated since 1946—have even worse records. In 1997 Sean Pattison, a stuntman, spoke movingly of what happened to him in making one of these movies: "On a non-union film I performed a stunt where I jumped off the First Street Bridge onto the back of a moving 24 foot truck. On the third jump, I hit the truck hard, resulting in a paralyzing spinal-cord injury. Medically speaking, I'm a quadriplegic."[54]

The proliferation of movie production in antiunion bastions like North Carolina also has compromised the health and safety of film workers. In March 1993 actor Brandon Lee died after he was shot in the abdomen during the filming in Wilmington of *The Crow*, released by Carolco Studio. The gun used in this fatal injury was placed in storage without being checked; when an actor pulled the trigger to "shoot" Lee, the explosion of a dummy round forced a bullet fragment out of the barrel, striking the twenty-eight-year-old son of Bruce Lee. In 1998 three were hurt, two critically, while filming a scene in *Black Dog*, starring Patrick Swayze.[55]

More than a half-century after the CSU's demise, Ken Abraham, a set dresser with IATSE Local 44 and a "prop person for the film and television industry," argued vehemently against proposals to change the conditions that led to Brent Hershman's auto accident. Rather than hire more workers, studios found it cheaper to pay studio labor time-and-a-half for overtime; the price paid—bone-tired weariness that could lead to fatal accidents—was rationalized as worth it.[56] Nikki Capshaw of Burbank argued just as vehemently that the problem was "due to the 'divide and conquer' nature of IATSE locals." Though bearing the earmarks of a horizontal industrial union, akin to the old CIO unions like the United Auto Workers, IATSE remains an uneasy alliance among often warring craft locals. Capshaw suggested that if these crafts could actually unite "to form one large union, this more powerful united front could negotiate a contract that provides wages more in line with the lucrative reality of the business as well as hours more conducive to physical and emotional health."[57]

By the 1990s worry about Communist influence in Hollywood had dropped sharply. Yet the party had not forgotten about the film industry. The Communists expressed concern about the attempt by Regal Cinemas, "the third largest theatrical chain in the United States," to replace the once powerful projectionists of IATSE with "low wage part-time workers with no benefits."[58] Though IATSE mounted a spirited objection to this démarche, odds were that this union—which, ironically, had been weakened as party influence in the industry dissipated—would not be able to meet the challenge of Regal.

Though the Lilliputian Communist Party has not forgotten about

Hollywood, apparently other forces on the left have. Michael Everett, a leader of "IA Progressives"—which has sought to emulate the example of CSU—expressed keen disappointment in mid-1999 when the left-leaning publication *The Nation* in a special issue on the industry, failed "to discuss the critical issues facing . . . workers. . . . [S]carcely do you mention that we even exist." Hollywood, he reminded, was a "factory town in deep distress . . . We're the rust belt of the new millennium. . . . [W]ages and working conditions are deteriorating." [59] Whereas Hollywood labor once served as a model and exemplar of militance, with the disappearance of CSU even those who styled themselves as prounion often acted as if moviemaking were a bit of magic, creating "products" without the deployment of workers.

★ In 1974 Richard Walsh, longtime leader of IATSE, stepped down; he had glaucoma. He had beaten back the challenge to his leadership from Roy Brewer, and in fact, was elected a vice president of the united AFL-CIO in 1955. In 1992 he died at the age of ninety-two. [60]

In 1975, as he was about to be called before a congressional committee investigating various CIA plots over the years—including agency ties to organized crime—Johnny Roselli was "asphixiated [*sic*] aboard a yacht, then his legs were sawed off so [he] would fit into an oil drum that was found floating near Miami." [61] Two years earlier, Herb Sorrell had passed away; his notoriety having faded, he died in virtual obscurity. [62]

Sorrell carried to his grave the burden of being regarded a Communist in a nation that elected his interlocutor, Ronald Reagan, as president on an explicitly anticommunist platform. During his tenure in the White House, the basis was laid for the dismantling of the Soviet Union and the weakening of Communist parties worldwide—including in the United States itself, where the party had fallen on hard times since the glory days of John Howard Lawson and Dalton Trumbo.

In 1997 there was a tsunami of press coverage marking the half-century since the onset of the blacklist, with apologies for this practice emerging far and wide. But some critics charged that this regret was misplaced, given that some of those blacklisted—like Lawson—were card-carrying Communists and, it was said, complicit in the crimes of Stalin. [63]

Pete Seeger, the singer who worked closely with People's Songs, the group that helped maintain strikers' morale on picket lines and in jails during the labor unrest of the 1940s, dissented vigorously. Sure, he said, he would apologize for Stalin, but, he continued, "I guess anyone who

[is] himself or herself a Christian should be prepared to apologize for the Inquisition, the burning of heretics by Protestants, the slaughter of Jews and Moslems by Crusaders." The United States "could consider apologizing for stealing land from Native Americans and enslaving blacks. Europeans could apologize for worldwide conquests, Mongolians for Genghis Khan. And supporters of Roosevelt could apologize for his support of Somoza, of Southern white Democrats, of Franco's Spain, for putting Japanese-Americans in concentration camps."[64] Lost in this discourse was the fact that although routing Reds was the ostensible basis for the blacklist, overwhelmingly the victims were non-Communists.

Whether one accepts this troubadour's contention or not, words uttered sixty years ago continue to ring true. "One movie that Hollywood has never produced and probably never will is the story of its own unionization. Any number of producers would be placed under physicians' care if the idea were seriously suggested."[65]

"Class Struggle in Hollywood" may be the greatest story never told —by the studios.

ARCHIVAL COLLECTIONS

Academy of Motion Picture Arts and Sciences, Los Angeles
    Alexander Knox Papers
    Oral History Transcripts
    Roger McDonald Papers
American Film Institute, Louis B. Mayer Library, Los Angeles
    Oral History Transcripts
Boston University Library
    Albert Maltz Papers
    Ralph De Toledano Papers
Brigham Young University, Provo, Utah
    Argosy Pictures Corporation Archives
    Bosely Crowther Papers
    Cecil B. DeMille Archives
California State Archives, Sacramento
    Earl Warren Papers
California State University, Northridge
    Los Angeles County Federation of Labor Papers
    Motion Picture Screen Cartoonists Guild Papers
Columbia University
    Federated Press Papers
    Laura Z. Hobson Papers
    Oral History Research Project
Cornell University
    Philip Taft Papers
Eastern Washington Historical Society
    Eric Johnston Papers

Estate of Canada Lee, Santa Barbara, California
    Canada Lee Papers
Franklin D. Roosevelt Library, Hyde Park, New York
    Franklin D. Roosevelt Papers
Hoover Institute, Palo Alto, California
    America First Papers
    Jay Lovestone Papers
    National Republic Papers
Library of Congress, Manuscript Division, Washington, D.C.
    Records of the NAACP
Meiklejohn Civil Liberties Institute, Berkeley
    Various legal records & documents
Museum of Modern Art, New York
    Sonia Volochova Papers
National Archives, College Park, Maryland
    Records of National War Labor Board
    Records of U.S. Federal Mediation and Conciliation Service
National Archives, Laguna Niguel, California, and College Park, Maryland
    National Labor Relations Board Papers
National Archives, New York City
    Nitti Transcript *(U.S. v. Frank Nitto, et al.)*
National Archives, Washington, D.C.
    Records of the Committee on Un-American Activities
    Van Deman Collection
New York City Office of the IATSE
    IATSE Records
New York Public Library
    Billy Rose Library
New York Public Library, Schomburg Library
    Pettis Perry Papers
New York University
    Actors Equity Papers
    American Guild of Musical Artists Papers
    American Guild of Variety Artists Papers
    Cedric Belfrage Papers
San Francisco State University, Labor Archives and Research Center
    Norman Leonard Papers
Screen Actors Guild Office, Los Angeles
    Screen Actors Guild Papers
Southern California Library for Social Studies and Research, Los Angeles
    Conference of Studio Unions Collection
    Hollywood Studio Strike Collection
    Leo Gallagher Papers

Southern Illinois University, Morris Library, Carbondale
  John Howard Lawson Papers
Stanford University, Stanford, California
  Huey P. Newton Foundation Records
State Historical Society of Wisconsin, Madison
    Dalton Trumbo Papers
    Dore Schary Papers
    Hollywood Democratic Committee Papers
    Howard Koch Papers
    Melvyn Douglas Papers
    Robert Kenny–Robert Morris Papers
    Teamsters Papers
    Walter Wanger Papers
Tamiment Institute Library, Robert F. Wagner Labor Archives, NYU
    Actors Equity Papers
    American Guild of Musical Artists Papers
    American Guild of Variety Artists Papers
    American Labor Unions' Constitutions, Proceedings, Officers' Reports
      and Supplementary Documents (American Labor Unions)
    Cedric Belfrage Papers
    Communist Activity in the Entertainment Industry
    Labor Research Association Papers
    Louis Weinstock Papers
    National Council on American-Soviet Friendship Papers
    United Scenic Artists, Local 829 of the Brotherhood of Painters,
      Decorators Papers (United Scenic Artists Papers)
University of California, Berkeley
    Clark Kerr Papers
    Hiram Johnson Papers
    James F. T. O'Connor Papers
    San Francisco CIO Papers
    Tom Mooney Papers
    William Randolph Hearst Papers
University of California, Los Angeles Libraries, Department of Special
      Collections
    Fox Collection (Twentieth-Century Fox Collection)
    UCLA Oral History Program
University of Southern California
    Edward G. Robinson Papers
    Jack Warner Collection
University of Texas at Austin, Harry Ransom Humanities Research Center
    David O. Selznick Collection

Wayne State University, Detroit
    Louis Ciccone Papers
    United Auto Workers, Local 216 Papers
Yivo Institute for Jewish Research, New York
    American Jewish Committee Papers

NOTES

PREFACE

1. Ellen Schrecker, *Many Are the Crimes: McCarthyism in America,* Boston: Little Brown, 1998, p. 398.
2. Karen Brodkin, *How Jews Became White and What That Says about Race in America,* New Brunswick, N.J.: Rutgers University Press, 1998.

INTRODUCTION

1. *Los Angeles Times,* 6 October 1945.
2. Affidavit of Douglas Tatum, 26 September 1946; affidavit of Arthur Maurer, 7 September 1945, Box 2734, Jack Warner Collection.
3. Ronald Reagan, *An American Life,* New York: Simon & Schuster, 1990, pp. 108–109, 114. See also Stephen Vaughn, *Ronald Reagan in Hollywood: Movies and Politics,* New York: Cambridge University Press, 1994; Gary Wills, *Reagan's America: Innocents at Home,* Garden City: Doubleday, 1987: Here will be found an account of a controversial 1962 investigation of labor corruption in Hollywood that touched directly on the fortunes of the future president; and Edgar Morin, *The Stars,* New York: Evergreen, 1960.
4. Jack Tenney to Earl Warren, 8 October 1945, File 3640: 2365, Earl Warren Papers.
5. Grace Dudley to Earl Warren, 9 October 1945, File 3640: 2365, Warren Papers.
6. Though an important union that supplied many leaders to the American Federation of Labor (AFL), IATSE has not received sufficient attention from scholars. See, e.g., Robert Osborne Baker, "The International Alliance of The-

atrical Stage Employees and Moving Picture Machine Operators of the U.S. and Canada," Ph.D. dissertation, University of Kansas, 1933, Tamiment Institute, New York University.

7. Michael Nielsen, "Motion Picture Craft Workers and Craft Unions in Hollywood: The Studio Era, 1912–1948," Ph.D. dissertation, University of Illinois, 1985, pp. 89, 179; *New York Times,* 9 May 1937.

8. Larry Ceplair and Steven Englund, *The Inquisition in Hollywood: Politics in the Film Community, 1930–1960,* Garden City, N.J.: Doubleday, 1980, p. 224. See also Murray Rose, *Stars and Strikes: Unionization of Hollywood,* New York: Columbia University Press, 1941; and Peter Steven, ed., *Jump Cut: Hollywood, Politics and Counter Cinema,* Westport, Conn.: Praeger, 1985.

9. Carey McWilliams, *The Education of Carey McWilliams,* New York: Simon and Schuster, 1979. See also Carey McWilliams, Oral History, 1982, 300/195, UCLA Oral History Program; Brett L. Abrams, "The First Hollywood Blacklist: The Major Studios Deal with the Conference of Studio Unions," *Southern California Quarterly,* 77 (Number 3, Fall 1995): 215–253.

10. Abraham Polonsky, Oral History, 1974, American Film Institute.

11. See, e.g., Lary May, *Screening Out the Past: The Birth of Mass Culture and the Motion Picture Industry,* New York: Oxford University Press, 1980; Lary May, ed., *Recasting America: Culture and Politics in the Age of Cold War,* Chicago: University of Chicago Press, 1989.

12. See, e.g., Ellen Schrecker, *Many Are the Crimes: McCarthyism in America,* Boston: Little, Brown, 1998. See also Michael Denning, *The Cultural Front: The Laboring of American Culture in the Twentieth Century,* New York: Verso, 1996.

13. Kevin J. Fernlund, ed., *The Cold War and the American West, 1945–1989,* Albuquerque: University of New Mexico Press, 1998, p. 1.

14. Motion Picture Producers and Distributors of America, Inc., *The Community and the Motion Picture: Report of National Conference on Motion Pictures, September 24–27, 1929,* New York: Jerome Ozer, 1971, pp. 16, 20, 31. See also Joel Swenson, "The Entrepreneur's Role in Introducing the Sound Motion Picture," *Political Science Quarterly,* 63 (September 1948): 404–423; Anthony Dawson, "Motion Picture Economics," *Hollywood Quarterly,* 3 (1948): 217–240; Colin Shindler, *Hollywood in Crisis: Cinema and American Society, 1929–1939,* New York: Routledge, 1996.

15. *Los Angeles Times,* 28 December 1921.

16. William Irving Greenwald, "The Motion Picture Industry: An Economic Study of the History and Practices of a Business," Ph.D. dissertation, New York University, p. 227; the author adds, "[T]here is no industry or segment of the American economy for which less empirical material is available than for the motion picture industry and its branches."

17. *In Fact,* 16 (Number 7, 17 November 1947), Box 27, Folder 4, John Howard Lawson Papers. See also Thomas Cripps, *Hollywood's High Noon: Moviemaking and Society before Television,* Baltimore: Johns Hopkins University Press, 1997.

18. Aida Arfan Hozic, "The Rise of the Merchant Economy: Industrial Change in the American Film Industry," Ph.D. dissertation, University of Virginia, 1997, p. 52.

19. Janet Wasko, *Movies and Money: Financing the American Film Industry*, Norwood, N.J.: Ablex, 1982, pp. xii. 110; *New York Daily News*, 26 November 1947. See also Greenwald, "The Motion Picture Industry," p. 59: "The financial houses of the east gained wide influence and control in Hollywood by having members on the boards of directors and financial committees of the [movie] companies"; Mae D. Huettig, *Economic Control of the Motion Picture Industry*, Philadelphia: University of Pennsylvania Press, 1944; and Janet Staiger, "The Hollywood Mode of Production: The Construction of Divided Labor in the Film Industry," Ph.D. dissertation, University of Wisconsin, Madison, 1981.

20. "IATSE Information Bulletin," 14 September 1945, IATSE Records, New York City Office.

21. *People's Daily World*, 24 January 1947.

22. Diana Altman, *Hollywood East: Louis B. Mayer and the Origins of the Studio System*, New York: Carol, 1992, p. xii.

23. John Izod, *Hollywood and the Box Office, 1895–1986*, New York: Columbia University Press, 1986, pp. 117, 119; according to the *Motion Picture Herald*, 5 February 1949, the number of films made in Hollywood fell from 567 in 1937 to 363 in 1947 and from 23,000 workers employed in 1945 to 13,000 in 1948. See also Linda Jo Gartley, "The American Film Industry in Transition: 1946–1956," Ph.D. dissertation, University of Michigan, 1972.

24. Aubrey Solomon, *Twentieth-Century Fox: A Corporate and Financial History*, Metuchen: Scarecrow Press, 1988, pp. 60, 61, 64, 65; Richard Maurice Hurst, *Republic Studios: Between Poverty Row and the Majors*, Metuchen: Scarecrow Press, 1979. The challenge of television caused the Screen Actors Guild, Actors Equity, and related unions to contemplate a merger: see Minutes of Council, 8 February 1944, Box 5, Reel 5043, Actors Equity Papers. Television also provided a challenge to CSU as IATSE moved rapidly to unionize the industry. See also *Variety*, 8 August 1945: IATSE charters Broadcasting Studio Union Local 794, and a "deal covering technicians employed by DuPont in New York is expected to be closed at an earlier date. . . . Sometime back Local 306 Moving Picture Machine Operators sought jurisdiction over television. This union as well as other projectionist and stagehand locals of the IA battled over television at last summer's IA convention in St. Louis."

25. *Forbes*, 15 January 1946.

26. "Jurisdictional Disputes in the Motion Picture Industry," 25–27 February, 1–5, 9–12, 15–17 March 1948. U.S. House of Representatives, 80th Congress, 2nd Session, Special Subcommittee of the Committee on Education and Labor, Hearings, Pursuant to HR 111. Washington, D.C.: Government Printing Office, 1948, p. 1586. Hereafter, "Jurisdictional Disputes." See also "Jurisdictional Disputes in the Motion Picture Industry," 11–14, 18–20, 22, 25–30 August 1947 and

2–3 September 1947, U.S. House of Representatives, 80th Congress, 1st Session, Special Subcommittee of the Committee on Education and Labor, Hearings, Pursuant to HR 111, volume I, Washington, D.C.: Government Printing Office, 1947. For larger estimates of weekly movie attendance, see Tino Balio, ed., *The American Film Industry,* Madison: University of Wisconsin Press, 1976.

27. Wasko, *Movies and Money,* p. 108. See also Philip French, *The Movie Moguls,* London: Weidenfeld and Nichols, 1969, p. 153; John Baxter, *Sixty Years of Hollywood,* South Brunswick, N.J.: A. S. Barnes, 1973, p. 155; and Carlo Curti, *Skouras: King of Fox Studios,* Los Angeles: Holloway House, 1967.

28. H. Mark Glancy, "Warner Brothers Film Grosses, 1929–1951: The William Schaefer Ledger," *Historical Journal of Film, Radio and Television,* 15 (Number 1, March 1995): 55–73, p. 65. See also H. Mark Glancy, "MGM Film Grosses, 1924–1948: The Eddie Mannix Ledger," *Historical Journal of Film, Radio and Television,* 12 (Number 2, June 1992): 127–144; and Richard B. Jewell, "RKO Film Grosses, 1929–1951: The C. J. Tevlin Ledger," *Historical Journal of Film, Radio and Television,* 14 (Number 1, March 1994): 37–49.

29. Editorial, *The Screen Writer,* 4 (Number 3, September 1948): 1.

30. Clayton R. Koppes and Gregory D. Black, *Hollywood Goes to War: How Politics, Profits, and Propaganda Shaped World War II Movies,* New York: Free Press, 1987, p. 4.

31. Izod, *Hollywood and the Box Office,* pp. 126, 128.

32. Greenwald, *The Motion Picture Industry,* p. 59.

33. Richard Lewis Ward, "A History of the Hal Roach Studios," Ph.D. dissertation, University of Texas at Austin, 1995, p. 362.

34. David Brody, *Workers in Industrial America: Essays on the 20th Century Struggle,* New York: Oxford University Press, 1980, pp. 178, 180, 225. See also Kevin Boyle, *The UAW and the Heyday of American Liberalism, 1945–1968,* Ithaca, N.Y.: Cornell University Press, 1995; Stephen Amberg, *The Union Inspiration in American Politics: The Autoworkers and the Making of a Liberal Industrial Order,* Philadelphia: Temple University Press, 1994; Robert Zieger, *American Workers, American Unions,* Baltimore: Johns Hopkins University Press, 1994; Martin Halpern, *UAW Politics in the Cold War Era,* Albany: State University of New York Press, 1988; and Bill Goode, *Infighting in the UAW: The 1946 Election and the Ascendancy of Walter Reuther,* Westport, Conn.: Greenwood, 1994.

35. Brody, *Workers in Industrial America,* p. 181; See also Howell John Harris, *The Right to Manage: Industrial Relations Policies of American Business,* Madison: University of Wisconsin Press, 1982.

36. Sumner H. Slichter, *Trade Unions in a Free Society,* Cambridge: Harvard University Press, 1947, p. 5.

37. Melvin Dubofsky, *The State and Labor in Modern America,* Chapel Hill: University of North Carolina Press, 1994, p. 192. See also Paul K. Edwards, *Strikes in the United States, 1881–1974,* New York: St. Martin's Press, 1981; Armand Thieblot and Thomas Haggard, *Union Violence: The Record and the Response by*

Courts, Legislatures and the NLRB, Philadelphia: Wharton, 1983; and Wilfred H. Crook, *Communism and the General Strike,* Hamden, Conn.: Shoe String Press, 1960.

38. Harris, *The Right to Manage,* p. 194; See also Patricia Sexton, *The War on Labor and the Left: Understanding America's Unique Conservatism,* Boulder, Colo.: Westview, 1991; and Robert N. Stern, et al., *The U.S. Labor Movement: References and Resources,* New York: G. K. Hall, 1996.

39. Elizabeth A. Fones-Wolf, *Selling Free Enterprise: The Business Assault on Labor and Liberalism, 1945-1960,* Urbana: University of Illinois Press, 1994, pp. 6, 53.

40. Louis B. Perry and Richard S. Perry, *A History of the Los Angeles Labor Movement, 1911-1941,* Berkeley: University of California Press, 1963, p. vii. See also Grace Heilman Stimson, *Rise of the Labor Movement in Los Angeles,* Berkeley: University of California Press, 1955. See also Rhonda F. Levine, *Class Struggle in the New Deal: Industrial Labor, Industrial Capital and the State,* Lawrence: University Press of Kansas, 1988.

41. Irving Richter, *Labor's Struggles, 1945-1950: A Participant's View,* New York: Cambridge University Press, 1994, p. xi.

42. Daniel Cornford, ed., *Working People of California,* Berkeley: University of California Press, 1995, pp. 7, 9, 15.

43. Hugh Lovell and Tasile Carter, *Collective Bargaining in the Motion Picture Industry: A Struggle for Stability,* Berkeley: University of California Press, 1955. See also Ian Jarvie, *Hollywood's Overseas Campaign: The North Atlantic Movie Trade, 1920-1950,* New York: Cambridge University Press, 1992; Emily Rosenberg, *Spreading the American Dream: American Economic and Cultural Expansion, 1890-1945,* New York: Hill and Wang, 1982.

44. Blaise Cendrars, *Hollywood: Mecca of the Movies,* Berkeley: University of California Press, 1995, p. 126.

45. David Prindle, *Risky Business: The Political Economy of Hollywood,* Boulder, Colo.: Westview, 1993, p. 133. See also Catherine Kerr, "Incorporating the Star: The Intersection of Business and Aesthetic Strategies in Early American Film," *Business History Review,* 64 (Number 3, Autumn 1990): 383–410; Russell Sanjek, *American Popular Music and Its Business: The First Four Hundred Years,* New York: Oxford University Press, 1988; and Kim McQuaid, *Uneasy Partners: Big Business in American Politics, 1945-1990,* Baltimore: Johns Hopkins University Press, 1994.

46. *Variety,* 4 September 1946; James Prickett, "Communist Conspiracy or Wage Dispute? The 1941 Strike at North American Aviation," *Pacific Historical Review,* 50 (1981): 215–233.

47. *Variety,* 3 January 1945. See also Allen Koenig, *Broadcasting and Bargaining: Labor Relations in Radio and T.V.,* Madison: University of Wisconsin Press, 1970.

48. *Motion Picture Herald,* 18 August 1945.

49. *Independent Film Journal,* 12 October 1946.

50. John Cogley, *Report on Blacklisting*, New York: Fund for the Republic, 1956, p. 60.

51. See, e.g., "Jurisdictional Disputes," U.S. House of Representatives, 80th Congress, 1st Session, 1947, p. 87; Seymour Z. Mann, "Congressional Behavior and National Labor Policy: Structural Determinants of the Taft-Hartley Act," Ph.D. dissertation, University of Chicago, 1951.

52. "Jurisdictional Disputes," U.S. House of Representatives, 80th Congress, 2nd Session, 1948, p. 1897.

53. Philip Dunne, Oral History, 1991, *Academy of Motion Picture Arts and Sciences*. See also Philip Dunne, *Take Two: A Life in Movies and Politics*, New York: McGraw-Hill, 1980.

54. *New York Times*, circa March 1948, Reel 544, National Republic Papers. See also Oliver Carlson, "The Communist Record in Hollywood," *American Mercury*, 66 (February 1948): 135–143.

55. "Jurisdictional Disputes," U.S. House of Representatives, 80th Congress, 2nd Session, 1948, p. 1919.

56. Ibid., p. 2125.

57. Herb Sorrell, Oral History, 1963, University of California, Los Angeles. Earlier, Sorrell stated, "I am not a Jew. But, of course, I have been accused of being a Jew, because I have been accused of being everything. . . . I am not saying that disparagingly, because some of the smartest people I know are Jews." "Jurisdictional Disputes," U.S. House of Representatives, 80th Congress, 2nd Session, 1948, p. 1884. See also p. 1593: Pat Casey, the chief labor negotiator for the studios also denied that Sorrell was a Communist; that this testimony came before a congressional committee considering legislation to further hamstring studio labor gives his words a further ring of credibility.

58. Ibid., p. 2031.

59. Ibid., p. 1838.

60. Ibid., p. 1842.

61. "Jurisdictional Disputes," U.S. House of Representatives, 80th Congress, 1st Session, 1947, p. 359.

62. Ben Dobbs, Oral History, 1990, University of California, Los Angeles.

63. Ben Margolis, Oral History, 1987, University of California, Los Angeles.

64. Nancy Lynn Schwartz, *The Hollywood Writers' Wars*, New York: Knopf, 1982.

65. *People's Daily World*, 15 March 1945. *New Masses*, a cultural journal that was close to the party, agreed; on 13 March 1945 it editorialized that such strikes were a blow "against our fighting men on the battlelines."

66. *People's Daily World*, 16 March 1945.

67. CSU included Painters Local 644; Set Designers Local 1421; Cinema Lodge Local 1185 (International Association of Machinists); International Brotherhood of Electrical Workers Local 40 (withdrew from CSU in February 1947); Screen Office Employees Guild (withdrew in April 1946); Carpenters Local 946;

Studio Guards and Set Watchmen Local 193 of Building Service Employees International Union (withdrew July 1947); Studio Janitors (withdrew April 1947); Screen Story Analysts Guild (withdrew 1946); Screen Publicists Guild (withdrew 1947); The Sheet Metal Workers were briefly part of CSU before the 1945 strike, while the Plumbers Local 78 and the Blacksmiths were intermittently close to CSU: See U.S. House of Representatives, 80th Congress, 2nd Session, "Jurisdictional Disputes," 1948, p. 1701. By one count there were 600 separate jobs in Hollywood and 43 different crafts. *Los Angeles Times,* 12 January 1947.

68. *People's Daily World,* 17 March 1945.

69. Ibid., 24 January 1947.

70. "Jurisdictional Disputes," U.S. House of Representatives, 80th Congress, 2nd Session, 1948, p. 2128.

71. *Hollywood Sun,* 10 July 1946; *People's Daily World,* 4 March 1948; clipping, circa 1948, Reel 544, National Republic Papers.

72. "Jurisdictional Disputes," U.S. House of Representatives, 80th Congress, 2nd Session, 1948, p. 1973.

73. Ibid., p. 1918.

74. Ibid., p. 2120.

75. *Los Angeles Examiner,* 14 March 1945; U.S. House of Representatives, Records of the Un-American Activities Committee, "Los Angeles Numbered Case Files . . . from Voters Record, Los Angeles County, May 1944," 59x-191, Record Group 233, Box 11.

76. See, e.g., Records of the Un-American Activities Committee, "Exhibits, Evidence, etc.," Record Group 233, Box 50.

77. David Caute, *The Great Fear: The Anti-Communist Purge under Truman and Eisenhower,* New York: Simon & Schuster, 1978, pp. 487–488.

78. U.S. House of Representatives, 82nd Congress, 2nd Session, Committee on Un-American Activities. *Communist Activities among Professional Groups in the Los Angeles Area—Part I,* 21 January 1952, p. 2444.

79. Samuel Sillen, "Culture and the Paycheck," *New Masses,* 56 (Number 3, 17 July 1946): 15–16.

80. Scott Forsyth, "Marxism, Film and Theory: From the Barricades to Postmodernism," in Leo Panitch, *Ruthless Criticism of All That Exists: The Socialist Register, 1997,* Atlantic Highlands, N.J.: Humanities Press, 1997, pp. 265–287. See also Herbert Biberman, *Salt of the Earth: The Story of a Film,* Boston: Beacon, 1965; Jonathan Buschbaum, *Cinema Engage: Film in the Popular Front,* Urbana: University of Illinois Press, 1988; Robert Sklar and Charles Musser, eds., *Resisting Images: Essays on Cinema and History,* Philadelphia: Temple University Press, 1990; Russell Campbell, *Cinema Strikes Back: Radical Filmmaking in the United States, 1930-1942,* Ann Arbor, Mich.: University of Michigan Press, 1982; David James and Rick Berg, eds., *The Hidden Foundation: Cinema and the Question of Class,* Minneapolis: University of Minnesota Press, 1996; Steven J. Ross, *Working-Class Hollywood: Silent Film and the Shaping of Class in America,* Princeton, N.J.:

Princeton University Press, 1998; Kay Sloan, *The Loud Silents: Origins of the Social Problem Film,* Urbana: University of Illinois Press, 1988; Peter Stead, *Film and the Working Class: The Feature Film in British and American Society,* London: Routledge, 1989; and Kevin Brownlow, *Behind the Mask of Innocence: Sex, Violence, Prejudice, Crime: Films of Social Conscience in the Silent Era,* New York: Knopf, 1990.

81. *Hollywood Reporter,* 12 February 1947.

82. Kathleen A. Brown, "Ella Reeve Bloor: The Politics of the Personal in the American Communist Party," Ph.D. dissertation, University of Washington, 1996, p. 290. See also James G. Ryan, *Earl Browder: The Failure of American Communism,* Tuscaloosa: University of Alabama Press, 1997; Belinda Corbus Bezner, "American Documentary Photography during the Cold War: The Decline of Tradition," Ph.D. dissertation, University of Texas at Austin, 1993; Judith Ellen Brussell, "Government Investigations of Federal Theater Project Personnel in the Works Progress Administration, 1935–1939," Ph.D. dissertation, City University of New York, 1993; and cf. Nina Fishman, *The British Communist Party and the Trade Unions, 1933–1945,* Brookfield, Ver.: Scolar, 1995.

83. "Special Report," U.S. Senate, Internal Security Subcommittee, 17 May 1943, R-6117c, B-31, Record Group 46, Box 32, Van Deman Collection. This collection, recently accessioned, contains some of the most detailed records on the Communist Party ever produced, including minutes to meetings, regular reports by intelligence operatives, and membership rosters. This collection has similarly rich holdings on various ethnic organizations in California as well. Ralph Van Deman was a San Diego surgeon who cooperated with military intelligence and maintained thousands of files compiled by his own private intelligence network. See *New York Times,* 7 September 1971. Though the House Un-American Activities Committee traditionally received more publicity, the Internal Security Subcommittee was described by the *New York Times* as a committee that "far overreaches" HUAC "as it far outreaches Senator Joseph McCarthy. . . . The mandate from the Senate is for practical purposes, limitless in the whole field of security." *New York Times,* 2 January 1997. See also, e.g., Christopher John Gerard, "A Program of Cooperation: The FBI, the Senate Internal Security Subcommittee, and the Communist Issue, 1950–1956," Ph.D. dissertation, Marquette University, 1993; Richard Charles Ehret, "A Descriptive Analysis of the Hearings Held by the House Committee on Un-American Activities in 1947 and 1951 on the Communist Infiltration of the Motion Picture Industry and Their Relationship to the Hollywood Labor Movement," M.A. thesis, University of California, Los Angeles, 1969.

84. William Z. Foster, *Strike Strategy,* Chicago: Labor Herald Library No. 18, TUEL, 1926. See also Bernard Johnpoll, ed., *A Documentary History of the Communist Party of the U.S.,* Westport, Conn.: Greenwood, 1992.

85. John Weber to Gerald Horne, 6 February 1999 (in possession of author).

86. *CSU Bulletin,* July–August 1944, Box 1, Screen Cartoonists Guild Collection.

87. Manohla Dargis, "Dark Side of the Dream," *Sight and Sound,* 6 (Number 8, August 1996): 15–19.

88. *Los Angeles Times,* 28 July 1948; *Los Angeles Examiner,* 26 August 1948.

89. Charles Rappleye and Ed Becker, *All-American Mafioso: The Johnny Roselli Story,* Garden City, N.J.: Doubleday, 1991, p. 120. See also "Third Interim Report on the Special Committee to Investigate Organized Crime in the Interstate Commerce, Pursuant to S. Resolution 202: A Resolution to Investigate Gambling and Racketeering Activities," Report Number 307, U.S. Senate, 82nd Congress, 1st Session, Washington, D.C.: Government Printing Office, 1951; Howard Kimeldorf, *Reds or Rackets: The Making of Radical and Conservative Unions on the Waterfront,* Berkeley: University of California Press, 1988; and Rich Cohen, *Tough Jews: Fathers, Sons and Gangster Dreams,* New York: Simon & Schuster, 1998.

90. Stephen Norwood, "Ford's Brass Knuckles: Harry Bennett, the Cult of Masculinity and Anti-Labor Terror, 1920–1945," *Labor History,* 37 (Number 3, Summer 1996): pp. 365–391. See also Laurie Caroline Pintar, "Herbert K. Sorrell as the Grade-B Hero: Militancy and Masculinity in the Studios," Ibid., pp. 392–416.

91. *Birmingham News,* 24 June 1956.

92. John Gerassi and Frank Browning, *The American Way of Crime,* New York: Putnam, 1986; David R. Johnson, *Illegal Tender: Counterfeiting and the Secret Service in Nineteenth-Century America,* Washington, D.C.: Smithsonian Institution Press, 1995.

93. David Johnson, "Homegrown Gangsters: Urban Crime in the 20th-Century West," *Journal of the West,* 34 (Number 3, July 1995): 49–58, p. 49.

94. Alan Balboni, *Beyond the Mafia: Italian Americans and the Development of Las Vegas,* Reno: University of Nevada Press, 1996, p. 61. See also C. Elizabeth Raymond, *George Wingfield: Owner and Operator of Nevada,* Reno: University of Nevada Press, 1993.

95. *New York Times,* 20 March 1943.

96. Lester Cole, *Hollywood Red: The Autobiography of Lester Cole,* Palo Alto, Calif.: Ramparts Press, 1981, p. 216.

97. *U.S. v. Frank Nitto, et al.,* #114–101, Volume 114, U.S. District Court for Southern District of New York; Case #19456–19460, Record Group 276, Archives Box 5809, U.S. Court of Appeals for Second Circuit, Transcript of Record, *U.S. v. Louis Compagna, Johnny Roselli, et al.,* pp. 1979, 1985, 1987, 1990, 1992, 2008. Hereafter referred to as "Nitti Transcript."

98. Dennis McDougal, *The Last Mogul: Lew Wasserman, MCA and the Hidden History of Hollywood,* New York: Crown, 1998, p. 264.

99. Hank Messick, *The Beauties and the Beasts: The Mob in Show Business,* New York: David McKay, 1973, pp. 49–50, 51–52, 57.

100. Leo Katcher, *The Big Bankroll: The Life and Times of Arnold Rothstein,* New York: Da Capo, 1994, pp. 165, 267.

101. Rappleye and Becker, *All-American Mafioso,* p. 60.

102. *New York Times,* 22 January 1996. See also McDougal, *The Last Mogul,* p. 326: Korshak "hobnobbed with the likes of Secretary of Labor Arthur Goldberg and former Truman Vice President Alben Barkley."

103. Vaughn, *Ronald Reagan in Hollywood,* p. 135.

104. CSU Flyer, circa 1946, Conference of Studio Unions Collection, Southern California Library for Social Studies and Research.

105. *Chicago Daily News,* 29 May 1946.

106. *Los Angeles Herald-Express,* 23 January 1947.

107. *Los Angeles Daily News,* 14 November 1947.

108. Ibid., 14 November 1947.

109. Otto Friedrich, *City of Nets: A Portrait of Hollywood in the 1940s,* New York: Harper & Row, 1986, p. 258.

110. Patrick McGilligan and Paul Buhle, *Tender Comrades: A Back Story of the Hollywood Blacklist,* New York: St. Martin's, 1997, p. 187.

111. See, e.g., Gerald Horne, "Rethinking the Lumpen: Gangsters and the Political Economy of Capitalism," in Herbert Shapiro, ed., *African-American History and Radical Historiography: Essays in Honor of Herbert Aptheker,* Minneapolis, Minn.: MEP Press, 1998, pp. 285–308.

112. See Michael Birdwell, *Celluloid Soldiers: Warner Bros. Campaign against Nazism,* New York: New York University Press, 1999.

113. William Sheafe Chase, *Catechism on Motion Pictures in Inter-State Commerce,* New York: New York Civic League, 1922, p. 10. See also Patricia Erens, *The Jew in the American Cinema,* Bloomington: Indiana University Press, 1984; Lester D. Friedman, *Hollywood's Image of the Jew,* New York: Ungar, 1982; and Les and Barbara Keyser, *Hollywood and the Catholic Church: The Image of Roman Catholicism in American Movies,* Chicago: Loyola University Press, 1984.

114. Nielsen, "Motion Picture Craft Workers," p. 272.

115. Letters to John Howard Lawson, circa October 1947, Box 27, Folder 3, John Howard Lawson Papers.

116. "Facts and Anti-Semitism," circa 1946, Hollywood Citizens' Fact-Finding Committee, Sonia Volochova Papers.

117. Ben Seligman, "They Came to Hollywood: How the Jews Built the Movie Industry," *Jewish Frontier,* 20 (1953): 19, 29; See also Steven Alan Carr, "The Hollywood Question: America and the Belief in Jewish Control over Motion Pictures before 1941," Ph.D. dissertation, University of Texas at Austin, 1994, p. 63.

118. Carr, "The Hollywood Question," p. 114. See also Henry Srebrnik, *London Jews and British Communism, 1933–1945,* London: Valentine/Mitchell, 1995.

119. Erens, *The Jew in the American Cinema,* pp. 192–193.

120. "Weekly Intelligence Summary," 18 February 1946, Record Group 46, Box 44, U.S. Senate, Internal Security Subcommittee, Van Deman Collection.

121. Memorandum on John Rankin and anti-Semitism, undated, Box 14, Robert Kenny–Robert Morris Papers. See also *Chicago Daily Tribune*, 5 June 1941; *PM*, 5 June 1941; *Congressional Record*, 29 March 1943, 2 December 1943, 18 December 1943, 26 June 1944.

122. Percy N. Friedlander to Frank Green, 23 June 1949, "Survey of Anti-Semitic Organizations Active in Los Angeles," Geo-Dom, Box 3, American Jewish Committee Papers, Yivo Institute.

123. Minutes of AJC-LA meeting, 10 January 1946, Box 5, American Jewish Committee Papers, Yivo Institute.

124. Izod, *Hollywood and the Box Office*, p. 112.

125. Paul Lenti, "Latin America Takes On Hollywood," *NACLA: Report on the Americas*, 27 (Number 2, September/October 1993): 4–9.

126. Thomas Guback, *The International Film Industry: Western Europe and America since 1945*, Bloomington: Indiana University Press, 1969. See also John T. Trumpbour, " 'Death to Hollywood': The Politics of Film in the United States, Great Britain, Belgium, and France, 1920–1960," Ph.D. dissertation, Harvard University, 1996.

127. *Los Angeles Times*, 12 March 1946.

128. *Daily Worker*, 2 December 1945.

129. *Los Angeles Times*, 3 June 1946.

130. Denise J. Youngblood, *Movies for the Masses: Popular Cinema and Soviet Society in the 1920s*, New York: Cambridge University Press, 1992; Peter Kenz, *Cinema and Soviet Society, 1917–1953*, New York: Cambridge University Press, 1993; Richard Stites, *Russian Popular Culture: Entertainment and Society since 1900*, New York: Cambridge University Press, 1992; Dmitry and Vladimir Shlapentokh, *Soviet Cinematography, 1918–1991*, New York: Aldine de Gruyter, 1993; Andrew Horton, ed., *Inside Soviet Film Satire: Laughter with a Lash*, New York: Cambridge University Press, 1993. In 1936 *New Masses* contrasted Paramount's release of *Wings over Ethiopia*—"in effect a tribute to the civilizing efforts of Mussolini"—with the Soviet Union's *Abyssinia*, which was seen as more supportive of Addis Ababa's fight against Italian colonialism.

131. Strikingly, when the Soviet Union in 1989 reportedly dispensed with the so-called Brezhnev Doctrine, which was said to have motivated and justified Moscow's intervention in the internal affairs of its Eastern European neighbors, Soviet spokesman Gennadi Gerasimov said this doctrine was now to be replaced with the "Frank Sinatra Doctrine," referring to "the singer's signature ballad, 'I did it my way.' " Thomas Blanton, "When Did the Cold War End?" *Cold War International History Project*, (Number 10, March 1998): 184–188.

132. Richard Pells, *Not Like Us: How Europeans Have Loved, Hated, and Transformed American Culture since World War II*, New York: Basic, 1997. See also Mark

Rupert, *Producing Hegemony: The Politics of Mass Production and American Global Power,* New York: Cambridge University Press, 1995.

133. Testimony of Eric Johnston before the Reciprocity Information Tariff Commission, 1 May 1947, Folder 19, Box 405, Cecil B. De Mille Archives.

134. Testimony of Eric Johnston, 6 February 1947, Folder 19, Box 405, De Mille Archives.

135. *Forbes,* 1 October 1947.

136. Ibid.

137. Lorraine M. Lees, *Keeping Tito Afloat: The United States, Yugoslavia and the Cold War,* University Park: Pennsylvania State University Press, 1997, p. 59.

138. "Jurisdictional Disputes," U.S. House of Representatives, 80th Congress, 2nd Session, p. 1681.

139. Hozic, *The Rise of the Merchant Economy,* p. 115.

140. *Motion Picture Herald,* 5 May 1945.

141. "Jurisdictional Disputes," U.S. House of Representatives, 80th Congress, 2nd Session, 1948, p. 2294.

142. Joseph Greco, "The File on Robert Siodmak in Hollywood: 1941–1951," Ph.D. dissertation, State University of New York, Stony Brook, 1995, p. 40.

143. Selznick Studio to Joseph Cotten, 23 June 1945, Box 876, Folder 2, David O. Selznick Collection.

144. Michael Denning, *The Cultural Front,* p. 320.

145. Memorandum from SAC-LA, FBI, 20 March 1945, Reel 2, Communist Activity in the Entertainment Industry: FBI Surveillance Files on Hollywood.

146. Memorandum from SAC-LA, FBI, 2 April 1945, Reel 2, Communist Activity in the Entertainment Industry.

147. Thurgood Marshall to Roy Wilkins, 30 October 1947, Group II, Box B73, NAACP Papers.

148. *Fortune,* November 1946, "Labor Clippings File," Academy of Motion Picture Arts and Science.

149. "Jurisdictional Disputes," U.S. House of Representatives, 80th Congress, 2nd Session, 1948, p. 2080.

150. "Jurisdictional Disputes," U.S. House of Representatives, 80th Congress, 1st Session, 1947, p. 485. Such films as *The Best Years of Our Lives, The Secret Life of Walter Mitty, It Happened on Fifth Avenue* and many others were wracked with jurisdictional disputes.

151. "Jurisdictional Disputes," U.S. House of Representatives, 80th Congress, 1st Session, 1947, p. 467.

152. Ibid., p. 6.

153. Collette A. Hyman, *Staging Strikes: Workers' Theatre and the American Labor Movement,* Philadelphia: Temple University Press, 1997, p. 4.

154. *Daily Worker,* 13 August 1943.

155. Thomas Guback, "Capital, Labor Power and the Identity of Film," in

Bruce Austin, ed., *Current Research in Film: Audiences, Economics and Law,* Volume V, 126–134, p. 127.

156. Michael Nielsen, "Toward a Workers' History of the U.S. Film Industry," in Vincent Mosco and Janet Wasko, eds., *The Critical Communications Review, Volume I: Labor, the Working Class and the Media,* Norwood, N.J.: Ablex, 1983, 47–83, p. 49.

157. See Michael Chanan, *Labour Power in the British Film Industry,* London: British Film Institute, 1976, passim.

158. Denise Hartsough, "Studio Labor Relations in 1939: Historical and Sociological Analysis," Ph.D. dissertation, University of Wisconsin, 1987, p. 224.

CHAPTER I

1. Melvyn Dubofsky, *The State and Labor in Modern America,* Chapel Hill: University of North Carolina Press, 1994, p. 76.

2. Robert M. Stanley, *The Celluloid Empire: A History of the American Movie Industry,* New York: Hastings, 1978, p. 109.

3. Ralph Edward Shaffer, "Radicalism in California, 1869–1929," Ph.D. dissertation, University of California, Berkeley, 1962, pp. 163, 215, 307, 380; See also Thomas Ralph Clark, "The Limits of Liberty: Courts, Police and Labor Unrest in California, 1890–1926," Ph.D. dissertation, University of California, Los Angeles, 1994.

4. Frank Donner, *Protecters of Privilege: Red Squads and Police Repression in Urban America,* Berkeley: University of California Press, 1990, pp. 59–64.

5. See, e.g., Jennifer Susan Palmer, "Cedric Belfrage: Anglo-American Nonconformist," Ph.D. dissertation, University of Delaware, 1993.

6. Interview with Cedric Belfrage on Thames Television, United Kingdom, circa 1973, Box 10, Cedric Belfrage Papers.

7. "Censored! A Record of Present Terror and Censorship in the American Theater," New York: National Committee Against Censorship of the Theater Arts, 1935, Reel 120, National Republic Papers.

8. W. B. Cullen to Mickey Richardson, 11 September 1930, File 3273, Earl Warren Papers.

9. Clipping file, circa 1930s, File 3273, Earl Warren Papers.

10. Motion Picture Producers and Distributors of America, Inc., *The Community and the Motion Picture: Report of National Conference on Motion Pictures, September 24–27, 1929,* New York: Jerome Ozer, 1971, p. 78.

11. "Jurisdictional Disputes," U.S. House of Representatives, 80th Congress, 1st Session, 1947, p. 508.

12. J. Staser, Division Manager of Pinkerton's, to General Manager of Universal Pictures, 16 February 1933, Box 8, Norman Leonard Papers.

13. See, e.g., "Los Angeles Police Dept. Radical Squad," Weekly Intelligence Report, 1–12 January 1924, Records of the House Un-American Activities Committee, Record Group 233, Box 43.

14. Frank Garbutt to Captain William Hynes, 26 September 1936, Box 8, Norman Leonard Papers.

15. Hermann Schwinn to William Hynes, 5 April 1934, Box 8, Norman Leonard Papers.

16. Luke Lane to C. Grimaldi, 27 December 1934, Box 8, Norman Leonard Papers.

17. Kaoru Nakashima to Homer Cross, 31 March 1937, Box 8, Norman Leonard Papers.

18. Nakano to L.A. County Sheriff, 2 August 1932, Box 8, Norman Leonard Papers.

19. William Hynes to General Ralph Van Deman, 3 October 1938, Norman Leonard Papers.

20. F. T. Murayama to "Red Squad," 2 November 1937, Box 8, Norman Leonard Papers.

21. Jay Rand, "Hitlerites in Hollywood," *New Masses,* 16 (Number 4, 23 July 1935): 29–30, p. 29.

22. *Los Angeles Times Magazine,* 19 June 1935.

23. *Los Angeles Examiner,* 31 October 1934.

24. Report to William Hynes, 25 September 1937, Record Group 233, Box 49, U.S. House of Representatives, Records of the Committee on Un-American Activities.

25. James G. Stewart, Oral History, 1976, American Film Institute.

26. Harold Smith to NRA, 14 December 1933, Record Group 25, Box 8, National Labor Relations Board Papers; See also Gordon Hall to William Crawford, 4 October 1933, Box FX-LR-1000, Fox Collection.

27. Dennis William Mazzocco, "Democracy, Power and Equal Rights: The AFL vs. CIO Battle to Unionize the United States Broadcast Technicians, 1926–1940," Ph.D. dissertation, University of California, San Diego, 1996, pp. 63–66.

28. Ed Ray, "Hollywood as Strikebreaker," *New Masses,* 17 (Number 5, 1 October 1935): 44; David Platt, "Paramount and Pinkerton," *New Masses,* 20 (Number 3, 14 July 1936): 29.

29. Stanley, *The Celluloid Empire,* p. 97.

30. Nitti Transcript, p. 1805.

31. Press Release, 14 October 1933, Record Group 25, Box 6, National Labor Relations Board Papers.

32. Edmond DePatie, Oral History, 1965, University of California, Los Angeles.

33. Press Release, 18 July 1941, Reel 9091, Federated Press Papers.

34. "Jurisdictional Disputes," U.S. House of Representatives, 80th Congress, 2nd Session, 1948, p. 1572.

35. Joseph North, "The New Hollywood," *New Masses,* 32 (Number 3, 11 July 1939): 14–16, p. 14.

36. Nitti Transcript, p. 1015.

37. Ibid., 1295.

38. *Chicago Tribune,* 12 June 1935.

39. *Chicago Daily News,* 19 July 1935.

40. Nitti Transcript, p. 1055.

41. Ibid., pp. 154, 156, 158, 171, 483, 503, 537, 621, 661, 671, 714, 730, 736, 738, 789, 813, 838.

42. Ibid., p. 1451.

43. Ibid., pp. 1226, 1229, 1242, 1249, 1253, 1270, 1274, 1279.

44. *New York Morning Telegraph,* 13 October 1941.

45. "Jurisdictional Disputes," U.S. House of Representatives, 80th Congress, 2nd Session, 1948, p. 2000. See also *Variety,* 9 November 1939.

46. *New York Times,* 19 October 1943; *New York Morning Telegraph,* 13 October 1941.

47. Florabel Muir, "'All Right Gentlemen, Do We Get the Money?' The Astonishing Success Story of Bad Boy Bioff in Movieland," *Saturday Evening Post,* 212 (Number 31: 27 January 1940): 9–11, 81–84.

48. Nitti Transcript, p. 1325.

49. Herbert Aller, *The Extortionists,* Beverly Hills: Guild-Hartford, 1972.

50. Nitti Transcript, p. 1951.

51. *Cincinnati Enquirer,* 25 October 1947.

52. Griffin Fariello, *Red Scare: Memories of the American Inquisition: An Oral History,* New York: Norton, 1995, p. 112.

53. Edward Newhouse, "Hollywood on Strike," *New Masses,* 23 (Number 9, 18 May 1937): 6–8.

54. Martin Porter, "Another Hollywood Picture," *New Masses,* 24 (Number 2, 5 October 1937): 19–21.

55. Andrew Collins, "Hollywood's Yes-Men Say," *New Masses,* 24 (Number 10, 3 August 1937): 15.

56. Muir, "All Right, Gentlemen," pp. 9–11, 81–84.

57. "Jurisdictional Disputes," U.S. House of Representatives, 80th Congress, 2nd Session, 1948, p. 1847.

58. Nitti Transcript, p. 2982.

59. Denise Hartsough, "Studio Labor Relations in 1939: Historical and Sociological Analysis," Ph.D. dissertation, University of Wisconsin, Madison, 1987, pp. 84–87.

60. Becky Marianna Nicolaides, "In Search of the Good Life: Community and Politics in Working-Class Los Angeles, 1920–1955," Ph.D. dissertation, Columbia University, 1993.

61. Clipping, circa 1937, Record Group 25, Box 1, National Labor Relations Board Papers.

62. Towne Nylander, 14 September 1937, Record Group 25, Box 1, National Labor Relations Board Papers.

63. J. W. McCluskey to Senator Robert LaFollette, 1 September 1937, Record Group 25, Box 1, National Labor Relations Board Papers.

64. Nitti Transcript, pp. 1895, 1935.

65. Ibid., p. 2841.

66. Memorandum, circa 1942, Group II, Box B89, NAACP Papers.

67. Report by Fred Rinaldo for the Hollywood Arts, Sciences and Professions Council, 26 April 1952, Box 40, Folder 5, John Howard Lawson Papers.

68. Anna C. Christian, *Meet It, Greet It and Defeat It: The Biography of Frances E. Williams,* Los Angeles: Milligan, 1999, pp. 108, 160.

69. Ossie Davis and Ruby Dee, *With Ossie and Ruby: In This Life Together,* New York: William Morrow, 1998, pp. 195, 199, 337.

70. Laurie Caroline Pintar, "Off-Screen Realities: A History of Labor Activism in Hollywood, 1933–1947," Ph.D. dissertation, University of Southern California, 1995, p. 129.

71. *Daily Worker,* 10 November 1943.

72. *Variety,* 15 July 1964. See also Karen Ward Mahar, "Women, Filmmaking and the Gendering of the American Film Industry, 1896–1928," Ph.D. dissertation, University of Southern California, 1995. In the early days of the industry, women "screenwriters represented at least half of the screenwriting trade in the silent era, and many became powerful producers, directors and supervisors as well." See Wendy Holliday, "Hollywood's Modern Women: Screenwriting, Work Culture and Feminism, 1910–1940," Ph.D. dissertation, New York University, 1995, p. 57; Boze Hadleigh, *Hollywood Lesbians,* New York: Barricade, 1994.

73. Report by George Browne, 8–11 June 1936, Proceedings of the 33rd Convention of IATSE of U.S. and Canada, Kansas City, Missouri, Reel 230, American Labor Unions' Constitutions, Proceedings, Officers' Reports and Supplementary Documents. See also Trevor Lummis, *The Labour Aristocracy, 1851–1914,* Aldershot, England: Scolar, 1994.

74. 6–9 June 1938, Cleveland, Ohio, Reel 230, American Labor Unions.

75. Larry Ceplair, "A Communist Labor Organizer in Hollywood: Jeff Kibre Challenges the IATSE, 1937–1939," *The Velvet Light Trap,* (Number 23, Spring 1989): 64–74.

76. Jeff Kibre Report, 23 April 1938, Reel 230, *American Labor Unions.* See also Denise Hartsough, "Crime Pays: The Studios' Labor Deals in the 1930s," *The Velvet Light Trap,* (Number 23, Spring 1989): 49–63.

77. George Browne Report, 3–6 June 1940, Louisville, Kentucky, Reel 230, American Labor Unions.

78. Nitti Transcript, p. 2854.

79. "Jurisdictional Disputes," U.S. House of Representatives, 80th Congress, 2nd Session, 1948, p. 1874.

80. Melvin Small, "How We Learned to Love the Russians: American Media and the Soviet Union during World War II," *The Historian,* 36 (Number 3, May 1974): 455–478.

81. Aller, *The Extortionists,* p. 141.

82. *New York Morning Telegraph,* 13 October 1941; *New Republic,* 27 October 1941; *Variety,* 5 November 1941.

83. Joseph Padway to Joseph Tuohy, 23 May 1941, Box 22, Teamsters Papers.

84. Memorandum from Ralph Clare, Secretary-Treasurer, Studio Transportation Drivers, 12 August 1943, Box 22, Teamsters Papers.

85. Marc Connelly to Teamsters, 12 June 1944, Box 22, Teamsters Papers.

86. *The Screen Actor,* 9 (Number 3, February 1943): 5.

87. Ibid., 9 (Number 4, March 1943): 1.

88. Ibid., 7 (Number 4, March 1942): 14.

89. Ibid., 8 (Number 2, July 1942): 8.

90. Ibid., 8 (Number 3, August 1942): 8, 10.

91. *Variety,* 20 December 1944.

92. Ella Winter, "Screen Writers Close Ranks," *New Masses,* 33 (Number 2, 3 October 1939): 27–28, p. 27.

93. *Variety,* 21 July 1942.

94. FBI Report, 10 July 1943, 100–157, Reel 2, *Communist Activity in the Entertainment Industry.*

95. *Daily Worker,* 7 August 1943; Al Richmond, *A Long View from the Left: Memoirs of an American Revolutionary,* Boston: Houghton Mifflin, 1973.

96. N. A. Daniels, "Hollywood Congress," *New Masses,* 49 (Number 1, 5 October 1943): 30–31.

97. *Variety,* 30 March 1942.

98. Michael Barrier, *Hollywood Cartoons: American Animation in Its Golden Age,* New York: Oxford University Press, 1999. Disney was one of the more hardnosed and obdurate studios during this battle; a decade later the company was being challenged by UPA (United Productions of America). However, many of UPA's cartoonists had left-wing sympathies, and in the hothouse atmosphere of the 1950s, such beliefs were unacceptable. The cartoonists were dismissed, UPA was wounded mortally, and Disney—which had truly earned an antilabor reputation—was catapulted into further prominence.

99. Harvey Deneroff, " 'We Can't Get Much Spinach': The Organization and Implementation of the Fleischer Animation Strike," *Film History: An International Journal,* 1 (Number 1, 1987): 1–14.

100. *Variety,* 8 January 1941.

101. Ibid., 6 January 1943; See also Mike Cormack, *Ideology and Cinematography in Hollywood, 1930–1939,* New York: St. Martin's, 1994.

102. Joseph Foster, "Changing Hollywood," *New Masses,* 54 (Number 6, 6 February 1945): 27.

CHAPTER 2

1. Michael Shull, "Tinted Shades of Red: The Popular American Cinematic Treatment of Militant Labor, Domestic Radicalism and Russian Revolutionaries, 1909–1929," Ph.D. dissertation, University of Maryland, 1994, pp. 153, 222, 269, 272. See also F. D. Klingender, *Marxism and Modern Art,* New York: International, 1945.

2. *Los Angeles Times,* 16 November 1997.

3. Burton Levine, "Professional Betrayers: The Secret World of Political Spies," Ph.D. dissertation, University of Pennsylvania, 1995, pp. 48–50, 53, 131.

4. Karl Marx, *Class Struggles in France, 1848–1850,* New York: International, 1964.

5. "Los Angeles Police Dept. Radical Squad," Weekly Intelligence Report, 1–12 January 1924, 13–29 January 1924, 23–29 August 1924, 13–19 September 1924, 27 September–3 October 1924, 4–10 October 1924, U.S. House of Representatives, Records of the Un-American Activities Committee, Record Group 233, Box 43.

6. William Hynes to Standard Oil, 5 November 1929, Box 8, Norman Leonard Papers.

7. Robert O'Hanlon to LAPD, 4 March 1930; T. S. Moodie to William Hynes, 31 October 1932, Box 8, Norman Leonard Papers.

8. R. C. Flournoy to "Dear Bill," 24 March 1934, Record Group 233, Box 45, "Reports and Memoranda Provided by the Intelligence Bureau, 1933–1938," U.S. House of Representatives, Records of the House Un-American Activities Committee.

9. "List of Meetings Broken Up by the Intelligence Bureau, 1933–1938," Records of the House Un-American Activities Committee.

10. Furniture Mfg. Assc. to William Hynes, 18 July 1935. Records of the House Un-American Activities Committee.

11. *Los Angeles Daily News,* 14 June 1939; *People's Daily World,* 15 June 1939.

12. J. Sultan to Karpiloff, 14 October 1930, Box 8, Norman Leonard Papers.

13. *Los Angeles Times,* 29 November 1937. See also "Major Activities of the Communists at Present," Intelligence Bureau—LAPD, 9 March 1936, Reel 96, National Republic Papers.

14. Memorandum, Sheriff's Office, Los Angeles County, 1 July 1932, Reel 95, National Republic Papers.

15. Pettis Perry, "How a Negro Came to Marxism," undated, Box 1, Folder 1, Pettis Perry Papers.

16. Brochure, circa 1934, Reel 125, National Republic Papers.

17. Undated clipping, Reel 125, National Republic Papers.

18. Report to LAPD Intelligence, 15 November 1935, Box 8, Norman Leonard Papers.

19. William Hynes, "The Communist Situation in Los Angeles," undated,

U.S. House of Representatives, Records of the Committee on Un-American Activities, Record Group 233, Box 49.

20. Advertisement, *New Masses,* 3 March 1935.

21. Report to LAPD Intelligence, 31 August 1935, Box 10, Norman Leonard Papers.

22. 12 September 1935, Box 10, Norman Leonard Papers.

23. Greg Mitchell, *The Campaign of the Century: Upton Sinclair's Race for Governor of California and the Birth of Media Politics,* New York: Random House, 1992.

24. Report to LAPD Intelligence, 14 May 1937, Box 10, Norman Leonard Papers.

25. Report to LAPD Intelligence, 6 August 1937, Box 10, Norman Leonard Papers.

26. Report to LAPD Intelligence, 30 December 1935, Box 10, Norman Leonard Papers.

27. "Resolutions and Proposals Adopted at L.A. County Convention," of Communist Party, 27–28 March 1937, Reel 96, National Republic Papers.

28. "The Communist Situation in California," Report of Sub-Committee on Subversive Activities of the Crime Prevention Committee, the Peace Officers Association, State of California, 17th Annual Convention, Oakland, California, 16–17 September 1937, Reel 96, National Republic Papers. See also "Materials on Communism in California," Submitted to Special Committee on Communism by the Bay Counties Peace Officers Association, by C.S. Morrill, Chief, Division of Criminal Identification and Investigation, 14 April 1932, Reel 96, National Republic Papers.

29. "Proceedings of the California Convention" of the Communist Party, 14–15 May 1938, Reel 96, National Republic Papers. See also "Report on Subversive Activities of the Crime Prevention Committee of the Peace Officers' Association, State of California," 20th Annual Convention, Fresno, California, 17–19 October 1940, Reel 96, National Republic Papers.

30. Ernest Jerome Hopkins, *What Happened in the Mooney Case,* New York: Brewer, Warren & Putnam, 1932; Robert Burke, *Olson's New Deal for California,* Berkeley: University of California Press, 1953.

31. Stationery, Hollywood Committee for the Freedom of Mooney and Billings, circa 1937, Carton 20, Tom Mooney Papers.

32. Petition to Lt. Governor Hatfield, 15 March 1937, Carton 20, Tom Mooney Papers.

33. William Z. Foster to "Dear Friend Tom," 26 September 1930?, Carton 7, Tom Mooney Papers.

34. "Browder Newton" to Tom Mooney, 30 May 1932, Carton 10, Tom Mooney Papers.

35. Upton Sinclair to Franklin D. Roosevelt, 12 May 1934, Carton 15, Tom Mooney Papers.

36. Upton Sinclair to Anna Mooney, 3 April 1931, Carton 15, Tom Mooney Papers.

37. George Bernard Shaw to Tom Mooney, 27 March 1933, Carton 15, Tom Mooney Papers.

38. Frederic March to Tom Mooney, 3 August 1936, Carton 17, Tom Mooney Papers.

39. Frederic March to Tom Mooney, 17 March 1937, Carton 22, Tom Mooney Papers.

40. Frederic March to Tom Mooney, 15 April 1937, Carton 22, Tom Mooney Papers.

41. J. R. Agnew, Secretary, Local 22, IATSE—San Diego, 11 July 1929, Carton 8, Tom Mooney Papers; Louis Rouse, Acting Assistant President, IATSE—New York City, 17 June 1930, Carton 8, Tom Mooney Papers.

42. Joseph Ellis, Secretary, Teamsters—Vallejo to Tom Mooney, undated, Carton 8, Tom Mooney Papers.

43. J. R. Hoisington, United Brotherhood of Carpenters and Joiners, Huntington Beach, California to Tom Mooney Campaign, 2 September 1931, Carton 15, Tom Mooney Papers.

44. Louis Weinstock to Tom Mooney, 6 January 1939, Carton 25, Tom Mooney Papers.

45. See Cartons 7, 10, 16, Tom Mooney Papers.

46. C. E. Ripple, Secretary, District Council 36 of Painters—Los Angeles to Governor Culbert Olson, 16 January 1939, Tom Mooney Papers.

47. J. W. Gillette, International Studio Representative, Musicians Mutual Protective Association, Local 47 of American Federation of Musicians to Tom Mooney, 11 March 1937; and Harry Baldwin to Tom Mooney, 27 July 1938, Carton 18, Tom Mooney Papers.

48. Assemblyman Jack Tenney to Mooney Defense Committee, 11 March 1937, Carton 23, Tom Mooney Papers.

49. Assemblyman Sam Yorty to Tom Mooney, 8 April 1938, Carton 23, Tom Mooney Papers.

50. Leo Gallagher to Tom Mooney, 7 December 1936, Carton 16, Tom Mooney Papers.

51. Leo Gallagher to Tom Mooney, 10 September 1937, Carton 20, Tom Mooney Papers.

52. Oliver Thornton to Campaign Manager, 17 August 1938, Carton 20, Tom Mooney Papers.

53. Report of Joint Fact-Finding Committee on Un-American Activities in California, California Legislature, 55th Session, 1943, pp. 63, 73, 78, 80, 91, 161, 158, 329.

54. Fourth Report on the Senate Fact-Finding Committee on Un-American Activities: Communist Front Organizations, California. Legislature. 60th Session, 1948, p. 364.

55. Undated clipping, circa 1940s, Reel 385, National Republic Papers.

56. Abraham Polonsky, Oral History, January 1974, American Film Institute.

57. Arnaud D'Usseau, "A Screenwriter Speaks," *New Masses,* 32 (Number 12, 12 September 1939): 29–31.

58. Marion Miller, *I Was a Spy,* Indianapolis: Bobbs-Merrill, 1960, p. 117.

59. Kim Chernin, *In My Mother's House: A Daughter's Story,* New York: Harper & Row, 1983.

60. Leroy Robinson, "John Howard Lawson—The Early Years" and "John Howard Lawson: Childhood," reprinted from "Bulletin of the Faculty of Arts, Nagasaki University Humanities," 19 (Number 1, 1979), Billy Rose Library.

61. Ibid. See also Leroy Robinson, "John Howard Lawson's 'Thunder Morning'," Billy Rose Library.

62. Autobiography, Box 98, Folder 3, John Howard Lawson Papers.

63. See, e.g., Harvey M. Teres, *Renewing the Left: Politics, Imagination and the New York Intellectuals,* New York: Oxford University Press, 1996.

64. Theodore Ward to John Howard Lawson, 3 August 1940, Box 34, Folder 4, John Howard Lawson Papers.

65. Thomas Cripps, *Making Movies Black: The Hollywood Message Movie from World War II to the Civil Rights Era,* New York: Oxford University, 1993.

66. *Daily Worker,* 15 October 1944.

67. Joseph Foster, "Current Films," *New Masses,* 50 (Number 11, 14 March 1944): pp. 28–33. See also Russell Campbell, *Cinema Strikes Back: Radical Filmmaking in the United States, 1930-1942,* Ann Arbor: UMI Research Press, 1982.

68. Charlotta Bass to John Howard Lawson, 18 July 1946, Box 12, Folder 3, John Howard Lawson Papers.

69. John Howard Lawson, "Can Anything Be Done About Hollywood?" *Masses & Mainstream,* 5 (Number 11, November 1952): 37–46. See also Scott Greer, "The Participation of Ethnic Minorities in the Labor Unions of Los Angeles County," Ph.D. dissertation, University of California, Los Angeles, 1952, pp. 9, 61, 112, 113: In that work, the writer refers to "various motion picture employees' organizations" such as the " 'white Jim Crow' unions." Some "lighter Mexicans" had few problems in securing employment, but "the darker ones are at a disadvantage." The oil workers' union rarely had minority members, a "reflection of an exclusionist policy on the part of management," while the packinghouse workers union, which had left and Communist leadership, had a "high proportion of Negroes."

70. George Willner to John Howard Lawson, 18 March 1949, Box 40, Folder 1, John Howard Lawson Papers.

71. See, e.g., Edward Callan, *Cry, the Beloved Country: A Novel of South Africa,* Boston: Twayne, 1991; Alan Paton, *Journey Continued: An Autobiography,* New York: Scribner, 1988; Peter F. Alexander, *Alan Paton: A Biography,* New York: Oxford University Press, 1994.

72. Memorandum, undated, Box 40, Folder 1, John Howard Lawson Papers.

See positive review in *New York Times*, 24 January 1952; *New York Journal-American*, 24 January 1952.

73. *Daily Worker*, 14 July 1943. See also Tom Zaniello, *Working Stiffs, Union Maids, Reds and Riffraff: An Organized Guide to Films about Labor*, Ithaca: ILR Press/Cornell, 1996.

74. Jason Joy to George Wasson, 26 July 1939, FX-LR-732, Fox Collection.

75. Vaughn, *Ronald Reagan in Hollywood*, pp. 150–151.

76. Anna C. Christian, *Meet It, Greet It and Defeat It: The Biography of Frances E. Williams:* Los Angeles: Milligan, 1999, pp. 147, 148, 164.

77. Helen Manfull, ed., *Additional Dialogue: Letters of Dalton Trumbo, 1942–1962*, New York: Bantam, 1972, p. 1.

78. Bruce Cook, *Dalton Trumbo*, New York: Scribner's, 1977, p. 147.

79. *Labor Herald*, 30 March 1945; *Dispatcher*, 6 April 1946.

80. Conference Program, 12 March 1947, Box 40, Folder 4, Dalton Trumbo Papers.

81. Dalton Trumbo, *The Time of the Toad: A Study of Inquisition in America*, New York: Harper & Row, 1972, pp. 42, 49, 60, 138.

82. Ibid.

83. Undated speech by Dalton Trumbo, Box 40, Folder 9, Dalton Trumbo Papers.

84. Rosalie Stewart to John Zinn, 13 September 1934, Box FX-LR-54, Fox Collection.

85. See also Lester Cole, *Hollywood Red: The Autobiography of Lester Cole*, Palo Alto: Ramparts, 1981; and see Carl Foreman, Oral History, April 1959, Columbia University.

86. Vaughn *Ronald Reagan in Hollywood*, p. 151.

87. Report, 31 December 1943, Record Group 46, Box 32, R-6701-a, U.S. Senate, Internal Security Subcommittee, Van Deman Collection.

88. Ibid., 31 December 1943, R6701-d.

89. Ibid., 30 December 1943, R6702-a.

90. Ibid., 31 December 1943, R6708-b.

91. D. M. Ladd to "The Director," 2 December 1944, Reel 1, *Communist Activity in the Entertainment Industry.* FBI and informer's reports—including those that form the basis for a good deal of this chapter—must be read cautiously. I surmise that they are 90 percent accurate in identifying individuals with "pro-Communist" views; however, they can be quite misleading in the homogenization of levels of commitment and in demonizing of activities carried out by individuals who hold such allegiances.

92. *The Screen Writer*, 2 (Number 4, September 1946): 2.

93. *Los Angeles Examiner*, 28 July 1946; *Los Angeles Herald Express*, 30 July 1946; *Los Angeles Times*, 31 July 1946; *Chicago Daily News*, 1 August 1946; *Los Angeles Daily News*, 6 August 1946.

94. Clipping, 25 October 1946, Reel 386, National Republic Papers; *New York Times*, 22 October 1946.

95. Ben Burns, *Nitty Gritty: A White Editor in Black Journalism*, Jackson: University Press of Mississippi, 1996, p. 75.

96. Pettis Perry, "Negroes in the 1944 Elections," Box 3, Folder 5, Pettis Perry Papers.

97. Patrick McGilligan and Paul Buhle, *Tender Comrades: A Back Story of the Hollywood Blacklist*, New York: St. Martin's, 1997, pp. 149, 164.

98. Vaughn, *Ronald Reagan in Hollywood*, p. 173.

99. "Special Report," 15 April 1945, Record Group 46, Box 40, R7714-a, U.S. Senate, Internal Security Subcommittee, Van Deman Collection.

100. "Special Report," 16 April 1945, Record Group 46, Box 40, R7714-e, U.S. Senate, Internal Security Subcommittee, Van Deman Collection.

101. *Los Angeles Sentinel*, 19 September 1946.

102. Minutes of Council Meeting, 25 June 1946, Box 5, Reel 5043, Actors Equity Association.

103. *California Eagle*, 7 November 1946.

104. *Los Angeles Sentinel*, 31 October 1946 and 7 November 1946.

105. *Daily Worker*, 6 February 1944.

106. *Daily Worker*, 18 January 1945.

107. V. J. Jerome, "The Negro in Hollywood Films," text of speech delivered 3 December 1950, Reel 1779, #4276, Tamiment Radical Pamphlet Series.

108. Review by David Platt, *Daily Worker* circa 28 January 1944, Reel 8, *Communist Activity in the Entertainment Industry*.

109. "Confidential" Report, 21 June 1946, Record Group 46, Box 45, R-8488-e, U.S. Senate, Internal Security Subcommittee, Van Deman Collection.

110. *Daily Worker*, circa February 1944, Reel 8, Communist Activity in the Entertainment Industry.

111. *Daily Worker*, 15 November 1944.

112. Margaret E. James to Robert Kenny, 9 August 1946, Robert Kenny Papers.

113. *Hollywood Reporter*, 13 June 1952.

114. Report, 24 February 1945, Record Group 46, Box 39, R7569-b, U.S. Senate, Internal Security Subcommittee, Van Deman Collection.

115. "Weekly Intelligence Summary," 18–25 October 1944, Record Group 46, Box 33, R6733-a, U.S. Senate, Internal Security Subcommittee, Van Deman Collection.

116. Report, 11 September 1943, Record Group 46, Box 39, R7596-a and b, U.S. Senate, Internal Security Subcommittee, Van Deman Collection.

117. *Variety*, 31 July 1946.

118. Frances Stonor Saunders, *Who Paid the Piper? The CIA and the Cultural Cold War*, London: Granta Books, 1999.

119. Albert Maltz, Oral History, 13 February 1975 through 26 January 1979, Box 11, Albert Maltz Papers.

120. Albert Maltz, "What Shall We Ask of Writers?" *New Masses,* 58 (Number 7, 12 February 1946): 19–22.

121. Howard Fast, "Art and Politics," *New Masses,* 58 (Number 9, 26 February 1946): 6–8; Joseph North, "No Retreat for the Writer," *New Masses,* 58 (Number 9, 26 February 1946): 8–10. Ironically, years earlier a critic in the *New Masses* had presented an analysis similar to that of Maltz without incurring the wrath of other writers. Peter Ellis, in analyzing Victor McLaglen's role in *The Informer,* determined it irrelevant that the actor himself was "reactionary and nurses fascist aspirations." An actor is an "artist," and "in the final analysis, a worker" with no say over the lines he spouts. See Peter Ellis, "On Calling Names," *New Masses,* 20 (Number 11, 28 July 1936): 29.

122. William Z. Foster, "People's Cultural Policy," *New Masses,* 59 (Number 4, 23 April 1946): 6–9.

123. Bernhard Stern to Albert Maltz, 18 February 1946, Box 15, Folder 14, Albert Maltz Papers.

124. Millard Lampel to Albert Maltz, 21 February 1946, Box 15, Folder 14, Albert Maltz Papers.

125. Louis Harap to Joseph North, 22 February 1946, Box 15, Folder 14, Albert Maltz Papers.

126. See also McGilligan and Buhle, *Tender Comrades.*

127. Trumbo, *The Time of the Toad,* p. 49.

128. McGilligan and Buhle, *Tender Comrades,* p. 6.

129. Harry Potamkin, "The Eyes of the Movie," New York: International Pamphlet No. 38, circa 1930s, Reel 117, National Republic Papers.

130. Archibald MacLeish, "The Cinema of Joris Ivens," *New Masses,* 24 (Number 9, 24 August 1937): 18.

131. Louis Harap, "Christopher Cauldwell," *New Masses,* 57 (20 November 1945): 22–23, p. 22.

132. Manfull, *Additional Dialogue,* Dalton Trumbo to Samuel Sillen, circa 1946, p. 22.

133. John Howard Lawson, *Theory and Technique of Playwriting and Screenwriting,* New York: Putnam's, 1949; John Howard Lawson, *Film: The Creative Process: The Search for an Audio-Visual Language and Structure,* New York: Hill and Wang, 1964; John Howard Lawson, *Film in the Battle of Ideas,* New York: Masses and Mainstream, 1953.

134. V. J. Jerome, *Culture in a Changing World: A Marxist Approach,* New York: New Century, 1947, p. 25. See also V. J. Jerome, "Grasp the Weapon of Culture!" (Text of his report to the 15th National Convention of the Communist Party, December 1950), Reel 1781, #4275, Tamiment Radical Pamphlet Series; U.S. House of Representatives, 82nd Congress, 1st Session, *Communist Infiltration of Hollywood Motion Picture Industry—Part I,* 8 March 1951.

135. *Daily Worker,* 16 April 1944.

136. See, e.g., *Daily Worker,* 18 April 1943.

137. Ibid., 9 April 1944.

138. Ibid., 18 December 1944.

139. Ibid., 21 January 1944.

140. See e.g. William Alexander, *Film on the Left: American Documentary Film from 1931 to 1942,* Princeton, N.J.: Princeton University Press, 1981; Peter Ellis, "Sights and Sounds," *New Masses,* 23 (Number 8, 11 May 1937): 30–32.

141. Peter Ellis, "Sights and Sounds," *New Masses,* 21 (Number 2, 6 October 1936): 29.

142. Report, 18 March 1945, Record Group 46, Box 44, R-8343, U.S. Senate, Internal Security Subcommittee, Van Deman Collection.

143. FBI Report, 100–15732, 12 March 1946, Reel 2, *Communist Activity in the Entertainment Industry.*

144. *Daily Worker,* 28 May 1944.

145. Reports, 9 November 1945 and 12 December 1945, Reel 2, *Communist Activity in the Entertainment Industry.*

146. "Jurisdiction Disputes," U.S. House of Representatives, 80th Congress, 2nd Session, 1948, p. 1937.

147. Nancy Lynn Schwartz, *The Hollywood Writers' Wars,* New York: Knopf, 1982, pp. 81, 86, 91, 192, 193; Kurt Schuparra, *Triumph of the Right: The Rise of the California Conservative Movement, 1945–1966,* Armonk: M. E. Sharpe, 1998.

148. Schwartz, *The Hollywood Writers' Wars.*

149. Report, 9 June 1945, Record Group 46, Box 44, R8342-c, U.S. Senate, Internal Security Subcommittee, Van Deman Collection.

150. Report, 6 March 1944, Record Group 46, Box 33, R6821-b, Van Deman Collection. The equation of Tuttle with De Mille as a director is subject to challenge.

151. Report, 4 February 1944, Record Group 46, Box 33, R6903-b, Van Deman Collection.

152. "Confidential" Report, 9 March 1944, Record Group 46, Box 44, R8368-c, Van Deman Collection.

153. Report, 10 February 1944, Record Group 46, Box 33, R6866-c, Van Deman Collection.

154. Report, 21 April 1945, Record Group 46, Box 40, 7700-a, Van Deman Collection. This evaluation of Garfield is misleading; however, like other bits of evidence proffered by the authorities, this one is striking not because of the truth of the matter asserted but because of what it reveals about their state of mind: in suggesting that Garfield's staunch liberalism was roughly equivalent to pro-communism, this report suggests that the impact—if not the purpose—of the anticommunist upsurge was to derail progressives generally.

155. Report, 11 January 1945, Record Group 46, Box 37, R7450-f, Van Deman Collection.

156. "Weekly Intelligence Summary," 15 June 1946, Record Group 46, Box 44, R8501, Van Deman Collection.

157. "Weekly Intelligence Summary," 19 July 1946, Record Group 46, Box 44, R8602, Van Deman Collection.

158. Report, 9 December 1943, Record Group 46, Box 39, R7649-b, Van Deman Collection. See also Wendy Smith, *Real Life Drama: The Group Theatre and America, 1931–1940,* New York: Grove Weidenfeld, 1990.

159. Report, 1 August 1944, Record Group 46, Box 36, R7189-b, Van Deman Collection. Others reported to be in the party included George H. Corey, a screenwriter at Columbia (Report, 22 September 1945, Record Group 46, Box 44, R8341-b); Richard Collins, screenwriter for MGM (Report, 18 December 1943, Record Group 46, Box 32, R6708-b); Robert Rossen, director, "called 'social significance Joe'" (Report, 5 January 1944, Record Group 46, Box 33, R6783-a); Ben Margolis, attorney for the party, was said to be a member of "the Hollywood Club" (Report, 10 April 1945, Record Group 46, Box 40, R7691-a); John Weber, alias Isador Weinstein, was a Communist "employed in the literary department of the William Morris Agency" (Report, 12 April 1945, Record Group 46, Box 40, R7691-f).

160. Report, 4 January 1944, Record Group 46, Box 33, R6783-b, Van Deman Collection.

161. Report, 11 January 1944, Record Group 46, Box 33, R6783-c, Van Deman Collection.

162. Report, 25 August 1945, Record Group 46, Box 42, R7998-b, Van Deman Collection.

163. Report, 1 June 1943, Record Group 46, Box 33, R6840-f, Van Deman Collection: Harold Buchman, a screenwriter at Fox, is listed as a "communist fellow traveller"; Abrams S. Burrows, radio scriptwriter for *Duffy's Tavern,* was "formerly a member of the cultural section" of the party and was reputed to be still involved; Report, 10 January 1944, Record Group 46, Box 33, R6846-a: Anna Revere, a "motion picture actress employed by" Fox, who had been "in numerous plays on Broadway" was reported to be a Communist; she was born 25 June 1907, had brown hair and blue eyes, and was 5'5" and 125 pounds.

164. Report, 30 October 1943, Record Group 46, Box 32, R6601, Van Deman Collection.

165. Report, 8 March 1946, Record Group 46, Box 43, R8319-a, Van Deman Collection.

166. Report, 18 March 1946, Record Group 46, Box 43, R8353, Van Deman Collection.

167. Report, 4 February 1946, Record Group 46, Box 44, R8262, Van Deman Collection.

168. Report, 29 June 1946, Record Group 46, Box 44, R8601, Van Deman Collection.

169. Report, 27 January 1944, Record Group 46, Box 35, R7091-c, Van Deman Collection.

170. "Weekly Intelligence Summary," 25 August 1945, Record Group 46, Box 41, 7955-d, Van Deman Collection.

171. Report, 17 June 1944, Record Group 46, Box 36, R7154-a, Van Deman Collection.

172. Report, 22 October 1943, Record Group 46, Box 32, R6651-c, Van Deman Collection.

173. Report, 9 August 1945, Record Group 46, Box 44, R8379-a; Report, 14 March 1944, Record Group 46, Box 33, R6820-b, Van Deman Collection.

175. Report, 6 March 1945, Record Group 46, Box 42, R8099-c, Van Deman Collection.

176. Louis Goldblatt, Oral History, 15 February 1978, Columbia University. Goldblatt worked with Jeff Kibre, dispatched by the longshore union to organize studio labor in the 1930s. Kibre later worked for the United Fishermen's Union, which was run out of business by the government in a case prosecuted by the future Supreme Court justice Thurgood Marshall.

177. Report, 11 September 1943, Record Group 46, Box 46, R8751-c, Van Deman Collection.

178. Report, 3 April 1944, Record Group 46, Box 35, R7052-a, Van Deman Collection.

179. Report, 9 March 1944, Record Group 46, Box 34, R6901-c, Van Deman Collection.

180. Report, 15 June 1944, Record Group 46, Box 44, R8408-d, Van Deman Collection.

181. Report, 25 December 1943, Record Group 46, Box 32, R6719-c, Van Deman Collection.

182. "Weekly Intelligence Summary," Record Group 46, Box 46, R8784, Van Deman Collection.

183. Catalogue of Courses, 24 January 1944, Record Group 46, Box 33, R6741, Van Deman Collection.

184. FBI Report, 100–1763, 29 February 1944, Record Group 46, Box 33, R6864, Van Deman Collection.

185. Ibid.

186. Report, 24 May 1944, Record Group 46, Box 35, R7110-a, Van Deman Collection.

187. See, e.g., Box 4, Folder 4, Hollywood Democratic Committee Papers.

188. N. A. Daniels, "Hollywood Congress," *New Masses,* 49 (Number 1, 5 October 1943): 30–31.

189. Report, 18 August 1946, Record Group 46, Box 45, R8606, Van Deman Collection.

190. Report, 1 April 1946, Record Group 46, Box 44, R8354, Van Deman Collection.

191. "Confidential War Department Report," 20 June 1945, Record Group 46, Box 41, R7832-a, Van Deman Collection.

192. Michael Denning, *The Cultural Front: The Laboring of American Culture in the Twentieth Century,* New York: Verso, 1996, p. 378.

193. Report on Southern California Communist Party meeting, 18 September 1945, Record Group 46, Box 42, R8021, Van Deman Collection.

194. "Report B—California," "Confidential Notes on CP," 23 April 1951, Record Group 233, Box 50, U.S. House of Representatives, Records of the Committee on Un-American Activities.

195. Report, 18 February 1946, Record Group 46, Box 43, R8288, U.S. House of Representatives, Records of the Committee on Un-American Activities.

196. Report to California State Convention of the Communist Party, 17 July 1948, Niebyl-Proctor Library.

197. Minutes of Council, 10 December 1946, Box 5, Reel 5043, Actors Equity Papers.

198. *Los Angeles Times,* 20 February 1942.

199. Interview with Lela Rogers, 3 May 1944, Record Group 233, Box 29, File 324, "Exhibits, Evidence, etc.," U.S. House of Representatives, Records of the Committee on Un-American Activities.

200. Clipping, circa August 1947, Reel 544, National Republic Papers.

201. Clipping, 1 November 1947, Reel 384, National Republic Papers.

202. Howard Suber, "The Anti-Communist Blacklist in the Hollywood Motion Picture Industry," Ph.D. dissertation, UCLA, 1968, p. 90.

203. *New York Times,* 1 October 1946.

204. Report, 17 May 1947, Box 584, Jay Lovestone Papers.

CHAPTER 3

1. Lester Cole, *Hollywood Red: The Autobiography of Lester Cole,* Palo Alto, Calif.: Ramparts Press, 1981. See also Claire Potter, *War on Crime: Bandits, G-Men and the Politics of Mass Culture,* New Brunswick: Rutgers University Press, 1998.

2. Stephen Norwood, "Ford's Brass Knuckles," *Labor History,* 37 (Number 3, Summer 1996): 365–391.

3. *Daily Worker,* 24 December 1935; See File on corruption in painters locals in New York City, 1932–1936, Box 1, Louis Weinstock Papers.

4. Philip S. Foner, *The Fur and Leather Workers Union: A Story of Dramatic Struggles and Achievements,* Newark: Nordan Press, 1950, pp. 396, 413.

5. Sidney Lens, *Left, Right and Center: Conflicting Forces in American Labor,* Hinsdale: Henry Regnery, 1949, p. 68.

6. See "Racketeering," File 7, Box 10, Philip Taft Papers.

7. Leo Katcher, *The Big Bankroll: The Life and Times of Arnold Rothstein,* pp. 239, 241, 261.

8. Michael J. Zuckerman, *Vengeance Is Mine: Jimmy 'The Weasel' Fratianno Tells How He Brought the Kiss of Death to the Mafia,* New York: MacMillan, 1987, p. 101.

9. David Scott Witwer, "Corruption and Reform in the Teamsters Union, 1890 to 1991," Ph.D. dissertation, Brown University, 1994, pp. 175, 233; in Manhattan the "Westies," an Irish-American gang, had "influence in various entertainment unions, especially theatrical Teamsters Local 817, which delivered props and equipment to film and television studios throughout the city. . . . [I]n the late 1940s the murderous John 'Cockeye' Dunn . . . had made efforts to take over Teamsters Local 804 by threatening the life of Joe Coffey, Sr. . . . [D]rivers for [Local] 817 became among the highest paid of any Teamster local in the city." See T. J. English, *The Westies: Inside the Hell's Kitchen Irish Mob,* New York: G. P. Putnam's, 1990, pp. 155, 159, 263.

10. Michael Denning, *The Cultural Front: The Laboring of American Culture in the Twentieth Century,* New York: Verso, 1996, pp. 375–376.

11. Sam and Chuck Giancana, *Double Cross: The Story of the Man Who Controlled America,* New York: Warner, 1992, p. 105.

12. Mark A. Stuart, *Gangster #2: Longy Zwillman, the Man who Invented Organized Crime,* Secaucus: Lyle Stuart, 1985, p. 127.

13. Jeff Gerth, "Richard Nixon and Organized Crime," in Sid Blumenthal and Harvey Yazijian, *Government by Gunplay: Assassination Theories from Dallas to Today,* New York: New American Library, 1976, pp. 130–151. On 1 June 1973 a *Los Angeles Times* editorial, "Nixon, the Teamsters and the Mafia," detailed the close ties between the premier anticommunist politician and organized crime figures stretching back to the era of CSU.

14. John Hutchinson, *The Imperfect Union: A History of American Trade Unions,* New York: Dutton, 1970, pp. 130–133. See also Leo Huberman, *The Labor Spy Racket,* New York: Modern Age, 1937; Sidney Howard, *The Labor Spy,* New York: Republic Publications, 1924.

15. Denning, *The Cultural Front,* p. 254. "Film noir," a major thematic trend closely identified with Hollywood, has been marked indelibly by the pervasive influence of organized crime. See, e.g., Jon Tuska, *Dark Cinema: American Film Noir in Cultural Perspective,* Westport, Conn.: Greenwood, 1984. In response to the perceived debasing of movies, in the early 1930s reformers sought to point Hollywood in a different direction. See "Personal" Memorandum by William Short, Director of Motion Picture Research Council, to Jane Addams, Ivy Lee, Gerard Swope, et al., 15 September 1933, Box 12, Motion Picture Research Council Papers. See also John McCarty, *Hollywood Gangland: The Movies' Love Affair with the Mob,* New York: St. Martin's, 1993.

16. Robert Lacey, *Little Man: Meyer Lansky and the Gangster Life,* Boston: Little, Brown, 1991, p. 148.

17. Michael Munn, *The Hollywood Connection: The True Story of Organized Crime in Hollywood,* London: Robson, 1993, p. 89. See also Marvin Wolf and Katherine Moder, *L.A. Crime,* New York: Facts on File, 1986.

18. Manohla Dargis, "Dark Side of the Dream," *Sight and Sound,* 6 (Number 8, August 1996): 15–19.

19. *New Yorker,* 21–28 October 1996. See also Arthur Miller, *Timebends: A Life,* New York: Grove Press, 1987.

20. Joseph Greco, "The File on Robert Siodmak in Hollywood: 1941–1951," Ph.D. dissertation, State University of New York, Stony Brook, 1995, pp. 179–180.

21. "Proceedings of Conference on Thought Control in the U.S.," sponsored by Hollywood Arts, Sciences and Professions Council, July 1947, Beverly Hills Hotel, p. 329, Labor Archives and Research Center, San Francisco State University.

22. Hank Messick, *The Beauties and the Beasts: The Mob in Show Business,* p. ix.

23. *New York Times,* 23 July 1997.

24. Speech by Eric Johnston, 27 January 1948, Box 411, File 15, Cecil B. De-Mille Archives.

25. *Granma Weekly,* 4 December 1996 (this Cuban newspaper was citing remarks made by Luciano to the Havana magazine *Bohemia* in 1957).

26. Andy Edmonds, *Bugsy's Baby: The Secret Life of a Mob Queen,* New York: Birch Lane, 1993, p. 72.

27. Earl Warren to Hiram Johnson, 23 October 1939, Part III, Box 79, Hiram Johnson Papers.

28. Warren Olney III to Earl Warren, 21 May 1946, F3640: 2631, Earl Warren Papers.

29. *San Francisco Examiner,* 31 May 1946.

30. Mrs. Don Hays to Earl Warren, 25 July 1946, F3640: 2631, Earl Warren Papers.

31. E. E. Stokes to Earl Warren, 4 October 1947, File 3640: 937–955, E5862, Earl Warren Papers.

32. Memorandum to Harold Huls, President, Public Utilities Commission, 12 December 1947, File 3640: 937–955, E5862, Earl Warren Papers.

33. *Los Angeles Daily News,* 8 November 1947, 13 November 1947.

34. Dennis Sprague to Vern Scoggins, 11 December 1947, File 3640: 937–955, E5862, Earl Warren Papers. See also *Los Angeles Daily News,* 4 December 1947.

35. Mickey Cohen, *Mickey Cohen: In My Own Words; The Autobiography of Michael Mickey Cohen as told to John Peter Nugent,* Englewood: Prentice-Hall, 1975, pp. 3, 74, 96, 99, 232, 233.

36. "Combined Reports of the Special Crime Study Commission on Organized Crime," Sacramento, November 1950, F3640: 955, Earl Warren Papers.

37. Michael Munn, *The Hollywood Connection: The True Story of Organized Crime in Hollywood,* Hollywood: Robson, 1993, p. 55.

38. Ibid., p. 62.

39. Zuckerman, *Vengeance Is Mine,* p. 7; Stuart, *Gangster #2,* p. 164.

40. *Variety,* 16 January 1940.

41. Charles Rappleye and Ed Becker, *All-American Mafioso: The Johnny Ro-selli Story,* Garden City, N.J.: Doubleday, 1991, p. 140: In Phoenix, Bioff—who had changed his name—became friendly with Barry Goldwater, with whom he consulted on "labor racketeering."

42. Elmer Irey, *The Tax Dodgers: The Inside Story of the T-Men's War with America's Political and Underworld Hoodlums,* Slocum, New York: Greenberg, 1948, p. 288.

43. Ovid Demaris, *The Last Mafioso: The Treacherous World of Jimmy Fratianno,* New York: Times Books, 1981, p. 29.

44. Cohen, *Mickey Cohen,* pp. 100, 106.

45. Nitti Transcript, pp. 2673, 2676, 2678.

46. Vincent J. Furriel, *Organized Crime: History and Control,* Sacramento: Chancellor's Office, California Community Colleges, California State Peace Officers' Training Series, 1976, pp. 88, 89, 102. Siegel also "supervised the Teamsters trucking and shipping operations at the studios." See Edmonds, *Bugsy's Baby,* p. 77.

47. Dan Moldea, *Dark Victory: Reagan, MCA and the Mob,* New York: Dutton, 1986, p. 69.

48. Giancana, *Double Cross,* p. 302.

49. *New York Herald Tribune,* 19 November 1943.

50. Nitti Transcript, p. 2387.

51. *Variety,* 10 January 1945.

52. Malcolm Johnson, *Crime on the Labor Front,* New York: McGraw-Hill, 1950, p. 30. See also Daniel Bell, *Capitalism Today,* New York: New American Library, 1971.

53. *Los Angeles Times,* 5 July 1987.

54. Giancana, *Double Cross,* p. 148.

55. Stuart, *Gangster #2,* p. 97.

56. Giancana, *Double Cross,* p. 34.

57. Cohen, *Mickey Cohen,* p. 59.

58. See, e.g., Martin Duberman, *Stonewall,* New York: Dutton, 1993; Leading L.A. mobster Mickey Cohen owned a number of "gay places" though he adds quickly: "I never had to go into them." See Cohen, *Mickey Cohen,* p. 196. Gary W. Potter, *The Porn Merchants,* Dubuque, Iowa: Kendall-Hunt, 1986, p. i. See also *Washington Post,* 12 April 1979: "[T]he pornography is controlled by organized crime. Phony names and dummy corporations are used, but behind them are the crime bosses." On the mob and music see Justine Picardie and Dorothy Wade, *Music Man: Ahmet Ertegun, Atlantic Records and the Triumph of Rock 'n' Roll,* New York: Norton, 1990: pp. 55, 163. Morris Levy, who owned the fabled jazz club Birdland "has never made any secret of his connections with the New York Mafia.

. . . [O]ne of the six major record companies that dominate the market today has had a mobster on its payroll and two other majors have been touched by . . . Mafia-related scandal." See also Ronald L. Morris, *Wait until Dark: Jazz and the Underworld, 1880–1940*, Bowling Green: Bowling Green Popular Press, 1980, pp. 4, 133: John Hammond "believed that no fewer than three in every four jazz clubs and cabarets of this distant period were either fronted, backed or in some way managed by Jewish and Sicilian mobsters." The author concludes, "The chief difficulty I experienced in conducting research for this study rests on this aspect of the code . . . stony silence" and wariness in discussing organized crime.

59. George Chauncey, *Gay New York: Gender, Urban Culture and the Making of the Gay Male World, 1890–1940*, New York: Basic, 1994, p. 450. Joseph Epstein, a leader of the mob in Chicago, was gay: See Edmonds, *Bugsy's Baby*, p. 34. A founding father of "beat" culture and an influence on William Burroughs and Jack Kerouac was Herbert Huncke, who formerly had been "a runner for the Capone gang" and a gay prostitute. He was the title character in Burrough's first book, *Junkie*, and was represented in Allen Ginsberg's *Howl* and Kerouac's *On the Road* (*New York Times*, 9 August 1996). In 1946 the L.A. City Council considered a measure to bar men "impersonating women" but "will not forbid women dressing as men." This trend was seen as an "increasing nuisance." *Los Angeles Times*, 18 December 1946. IATSE leader Roy Brewer charged that Sorrell and CSU ally Father George Dunne were lovers. See George Dunne, Oral History, 1981, UCLA Oral History Program. See also Robert Corber, *Homosexuality in Cold War America*, Durham: Duke University Press, 1997; William J. Mann, *Wisecracker: The Life and Times of William Haines, Hollywood's First Openly Gay Star*, New York: Viking, 1998; Andrew Hewitt, *Political Inversion: Homosexuality, Fascism and the Modernist Imaginary*, Stanford: Stanford University Press, 1996.

60. English, *The Westies*, p. 346: "Then Kelly and Shannon unzipped their pants and masturbated all over the guy." See also Giancana, *Double Cross*, pp. 100, 148, 397: A favored tactic of mobsters was shoving a poker "right up [the] ass" of opponents. Once Giancana put a gun in the rectum of an antagonist and threatened to pull the trigger. When William Jackson was murdered by the mob, they "rammed an electric prod up his rectum." The mob's entree into gay male culture provided them with leverage among certain elites. In 1952, for example, the *Las Vegas Sun* "listed men and dates of homosexual encounters between [Senator Joseph] McCarthy and other men." See Perry Bruce Kaufman, "The Best City of Them All: A History of Las Vegas, 1930–1960," Ph.D. dissertation, University of California, Santa Barbara, 1974, p. 506. See also *Las Vegas Sun*, 25 October 1952.

61. Rappleye and Becker, *All-American Mafioso*.

62. Stuart Timmons, *The Trouble with Harry Hay: Founder of the Modern Gay Movement*, Boston: Alyson, 1990, p. 61. See also Raymond Strait, *Star Babies: The Shocking Lives of Hollywood Children*, New York: St. Martin's, 1979; Harry Hay, *Radically Gay: Gay Liberation in the Words of Its Founder*, Boston: Beacon, 1996.

63. See, e.g., Michael Paul Rogin, *Black Face, White Noise: Jewish Immigrants and the Hollywood Melting Pot,* Berkeley: University of California Press, 1996; Daniel Bernardi, ed., *The Birth of Whiteness: Race and the Emergence of U.S. Cinema,* New Brunswick: Rutgers University Press, 1996; Maria Joy Bergstrom, "'Old Glory and Old Races': Whiteness and Gender in Narratives of the American West," Ph.D. dissertation, University of Michigan, 1996; Neil Foley, *The White Scourge: Mexicans, Blacks and Poor Whites in Texas Cotton Culture,* Berkeley: University of California Press, 1997; Paul Maria Stathakis, "Almost White: Greek and Lebanese-Syrian Immigrants in North and South Carolina, 1900–1940," Ph.D. dissertation, University of South Carolina, 1991.

64. English, *The Westies,* p. 160.

65. See Gerald Horne, *Fire This Time: The Watts Uprising and the 1960s,* Charlottesville: University Press of Virginia, 1995, passim.

66. Daniel Bell, *The End of Ideology,* Glencoe, Illinois: Free Press, 1960, p. 147. See also James O'Kane, *The Crooked Ladder: Gangsters, Ethnicity and the American Dream,* New Brunswick, N.J.: Transaction, 1992; Robert A. Rockaway, *But He Was Good to His Mother: The Lives and Crimes of Jewish Gangsters,* Jerusalem: Gefen Publishing House, 1993; Raymond Lee, *Gangsters and Hoodlums: The Underworld and Cinema,* South Brunswick, N.J.: A. S. Barnes, 1971; President's Commission on Organized Crime, *The Edge: Organized Crime, Business and Labor Unions,* Report to the President and Attorney General, Washington, D.C.: Government Printing Office, 1986; Rich Cohen, *Tough Jews,* New York: Simon & Schuster, 1998.

67. Stuart, *Gangster #2,* pp. 50, 188.

68. Edmonds, *Bugsy's Baby,* p. 155.

69. Demaris, *The Last Mafioso,* p. 105.

70. Frank Ragano and Selwyn Raab, *Mob Lawyer,* New York: Scribners, 1994, p. 19.

71. Lacey, *Little Man,* p. 337.

72. Zuckerman, *Vengeance Is Mine,* p. 84.

73. "Combined Reports of the Special Crime Study Commission."

74. *Los Angeles Times,* 20 June 1997: Eddie Cannizzaro, a "gofer for . . . Jack Dragna," admits that he murdered Siegel.

75. Cohen, *Mickey Cohen,* pp. 35, 43, 52, 67, 68, 91.

76. Ed Reid, *Mickey Cohen: Mobster,* New York: Pinnacle, 1973, pp. 171, 182.

77. See generally, Rogin, *Black Face, White Noise,* passim.

78. Munn, *The Hollywood Connection,* p. 32; See also Lewis Yablonsky, *George Raft,* San Francisco: Mercury House, 1974, pp. 4, 222.

79. Giancana, *Double Cross,* pp. 107, 263.

80. Demaris, *The Last Mafioso,* 109.

81. Stuart, *Gangster #2,* p. 142.

82. Ragano and Raab, *Mob Lawyer,* pp. 215, 314.

83. Jon Wiener, *Professors, Politics and Pop,* New York: Verso, 1991. See also *New Republic,* 31 March 1986: As late as 1960 Sinatra tried to defy the blacklist by hiring Albert Maltz for a writing assignment.

84. Cohen, *Mickey Cohen,* p. 86, 188.

85. *Washington Times-Herald,* 26 September 1947; *Washington Post,* 3 October 1947.

86. See "The Strikers," circa 1945–1946, "Union Related Items," Sonia Volochova Papers. This lengthy list also included Betty Grable, Dorothy Lamour, Irene Dunne, Greer Garson, Claudette Colbert, Linda Darnell, Shirley Temple, Esther Williams, June Allyson, Marjorie Main, Donna Reed, Larraine Day, Lana Turner, Barbara Stanwyck, Edward Arnold, Alan Hale, Bing Crosby, Brian Donlevy, Bud Abbott & Lou Costello, Rudy Vallee, Van Johnson, Fred Astaire, Walter Pidgeon, John Payne, Harry James, Dick Haymes, Cornell Wilde, Caesar Romero, Errol Flynn, Dennis Morgan, Robert Benchley, Adolf Menjou, and Pat O'Brien.

87. Ibid.

88. Edwin Greenwald to Ingrid Bergman, 21 May 1945, Box 597, Folder 17, David O. Selznick Collection.

89. *Hollywood Sun,* 25 July 1945. See also "The Picket Line," 21 September 1945, Roger McDonald Papers.

90. Danae Clark, *Negotiating Hollywood: The Cultural Politics of Actors' Labor,* Minneapolis: University of Minnesota Press, 1995, pp. 23, 71.

91. Charles Higham, *Merchant of Dreams: Louis B. Mayer, MGM and the Secret Hollywood,* New York: Donald I. Fine, 1993.

92. *Daily Worker,* 8 February 1944.

93. Program from L.A. Council event, 16 November 1943, Box 5, National Council of American-Soviet Friendship Papers. Other patrons included Charlotta Bass, Mayor Fletcher Bowron, Sidney Buchman, Theodore Dreiser, Helen Gahagan, E. Y. Harburg, Joris Ivens, Howard Koch, Albert Maltz, Carey McWilliams, Clarence Muse, and John Wexley.

94. Marjorie De Armand, "Hollywood Town Meeting," *New Masses,* 54 (Number 11, 13 March 1945): 29.

95. *Time,* 9 September 1946.

96. Edward G. Robinson to Robert Kenny, 17 December 1945, Robert Kenny Papers.

97. Edward G. Robinson to Jessica Smith, 13 February 1943, Box 29, Folder 7, Edward G. Robinson Papers.

98. "Shrine Talk" by Edward G. Robinson, 26 August 1943, Box 30, Folder 6, Edward G. Robinson Papers.

99. Edward G. Robinson to Nate Spingold, 5 May 1952, Box 18, Folder 8, Ralph De Toledano Papers. This file also includes groveling apologies for past leftism from, e.g., Henry and Phoebe Ephron, and Michael Blankfort.

100. Clipping, December 1946, Reel 384, National Republic Papers.

101. Myron Fagan, *Unmasking the Reds in Hollywood,* Hollywood: Cinema Educational Guild, 1949, Reel 226, National Republic Papers.

102. "Confidential 11ND 24427," circa 1943, Record Group 46, Box 32, R6643-a, U.S. Senate, Internal Security Subcommittee, Van Deman Collection.

103. Walter Reuther to Melvyn Douglas, 18 February 1946, Box 13, Folder 2, Melvyn Douglas Papers. See also *Detroit News,* 15 February 1946; *Detroit Free Press,* 15 February 1946.

104. Melvyn Douglas to PCA, 15 February 1947, Box 13, Folder 2, Melvyn Douglas Papers.

105. See Pamphlet by Patriotic Society of St. Louis, *Red Stars in Hollywood,* circa 1947, Box 13, Folder 2, Melvyn Douglas Papers.

106. Clipping, 18 August 1934, Reel 95, National Republic Papers.

107. *San Francisco Examiner,* 10 May 1944.

108. *Daily Worker,* 5 May 1944.

109. Patrick J. McGrath, *John Garfield: The Illustrated Career in Films and on Stage,* London: McFarland, 1993, p. 92.

110. "The Hollywood Closeup," 7 November 1945, Sonia Volochova Papers.

111. "The Hollywood Closeup," 1 November 1945, Southern California Library for Social Studies and Research.

112. Clipping, 10 December 1947, Reel 385, National Republic Papers. Boris Karloff also supported CSU: See Anne Edwards, *Early Reagan,* New York: William Morrow, 1987, p. 309.

113. Edward Dmytryk, Oral History, June 1959, Columbia University. See also Edward Dmytryk, *Odd Man Out: A Memoir of the Hollywood Ten,* Carbondale: Southern Illinois University Press, 1996. Contemporary entertainment executive Barry Diller has suggested that the "creative process forces you to be somewhat humanistic. . . . It comes with the work"; an artist must have "empathy with other people" and these forces drive artists ineluctably to the left. See David Prindle, *Risky Business: The Political Economy of Hollywood,* Boulder, Colo.: Westview, 1993, p. 95. See also Vincent Sherman, *My Life as a Film Director,* Lexington: University Press of Kentucky, 1997; Stephen Vaughn, *Ronald Reagan in Hollywood: Movies and Politics,* New York: Cambridge University Press, 1994, p. 188: psychological profiles portrayed actors as "driven by 'inner fears' or as 'neurotic, unstable and asocial' and prone to homosexuality."

114. *The Screen Writer,* 3 (Number 1, June 1947):3.

115. Vaughn, *Ronald Reagan in Hollywood,* p. 130.

116. Ronald Reagan with Richard G. Hubler, *Where's the Rest of Me: The Autobiography of Ronald Reagan,* New York: Karz, 1981, pp. 126, 159, 184.

117. Philip Dunne, Oral History, 1991, Academy of Motion Picture Arts and Sciences.

118. George Dunne, *King's Pawn: The Memoirs of George H. Dunne, S.J.,* Chicago: Loyola University Press, 1990, pp. 137, 142.

119. *CSU News,* 1 (Number 11, 18 January 1947): 1, Roger McDonald Papers.

120. Charles Chaplin, *My Autobiography,* New York: Simon & Schuster, 1964, p. 450.

121. *Daily Worker,* 16 February 1944.

122. Ibid., 14 January 1946.

123. Ibid., 5 March 1944.

124. Norman Jacoby of *Alert,* "the weekly report on Communism in California," to Donald MacLean, Cecil B. DeMille Productions, 29 December 1951, Box 1159, Folder 4, Cecil B. DeMille Archives. See also Thom Anderson, "Red Hollywood," in Suzanne Ferguson and Barbara Groseclose, eds., *Literature and the Visual Arts in Contemporary Society,* Columbus: Ohio State University Press, 1985, 141–196.

125. Eric Bentley, *Are You Now or Have You Ever Been? The Investigation of Show Business by the Un-American Activities Committee, 1947–1958,* New York: Harper & Row, 1972, p. 62. See also Sterling Hayden, *Wanderer,* New York: Knopf, 1963.

126. Bentley, *Are You Now or Have You Ever Been?* p. 121.

127. Walter Bernstein, Oral History, 10 February 1983, Columbia University.

128. *Daily Worker,* 9 September 1939. See also Victor Navasky, *Naming Names,* New York: Penguin, 1991.

129. Zuckerman, *Vengeance Is Mine,* p. 2.

130. Lacey, *Little Man,* p. 146.

131. Cohen, *Mickey Cohen,* p. 83. See also *People,* 21 October 1996.

132. *People,* 21 October 1996.

133. Kaufman, "The Best City of Them All," p. 367: "For a long period of time black entertainers at the resort hotels could not even stay at the hotels where they [performed]."

CHAPTER 4

1. Robert Lacey, *Little Man: Meyer Lansky and the Gangster Life,* Boston: Little Brown, 1991, p. 80.

2. Mark A. Stuart, *Gangster #2: Longy Zwillman, The Man Who Invented Organized Crime,* Secaucus: Lyle Stuart, 1985, pp. 88–89, 90.

3. Sam and Chuck Giancana, *Double Cross: The Story of the Man Who Controlled America,* New York: Warner, 1992, pp. 409, 434.

4. Andy Edmonds, *Bugsy's Baby: The Secret Life of a Mob Queen,* New York: Birch Lane, 1993, p. 111.

5. Sam Kashner and Nancy Schoenberger, *Hollywood Kryptonite: The Bulldog, the Lady and the Death of Superman,* New York: St. Martin's, 1996, pp. 6, 160, 185.

6. Mickey Cohen, *Mickey Cohen: In My Own Words; The Autobiography of Michael Mickey Cohen as told to John Peter Nugent,* Englewood: Prentice-Hall, 1975, p. 196.

7. Nitti Transcript, pp. 3255, 3275.

8. Ibid., pp. 3228, 3495.

9. *Labor Herald,* 15 February 1946.

10. *Daily Worker,* 23 February 1944.

11. "Dan Georgakas, "The Screen Playwright as Author: An Interview with Budd Schulberg," *Cineaste,* 2 (Number 4, 1982): 6–15, p. 11. With some justification, the actor Tony Curtis has claimed that criticism of his accent when he performs in Shakespeare's plays is both anti-Jewish and anti-New York since no one, he suggests, criticizes Sir Laurence Olivier when he uses his British accent while playing a Roman emperor: Tony Curtis, Interview, 9 November 1993, WNYC-AM, New York City.

12. Patriotic Tract Society, *Jew Stars over Hollywood,* St. Louis, circa 1940, California State Library, Sacramento.

13. *The Nation,* 17 April 1935; *New Masses,* 30 April 1935.

14. Michael Denning, *The Cultural Front: The Laboring of American Culture in the Twentieth Century,* New York: Verso, 1996, p. 197.

15. Steven Alan Carr, "The Hollywood Question: America and the Belief in Jewish Control over Motion Pictures before 1941," Ph.D. dissertation, University of Texas at Austin, 1994, p. 114.

16. Ivor Montague, *With Eisenstein in Hollywood,* New York: International, 1974, p. 68.

17. Stuart Timmons, *The Trouble with Harry Hay: Founder of the Modern Gay Movement,* Boston: Alyson, 1990, p. 29.

18. *New York Times,* 2 March 1997. See also Annette Insdorf, *Indelible Shadows: Film and the Holocaust,* New York: Cambridge University Press, 1989.

19. Anthony Slide, "Hollywood's Fascist Follies," *Film Comment,* 27 (Number 4, July-August 1991): 1–8. See also Gloria Lothrop, "A Shadow on the Lance: The Impact of Fascism on Los Angeles Italians," *California History,* 75 (Number 4, 1996): 322–353.

20. Gregory Black, *Hollywood Censored: Morality Codes, Catholics and the Movies,* New York: Cambridge University Press, 1994, p. 70–71.

21. John Russell Taylor, *Strangers in Paradise: The Hollywood Emigres, 1933–1950,* New York: Holt, Rinehart and Winston, 1983.

22. David Platt, "The Hollywood Witchhunt of 1947: A Thirtieth Anniversary," in David Platt, ed., *Celluloid Power: Social Film Criticism from 'The Birth of a Nation' to 'Judgment at Nuremberg,'* Metuchen: Scarecrow, 1992.

23. Press Release, 9 October 1941, Reel 9091, Federated Press Papers.

24. *Hollywood Reporter,* 18 August 1941.

25. *New York Times,* 23 July 1997.

26. R. E. Wood to Walter Braunschwiger, 11 August 1941, Box 269, America First Papers.

27. United Press International dispatch, 20 December 1940, Reel 94, National Republic Papers.

28. Undated Petition from Allan W. "Bill" Wells, National Republic Papers.

29. Robert N. Nodurft, "Hollywood's Road to War: The Film Industry and the Great Debate over Intervention," Ph.D. dissertation, Purdue University, 1995. See also Clayton R. Koppes and Gregory D. Black, *Hollywood Goes to War: How Politics, Profits and Propaganda Shaped World War II Movies,* New York: Free Press, 1987.

30. *New York Times,* 18 July 1940.

31. Bruce Minton, "Blackmailing Hollywood," *New Masses,* 52 (Number 7, 15 August 1944): 11–12.

32. Unsigned letter to Robert Stripling, 20 February 1942, Record Group 233, Box 1, "Los Angeles Office, Numbered Case Files," U.S. House of Representatives, Records of the Committee on Un-American Activities.

33. Memorandum to William Cline, 21 May 1942, Record Group 233, Box 11, File 60, U.S. House of Representatives, Records of the Committee on Un-American Activities.

34. Rosemary Foley to Dr. Israel Goldstein, 20 January 1943, Box 10, Folder 42, Walter Wanger Papers.

35. Henry Montor to Walter Wanger, 12 April 1943, Walter Wanger Papers.

36. Harry Cohn to Walter Wanger, 9 July 1943, Walter Wanger Papers.

37. Dinner program, 22 July 1943, Walter Wanger Papers.

38. Will Rogers, Jr., to Walter Wanger, 5 October 1943, Walter Wanger Papers.

39. Letter from Walter Wanger, et al., 7 October 1943, Walter Wanger Papers.

40. Walter White to Walter Wanger, 22 October 1940, Box 14, Folder 9, Walter Wanger Papers.

41. Memorandum from David O. Selznick Productions, 8 November 1939, Box 185, Folder 16, David O. Selznick Collection.

42. Selznick to John Hay Whitney, 10 February 1939, David O. Selznick Collection.

43. Rabbi Barnett Brickner to Selznick, 17 May 1938, David O. Selznick Collection.

44. Val Lewton to Selznick, 9 June 1939, David O. Selznick Collection.

45. Selznick to John P. Wharton, 19 January 1940, David O. Selznick Collection. See also Gerald Horne, *Black Liberation/Red Scare: Ben Davis and the Communist Party,* Newark: University of Delaware Press, 1994.

46. Speech by Canada Lee, circa 1949, Box 1, Canada Lee Papers.

47. Edward Margolies and Michel Fabre, *The Several Lives of Chester Himes,* Jackson: University Press of Mississippi, 1997, p. 47.

48. Neal Gabler, *An Empire of Their Own: How the Jews Invented Hollywood,* New York: Crown, 1988, pp. 365, 381.

49. FBI Report, 12 December 1946, Reel 2, Communist Activity in the Entertainment Industry.

50. FBI Report, 9 August 1946, Reel 2, Communist Activity in the Entertainment Industry.

51. Flyer by "Committee on Unemployment, Hollywood Actors and Technicians," circa 1939, Record Group 233, Box 13, U.S. House of Representatives, Records of the Committee on Un-American Activities.

52. *Los Angeles Times,* 23 March 1945. See also Charles P. Larrowe, *Harry Bridges: The Rise and Fall of Radical Labor in the U.S.,* New York: Lawrence Hill, 1972.

53. Report Delivered to the First National Convention of the American Jewish Labor Council by Max Steinberg, 15 June 1946, New York City, Niebyl-Proctor Library.

54. *People's Daily World,* 7 March 1945.

55. "Confidential" Report, "Weekly Intelligence Summary," Number 112, 16 February 1946, Record Group 46, Box 44, U.S. Senate, Internal Security Subcommittee, Van Deman Collection.

56. Memorandum, 17 June 1946, Record Group 46, Box 45, R8547-a, Van Deman Collection.

57. Memorandum, 16 June 1946, Record Group 46, Box 45, R8547-b, Van Deman Collection.

58. Memorandum, 29 June 1946, Record Group 46, Box 45, R8601, Van Deman Collection.

59. Arthur Liebman, *Jews and the Left,* New York: John Wiley, 1979, p. 1. See also Adam M. Weisberger, *The Jewish Ethic and the Spirit of Socialism,* New York: Peter Lang, 1997; Joy Torstrup McAllister, "A Study of Delinquent Jewish Youth in Los Angeles County," Ed.d. dissertation, University of California, Los Angeles, 1968.

60. See, generally, Gerald Horne, *Black Liberation/Red Scare: Ben Davis and the Communist Party,* Newark: University of Delaware Press, 1994.

61. Resolution, 15 June 1948, Box 112, Folder 4, Dore Schary Papers.

62. Undated Statement from JCRC, Box 92, Folder 9, Dore Schary Papers.

63. Myron Fagan, *Moscow over Hollywood,* Los Angeles: Cary, 1948.

64. Unsigned Memorandum, 17 February 1949, Box 92, Folder 9, Dore Schary Papers.

65. Daryl Zanuck to Laura Z. Hobson, 27 May 1947, Box 21, Laura Z. Hobson Papers.

66. "Mrs. Dalton" to Laura Z. Hobson, 7 February 1947, Laura Z. Hobson Papers.

67. George F. Custen, *Twentieth Century's Fox: Darryl F. Zanuck and the Culture of Hollywood,* New York: Basic, 1997, p. 303.

68. Nitti Transcript, pp. 1547, 1587, 1612, 1647, 1684. See also Tino Balio, *The American Film Industry,* Madison: University of Wisconsin Press, 1976.

69. "Open Letter to Jack Warner," *New Masses,* 57 (Number 4, 23 October 1945): 20.

70. *Daily Worker,* 8 November 1943.

71. Jack Warner to James F. T. O'Connor, 3 October 1944, Volume 20, James F. T. O'Connor Papers.

72. Hollywood for Roosevelt, circa 1940, 7024, Personal File, Franklin D. Roosevelt Papers. See also the group's full-page advertisement in the *New York Times,* 30 October 1940.

73. Invitation, 30 April 1942, Office of Social Entertainment, Box 103, Franklin D. Roosevelt Papers.

74. Jack Warner to James F. T. O'Connor, 20 November 1944, Volume 20, James F. T. O'Connor Papers.

75. Ethan Mordden, *The Hollywood Studios: House Style in the Golden Age of the Movies,* New York: Knopf, p. 230.

76. *Daily Worker,* 24 April 1944; David Platt article, 1944, Reel 8, #128, *Communist Activity in the Entertainment Industry.*

77. Jack Young, "Washington Talks to Hollywood," *New Masses,* 43 (Number 13, 30 June 1942): 10–12.

78. Griffin Fariello, *Red Scare: Memories of the American Inquisition: An Oral History,* New York: Norton, 1995, p. 117.

79. Howard Koch, Oral History, April 1974, American Film Institute. See also Ian Hamilton, *Writers in Hollywood, 1915–1951,* New York: Harper & Row, 1990.

80. Joseph Davies to Congressman Parnell Thomas, 10 June 1947; Joseph Davies to Howard Koch, 1 October 1947, Box 3, Howard Koch Papers. See also Robert Brent Toplin, ed., *Hollywood as Mirror: Changing Views of 'Outsiders' and 'Enemies' in American Movies,* Westport, Conn.: Greenwood, 1993.

81. *Hollywood Reporter,* 3 May 1943: "N.Y. Critics Heap Praise on 'Moscow' and Warners."

82. *Variety,* 26 September 1945.

83. Stephen Vaughn, *Ronald Reagan in Hollywood: Movies and Politics,* New York: Cambridge University Press, 1994, p. 159.

84. Patrick McGilligan and Paul Buhle, *Tender Comrades: A Back Story of the Hollywood Blacklist,* New York: St. Martin's, 1997, p. 712. See also Jack Warner, *My First Hundred Years in Hollywood,* New York: Random House, 1965.

85. Vaughn, *Ronald Reagan in Hollywood,* p. 75.

86. Michael Drosnin, *Citizen Hughes: In His Own Words—How Howard Hughes Tried to Buy America,* New York: Holt, Rinehart & Winston, 1985, pp. 162–166.

87. Charles Higham, *Merchants of Dreams: Louis B. Mayer, MGM and the Secret Hollywood,* New York: Donald I. Fine, 1993, pp. 287–288.

88. Marc Eliot, *Walt Disney: Hollywood's Dark Prince,* New York: Birch Lane, 1993, pp. xii, xx, 84, 108, 120, 123. Disney's distaste for the Laemmles may have been motivated by this family's staunch support of Jewish refugees during the

war years. See, e.g., Udo Bayer, "Laemmle's List: Carl Laemmle's Affidavits for Jewish Refugees," *Film History,* 10 (Number 4, 1998): 501–521.

89. "Jurisdictional Disputes," U.S. House of Representatives, 80th Congress, 1st Session, 1948, p. 1917. See also Steven Watts, *The Magic Kingdom: Walt Disney and the American Way of Life,* New York: Houghton Mifflin, 1997.

90. Ring Lardner, Jr., "The Sign of the Boss," in Platt, *Celluloid Power,* pp. 383–394.

91. Ayn Rand to DeMille, 3 July 1934, Box 315, Folder 5, Cecil B. DeMille Archives.

92. Memorandum, 14 November 1945, Box 1199, Folder 45, Cecil B. DeMille Archives.

93. A. G. Arnoll to Cecil B. DeMille Productions, 2 December 1937, Box 73, Folder 8, Cecil B. DeMille Papers.

94. R. B. Hood, FBI Special Agent in Charge, Los Angeles, to Florence Cole, 18 October 1947; J. Edgar Hoover to Cecil B. DeMille, 30 June 1947; Cecil B. DeMille to "Cousin Hunter," 18 April 1947, Box 407, Folder 15, Cecil B. DeMille Archives.

95. R. B. Hood to Florence Cole, 28 November 1940, Box 360, Folder 20, Cecil B. DeMille Archives.

96. Memorandum from "GR," 5 January 1942, Box 115, Folder 39, Cecil B. DeMille Archives.

97. *Hollywood Reporter,* 3 November 1947.

98. Memorandum from Donald MacLean, 8 December 1953, Box 1172, Folder 5, Cecil B. DeMille Archives.

99. George Shellenberger to Donald MacLean, 5 May 1955, Box 1192, Folder 15, Cecil B. DeMille Archives.

100. DeMille to Arthur DeBra, 14 June 1948, Box 411, Folder 15, Cecil B. DeMille Archives.

101. H. L. Hunt to DeMille, 27 May 1946; H. L. Hunt to Cecil B. DeMille, 7 August 1950; DeMille to H. L. Hunt, 18 August 1950; DeMille to H. L. Hunt, 3 March 1952, Box 1164, Folder 5, Cecil B. DeMille Archives.

102. Statement by DeMille, 14 February 1947, Box 1198, Folder 16; "Stenographic Transcript" of House Education and Labor Committee hearing, 11 May 1948, Box 1198, Folder 29, Cecil B. DeMille Archives.

103. Gladys Rosson to Herman Darstein, 13 October 1949, Box 908, Folder 24, Cecil DeMille Archives.

104. Michael Jeffers to Donald Hayne, 28 August 1948, Box 1207, Folder 5, Cecil B. DeMille Archives.

105. Earl Warren to DeMille, 8 July 1944, Box 111, Folder 11, Cecil B. DeMille Archives.

106. Herbert Brownell to DeMille, 16 September 1944, Box 111, Folder 11, Cecil B. DeMille Papers.

107. Dave E. Morris to Hiram Johnson, 30 July 1926, Part III, Box 78, Hiram Johnson Papers. See also Richard Coke Lower, *A Bloc of One: The Political Career of Hiram W. Johnson,* Stanford: Stanford University Press, 1993.

108. Louis B. Mayer to Hiram Johnson, 29 September 1931, Part III, Box 58, Hiram Johnson Papers.

109. Louis B. Mayer to James F. T. O'Connor, 5 September 1936, Volume 13, James F. T. O'Connor Papers.

110. See file "Motion Picture Controversies," circa 1938, File 3273, Earl Warren Papers.

111. File on Robert Kenny, circa 1946, File 3640: 571, Earl Warren Papers.

112. Earl Warren to Hiram Johnson, 27 March 1940, Part III, Box 79, Hiram Johnson Papers.

113. Giuliana Muscio, *Hollywood's New Deal,* Philadelphia: Temple University Press, 1997.

114. Selznick to Earl Warren, 23 October 1946, Box 2365, Folder 1, David O. Selznick Collection.

115. R. W. Hanley to Earl Warren, 24 October 1945, File 3640: 2365, Earl Warren Papers.

116. Louella Parsons to William Randolph Hearst, 25 February 1932, Carton 15, William Randolph Hearst Papers.

117. Louella Parsons to William Randolph Hearst, 26 April 1937, Carton 22, William Randolph Hearst Papers.

118. Arthur Lubin to Bosley Crowther, 2 June 1941, Box 6, Folder 5, Bosley Crowther Papers.

119. Clifton Fadiman to Bosley Crowther, 20 June 1944, Box 6, Folder 5, Bosley Crowther Papers.

120. Hollywood Arts, Sciences and Professions Council, *Thought Control in USA: Toward Freedom of Thought,* Los Angeles: HASPC, 1947, San Francisco State University, Labor Archives and Research Center.

121. *Los Angeles Examiner,* 18 March 1945.

122. Mordden, *The Hollywood Studios,* pp. 12, 24, 89, 323. See also Rudy Behlmer, ed., *Inside Warner Bros.,* New York: Viking, 1985; Bosley Crowther, *Hollywood Rajah: The Life and Times of Louis B. Mayer,* New York: Holt, Rinehart and Winston, 1960; Samuel Marx, *Mayer and Thalberg: The Make-Believe Saints,* New York: Random House, 1975; Gilbert Seldes, *The Movies Come from America,* New York: Scribner's, 1937; Bob Thomas, *Thalberg: Life and Legend,* Garden City, N.J.: Doubleday, 1969; Ronald Davis, *The Glamour Factory: Inside Hollywood's Big Studio System,* Dallas: Southern Methodist University Press, 1993.

123. Vaughn, *Ronald Reagan in Hollywood,* p. 45.

124. *Los Angeles Times,* 5 February 1944. See also *New York Sun,* 5 February 1944.

125. Robert Vogel, Oral History, 1991, Academy of Motion Picture Arts & Sciences.

126. N. A. Daniels, "Hollywood Letter," *New Masses,* 50 (Number 10, 7 March 1944): 29–30.

127. Roger Baldwin to Crowther, 5 October 1945, Box 6, Folder 6, Bosley Crowther Papers.

128. Nodurft, "Hollywood's Road to War," pp. 83, 88.

129. James Dugan, "Sights and Sounds," *New Masses,* 36 (Number 1, 25 June 1940): 30–31.

130. Press Release from War Production Board, 6 January 1945, Box 1016, Folder 8, David O. Selznick Collection.

131. Campaign Material, 1940, Box 1, Folder 19, Eric Johnston Papers.

132. Literature, circa 1945, Box 2, Folder 43, Eric Johnston Papers.

133. *Variety,* 5 June 1946.

134. Ibid., 18 September 1946.

135. Ibid., 18 September 1946. See also Joseph Foster, "Exit Hays, Enter Johnston," *New Masses,* 57 (Number 11, 9 October 1945): 29–30.

136. Ina Johnston, Oral History, circa 1977, Eastern Washington Historical Society.

137. *Variety,* 19 September 1945.

138. Eric Johnston to Ina Johnston, 18 November 1946, Box 8, Folder 1, Eric Johnston Papers.

139. Eric Johnston to "Ina and girls," 22 July 1947, Box 8, Folder 1, Eric Johnston Papers.

140. Eric Johnston to "Dear Mother," 12 March 1948, Box 8, Folder 1, Eric Johnston Papers.

141. *The Screen Writer,* 2 (Number 4, September 1946): 2.

142. Statement by Eric Johnston, circa 1949, Box 6, Folder 7, Eric Johnston Papers.

143. John Ruffato, Oral History, 15 September 1978, Eastern Washington Historical Society.

144. *Variety,* 26 September 1945.

145. *New York Sun,* 28 October 1947.

146. Eric Johnston, Oral History, 1959, Columbia University.

147. John Ruffato, Oral History, 15 September 1978, Eastern Washington Historical Society.

148. Joseph Foster, "Movies in Mexico," *New Masses,* 54 (Number 7, 20 February 1945): 28–30.

149. See, e.g., Donald Leroy Perry, "An Analysis of the Financial Plans of the Motion Picture Industry for the Period 1929 to 1962," Ph.D. dissertation, University of Illinois, 1966; Margaret Dickinson and Sarah Street, *Cinema and State: The Film in Industry and Government, 1927–1984,* London: British Film Institute, 1985; Stephen G. Jones, *The British Labour Movement and Film, 1918–1939,* New York: Routledge, 1987; Randal Johnson, *The Film Industry in Brazil: Culture and the State,* Pittsburgh: University of Pittsburgh Press, 1987; Jonathan Buchs-

baum, *Cinema Engage: Film in the Popular Front,* Urbana: University of Illinois Press, 1988; Robert Burnett, *The Global Jukebox: The International Music Industry,* New York: Routledge, 1996; Abe Mark Nornes and Fukushima Yukio, eds., *The Japan/America Film Wars: World War II Propaganda and Its Cultural Contexts,* Chur, Switzerland: Harwood, 1994; *Daily Worker,* 28 August 1944; Albert Moran, ed., *Film Policy: International, National and Regional Perspectives,* London: Routledge, 1996; Martine Danan, "From Nationalism to Globalization: France's Challenge to Hollywood's Hegemony," Ph.D. dissertation, Michigan Technical University, 1994; Lary May, *Screening Out the Past: The Birth of Mass Culture and the Motion Picture Industry,* New York: Oxford, 1980.

150. Selznick to Morris Ernst, 3 April 1945, Box 1321, Folder 3, David O. Selznick Collection. See also Kristin Thompson, *Exporting Entertainment: America in the World Film Market, 1907–1934,* London: British Film Institute, 1985; Steven S. Wildman and Stephen E. Siwek, *International Trade in Films and Television Programs,* Cambridge: Ballinger, 1988.

151. Morris Ernst to Selznick, 17 August 1945, Box 1321, Folder 3, David O. Selznick Collection.

152. Selznick to Morris Ernst, 3 April 1945, Box 597, Folder 17, David O. Selznick Collection.

153. Selznick to Ernst, 22 March 1945, Box 1321, Folder 3, David O. Selznick Collection.

154. Selznick to Earl Warren, 21 April 1945, Box 597, Folder 17, David O. Selznick Collection.

CHAPTER 5

1. P. K. Edwards, *Strikes in the United States, 1881–1974,* New York: St. Martin's, 1981, pp. xiii, 3, 7. See also Bernard Karsh, *Diary of a Strike,* Urbana: University of Illinois Press, 1958, p. v: "The strike is among the most highly publicized and the least studied social phenomena of our time."

2. "Jurisdictional Disputes," U.S. House of Representatives, 80th Congress, 2nd Session, 1948, p. 1919.

3. K. G. J. C. Knowles, *Strikes—A Study in Industrial Conflict,* New York: Philosophical Library, 1952, p. 1.

4. William Z. Foster, *Strike Strategy,* Chicago: TUEL, Labor Herald Library, 1926, p. 3.

5. John Steuben, *Strike Strategy,* New York: Gaer, 1950, p. 63. See also Harold Hart, ed., *The Strike: For and Against,* New York: Harold Hart, 1971; Wyndham Mortimer, *Organize! My Life as a Union Man,* Boston: Beacon, 1971.

6. Nelson Lichtenstein, *Labor's War at Home: The CIO in World War II,* New York: Cambridge University Press, 1982.

7. Howell Harris, *The Right to Manage: Industrial Relations Policies of American Business in the 1940s*, Madison: University of Wisconsin Press, pp. 3–4.

8. Sally M. Miller and Daniel A. Cornford, eds., *American Labor in the Era of World War II*, Westport, Conn.: Greenwood, 1995.

9. Timothy Alan Willard, "Labor and the National War Labor Board, 1942–1945: An Experiment in Corporatist Wage Stabilization," Ph.D. dissertation, University of Toledo, 1984, p. 410.

10. Richard P. Boyden, "The San Francisco Machinists and the National War Labor Board," in Miller and Cornford, *American Labor in the Era of World War II*, pp. 105–119. See also "Weekly News Letter from California State Federation of Labor," 12 December 1945, Southern California Library for Social Studies and Research: The AFL assailed "raiding" by CIO and its "campaign of jurisdictional warfare."

11. "Jurisdictional Disputes," U.S. House of Representatives, 80th Congress, 1st Session, 1947, p. 104.

12. "Jurisdictional Disputes," U.S. House of Representatives, 80th Congress, 2nd Session, 1948, p. 1562.

13. Nitti Transcript, p. 1332.

14. "Information Bulletin," 7 September 1945, IATSE Records—New York City Office.

15. "Jurisdictional Disputes," U.S. House of Representatives, 80th Congress, 2nd Session, 1948, p. 1790.

16. *Variety*, 16 May 1945.

17. "Jurisdictional Disputes," U.S. House of Representatives, 80th Congress, 2nd Session, 1948, p. 1562. See also Gorham Kindem, ed., *The American Movie Industry: The Business of Motion Pictures*, Carbondale: Southern Illinois University Press, 1982.

18. "Jurisdictional Disputes," U.S. House of Representatives, 80th Congress, 1st Session, 1947, pp. 476–486.

19. Tom Murtha to Karen Pezutto, undated, IATSE Records—New York City Office: There were conflicts within and without Local 44 of IATSE involving, e.g., Nurserymen, Drapers, and Upholsterers; an accompanying document sought to distinguish "property-making and miniature work" versus "special effects or general effects" versus "upholsterers and drapers" versus "nursery set dressers," etc. See also Thomas Murtha, Chairman, Adjustment Committee, to George Browne, 10 September 1940, re: Conflicts between IATSE Local 27, Laborers versus other IATSE Locals—e.g., grips. "The grips especially have made violent protests."

20. Ibid., p. 104.

21. Ibid., p. 2050.

22. "Jurisdictional Disputes," U.S. House of Representatives, 80th Congress, 2nd Session, 1948, pp. 2033–2040. See also Christina Kathleen Wilson, "Cedric Gibbons and Metro-Goldwyn-Mayer: The Art of Motion Picture Set Design," Ph.D. dissertation, University of Virginia, 1998.

23. Transcript of Proceedings before the National War Labor Board, "In the Matter of Loew's (MGM) and Screen Cartoonists Guild, Local 852, AFL," Los Angeles, 5 March 1945, Box 85, Clark Kerr Papers.

24. See also Columbia Pictures, etc., and Screen Publicists Guild, Case No. 111–12307-D, Hearings Held 2 January 1945, Box 85, Clark Kerr Papers.

25. "Records Relating to Strikes," 2 March 1945, Record Group 202, Box 966, Records of National War Labor Board. See also "Motion Picture Producers Association v. Screen Office Employees Guild, Local 1391," 25 November 1944, Record Group 280, Box 1517, Records of U.S. Federal Mediation and Conciliation Service; File on 1945, 111–11414–111–11519, Record Group 202, Box 581, Records of National War Labor Board.

26. "Jurisdictional Disputes," U.S. House of Representatives, 80th Congress, 1st Session, 1947, p. 65.

27. Ibid., p. 825.

28. Minutes of Screen Actors Guild meeting, 16 March 1945, Screen Actors Guild Papers.

29. *New York World-Telegram,* 11 November 1941; *Variety,* 16 August 1939.

30. Lester Cole, *Hollywood Red: The Autobiography of Lester Cole,* Palo Alto, Calif.: Ramparts, 1981, p. 212.

31. William Green to Herb Sorrell, 16 March 1945, Screen Actors Guild Papers.

32. "Jurisdictional Disputes," U.S. House of Representatives, 80th Congress, 2nd Session, 1948, p. 2220.

33. "Jurisdictional Disputes," U.S. House of Representatives, 80th Congress, 1st Session, 1947, p. 856.

34. Mike Nielsen and Gene Mailes, *Hollywood's Other Blacklist: Union Struggles in the Studio System,* London: British Film Institute, 1995, p. 167.

35. Hans Burkhardt, Oral History, 1977, UCLA Oral History Program.

36. Undated note, Box 1199, Folder 44, Cecil B. DeMille Archives.

37. Ibid.

38. Karl Struss to Frances Perkins, 23 April 1945, Record Group 280, Case File 444/3763–444/3823, Box 1525, Records of U.S. Federal Mediation and Conciliation Service.

39. *International Juridical Association Monthly,* 5 (Number 7, January 1937): 75; *People of the State of California v. Mrs. Charlotte Duncan,* Superior Court, L.A. County, Appellate Department, Cr.A. 1369, 28 December 1936, Meiklejohn Civil Liberties Institute. See also Hosoon Chang, "Labor Picketing and the First Amendment: Union Members' Right to Picket, Public Opinion and the U.S. Supreme Court," M.A. thesis, University of North Carolina, Chapel Hill, 1990.

40. Memorandum from K. B. Anger, "Picket Chief," and Eugene Judd, Secretary, 7 December 1945, Box 1, Louis Ciccone Papers.

41. Letter to Roger McDonald from spouse, undated, circa 1945, Roger McDonald Papers.

42. "The Ten Commandments of the Pickets," circa 1945, Roger McDonald Papers.

43. *Motion Picture Herald,* 7 July 1945.

44. *Hollywood Atom,* 16 August 1945, Hollywood Studio Strike Collection, Southern California Library for Social Studies and Research.

45. Press Release, 3 October 1945, Reel 9091, Federated Press Papers.

46. *Hollywood Atom,* 31 August 1945, Roger McDonald Papers.

47. *Hollywood Sun,* 8 June 1945, Roger McDonald Papers.

48. "Picket Line Slogans," 1945, Roger McDonald Papers.

49. "The Ten Commandments of the Picket Line," circa 1945–1946, Sonia Volochova Papers.

50. "Union Related Items," circa 1945–1946, Sonia Volochova Papers.

51. "Jurisdictional Disputes," U.S. House of Representatives, 80th Congress, 1st Session, 1947, p. 116.

52. "Summons," *Warner Brothers v. Local 1421,* circa 1945, Roger McDonald Papers.

53. "Jurisdiction Disputes," U.S. House of Representatives, 80th Congress, 1st Session, 1948, p. 1923.

54. *Motion Picture Herald,* 2 June 1945.

55. Ibid., 5 May 1945.

56. Daniel O'Shea to Morris Ernst, 27 April 1945, Box 597, Folder 17, David O. Selznick Collection.

57. "Picket Line," 21 April 1945, Box 597, Folder 17, David O. Selznick Collection.

58. Dick Hungate to Selznick, 14 May 1945, Box 597, Folder 17, David O. Selznick Collection. See also flyer issued by "Autonomy Alliance Organized to Fight for Clean Unionism Free of Gangsterism and Dictatorship," Box 597, Folder 17, David O. Selznick Collection: Here IATSE's Richard Walsh was accused of placing B. C. 'Cappy' Duval—"whose career in Hollywood began as a collector for Bioff's 2% assessment racket"—in control of a local. "Thousands are spent to force new people into the IATSE—not one cent has been spent to help [represent] IATSE members!!" Walsh, it was said, "has incurred the hatred of other [IA] unions for the IATSE. Only last week delegates from many diversified unions voted against affiliation of an IATSE local in the Central Labor Council. The local was No. 80, Studio Grips."

59. *Hollywood Reporter,* 13 November 1946.

60. "Charles" to "Dan," undated, Box 597, Folder 17, David O. Selznick Collection.

61. "Jurisdictional Disputes," 80th Congress, 2nd Session, U.S. House of Representatives, 1948, pp. 1774, 1783.

62. L. T. Sheppard to "the two Warner Brothers," undated, Box 6, Folder 10, Jack Warner Collection.

63. Warner to John Cromwell, 15 October 1945, Box 6, Folder 10, Jack Warner Collection.

64. Ross F. Walker to Warner, 8 October 1945, Box 6, Folder 10, Jack Warner Collection.

65. Howard Emmett Rogers to Warner, 19 October 1945, Box 6, Folder 10, Jack Warner Collection.

66. Jacob Solomon to Warner Bros., circa 1945, Box 6, Folder 10, Jack Warner Collection.

67. *Los Angeles Times,* 10 August 1945.

68. Transcript of Conversation between Steve Trilling and Jack Dales, undated, Box 8, Folder 6, Jack Warner Collection.

69. A. M. Sperber and Eric Lax, *Bogart,* New York: Morrow, 1997, p. 316.

70. Fred Meyer to Warner, 4 June 1945, Box 6, Folder 9, Jack Warner Collection.

71. Marjorie Penn Lasky, "Off Camera: A History of the Screen Actors Guild During the Era of the Studio System," Ph.D. dissertation, University of California, Davis, 1992, pp. 207, 214, 223, 238.

72. *Los Angeles Times,* 13 March 1945.

73. *People's Daily World,* 17 March 1945.

74. Ibid., 23 March 1945.

75. "Officers' and Committee Reports," 28 September 1945, Box 1, Folder 1, Hollywood Democratic Committee Papers.

76. *People's Daily World,* 24 March 1945.

77. Ibid., 9 April 1945.

78. *Los Angeles Times,* 23 March 1945.

79. Ibid., 18 March 1945 and 24 March 1945.

80. Ibid., 23 March 1945.

81. *Variety,* 14 March 1945.

82. Ibid., 4 April 1945.

83. *Los Angeles Daily News,* 21 March 1945.

84. *Los Angeles Times,* 18 March 1945.

85. *Variety,* 23 May 1945, 13 June 1945.

86. *People's Daily World,* 10 October 1945.

87. Ibid., 16 October 1945.

88. Flyer, circa 1945, Roger McDonald Papers.

89. *People's Daily World,* 19 October 1945.

90. John Cromwell to Warner, 12 October 1945, Box 6, Folder 10, Jack Warner Collection.

91. *Variety,* 20 June 1945.

92. *Los Angeles Times,* 20 August 1945.

93. *Variety,* 4 July 1945.

94. *Los Angeles Times,* 16 April 1945.

95. Ibid., 1 April 1945 and 17 April 1945.

96. *Los Angeles Herald-Express,* 4 April 1945.

97. *Variety,* 2 May 1945.

98. *Los Angeles Times,* 30 May 1945.

99. *Variety,* 6 June 1945.

100. *Los Angeles Times,* 1 June 1945.

101. Ibid., 25 July 1945.

102. *Variety,* 25 July 1945.

103. *Los Angeles Times,* 14 August 1945.

104. Ibid., 14 August 1945.

105. *People's Daily World,* 30 July 1945.

106. Ibid., 28 September 1945.

107. *Variety,* 13 June 1945.

108. Ibid., 8 August 1945.

109. Press Release, 3 October 1945, Reel 9091, Federated Press Papers.

110. Herb Sorrell to Pepe Ruiz, 7 June 1945, Box 1, Screen Cartoonists Guild Collection.

111. *Variety,* 8 August 1945.

112. Ibid., 1 August 1945.

113. Joe Tuohy to Daniel Tobin, circa May 1945, Box 22, Teamsters Papers.

114. Joe Tuohy to Daniel Tobin, 24 May 1945, Box 22, Teamsters Papers.

115. Daniel Tobin to Joe Tuohy, 8 August 1945, Box 22, Teamsters Papers. See also Steven Brill, *The Teamsters,* New York: Simon & Schuster, 1978; Donald Garnel, *The Rise of Teamster Power in the West,* Berkeley: University of California Press, 1972.

116. Joe Tuohy to Daniel Tobin, 8 August 1945, Box 22, Teamsters Papers.

117. "Information Bulletin," 15 June 1945, IATSE Records—New York City Office.

118. See "Our Stand as 'IA' Men," 1 (Spring 1945), Hollywood Studio Strike Collection, Southern California Library for Social Studies and Research.

119. Report of 38th National Convention of IATSE, 22–26 July 1946, Reel 230, American Labor Unions' Constitutions, Proceedings, Officers' Reports and Supplementary Documents.

120. "Jurisdictional Disputes," U.S. House of Representatives, 80th Congress, 2nd Session, 1948, p. 2372.

121. Testimony of Richard Walsh, 1939, IATSE Records—New York City Office.

122. Roy Brewer to Daniel Tobin, 25 September 1945, Reel 77, Box 4, Teamsters Papers.

123. R. B. Hood to J. Edgar Hoover, 6 November 1945, Reel 2, Communist Activity in the Entertainment Industry.

124. *Los Angeles Times,* 27 September 1945.

125. "Photostatic Copies of Communist Party Documents and Exemplars of the Handwriting of Herbert K. Sorrell," circa 1946, Screen Actors Guild Papers.

126. "Jurisdictional Disputes," U.S. House of Representatives, 80th Congress, 2nd Session, 1948, pp. 1900, 1917.

127. Robert Hethmon interview with John Howard Lawson, 1964, Box 39, Folder 1, John Howard Lawson Papers.

128. See generally, Gerald Horne, *Black Liberation/Red Scare: Ben Davis and the Communist Party*, Newark: University of Delaware Press, 1994, passim. See also Donald Ranstead, "District 13: A History of the Activities of the California Communist Party, 1929–1940," M.A. thesis, University of California, Davis, 1962.

129. Memo from Emil Freed, circa 1945, Hollywood Studio Strike Collection, Southern California Library for Social Studies and Research.

130. "Jurisdictional Disputes," U.S. House of Representatives, 80th Congress, 2nd Session, 1948, pp. 1570, 1589.

131. "Special Report . . . Prepared for Members of the Research Institute of America," circa 1945, Record Group 46, Box 45, R-8503, Van Deman Collection.

132. George to Roger McDonald, 26 September 1945, Roger McDonald Papers.

133. *Hollywood Atom*, 10 October 1945, Hollywood Studio Strike Collection, Southern California Library for Social Studies and Research.

134. David Oberweiser, Jr., "The CIO: Vanguard for Civil Rights in Southern California, 1940–1946," in Miller and Cornford, eds., *American Labor in the Era of World War II*, pp. 200–216.

135. Undated, unreferenced document, Roger McDonald Papers.

136. Report by McDonald, 1956, Roger McDonald Papers.

137. Herb Sorrell to McDonald, 19 September 1945, Roger McDonald Papers.

138. Report by McDonald, 1956, Roger McDonald Papers.

139. "Confidential Report," 25 September 1945, Roger McDonald Papers.

140. Herb Sorrell to McDonald, 14 September 1945, Roger McDonald Papers.

141. Herb Sorrell to Pepe Ruiz, 3 October 1945, Box 1, Screen Cartoonists Guild Collection.

142. Herb Sorrell to McDonald, 3 October 1945, Roger McDonald Papers.

143. *Los Angeles Times*, 5 September 1945.

144. *Variety*, 26 September 1945.

145. *Los Angeles Times*, 15 September 1945.

146. Irma Mae Ross to Warner, 17 October 1945, Box 6, Folder 10, Jack Warner Collection.

147. Petition, 17 October 1945, Box 6, Folder 10, Jack Warner Collection.

148. Notes from meeting, circa October 1945, Box 6, Folder 10, Jack Warner Collection.

149. *Variety*, 3 October 1945. See also "In the Matter of Columbia Pictures Corporations," et al. and Local 1421, Case No. 21-re-20, circa 1945, Roger McDon-

ald Papers: "[T]he sole issue" is "the eligibility of the voters (strikers and alleged replacements) in the election held on May 24, 1945."

150. *People's Daily World,* 5 October 1945.

151. *Hollywood Sun,* 5 December 1945, Roger McDonald Papers.

152. To "Dearest Roger," 4 October 1945, Roger McDonald Papers.

153. "Jurisdictional Disputes," U.S. House of Representatives, 80th Congress, 2nd Session, 1948, p. 1920.

154. *Los Angeles Times,* 9 October 1945.

155. *People's Daily World,* 9 October 1945.

156. Ibid., 11 October 1945.

157. *Los Angeles Times,* 10 October 1945.

158. *Variety,* 10 October 1945.

159. "Jurisdictional Disputes," U.S. House of Representatives, 80th Congress, 2nd Session, 1948, p. 1920.

160. Elaine Spiro, "Hollywood Strike—October 1945," *Film History,* 10 (Number 3, 1998): pp. 415–418.

161. *Hollywood Citizen-News,* 5 October 1945 and 8 October 1945.

162. *Los Angeles Examiner,* 9 October 1945.

163. *Los Angeles Times,* 9 October 1945.

164. *Hollywood Atom,* 9 October 1945, Hollywood Studio Strike Collection, Southern California Library for Social Studies and Research.

165. *Los Angeles Times,* 7 October 1945.

166. To McDonald, 9 October 1945, Roger McDonald Papers.

167. Joe Tuohy to Daniel Tobin, 8 October 1945, Box 22, Teamsters Papers.

168. Edward Mussa to McDonald, 12 October 1945, Roger McDonald Papers.

169. Hollywood Strikers to New York City, 9 October 1945, Roger McDonald Papers.

170. Press Release, 15 October 1945, Reel 9091, Federated Press Papers.

171. A. M. Sperber and Eric Lax, *Bogart,* New York: Morrow, 1997, p. 316.

172. Spiro, "Hollywood Strike," pp. 417–418.

173. W. T. Sweiger to Warren, 5 October 1945, File 3640: 2365, Earl Warren Papers.

174. D. Pearce to "Miss MacGregor," 8 October 1945, File 3640: 2365, Earl Warren Papers.

175. Memorandum, 9 October 1945, File 3640: 2365, Earl Warren Papers.

176. Mrs. Cole to Warren, 10 October 1945, File 3640: 2365, Earl Warren Papers.

177. Alfred Haddock to Warren, 9 October 1945, File 3640: 2365, Earl Warren Papers.

178. Helen MacGregor to W. T. Sweigert, 11 October 1945, File 3640: 2365, Earl Warren Papers.

179. *Hollywood Atom,* 24 August 1945, Hollywood Studio Strike Collection, Southern California Library for Social Studies and Research.

180. George Pepper to Robert Hannegan, 20 September 1945, Box 4, Folder 4, Hollywood Democratic Committee Papers.

181. Roy Fulwinder to ICC, October 1945, Box 4, Folder 4, Hollywood Democratic Committee Papers.

182. *Hollywood Citizen-News,* 17 October 1945; ibid., 13 October 1945.

183. Ibid., 11 October 1945.

184. To "Dearest Roger," circa October 1945, Roger McDonald Papers.

185. *Los Angeles Examiner,* 10 October 1945.

186. To "Dearest Honey," 10 October 1945, Roger McDonald Papers.

187. To "Dearest Roger," circa October 1945, Roger McDonald Papers.

188. *Los Angeles Examiner,* 15 October 1945.

189. Ibid., 9 November 1945.

190. Ibid., 10 October 1945.

191. *Los Angeles Times,* 31 January 1946.

192. *Variety,* 24 October 1945.

193. *Los Angeles Times,* 17 October 1945.

194. *People's Daily World,* 12 October 1945.

195. *Los Angeles Times,* 24 October 1945.

196. "Phyllis" to "Dear Mac," 15 October 1945, Roger McDonald Papers.

197. Morris Cohn to Herb Freston, 18 October 1945, Box 2374, Jack Warner Collection.

198. *Los Angeles Times,* 8 October 1945.

199. *Los Angeles Herald-Express,* 9 October 1945.

200. *Los Angeles Times,* 12 October 1945.

201. *People's Daily World,* 13 October 1945.

202. TRO No. 506788, Superior Court of State of California, Los Angeles County, *RKO v. Sorrell,* Hollywood Studio Strike Collection, Southern California Library for Social Studies and Research.

203. *Hollywood Reporter,* 7 November 1945.

204. *Los Angeles Times,* 23 October 1945.

205. Ibid., 26 October 1945.

206. *Variety,* 31 October 1945.

207. Ibid., 21 November 1945.

208. Ibid., 14 November 1945.

209. Ibid., 28 November 1945.

210. Ibid., 31 October 1945.

211. "Report of Special Agent," 10 October 1945, Reel 2, Communist Activity in the Entertainment Industry.

212. *People's Daily World,* 31 October 1945; Press Release, 31 October 1945, Reel 9091, Federated Press Papers.

213. *Los Angeles Times,* 31 October 1945.

214. "Jurisdictional Disputes," U.S. House of Representatives, 80th Congress, 2nd Session, 1948, p. 1900.

215. *Variety,* 28 November 1945.

216. "Jurisdictional Disputes," U.S. House of Representatives, 80th Congress, 1st Session, 1947, p. 825.

217. Joe Tuohy to Daniel Tobin, 23 November 1945, Box 22, Teamsters Papers.

218. *People's Daily World,* 7 November 1945.

219. Ibid., 13 November 1945.

220. *Los Angeles Times,* 16 November 1945.

221. Ibid., 30 November 1945.

222. Ibid., 15 December 1945.

223. Ibid., 7 November 1945.

224. "Jurisdictional Disputes," U.S. House of Representatives, 80th Congress, 2nd Session, 1948, p. 1921.

225. *Los Angeles Times,* 27 December 1945.

226. Ibid., 8 November 1945.

227. Ibid., 9 November 1945.

228. Ibid., 11 November 1945.

229. Ibid., 10 November 1945.

CHAPTER 6

1. "Jurisdictional Disputes in the Motion-Picture Industry," U.S. House of Representatives, Special Subcommittee of the Committee on Education and Labor, Hearings, 80th Congress, 2nd Session, Pursuant to HR 111, 1948, p. 2060. Other CSU members thought less of Casey than did Sorrell: "Ever sit in on a negotiating meeting with the producers? Well, you have your team and they have theirs and you face each other. Pat ('Silver-Dollar-Shuffler') Casey carries the ball. Then, when going gets rough, comes the fastest triple pass you ever saw, Casey to [Fred] Pelton to [Eddie] Mannix; the ball disappears and you're back where you started which is nowhere! That's the kind of hide-and-seek game they've been playing with us for two and a half years." *Hollywood Reporter,* 11 November 1946.

2. Memorandum to J. Edgar Hoover, 27 November 1945, Reel 2, Communist Activity in the Entertainment Industry.

3. *Los Angeles Times,* 28 November 1945.

4. Ibid., 10 January 1946.

5. Ibid., 12 February 1945 and 13 February 1945. See also *Variety,* 9 January 1946.

6. *Los Angeles Times,* 15 February 1945 and 19 February 1945.

7. Ibid., 9 February 1946.

8. Ibid., 27 February 1946.

9. Ibid., 6 August 1946.

10. Ibid., 7 January 1947.

11. Ibid., 19 September 1946.

12. Ibid., 1 February 1946.

13. Ibid., 3 January 1946.

14. *Variety,* 9 January 1946.

15. Ibid.

16. *Los Angeles Times,* 3 January 1946.

17. *Variety,* 13 March 1946.

18. *Labor Herald,* 25 January 1946.

19. Ibid., 29 March 1946.

20. Carl Morgen, "Destroying the CIO Council," in Ann Fagan Ginger and David Christiano, *The Cold War against Labor,* volume I, Berkeley: Meiklejohn, 1987, pp. 430–437. The very existence of the CIO acted as a positive prod on the AFL. In 1944 Kenneth Wester, secretary treasurer of the Produce Driver and Employees Union Local 630 of the Teamsters on the West Coast, wanted to bar Japanese-Americans from his union. But Teamsters leader Dave Beck reminded him that when they barred Japanese-Americans in Denver, the CIO moved in, accepted them, and "thus got a foothold in the produce market." See Dave Beck to Kenneth Weston, 31 May 1944, Box 58, Teamsters Papers.

21. Paul Pinsky, Research Director, California—CIO Council to Robert Dunn, 25 June 1946, Box 1, Labor Research Association Papers.

22. Becky Marianna Nicolaides, "In Search of the Good Life: Community and Politics in Working Class Los Angeles, 1920–1955," Ph.D. dissertation, Columbia University, 1993, pp. 161, 365, 368.

23. *Los Angeles Times,* 28 March 1946.

24. Ibid., 13 April 1946. The painters, set decorators, story analysts, carpenters, electricians, and machinists were among those voting to strike.

25. Ibid., 7 May 1946 and 20 June 1946.

26. Ibid., 24 May 1946 and 29 May 1946.

27. "Jurisdictional Disputes," U.S. House of Representatives, 80th Congress, 2nd Session, 1948, p. 2093.

28. *Los Angeles Times,* 5 June 1946.

29. Ibid., 22 June 1946.

30. *Los Angeles Examiner,* 2 July 1946.

31. *Los Angeles Times,* 4 July 1946. See full-page ad in *Los Angeles Daily News,* 2 July 1946, attacking Sorrell before the strike's conclusion.

32. "Jurisdictional Disputes," U.S. House of Representatives, 80th Congress, 2nd Session, 1948, p. 2093. See also "United States of America before the National Labor Relations Board," "In the Matter of," CSU, "Combined Motions, Appeal, Objections and Briefs of Individual Practitioners in Intervention," (Exhibit B-9 includes treaty of Beverly Hills), Box 854, Folder 3, David O. Selznick Collection.

33. *Los Angeles Times,* 20 July 1946.

34. Ibid., 23 July 1946.

35. *People's Daily World,* 6 February 1946.

36. *Los Angeles Times,* 25 July 1946.

37. *The Screen Writer,* 2 (Number 2, July 1946): 40.

38. *Variety,* 31 July 1946.

39. Paul Dullzell, executive secretary, Actors Equity Association to Hyman Faine, AGMA 2 October 1946, Box 3, Reel 5161, American Guild of Musical Artists Papers.

40. *Hollywood Citizen-News,* 16 December 1946.

41. Memorandum, 9 August 1946, Record Group 46, Box 46, R-8634-b, Van Deman Collection.

42. Memorandum, "confidential," 27 September 1946, Record Group 46, Box 46, R-8697, Van Deman Collection.

43. *Los Angeles Times,* 10 August 1946.

44. Memorandum, 11 March 1946, Record Group 46, Box 46, R-8385, U.S. Senate, Internal Security Subcommittee, Van Deman Collection.

45. Leaflet, circa 1946, Sonia Volochova Papers.

46. "Weekly News Letter from California State Federation of Labor," 24 July 1946, Southern California Library for Social Studies and Research.

47. Ibid.

48. Gene B. Tipton, "The Labor Movement in the Los Angeles Area During the 1940s," Ph.D. dissertation, UCLA, 1953, pp. 27, 218, 263, 269.

49. *Los Angeles Times,* 24 August 1946.

50. *Labor Herald,* 6 September 1946.

51. *Variety,* 4 September 1946.

52. Ibid., 28 August 1946.

53. Undated Memorandum, Series III, Box 12, Los Angeles County Federation of Labor Papers.

54. "Jurisdictional Disputes," U.S. House of Representatives, 80th Congress, 1st Session, 1947, p. 14.

55. George Dunne, *Hollywood Labor Dispute: A Study in Immorality,* Los Angeles: Conference Publishing Company, undated, circa 1949, p. 22.

56. "Jurisdictional Disputes," U.S. House of Representatives, 80th Congress, 1st Session, 1947, p. 420.

57. Ibid., p. 14.

58. "Jurisdictional Disputes," U.S. House of Representatives, 80th Congress, 2nd Session, 1948, p. 2062.

59. "Jurisdictional Disputes," U.S. House of Representatives, 80th Congress, 1st Session, 1947, p. 71.

60. Walter Galenson, *The United Brotherhood of Carpenters: The First Hundred Years,* Cambridge: Harvard University Press, 1983, p. 293.

61. "Jurisdictional Disputes," U.S. House of Representatives, 80th Congress, 1st Session, 1947, p. 573.

62. Ibid., p. 537.

63. "Jurisdictional Disputes," U.S. House of Representatives, 80th Congress, 2nd Session, 1948, p. 1799.

64. "Jurisdictional Disputes," U.S. House of Representatives, 80th Congress, 1st Session, 1947, p. 971.

65. George Dunne, Oral History, 1981, UCLA Oral History Program.

66. Release, 20 August 1947, Reel 9091, Federated Press Papers.

67. "Jurisdictional Disputes," U.S. House of Representatives, 80th Congress, 2nd Session, 1948, pp. 2228, 2230, 2273. The 1946 lockout created a morass of distinctions between and among the "Cincinnati directive" of October 1945 when the AFL intervened in the strike; the "December decision" of December 1945 when the 3 man committee favored IATSE; the "July contract" arising out of the July 1946 strike; the "August clarification" when the AFL basically altered its "December decision"; and the alleged September "ultimatum" when CSU supposedly threatened it would walk out immediately rather than work on "hot" sets.

68. *Variety,* 30 October 1946.

69. *Hollywood Reporter,* 25 October 1946; *Variety,* 4 November 1946.

70. *Los Angeles Times,* 9 September 1946.

71. *Independent Film Journal,* 12 October 1946.

72. Leaflet, undated, "to: Mr. Paul Harvey," Screen Actors Guild Papers.

73. *Variety,* 9 October 1946.

74. *People's Daily World,* 4 October 1946.

75. *Los Angeles Times,* 3 October 1946.

76. *Variety,* 25 September 1946.

77. *The Screen Writer,* 2 (Number 6, November 1946): 34–35.

78. Ibid., 2 (Number 5, October 1946): 32.

79. Report of Membership Meeting of Screen Writers Guild, 17 August 1945, Hollywood Studio Strike Collection, Southern California Library for Social Studies and Research.

80. *Hollywood Citizen-News,* 27 September 1946.

81. *Variety,* 30 September 1946.

82. *Hollywood Citizen-News,* 28 September 1946.

83. "Jurisdictional Disputes," U.S. House of Representatives, 80th Congress, 2nd Session, 1948, p. 2124.

84. *Hollywood Citizen-News,* 26 September 1946.

85. *Variety,* 2 October 1946.

86. *Hollywood Reporter,* 27 September 1946.

87. *Los Angeles Times,* 6 October 1946.

88. Ibid., 26 September 1946.

89. Ibid., 27 September 1946.

90. Paramount Newsreel, October 1946, Grinberg Film Library—New York.

91. *Variety,* 2 October 1946.

92. *Los Angeles Daily News,* 1 October 1946.

93. *Hollywood Citizen-News,* 1 October 1946.

94. *Los Angeles Times,* 2 October 1946.

95. Ibid.

96. *Los Angeles Times,* 28 September 1946.

97. *Time,* 7 October 1946.

98. "Jurisdictional Disputes," U.S. House of Representatives, 80th Congress, 1st Session, 1947, p. 432.

99. *Los Angeles Times,* 6 October 1946.

100. *People's Daily World,* 12 October 1946.

101. Ibid., 12 November 1946.

102. *Variety,* 30 October 1946.

103. Ibid., 13 November 1946.

104. "Communist Infiltration of the Hollywood Motion Picture Industry," Testimony of Roy Brewer, 17 May 1951, U.S. House of Representatives, 82nd Congress, 1st Session, Washington, D.C.: Government Printing Office, p. 515.

105. *Los Angeles Times,* 19 October 1946 and 24 October 1946.

106. Ibid., 12 October 1946.

107. *People's Daily World,* 9 November 1946.

108. Ibid., 15 November 1946.

109. *Los Angeles Times,* 23 September 1946.

110. Ibid., 14 November 1946.

111. Ibid., 2 November 1946.

112. *Hollywood Citizen-News,* 12 November 1946.

113. *Los Angeles Daily News,* 14 November 1946.

114. *Los Angeles Times,* 14 December 1946.

115. Ibid., 6 November 1946.

116. Ibid., 10 December 1946.

117. Ibid., 14 November 1946.

118. Ibid., 17 November 1946.

119. Ibid., 6 November 1946.

120. Ibid., 16 November 1946.

121. Ibid., 23 November 1946.

122. "Jurisdictional Disputes," U.S. House of Representatives, 80th Congress, 2nd Session, 1948, p. 2128; *Picket Line,* 4 March 1947, Hollywood Studio Strike Collection, Southern California Library for Social Studies and Research.

123. *New York Herald Tribune,* 4 March 1947.

124. *Los Angeles Times,* 30 November 1946.

125. Ibid., 2 December 1946.

126. Ibid., 24 November 1946.

127. *Paul Perlin v. Local 80, IATSE, Roy Brewer, et al.,* in Superior Court of California, Los Angeles County, "Order to Show Cause," Affidavit of Paul Perlin, circa October 1946, Roger McDonald Papers.

128. "City-Wide Strike Strategy Committee, 1946," Minutes, 4 February 1946, Box 25, UAW, Local 216 Papers.

129. Bruce Nelson, *Workers on the Waterfront: Seamen, Longshoremen and Unionism in the 1930s,* Urbana: University of Illinois Press, 1988, pp. 71, 130.

130. Deposition of Rex Zimmerman, circa 1947, Box 40, Folder 10, Dalton Trumbo Papers.

131. *Flashes,* January 1947, Box 10, John Howard Lawson Papers.

132. *People's Songs,* 1 (Number 11, December 1946), Reel 117, National Republic Papers.

133. *People's Songs,* 2 (Number 4, May 1947), Reel 117, National Republic Papers.

134. Article by Ross Kavner, undated, Reel 117, National Republic Papers; See also Robbie Lieberman, *My Song Is My Weapon: People's Songs, American Communism and the Politics of Culture, 1930–1950,* Urbana: University of Illinois Press, 1995.

135. George Dunne, Oral History, 1981, UCLA Oral History Program.

136. Report from Pat Somerset, 16 October 1946, Screen Actors Guild Papers.

137. Transcript of Meeting, 24 October 1946, Screen Actors Guild Papers.

138. Charles Wilson to Robert Montgomery, 15 November 1946, Screen Actors Guild Papers.

139. Transcript of SAG meeting, 19 December 1946, Screen Actors Guild Papers.

140. Jack Dales, Oral History, 1981, UCLA.

141. David Prindle, *The Politics of Glamour: Ideology and Politics in the Screen Actors Guild,* Madison: University of Wisconsin Press, p. 48.

142. Duke Wales to Buck Harris, 29 January 1947, Screen Actors Guild Papers.

143. Jack Dales to WFTU, et al., 10 February 1947, Screen Actors Guild Papers.

144. W. Schevenel to "Dear Comrades," 26 February 1947, Screen Actors Guild Papers.

145. R. H. Cricks to SAG, 26 February 1947, Screen Actors Guild Papers.

146. George Kuvakus, Oral History, 10 March 1992, California State University, Northridge.

147. "Jurisdictional Disputes," U.S. House of Representatives, 80th Congress, 1st Session, 1947, pp. 222, 304, 366.

148. *CSU News,* 7 December 1946, Hollywood Studio Strike Collection, Southern California Library for Social Studies and Research.

149. *Los Angeles Daily News,* 29 October 1946.

150. *People's Daily World,* 22 November 1946.

151. *CSU News,* 3 May 1947, Hollywood Studio Strike Collection, Southern California Library for Social Studies and Research.

152. Ibid., 5 April 1947 and 18 December 1946.

153. Ibid., 20 December 1946.

154. *Picket Line,* 13 January 1947, Hollywood Studio Strike Collection, Southern California Library for Social Studies and Research.

155. Ibid., 19 April 1947.

156. *People's Daily World,* 29 November 1946.

157. Ibid., 12 December 1946.

158. *Variety,* 4 December 1946. See also Memorandum, 7 May 1946, Record Group 46, Box 46, R-8433, U.S. Senate, Internal Security Subcommittee, Van Deman Collection: The Communist Party in Southern California meeting with Toledano in "Tia Juana" was noted by military intelligence.

159. FBI Report, 10 February 1947, Reel 2, Communist Activity in the Entertainment Industry.

160. *Picket Line,* 21 November 1946, Hollywood Studio Strike Collection, Southern California Library for Social Studies and Research.

161. *Variety,* 18 December 1946.

162. *Los Angeles Times,* 17 December 1946.

163. Ibid., 20 December 1946.

164. Ibid., 18 December 1946.

165. Ibid., 9 January 1947; See *People v. Gustanes Ancker, et al.,* CR A2276, Trial Court No. 47, 661, Superior Court, Los Angeles County, Hollywood Studio Strike Collection, Southern California Library for Social Studies and Research.

166. *Los Angeles Herald,* 24 March 1947. See also Transcript of *People of State of California v. Homer L. Bartchy, et al.,* 1947, Box 2, Leo Gallagher Papers.

167. *Los Angeles Times,* 30 December 1947.

168. Ibid., 20 December 1947.

169. Joe Tuohy to Daniel Tobin, 6 November 1946, Box 22, Teamsters Papers.

170. Ibid., 10 December 1946.

171. *San Francisco Chronicle,* 11 December 1946.

172. Ibid.

173. *Picket Line,* 14 February 1947, Hollywood Studio Strike Collection, Southern California Library for Social Studies and Research.

174. "Jurisdictional Disputes," U.S. House of Representatives, 80th Congress, 1st Session, 1947, p. 1005. See also Thomas Schatz, *Boom and Bust: American Cinema in the 1940s,* Berkeley: University of California Press, 1999.

175. *Hollywood Reporter,* 19 June 1947.

176. *Los Angeles Times,* 21 June 1947.

177. Release, 28 August 1947, Reel 9091, Federated Press Papers.

178. *New York Times,* circa 8 July 1952, Reel 544, National Republic Papers.

179. "Jurisdictional Disputes," U.S. House of Representatives, 80th Congress, 1st Session, 1947, p. 47.

180. Releases, 21 March 1947 and 25 February 1946, Reel 9091, Federated Press Papers.

181. Release, 3 January 1951, Reel 9091, Federated Press Papers.

182. Minutes, Meeting of LA-CIO Council, 5 September 1947, Carton 8, San Francisco-CIO Papers.

183. Release, 28 October 1947, Reel 9091, Federated Press Papers.

184. Release, 27 October 1947, Reel 9091, Federated Press Papers.

185. Press Release from MPAA, 25 November 1947, Box 405, Folder 19, Cecil B. DeMille Archives. See also *New York Herald Tribune,* 22 October 1947; *New York Times,* 23 October and 2 November 1947; *Washington Post,* 5 November 1947.

186. Directors Guild members to Speaker of House and Chairman of HUAC, 20 October 1947, Box 9, Folder 1, Argosy Pictures Corporation Archives.

187. *Hollywood Reporter,* 24 December 1947; *Los Angeles Daily News,* 24 December 1947; *Hollywood Reporter,* 13 January 1948; *Daily Variety,* 13 January 1948; *Hollywood Reporter,* 11 February 1948.

188. *The Screen Writer,* 4 (Number 1, June–July 1948): 1.

189. Ibid., 4 (Number 4, October 1948): 18.

190. Campaign against *The Iron Curtain,* circa 1947, Box 5, National Council of American-Soviet-Friendship Papers.

191. John Dales, Jr., to International Board of Associated Actors and Artistes of America and the Governing Bodies of the Actors' Equity Association, Chorus Equity Association, American Federation of Radio Artists, American Guild of Musical Artists, and American Guild of Variety Artists, 16 August 1949, Box 403, American Guild of Variety Artists Papers.

192. Ronald Reagan to Paul Dullzell, 19 October 1949, Box 434, American Guild of Variety Artists Papers.

193. Pepe Ruiz to Herb Sorrell, 15 January 1947, Box 1, Motion Picture Screen Cartoonists Guild Papers.

194. "Julie" to Pepe Ruiz, 17 March 1947, Box 1, Motion Picture Screen Cartoonists Guild Papers.

195. Herb Sorrell to Pepe Ruiz, 27 March 1947, Box 1, Motion Picture Screen Cartoonists Guild Papers.

196. Herb Sorrell to Pepe Ruiz, 16 July 1947, Box 1, Motion Picture Screen Cartoonists Guild Papers. See also Roger A. Fischer, *Them Damned Pictures: Explorations in American Political Cartoon Art,* North Haven, Conn.: Archon, 1996.

197. *People's Daily World,* 17 April 1947.

198. Clipping, undated, Reel 544, National Republic Papers.

199. *Proceedings of Conference, Thought Control in USA: Toward Freedom of Thought:* Los Angeles, Hollywood Arts, Sciences and Professions Council, 1947, Labor Archives and Research Center, San Francisco State University. See "Case Files," 487/2439–487/2531, #2456, "Confidential," "Final Report," 17 August 1948, Motion Picture Producers Association, "Employer" and "Building Service Employees, Local 278, AFL," Record Group 280, Box 2479, U.S. Federal Mediation and Conciliation Service Records: "Parties reached final agreement and the union has signed the contract and said contract is now in the process of being

signed by each individual company. Contract is to continue for 5 years . . . provides for a very tight seniority clause and also provides that whatever wage increase is given to members of the IATSE will be granted the employees represented by the above named union. The contract also provides for a union shop." "CASE CLOSED." See also Harry Malcolm, Commissioner, to E. P. Marsh, Regional Director, "Case Files," 487/1101–487/1183, 22 April 1948, Record Group 280, Box 2479, U.S. Federal Mediation and Conciliation Service Records: The AFL dispute with Fox, Republic, Paramount, United Artists, RKO, etc. "has been settled satisfactorily"; the "union has been recognized as the bargaining agent for the past two years, and that the relationship is very good."

200. *1421 Bulletin*, 3 April 1947, Roger McDonald Papers.

201. Release, 30 October 1947, Reel 9091, Federated Press Papers.

202. *Variety*, 26 September 1947; *New York Times*, 2 November 1947.

203. "Jurisdictional Disputes," U.S. House of Representatives, 80th Congress, 1st Session, 1947, pp. 587, 591, 726.

204. "Marvin Bauman and Soren P. Thorsen, Petitioners," "In the Supreme Court of the State of California," "Petition for Writ of Mandate and Brief in Support Thereof," Hollywood Studio Strike Collection, Southern California Library for Social Studies and Research. See also Release, 22 March 1949, Reel 9037, Federated Press Papers.

205. Memorandum, 20 December 1946, Record Group 46, Box 46, R-8801-a, U.S. Senate, Internal Security Subcommittee, Van Deman Collection.

206. Ibid., Memorandum, 17 January 1947, Record Group 46, Box 46, R-8845-b.

207. Philip M. Connelly to Albert T. Lunceford, 10 September 1947, Box 8, R-8845-b, File-LA, San Francisco CIO Papers.

208. Memorandum, 20 March 1947, Box 4, United Scenic Artists, Local 829 of the Brotherhood of Painters, Decorators Papers.

209. Release, 9 March 1948, Reel 9091, Federated Press Papers.

210. Release, 20 August 1947, Reel 9091, Federated Press Papers.

211. Release, 22 August 1947, Reel 9091, Federated Press Papers.

212. *CSU News*, 28 June 1948, Roger McDonald Papers.

213. "Jurisdictional Disputes," U.S. House of Representatives, 80th Congress, 2nd Session, 1948, p. 1802.

214. Report from McDonald, 1947, Roger McDonald Papers.

215. "Jurisdictional Disputes," U.S. House of Representatives, 80th Congress, 2nd Session, 1948, p. 1889.

216. Release, 9 April 1948, Reel 9091, Federated Press Papers.

217. Releases, 20 December 1948, 19 October 1949, and 28 November 1950, Reel 9091, Federated Press Papers.

218. Edmond DePatie, Oral History, 1965, UCLA Oral History Program.

219. Memorandum of Conference, 28 July 1950, Box 2734, Jack Warner Collection.

220. *New York Times,* 3 June 1954.

221. Ibid., 15 April 1954.

222. Ibid., 22 January 1952.

223. Release, 10 April 1952, Reel 9091, Federated Press Papers.

224. Clipping, circa February 1948, Reel 544, National Republic Papers.

225. Release, 13 June 1950, Reel 9037, Federated Press Papers.

226. *People's Daily World,* 4 March 1948. See also Lary May, ed., *Recasting America: Culture and Politics in the Age of Cold War,* Chicago: University of Chicago Press, 1989.

227. *CSU v. Loew's,* 342 U.S. 919, 72 S.Ct. 367 (1952), cert. denied below: 193 F2d 51. See also *Schatte v. IATSE,* 182 F2d 158 (1950); *NLRB v. Warner Bros.,* 191 F2d 217 (1951).

228. *CSU v. Loew's,* 24 July 1947, "FSM" to George Wasson, 11 October 1948; Robert Patton to Fred Metzler; Box FX-LR-158, Fox Collection.

229. *Hollywood Sun,* 18 June 1947.

230. *Lawless, et al. v. Brotherhood of Painters, Decorators and Paperhangers,* 143 Cal. App. 2d 474, 300 P2d 159 (1956).

231. Memorandum, undated, Box 40, Folder 10, Dalton Trumbo Papers.

232. Dan Biederman to "Mrs. Schwartz," 25 April 1982, Alexander Knox Papers.

233. *People's Daily World,* 1 November 1946.

234. *The Painter and Decorator,* 60 (Number 11, November 1946): 11.

235. *Los Angeles Times,* 3 July 1946.

236. Release, 29 October 1948, Reel 9091, Federated Press Papers.

237. *People's Daily World,* 20 October 1945.

238. Glenn Pratt to Roger McDonald, October 1945, Roger McDonald Papers.

239. *Picket Line,* 16 April 1945, Box 1000, Folder 18, David O. Selznick Collection.

240. Roy Wilkins to Miss Wasem, 9 May 1947; Julia Baxter to Roy Wilkins; Walter White to David O. Selznick, 21 May 1947, Group II, Box A280, NAACP Papers. Actors such as Hattie McDaniel were concerned that attacking racial stereotypes would cause blacks' roles to disappear. See also Marjorie Lasky, "Off Camera: A History of the Screen Actors Guild During the Era of the Studio System," Ph.D. dissertation, University of California, Davis, 1992, p. 321.

241. Thurgood Marshall to Walter White, 20 December 1948, Group II, Box B73, NAACP Papers. See also Matthew Bernstein, *Walter Wanger, Hollywood Independent,* Berkeley: University of California Press, 1994.

242. "Loyalty Case No. 37," filed by Loren Miller, 1948, Group II, Box B12, NAACP Papers.

243. Walter White to Nicholas Schenck, 7 November 1947; Thurgood Marshall to Walter White, 20 December 1948, Group II, Box B73, NAACP Papers.

244. *Hollywood Atom,* 31 August 1945, Roger McDonald Papers.

245. See, e.g., William Berman, *America's Right Turn: From Nixon to Clinton,* Baltimore: Johns Hopkins University Press, 1998.

246. David Plotke, *Building a Democratic Political Order: Reshaping American Liberalism in the 1930s and 1940s,* New York: Cambridge University Press, 1996; James A. Gross, *Broken Promises: The Subversion of U.S. Labor Relations Policy, 1947–1994,* Philadelphia: Temple University Press, 1995; Walter Galenson, *The American Labor Movement, 1955–1995,* Westport, Conn.: Greenwood, 1996.

247. See, e.g., Staughton Lynd, ed., *'We Are All Leaders': The Alternative Unionism of the Early 1930s,* Urbana: University of Illinois Press, 1996.

EPILOGUE

1. *The Economist,* 31 May 1997.

2. *Los Angeles Sentinel,* 16 September 1993.

3. *Los Angeles Times,* 20 May 1997.

4. *New York Times,* 2 January 1998.

5. *Washington Post National Weekly Edition,* 12 January 1998.

6. *New York Times,* 3 July 1998.

7. Ibid., 4 August 1997; See also Geoffrey Nowell-Smith and Steven Ricci, eds., *Hollywood and Europe: Economics, Culture, National Identity: 1945–95,* London: British Film Institute, 1998.

8. *Financial Times,* 15 December 1998; *Los Angeles Sentinel,* 28 January 1999.

9. *LA Weekly,* 13–19 August 1999.

10. *New Yorker,* 19 January 1997; Tom Peters, *The Circle of Innovation,* New York: Knopf, 1998.

11. *New York Times,* 22 January 1998.

12. *Financial Times,* 13–14 June 1998.

13. *New York Times,* 5 February 1999.

14. *Business Week,* 14 March 1994.

15. Lois Gray and Ronald L. Seeber, eds., *Under the Stars: Essays on Labor Relations in Arts and Entertainment,* Ithaca, N.Y.: Cornell University Press, 1996, p. 1.

16. *Los Angeles Times,* 17 June 1998. In late 1999, IATSE activist Michael Everett led a demonstration in Los Angeles at a dinner sponsored by the Motion Picture Association of America honoring U.S. commerce secretary William Daley. The sound technicians, prop workers, and others in attendance were protesting trade agreements that—they charged—were leading to job loss and making Hollywood part of the "rustbelt." *LA Weekly,* 26 November–2 December 1999.

17. Kyoko Hirano, *Mr. Smith Goes to Tokyo: Japanese Cinema under the American Occupation, 1945–1952,* Washington: Smithsonian Institution Press, 1992, pp. 205, 237, 257.

18. Junichi Saga, *Confessions of a Yakuza: A Life in Japan's Underworld,* New York: Kodansha, 1991, p. 195.

19. *New York Times,* 11 June 1997.

20. *Los Angeles Times,* 20 July 1997.

21. *The Economist,* 21 June 1997.

22. *New York Times,* 27 March 1997.

23. Ibid., 1 January 1998.

24. *Far Eastern Economic Review,* 1 May 1997.

25. Frederic Dannen, "Partners in Crime: China Bonds with Hong Kong's Underworld," *New Republic,* 217 (Numbers 2 & 3, 14–21 July 1997): 18–24, p. 23. See also Frederic Dannen and Barry Long, *Hong Kong Babylon: An Insider's Guide to the Hollywood of the Far East,* New York: Hyperion, 1997.

26. Frederic Wakeman, *Policing Shanghai, 1927–1937,* Berkeley: University of California Press, 1994. See also Clive Emsley and Louis A. Knafla, eds., *Crime History and Histories of Crime: Studies in the Historiography of Crime and Criminal Justice in Modern History,* Westport, Conn.: Greenwood, 1996. In Afghanistan a soldier turned outlaw came to power: See Fayz Muhammad, *Kabul under Siege: An Inside Account of the 1929 Uprising,* Princeton, N.J.: Markus Wiener, 1997.

27. Laurie Gunst, *Born Fi' Dead: A Journey through the Jamaican Posse Underworld,* New York: Henry Holt, 1995, pp. xiv, xv, 9, 74, 81.

28. *New York Times,* 21 August 1997.

29. *Los Angeles Times,* 21 November 1997.

30. Robert Evans, *The Kid Stays in the Picture,* New York: Hyperion, 1994, p. 4.

31. *New York Times,* 22 January 1996; *Los Angeles Times,* 22 January 1996.

32. Michael J. Zuckerman, *Vengeance Is Mine: Jimmy 'The Weasel' Fratianno Tells How He Brought the Kiss of Death to the Mafia,* New York: Macmillan, 1987, p. 157. See also Peter Maas, *Underboss: Sammy the Bull Gravano's Story of Life in the Mafia,* New York: HarperCollins, 1997.

33. *New York Newsday,* 24 November 1996.

34. Michel Chossudovsky, "The Business of Crime and the Crimes of Business," *Covert Action Quarterly,* (Number 58, Fall 1996): 24–30, 54.

35. *Business Week,* 16 December 1996, 15 December 1997; *New York Times,* 19 March 1997.

36. *New York Times,* 13 June 1997.

37. Ibid., 21 February 1984; *Business Week,* 14 February 1983; *Wall Street Journal,* 5 October 1982; *San Francisco Examiner,* 9 May 1978; *U.S. News & World Report,* 9 September 1980; *National Law Journal,* 29 February 1988.

38. *San Francisco Bay Guardian,* 20–26 January 1999.

39. Contract, 1 November 1970, Series 2, Box 27, Huey P. Newton Foundation Records.

40. Irma Watkins-Owens, *Blood Relations: Caribbean Immigrants and the Harlem Community, 1900–1930,* Bloomington: Indiana University Press, 1996, p. 146.

41. *New York Times,* 7 July 1997.

42. *LA Weekly,* 7–13 February 1997.

43. Memo from Perry, circa 1958, Box 2, Folder 11, Pettis Perry Papers.

44. *New York Times,* 28 July 1963.

45. *Los Angeles Sentinel,* 8 July 1999; See also Anna Christian, *Meet It, Greet It and Defeat It: The Biography of Frances E. Williams,* Los Angeles: Milligan Books, 1999, p. 176.

46. F. C. Duke Zeller, *Devil's Pact: Inside the World of the Teamsters Union,* Secaucus: Birch Lane, 1996, pp. 169, 170, 171.

47. *Los Angeles Times,* 24 March 1997.

48. Marc Cooper, "Concession Stand . . . Can Hollywood Unions Survive," *American Film,* 13 (Number 3, December 1987): 32–39.

49. *Los Angeles Times,* 22 May 1997. This was not a unique development. Early in 1999 William Charles Skeen, a stuntman on the television show *Walker, Texas Ranger,* died during the filming of a dangerous car chase. *Washington Post,* 13 January 1999.

50. *LA Weekly,* 6–12 June 1997.

51. *Los Angeles Times,* 1 July 1997.

52. *LA Weekly,* 25–31 July 1997.

53. One of the possible negatives—from the point of view of management—of production abroad is that foreign laborers often are not as quiescent as their U.S. counterparts. The union that declared a strike at the Baja California, Mexico, movie lot where *Titanic* was filmed withdrew its labor for two weeks in June 1999. Twentieth-Century Fox studios "was shuttered with some employees inside," *Los Angeles Times,* 25 June 1999.

54. *LA Weekly,* 15–21 August 1997.

55. *Raleigh News & Observer,* 7 January 1998.

56. *Los Angeles Times,* 19 April 1997.

57. Ibid.

58. *People's Weekly World,* 17 January 1998.

59. *The Nation,* 268 (Number 24, 28 June 1999): 2.

60. *Variety,* 3 April 1974 and 24 August 1992.

61. Carlos Clarens, *Crime Movies: An Illustrated History,* New York: Norton, 1980, p. 168.

62. *Variety,* 16 May 1973.

63. Michael J. Ybarra, "Blacklist Whitewash: The Real Story of the Hollywood Ten," *New Republic,* 218 (Numbers 1, 2, 5, & 12 January 1998): 20–23. See also Stephen Schwartz, *From West to East: California and the Making of the American Mind,* New York: Free Press, 1998.

64. *Los Angeles Times,* 16 November 1997. See also Pete Seeger, *Where Have All the Flowers Gone: A Singer's Stories,* New York: Sing Out, 1993.

65. Release, 24 December 1941, Reel 9091, Federated Press Papers.

INDEX

Knight, Marion "Suge," 235
Knox, Alexander, 212–213
Koch, Edward, 134, 278n93
Koppes, Clayton, 10
Korda, Alexander, 177
Korshak, Sidney, 24, 46, 111, 234
Kuhn, Fritz, 124
Ku Klux Klan, 16, 62, 78, 79, 129, 131
Kuvakus, George, 213

Labor, xii, 10, 35, 68, 73, 82, 97, 155, 192,
193; and Communists, vii–viii, 4,
21, 6, 93, 171, 173; studio, viii, xii,
13, 44, 45, 49–50, 53, 54, 58, 63,
67, 122, 142, 156, 160, 172, 175, 197,
207, 209, 210, 218, 223, 230, 232,
237, 271n176, 307n16; radicalism of,
xiii, 18, 44, 49, 137, 153, 229; and
moguls, xiii, 128, 136; weakened
role of, xiii, 239; postwar concerns
regarding, 11; unrest, 12, 39, 49,
121, 229; and violence, 12, 197;
and anti-Semitism, 26; repression
of, 39–43; and police, 41, 51, 136;
and organized crime, 49, 51, 54,
98; in circuses, 53; in nightclubs,
53; in theaters, 53; and seasonal
unemployment, 54; in auto industry, 63; corruption in, 98, 245n3,
275n41; and Wagner Act, 154;
and World War II, 154; divisions
within, 156, 179; and layoffs, 176–
177; surpluses, 179; and open shop
rules, 200; foreign, 309n53. *See also*
Lockout of 1946; Strike of 1945;
Strikes; Unions
Labor Non-Partisan League, 16
Lady on a Train, 162
Laemmle, Carl, Jr., 120, 136, 284n88
LaFollette, Robert, 40, 51
Lamar, Dorothy, 133
Lampel, Millard, 82
Landis, John, 237
Lang, June, 22
Lansky, Meyer, 100, 108, 109, 117, 120,
235
Lardner, Ring, Jr., ix, 66, 74, 113
Laski, Harold, 145
Laughton, Charles, 113, 189
Lawson, Belle Hart, 70
Lawson, John Howard, ix, 7, 41, 49, 64,
70, 75, 77, 81, 85–86, 92, 116, 122,
126, 131, 135, 184, 187, 239; as leader
of Hollywood Communists, xi,
15, 26, 71; and anti-Semitism, 26;
biography of, 70, 71; early writings
of, 71; and Scottboro 9 case, 71;
relationship to non-Communists,
72; and African Americans, 72, 74;
backs CSU, 73; blacklisting of, 73;
and portrayal of labor, 73; opposes
racism, 73–74; debates Jerome, 83;
jailing of, 110; walks picket lines,
175
Lawson, Simeon, 70
Leah the Forsaken, 122
Lechner, John, 129
Lederer, Francis, 127
Lee, Brandon, 238
Lee, Canada, 79, 127
Lee, "Gypsie" Rose, 113
Lee, Spike, 235, 236
Leigh, Janet, 111
Lesher, Bernice M., 186
Levine, Burton, 61
Levitt, Helen Joy, 87
Lewin, Jean, 80
Lewis, John L., 18, 167
Lewton, Val, 127
Library of Congress: Legislative Re-
search Service, 9
Liebman, Arthur, 130
Lifeboat, 79
Life of Emile Zola, 128
Lindbergh, Charles, 124
Lindelof, Lawrence, 178
Little Caesar, 132
Little Women, 44
Locke, Alain, 72
Lockout of 1946, vii, xii, 3, 7, 9, 12, 14,
17–18, 35, 39, 75, 81, 85, 91, 105, 113,
115, 128, 141, 159, 188, 225, 300n67;
and film production, 14, 205, 215;
and jurisdictional disputes, 15; and
links between moguls and organized crime, 26; and anti-Semitism,
27; bellweathers of, 197; and Carpenters, 197; plans for, 198, 200;
and film quality, 201; tactics used
during, 202–204; and violence,
202–207; and public opinion, 203,
206; and women, 205–206; and

9, 149, 164–166; and declining film production, 9–10; "Big Eight" identified, 10; as factory towns, 13; collaborate with IATSE, 18, 46, 159, 160, 164, 170–171, 207, 214, 220, 224; and organized crime, 23–25, 46–48, 51, 120, 121, 214; and anti-Semitism, 26; and 1946 lockout, 39, 198, 200–205, 211, 215, 216; and labor, 41–42, 137, 142, 155, 156; repression of unions by, 44; small, 44; and payments to Bioff and Browne, 48; oppose 1937 strike, 49; filming schedules of, 50, 54; pressure actors to stop union support, 115; and the press, 141; economic troubles of, 141, 142, 144; use of foreign production by, 148; and film backlog, 157–158, 167, 201; and 1945 strike, 158–186 passim; collaborate with Walsh, 159; and informants, 165; and Communists, 184; efforts to purge CSU, 194–195, 223; and NLRB, 195; and Sorrell, 195; and new design techniques, 198; and public opinion, 207; and police, 208; and layoffs, 217; and wages, 217–218; and profits, 218; lawsuits against, 223, 224; independent, 223, 224, 230. *See also* Moguls; *names of individual studios*

Studs Lonigan, 82
Sullivan, Ed, 111
Sullivan, Ernest, 128
Sun Valley Serenade, 215
Swayze, Patrick, 238
Swift, Wesley, 27, 131
Synagogue Council of America, 126

Taft-Hartley Act, 15, 19, 138, 160, 213, 222
Taiwan: organized crime in, 233
Tatum, Douglas, 3
Teamsters, 24, 44, 56, 67, 90, 174, 182, 189, 197, 209, 216, 217, 234; and organized crime, 99, 105, 236, 275n46; refuse to observe CSU picket lines, 105, 195; and 1945 strike, 168; oppose CSU, 172–173; endorse blacklist, 219; Local 804,

273n9; Local 817, 273n9; Local 630, 298n20
Technicolor Film Corporation, 156, 204, 205
Television, viii, 10, 247n24
The Ten Commandments, 160
Tender Comrade, 76, 93
Tenney, Jack, 4, 68, 69, 128, 174, 190
Theaters, 9, 10, 53; picketing of, 161–163, 171, 177, 180; boycotts of, 162, 171
Thirty Seconds over Tokyo, 60
Thomas, Julius, 204
Thomas, Madelyn, 204
Thompson, Clarence, 19
Thomsen, Hans, 124
Three Little Pigs, 136
Three Stooges, 112
Tiffany Pictures, 44
Till the Clouds Roll By, 33
Time magazine, 113
Titanic, 237, 309n53
T-Men, 22
Tobin, Daniel, 172–174, 209
Toho Studios, 232
Toledano, Vincente Lombardo, 215
Tomorrow the World, 113
Tongue, Thomas, 159
Trade Union Education League, 61
Trafficante, Santo, 111
Trilling, Steve, 166
Truman, Harry S., 78, 106, 114, 187
Trumbo, Dalton, ix, 60, 70, 74–77, 81–83, 88, 93, 115, 128, 187, 224, 239
Tuohy, Joseph, 56, 172, 173, 182, 189, 195, 216
Turkey: organized crime in, 232
Turner, Lana, 111
Tuttle, Frank, 86–87, 269n150
Twentieth Century Fox, 7, 10, 24, 46, 47, 54, 75, 89, 121, 125, 146, 156, 161, 165–167, 177, 201, 215, 218, 237, 305n199, 309n53
Twilight Zone—The Movie, 237

Underwood, Aggie, 105
Unfinished Dance, 33
Unions, 5, 59, 61, 66, 68, 74, 107, 126, 135, 155, 191, 229, 232, 309n53; progressivism of, vii; craft, vii, 8, 13–14, 39, 48, 51, 191; militance of, viii, 231; conflicts between, ix, 159,

Printed and bound by CPI Group (UK) Ltd, Croydon, CR0 4YY

16/04/2025

14658534-0001